PLANNING-PROGRAMMING-BUDGETING
Second Edition

PLANNING
PROGRAMMING
BUDGETING
A Systems Approach to Management
SECOND EDITION

edited by
FREMONT J. LYDEN
and
ERNEST G. MILLER
Graduate School of Public Affairs
University of Washington

MARKHAM PUBLISHING COMPANY/ Chicago

MARKHAM POLITICAL SCIENCE SERIES
Aaron Wildavsky, Editor

Axelrod, *Conflict of Interest: A Theory of Divergent Goals with Applications to Politics*

Barber, *Citizen Politics: An Introduction to Political Behavior*, Second Edition

Barber, ed., *Power to the Citizen: Introductory Readings*

Barber, ed., *Readings in Citizen Politics: Studies of Political Behavior*

Cnudde and Neubauer, eds., *Empirical Democratic Theory*

Coplin, *Introduction to International Politics: A Theoretical Overview*

Coplin, ed., *Simulation in the Study of Politics*

Coplin and Kegley, eds., *A Multi-method Introduction to International Politics: Observation, Explanation, and Prescription*

Dolbeare and Dolbeare, *American Ideologies: The Competing Political Beliefs of the 1970's*

Dvorin, ed., *The Senate's War Powers: Debate on Cambodia from the Congressional Record*

Greenstein, *Personality and Politics: Problems of Evidence, Inference, and Conceptualization*

Greenstein and Lerner, eds., *A Source Book for the Study of Personality and Politics*

Lane, *Political Thinking and Consciousness: The Private Life of the Political Mind*

Lyden and Miller, eds., *Planning-Programming-Budgeting: A Systems Approach to Management*, Second Edition

McDonald, *Party Systems and Elections in Latin America*

Mitchell, *Public Choice in America: An Introduction to American Government*

Mitchell, *Why Vote?*

Payne, *The American Threat: The Fear of War as an Instrument of Foreign Policy*

Ranney, ed., *Political Science and Public Policy*

Ross, *American National Government: An Introduction to Political Institutions*

Ross, ed., *Public Choice and Public Policy: Seven Cases in American Government*

Ross and Mitchell, eds., *Introductory Readings in American Government: A Public Choice Perspective*

Russett, ed., *Economic Theories of International Politics*

Sharkansky, *Public Administration: Policy-Making in Government Agencies*, Second Edition

Sharkansky, ed., *Policy Analysis in Political Science*

Strickland, Wade, and Johnston, *A Primer of Political Analysis*, Second Edition

Contributors

PAUL L. BROWN is Administrator of the Division of Facilities and Services, Wisconsin Department of Administration, and was formerly Director of the Wisconsin Bureau of Budget and Management.

JESSE BURKHEAD is Maxwell Professor of Economics in the Maxwell School, Syracuse University.

C. WEST CHURCHMAN is Professor of Business Administration and Research Philosopher at the Space Sciences Laboratory, University of California, Berkeley.

O. LYNN DENISTON is Research Associate and Lecturer in Public Health Administration in the Department of Community Health Services, School of Public Health, University of Michigan.

JAMES S. DYER is Assistant Professor of Operations Management and Public Systems in the Graduate School of Business Administration, University of California, Los Angeles, and consultant to The Rand Corporation in the area of Educational Planning.

JOHN W. EVANS is Assistant Commissioner for Program Planning and Evaluation in the Office of the United States Department of Health, Education and Welfare.

GENE H. FISHER is Head of the Resource Analysis Department, The Rand Corporation.

V. A. GETTING is Professor of Public Health Administration in the Department of Community Health Services, School of Public Health, University of Michigan.

HARRY P. HATRY is Director of the State-Local Government Research Program in the Urban Institute and was formerly Deputy Director of the State-Local Finances Project, the George Washington University.

JAMES E. JERNBERG is Associate Professor and Associate Director, School of Public Affairs, University of Minnesota.

PERRY LEVINSON is Research and Demonstration Specialist in the Social and Rehabilitation Service, Atlanta Regional Office of the United States Department of Health, Education and Welfare.

VERNE B. LEWIS is a management consultant and was formerly Deputy U. S. Representative to the International Atomic Energy Agency in Vienna and served as budget officer in several federal agencies.

ROBERT A. LUTHER is Budget Officer of Fairfax County, Virginia.

FRANCIS E. MCGILVERY was president of the Management Assistance Corporation of Washington, D.C.

CHARLES M. MOTTLEY is Special Assistant to the Vice President for

v

Planning, The Pennsylvania State University, and was formerly an Operations Research Scientist in the Office of the Director, Bureau of Mines.

ATTIAT F. OTT is Professor of Economics at Clark University.

DAVID J. OTT is Professor of Economics at Clark University.

E. S. QUADE is Head of the Mathematics Department, The Rand Corporation.

IRWIN M. ROSENSTOCK is Professor of Public Health Administration, Department of Community Health Services, School of Public Health, University of Michigan.

A. H. SCHAINBLATT is a consultant to the General Electric Company, Santa Barbara, California.

ALLEN SCHICK is a Senior Fellow at The Brookings Institution and has served as a consultant to the U.S. Bureau of the Budget.

DAVID R. SEIDMAN is Assistant Chief, Division of Organization and Management Planning in the Office of Budget and Executive Management, Government of the District of Columbia, and was formerly a Senior Health Analyst in the Office of the Secretary, United States Department of Health, Education and Welfare.

WILLIAM WELCH is Research Assistant in the Office of Institutional Research, School of Business Administration, University of Michigan.

MICHAEL J. WHITE is Assistant Professor of Political Science at the University of Georgia.

WALTER WILLIAMS is Professor of Public Affairs and Director of Research of the Institute of Governmental Research in the Graduate School of Public Affairs, University of Washington, and was formerly Chief of the Research and Plans Division in the Office of Research, Plans, Programs, and Evaluation in the United States Office of Economic Opportunity.

Contents

Introduction to the Second Edition

When the first edition of this reader was published in 1968, government agencies had had little experience with PPB. Most federal agencies were still trying to figure out what was really involved in PPB and not many had made impressive progress in implementation. Few state and local governments were knowledgeable about the approach. Now, four years later, PPB is a familiar term at all levels of American government and in countries outside the United States as well.

The State-Local Finances Project (5-5-5) of the George Washington University was instrumental in introducing American state and local governments to the potentialities of this comprehensive budgetary approach.[1] As early as 1968, 28 states and 60 local governments reported that they were taking steps toward the implementation of a PPB system, and an additional 155 local governments reported that they were considering implementation.[2] School districts and institutions of higher education, especially the larger ones, have also adopted PPB systems, and a textbook for use in schools was published in 1968.[3] Outside the United States such countries as Belgium, Great Britain, Canada, and Japan have moved toward adoption of PPB systems in one form or another.[4] In 1969 the first edition of this reader was translated into Japanese.[5]

Not that PPB has been universally accepted. A survey conducted in mid-1968 (the *Rouse Report*) revealed a great deal of reluctance or indifference toward applying PPB in many of the federal agencies.[6] Even within the Bureau of the Budget (BOB) resistance to PPB was apparent. It received solid topside support, but many BOB examiners continued to evaluate agency programs on the basis of traditional criteria rather than on PPB-generated information.[7] In Congress, the Jackson Subcommittee[8] was apprehensive that PPB would lead to an emphasis on pseudo-expertise and meretricious claims for technical rather than political inputs and analysis in policy-making. On the other hand however, the Proxmire Subcommittee[9] saw positive advantages in the better and more com-

1

prehensive information that could be gained from this new approach to budgeting, for Congress as well as for the executive branch.

Confusion about what PPB really was and how it could be operationalized in different agency contexts also contributed to the resistance against PPB. BOB's first implementing directive, Bulletin 66-3 (October 12, 1965), called for submission of far more information than could be assembled. Every agency was required to prepare a Program Memorandum (PM) annually for each of its program categories. Though greatly understaffed, many agencies attempted to comply. The result was a flood of PMs, often completed too late to influence budget decisions. In Bulletins 68-2 (July 18, 1967) and 68-9 (April 12, 1968) BOB attempted to rectify this problem by limiting the number and length of PMs each agency was expected to submit. Much of the damage had already been done, however, and in the minds of many, PPB had become identified with the production of useless reports for people who would never read them.

At the state and local levels there has also been some disenchantment with PPB. In the 1968 State-Local Finances Survey, 73 local governments responded that they had rejected the idea of installing PPB. Usually, the reasons given were lack of resources or authority rather than lack of interest.[10] More recently, the states of New York and California appear to be cutting back on their efforts to implement PPB. By and large, however, enthusiasm for PPB remains very high at both state and local levels.

In the federal government a few agencies have made major strides toward implementing a workable PPB system. According to the *Rouse Report,* five of the sixteen agencies surveyed (HEW, USDA, OEO, AEC, and the Corps of Engineers-Civil Works) were receiving topside support in the development of these capabilities, and one (Commerce) was beginning to give increased impetus to its PPB efforts.[11]

In President Nixon's explanation of Reorganization Plan No. 2 of 1970, establishing the Domestic Council and the Office of Management and Budget, it seems clear that the essential purposes and substance of the PPB approach are to be continued and developed. But there are indications that President Nixon's views toward federal-state and federal-local relations may result in modifications and new emphases that will have an important effect on the future role of PPB.[12] In a recent statement, William A. Niskanen, who heads the program evaluation work in the Office of Management and Budget (formerly the Bureau of the Budget), argued that a "coherent bureaucracy" is one in which the *activities* of the subordinate units are consistent with the *objectives* of the superior organization.[13] "Coherence," he continued, "does not mean that the objectives of subordinate and superior units need be consistent, although they may be; rather it means that the activities of the subordinate unit must contribute to the objectives of the superior unit." If this philosophy were incorporated in PPB, it would encourage operating units of government to vie with each other in providing outputs for the accomplishment of superordinate level government goals. The superordinate level need not be concerned with the way the subordinate unit does this (as long as it is legal), but only with the output yield. The advantage of this approach is that the whole federal government would not be bound to a complicated chain of subgoals stretching from the lowest levels of operating agencies to the Chief Executive level. This approach, of course, would not obviate the need for goal setting by the operating organizations since each operating agency has its own clientele whose needs it must satisfy. It would mean that the operating agencies would have to justify their budget requests to OMB not in terms of their own goals, but in terms of how well their outputs met higher level goals. The review process would be simplified for OMB, and more alternative means of accomplishing national goals would be identified.

There are problems associated with this approach. For example, clientele needs to be met by the operating agency and national goal needs defined at the Presidential level are not distinct. The president must enlist clientele support to get his goals endorsed by Congress, and in return, clientele groups will demand presidential support for operating agency goals.

But there are indications that increased emphasis is being given to this approach in OMB. Procedural PPB requirements are being deemphasized. Agencies are encouraged to continue the institutionalization of PPB, but with increasing emphasis on within-agency development. In part, this action is undoubtedly a response to the dysfunctions that have emerged from the overproceduralization of PPB in the past. This tendency toward excessive emphasis procedures has been all too common among agencies, and many have fallen into the trap of proliferating implementary procedures until they have become immobilized by their own machinery. OMB appears now to be arguing that it hopes to save the real virtues of PPB by allowing agencies to disentangle themselves from the red tape the system has generated. It is likely that larger state and local jurisdictions that have adopted PPB are experiencing similar procedural problems.

At any rate, PPB appears to be moving into a new phase in its development that will undoubtedly have eventual consequences at state and local levels as well. Consequently, this second edition, *Planning-Programming-Budgeting: A Systems Approach to Management,* represents a major departure from its predecessor. Only four of the nineteen chapters included in the first edition have been retained. In order to appreciate the focus of this edition, it is necessary to consider some of the problems that have been associated with the implementation of PPB.

The first problem confronting an implementing organization is whether to direct initial attention to the development of a program structure or to the employment of analytical skills for dealing with specific program issues. It is tempting to choose the latter approach, which avoids getting bogged down in tangled theoretical and terminological problems involved in identifying goals, subgoals, activities, and so forth and their complicated means-ends relationships. Following the issues approach, one can quickly show the relevance of PPB by demonstrating its problem-solving capabilities in dealing with specific tangible decisions. There is, however, a major weakness in this approach. Unless the end results can be related to some kind of goal structure for the agency, the relevance of taking any action at all is indeterminable. As spokesmen in Dayton, one of the 5-5-5 Project cities, commented in a progress report: "Hindsight now shows us that we apparently spent an inordinate amount of time on developing our program analysis abilities (Task Force issue papers and our in-depth analysis project) in proportion to the time spent on some of the basic cornerstones of the PPBS process—namely, the program structure."[14]

The development of a program structure, however, is no easy undertaking. There are few guidelines or analytic approaches available to assist the administrator. Perhaps the most sophisticated work has been done in program planning and analysis, but many of the skills developed in this context have been learned on the job and transferred to others through apprenticeship. It was therefore recognized fairly early by those implementing PPB that analytic approaches would have to be developed for the design of program structures. Figures 1 and 2 reflect the rationale employed in the design of Pennsylvania's PPB system. Goals are identified as major state programs such as the protection of persons and property. Subgoals are the more specific program categories for the accomplishment of state goals (for example, control and reduction of crime). Objectives, then, become the more specific ends for accomplishing subgoals—more specific in that it is now possible at this level to identify their impacts. Finally, the program elements become the activities undertaken to accomplish objectives. Since these are activity-efforts, outputs achieved in relationship to perceived need can be identified. While the terminology used will differ for other jurisdictions implementing PPB, the basic logic reflected in the Pennsylvania program structure reflects the rationale aimed at by most jurisdictions.

FIGURE 1
Sample Program Structure
Commonwealth Program II
Protection of Persons and Property

Category	Subcategory	Element
General administration and support		
Traffic safety and supervision		
Control and reduction of crime	Crime prevention	
Maintenance of public order	Criminal law enforcement	
Provision of public services to local governments	Reintegration of adult offenders	Maintenance of inmate security
Water damage control and prevention		Maintenance of inmates' physical-mental health
Protection of the forest resource		Counseling of inmates for personal and social problems
Occupational health and safety		Education of inmates
Consumer protection		Occupational and vocational training of inmates
Community and housing hygiene and safety		Inspection of county and municipal institutions
		Social investigation
		Supervision for social and personal change
		Financial and professional assistance to county probation departments
		Screening to determine risk

Source: Robert J. Mowitz, *The Design and Implementation of Pennsylvania's Planning, Programming, Budgeting System* (University Park: Pennsylvania State University, Institute of Public Administration, n.d.), p. 52.

FIGURE 2
Sample Program Structure Statements and Program Plan Logic

Commonwealth program—protection of persons and property
Goal: To provide an environment and social system in which the lives of individuals, and the property of individuals and organizations are protected from natural and man-made disasters, and from illegal and unfair action.

Program category—control and reduction of crime
Subgoal: To provide a high degree of protection against bodily injury, loss of life, and loss of property resulting from unlawful or unfair actions by individuals or organizations; to provide a sufficiently secure setting for offenders in order to safeguard the community and provide for their health and well being; and to cure or alleviate the socially aberrant behavior of the offender and to assist the offender to function to the best of his potential upon release from an institution or while on probation.

Program subcategory—reintegration of offenders
Objective: To decrease the recurrence of crime by replacing criminal behavior with socially acceptable behavior

Impacts: Number and percent of persons released convicted for new crimes
Number and percent of evaluations of inmates reflecting gain in social skills and emotional controls
Number of releases under supervision of court parole or Pennsylvania Board of Parole
Number of admissions who are parole violators

Program element—counseling for personal and social problems
Outputs: Number of inmates receiving recommended individual counseling
Number of inmates receiving recommended group counseling
Number of inmates receiving recommended self improvement group counseling
Number of inmates receiving recommended psychiatric treatment

Need and/or demand: Number of inmates recommended for individual counseling
Number of inmates recommended for group counseling
Number of inmates recommended for self improvement group counseling
Number of inmates recommended for psychiatric treatment   Program statement

Funds required: Direct state activities
Payments to jurisdictions   Financial statement

Manpower required: Man years
Funds required   Manpower statement

Source: Robert J. Mowitz, *The Design and Implementation of Pennsylvania's Planning, Programming, Budgeting System* (University Park: Pennsylvania State University, Institute of Public Administration, n.d.), p. 53.

Another problem associated with program structure is whether one should attempt to develop a program format that will replace existing budget formats. The reform tradition associated with budgetary development has always stressed replacement of existing, inadequate formats with *better* formats. Thus, at the turn of the century, governments were urged to adopt the line-item budget in place of the then existing piecemeal budgets to facilitate accountability. The Hoover Commission later urged adoption of a performance budget in place of a line-item budget to facilitate the efficient management of resources. Many early PPBers recommended replacement of existing budget forms with a program structure. As these reformers began to understand the multiple purposes served by budgets in the political and managerial decision-making process, some of them began to question the utility of employing any single budget format for all purposes. Thus, in 1960, Charles Hitch was urging replacement of Defense program and budget formats then being used by a unified budget format.[15] By 1965, however, writing in *Decision-Making for Defense,* he was arguing: "I now feel that the advantages of the existing budget structure far outweigh the disadvantages which are principally mechanical, namely the need to translate program categories into budget categories and vice versa. This is the sort of disadvantage that modern high-speed computers are well designed to overcome."[16] While a program budget may be the best format for making decisions about effectiveness, the performance budget may be far superior in dealing with questions concerning the efficient use of resources and the line-item budget may yield the most appropriate information for decisions concerning accountability.

Each of these three budget formats yields different information, but the information provided by each is highly interdependent on the information provided by the others, as demonstrated schematically in Figure 3. To understand the operation of an organization we must know its goals, the activities it carries on to accomplish these goals, the resource mixes that are used, the responsible organizational units that produce these mixes, the outputs they yield, and the impacts that they have on society. The PPB or program budget concentrates on the goal and impact aspects of the process, the performance budget on the throughput (activities and outputs), and the line-item or object budget on the goods and services furnished.

It seems, then, that what is needed is not a program structure budget that *replaces* existing budget formats, but one that *supplements* them by providing information on goal direction and impact. The development of crosswalks to interrelate the information provided by each budget format is thus essential so that one may know how a decision made from one

FIGURE 3
Informational Orientations Emphasized by PPB, Performance, and Object Budget Formats

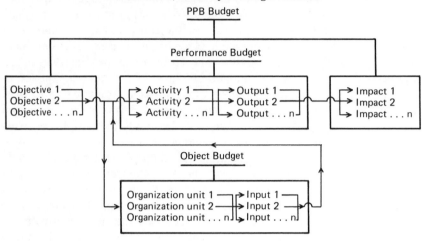

budget format will affect the cost represented by the other formats. As Hitch says, we now have the computer capabilities to accomplish this cross-tabulation.

Another problem in implementing PPB centers around the use of analytic methods. The method used conditions the way a problem is perceived. Every analytic method has its own value set. PPB has attempted to overcome this problem by using a variety of analytic tools, some based on microeconomics, some on operations research, others on sensitivity analysis, and so forth. Yet the mixture of these methods selected to consider any given issue has, for the most part, been justified on pragmatic grounds. The PPBers reply to this criticism by admitting that their methods will consider only those aspects of issue implications that are amenable to systematic analysis (for example, economic but not political). The end result is not intended to make a decision for a decision-maker, but merely to provide him with a better organization of some of the aspects of the situation. The decision-maker still must weigh the importance of the analytic inputs with information he will get on other dimensions of the situation from other sources (such as parties, and clientele) to arrive at his own decision. The problem posed by this line of reasoning is that the weight of the systematically analyzed evidence is likely to direct consideration away from those aspects of the situation that cannot be subjected to such rigorous systematization.

Closely related to this problem is the question of how program impact is to be measured. Since short-term program outcomes are easiest to identify and quantify, they are the most tempting to use in systematic analysis. Yet these short-term outcomes are likely to be no more than indicators of activity effort which may or may not have a significant impact on society in broad policy terms. Attempts to use long-range impact indicators, on the other hand, involve making subjective assumptions that may bring the validity of the whole methodological approach used into question. Whether one opts for the short-range or long-range impact indicators, it seems apparent that the results of a PPB analysis will be subject to a good deal of political buffeting in the dynamics of the public policy decision-making process.

These are some of the major problems that have confronted implementers of PPB. It seems logical, then, that this revised edition of the reader should incorporate selections that will best help practitioners to deal with such problems. Consequently, this edition has given greater attention to the political milieu of PPB, program planning and analysis, the design of program structures, the relation of systems to goals, crosswalking, and the experiences of implementers in various settings.

PPB is first considered in terms of its historical setting, as discussed by Allen Schick. It is then placed in its institutional setting, as illustrated by the role it plays in the annual budget process in the federal government (Ott and Ott).

Once PPB has been set in its historical and institutional perspective, consideration is given to the way it relates to the political process. Burkhead discusses the public expenditure theories that have been developed—the macroeconomic approach taken by Musgrave and others, and the microeconomic-political bargaining approach propounded by Lindblom, and Wildavsky et al. Schick argues in the following chapter that the latter approach, justified on the basis of "the way decisions are actually made," offers no assurance that societal needs are met and lacks the consideration of frames of reference broader than those held by the political bargainers. Jernberg, in Chapter 5, provides empirical evidence that the type of budget information—performance, program, and objects of expenditure, for example—most relevant to a congressional committee depends on the type of mission of the reporting agency. These findings indicate that no single type of budget format will meet the needs of all congressional committees, thus emphasizing the need for budget cross-walks.

The program planning and evaluation base of budgeting is discussed by Mottley and Deniston et al. in Chapters 6, 7 and 8. Mottley demonstrates that planning must lay the foundation for programming. Deniston et al. then discuss how programs can be designed to measure effectiveness and efficiency, respectively, and the relation between program planning and program evaluation.

Chapters 9 and 10 deal with the incorporation of program plans into the PPB budgeting format. Brown explains the method developed in Wisconsin for logically constructing a program structure. Hatry discusses the problems involved in developing criteria to measure program accomplishment in reference to such a program structure.

In the next three chapters, Lewis, Quade, and Fisher explain the rationale underlying three of the major analytic techniques employed in a PPB approach. Lewis sets forth the concept of opportunity costs based on marginal utility analysis, Quade discusses the systems analysis mode, and Fisher explains cost-utility analysis.

Chapters 14 and 15 deal with the problem of crosswalking information. Levinson points up the need for relating the goal structure of a PPB budget to the system needs of the implementing machinery. Churchman and Schainblatt then illustrate how different budget formats can be crosswalked to provide for these differential needs.

Section seven (Chapters 16–20) considers problems and experiences faced in the implementation of PPB. Seidman reports on the experience of HEW, a federal department that has made a major investment in the application of PPB. McGilvery is concerned with the inevitable problem that faces every agency installing a PPB system—reconciling the budgeting system with the accounting system. Luther examines the various problems involved in implementing PPB at the local government level. Dyer provides insight into the design of a budget in educational administration that can furnish information on effectiveness as well as efficiency. Williams and Evans illustrate the advantages, but also the difficulties, involved in conducting program evaluation. [17]

Finally, in Chapter 21, White discusses the future potentialities of PPB in view of the various schools of criticism that have emerged. His conclusion that none of these forms of criticism invalidate PPB as a useable management tool suggests that the philosophy embodied in PPB is likely to have a lasting effect on management regardless of the fate of the label.

Notes

[1] The State-Local Finances Project of the George Washington University, under the directorship of Selma J. Mushkin, was financed by a grant from the Ford Foundation. The so-called 5-5-5 project was begun in 1966 and involved five states, five cities, and five counties as program participants to adapt PPB processes to problems of their governments, with the idea that their efforts would serve also as a body of experience on which other governments might draw. The participating governments were California, Michigan, New York, Vermont, Wisconsin, Dade County (Florida), Los Angeles County (California), Nashville-Davidson County (Tennessee), Nassau County (New York), Wayne County (West Virginia), and the cities of Dayton, Denver, Detroit, New Haven, and San Diego. The major relevant publications of the State-Local Finances Project are: *PPB Notes* 1-11; *Program Planning for State, County, City*, (January 1967), by Harry Hatry and John Cotton; and *Implementing PPB in State, City, and County: A Report on the 5-5-5 Project* (June 1969).

[2] State-Local Finances Project, *Implementing PPB . . .*, pp. 132, 140.

[3] Harry J. Hartley, *Educational Planning-Programming-Budgeting: A Systems Approach* (Englewood Cliffs, N. J.: Prentice-Hall, 1968).

[4] See reports in the *Manchester Guardian Weekly* (October 24, 1970), and *The Economist* (April 25, 1970) for Great Britain. Information pertaining to other countries was obtained by personal interviews with officials from those countries.

[5] *PPBS to Shisutemu Bunseki*, trans. Tadao Miyakawa (Tokyo: Nihon Keizai Shinbunsha, 1969).

[6] Edwin L. Harper, Fred A. Kramer, and Andrew M. Rouse, *Implementation and Use of PPB in 16 Federal Agencies* (Washington, D.C.: U.S. Bureau of the Budget, April 1969). A revised version of this report appeared in the *Public Administration Review* (November/December 1969), 623–632.

[7] Stanley B. Botner, "Four Years of PPBS: An Appraisal," *Public Administration Review* (July/Aug. 1970), 423–431.

[8] The hearings, comments, memoranda, reports, and documents of the Jackson Subcommittee are conveniently collected in one volume, U.S. Congress, Senate, *Planning-Programming-Budgeting: Inquiry of the Subcommittee on National Security and International Operations* (Washington, D.C.: Government Printing Office, 1970). Senator Henry M. Jackson is Chairman for the Senate Committee on Government Operations.

[9] The major reports of the Proxmire Subcommittee are the following: U.S. Congress, *The Planning-Programming-Budgeting System: Progress and Potential*, Hearings Before the Subcommittee on Economy in Government of the Joint Economic Committee, 90th Cong., 1st sess., 14, 19, 20, 21 September, 1967; and *The Analysis and Evaluation of Public Expenditures: The PPB System*, A Compendium of Papers submitted to the Subcommittee on Economy in Government of the Joint Economic Committee, 91st Cong., 1st sess. (1969).

[10] State-Local Finances Project, *Implementing PPB . . .*, p. 140.

[11] Edwin L. Harper, Fred A. Kramer, and Andrew M. Rouse, "Implementation and Use of PPB in 16 Federal Agencies," *Public Administration Review* (November/December 1969), 626.

[12] President Richard Nixon, *Reorganization Plan No. 2 of 1970* (The White House, March 12, 1970). Reprinted in *Public Administration Review*, 30:6 (November/December 1970) 611–19. See especially the language on pp. 613–14.

[13] William A. Niskanen, "Toward a Coherent Bureaucracy," paper presented at the National meeting of the American Society for Public Administration, Denver, Colorado (April 20, 1971).

[14] State-Local Finances Project, *PPB Pilot Project Reports* (Washington, D.C.: George Washington University, February 1969), p. 107.

[15] Charles J. Hitch and Roland McKean, *The Economics of Defense in the Nuclear Age* (Cambridge, Mass.: Harvard University Press, 1960).

[16] Charles J. Hitch, *Decision-Making for Defense* (Berkeley: University of California Press, 1965), p. 30.

[17] For those interested in obtaining case study material dealing with various aspects of analysis and implementation, a variety of such cases is available from the Intercollegiate Case Clearing House, Soldiers Field Post Office, Boston, Massachusetts 02163. The Clearing House has an annotated list of cases and a price schedule.

I

PPB IN PERSPECTIVE

1

The Road to PPB:
The Stages of Budget Reform

ALLEN SCHICK

Among the new men in the nascent PPB staffs and the fellow travelers who have joined the bandwagon, the mood is of "a revolutionary development in the history of government management." There is excited talk about the differences between what has been and what will be; of the benefits that will accrue from an explicit and "hard" appraisal of objectives and alternatives; of the merits of multi-year budget forecasts and plans; of the great divergence between the skills and role of the analyst and the job of the examiner; of the realignments in government structure that might result from changes in the budget process.

This is not the only version, however. The closer one gets to the nerve centers of budget life—the Divisions in the Bureau of the Budget and the budget offices in the departments and agencies—the more one is likely to hear that "there's nothing very new in PPB; it's hardly different from what we've been doing until now." Some old-timers interpret PPB as

Reprinted from the *Public Administration Review*, 26, No. 4 (December 1966): 243–58, by permission of the author and publisher.

The author is indebted to Henry S. Rowen and Paul Feldman of the Bureau of the Budget and to the many federal officials who guided him through a summer's sojourn along the road to PPB.

a revival of the performance budgeting venture of the early 1950s. Others belittle the claim that before PPB, decisions on how much to spend for personnel or supplies were made without real consideration of the purposes for which these inputs were to be invested. They point to previous changes that have been in line with PPB, albeit without PPB's distinctive package of techniques and nomenclature. Such things as the waning role of the "green sheets" in the central budget process, the redesign of the appropriation structure and the development of activity classifications, refinements in work measurement, productivity analysis, and other types of output measurement, and the utilization of the Spring Preview for a broad look at programs and major issues.

Between the uncertain protests of the traditional budgeteer and the uncertain expectations of the *avant garde*, there is a third version. The PPB system that is being developed portends a radical change in the central function of budgeting, but it is anchored to half a century of tradition and evolution. The budget system of the future will be a product of past and emerging developments; that is, it will embrace both the budgetary functions introduced during earlier stages of reform as well as the planning function which is highlighted by PPB. PPB is the first budget system *designed* to accommodate the multiple functions of budgeting.

The Functions of Budgeting

Budgeting always has been conceived as a process for systematically re-lating expenditure of funds to accomplishment of planned objectives. In this important sense, there is a bit of PPB in every budget system. Even in the initial stirrings of budget reform more than fifty years ago, there were cogent statements on the need for a budget system to plan the objectives and activities of government and to furnish reliable data on what was to be accomplished with public funds. In 1907, for example, the New York Bureau of Municipal Research published a sample "program memoran-dum" that contained some 125 pages of functional accounts and data for the New York City Health Department.[1]

However, this orientation was not *explicitly* reflected in the budget systems—national, state, or local—that were introduced during the first decades of this century, nor is it *explicitly* reflected in the budget systems that exist today. The plain fact is that planning is not the only function that must be served by a budget system. The *management* of ongoing activities and the *control* of spending are two functions which, in the past, have been given priority over the planning function. Robert Anthony identifies three distinct administrative processes, strategic planning, management control, and operational control.

> Strategic planning is the process of deciding on objectives of the organization, on changes in these objectives, on the resources used to attain these objectives, and on the policies that are to govern the acquisition, use, and disposition of these resources.
>
> Management control is the process by which managers assure that resources are obtained and used effectively and efficiently in the accomplishment of the organization's objectives.
>
> Operational control is the process of assuring that specific tasks are carried out effectively and efficiently. [2]

Every budget system, even rudimentary ones, comprises planning, management, and control processes. Operationally, these processes often are indivisible, but for analytic purposes they are distinguished here. In the context of budgeting, *planning* involves the determination of objectives, the evaluation of alternative courses of action, and the authorization of select programs. Planning is linked most closely to budget preparation, but it would be a mistake to disregard the management and control elements in budget preparation or the possibilities for planning during other phases of the budget year. Clearly, one of the major aims of PPB is to convert the annual routine of preparing a budget into a conscious appraisal and formulation of future goals and policies. Management involves the programming of approved goals into specific projects and activities, the design of organizational units to carry out approved programs, and the staffing of these units and the procurement of necessary resources. The management process is spread over the entire budget cycle; ideally, it is the link between goals made and activities undertaken. *Control* refers to the process of binding operating officials to the policies and plans set by their superiors. Control is predominant during the execution and audit stages, although the form of budget estimates and appropriations often is determined by control considerations. The assorted controls and reporting procedures that are associated with budget execution—position controls, restrictions on transfers, requisition procedures, and travel regulations, to mention the more prominent ones —have the purpose of securing compliance with policies made by central authorities.

Very rarely are planning, management, and control given equal attention in the operation of budget systems. As a practical matter, planning, management, and control have tended to be competing processes in budgeting with no neat division of functions among various participants. Because time is scarce, central authorities must be selective in the things they do. Although this scarcity counsels the devolution of control responsibilities to operating levels, the lack of reliable and relied-on internal control systems has loaded central authorities with control functions at the expense of the planning function. Moreover, these processes often require different skills and generate different ways of handling the budget mission, so that one type of perspective tends to predominate over the others. Thus, in the staffing of the budget offices, there has been a shift from accountants to administrators as budgeting has moved from a control to a management posture. The initial experience with PPB suggests that the next transition might be from administrators to economists as budgeting takes on more of the planning function.

Most important, perhaps, are the differential informational require-ments of planning, control, and management processes. Informational needs differ in terms of time spans, levels of aggregation, linkages with organizational and operating units, and input-output foci. The apparent solution is to design a system that serves the multiple needs of budgeting. Historically, however, there has been a strong tendency to homogenize informational structures and to rely on a single classification scheme to serve all budgetary purposes. For the most part, the informational system has been structured to meet the purposes of control. As a result, the type of multiple-purpose budget system envisioned by PPB has been avoided.

An examination of budget systems should reveal whether greater emphasis is placed *at the central levels* on planning, management, or control. A *planning orientation* focuses on the broadest range of issues: What are the long-range goals and policies of the government and how are these related to particular expenditure choices? What criteria should be used in appraising the requests of the agencies? Which programs should be initiated or terminated, and which expanded or curtailed? A *manage-ment orientation* deals with less fundamental issues: What is the best way to organize for the accomplishment of a prescribed task? Which of several staffing alternatives achieves the most effective relationship between the central and field offices? Of the various grants and projects proposed, which should be approved? A *control orientation* deals with a relatively narrow range of concerns: How can agencies be held to the expenditure ceilings established by the legislature and chief executive? What reporting procedures should be used to enforce propriety in expenditures? What limits should be placed on agency spending for personnel and equipment?

It should be clear that every budget system contains planning, management, and control features. A control orientation means the subordination, not the absence, of planning and management functions. In the matter of orientations, we are dealing with relative emphases, not with pure dichotomies. The germane issue is the balance among these vital functions at the central level. Viewed centrally, what weight does each have in the design and operation of the budget system?

The Stages of Budget Reform

The framework outlined above suggests a useful approach to the study of budget reform. Every reform alters the planning-management-control balance, sometimes inadvertently, usually deliberately. Accordingly, it is possible to identify three successive stages of reform. In the first stage, dating roughly from 1920 to 1935, the dominant emphasis was on developing an adequate system of expenditure control. Although planning and management considerations were not altogether absent (and indeed occupied a prominent role in the debates leading to the Budget and Accounting Act of 1921), they were pushed to the side by what was regarded as the first priority, a reliable system of expenditure accounts. The second stage came into the open during the New Deal and reached its zenith more than a decade later in the movement for performance budgeting. The management orientation, paramount during this period, made its mark in the reform of the appropriation structure, development of management improvement and work measurement programs, and the focusing of budget preparation on the work and activities of the agencies. The third stage, the full emergence of which must await the institutionalization of PPB, can be traced to earlier efforts to link planning and budgeting as well as to the analytic criteria of welfare economics, but its recent development is a product of modern informational and decisional technologies such as those pioneered in the Department of Defense.

PPB is predicated on the primacy of the planning function; yet it strives for a multi-purpose budget system that gives adequate and necessary attention to the control and management areas. Even in embryonic stage, PPB envisions the development of crosswalk grids for the conversion of data from a planning to a management and control framework, and back again. PPB treats the three basic functions as compatible and complementary elements of a budget system, though not as co-equal asepcts of central budgeting. In ideal form, PPB would centralize the planning function and delegate *primary* managerial and control responsibilities to the supervisory and operating levels respectively.

In the modern genesis of budgeting, efforts to improve planning, management, and control made common cause under the popular banner of the executive-budget concept. In the goals and lexicon of the first reformers, budgeting meant executive budgeting. The two were inseparable. There was virtually no dissent from Cleveland's dictum that "to be a budget it must be prepared and submitted by a responsible executive. . . ."[3] Whether from the standpoint of planning, management or control, the executive was deemed in the best position to prepare and execute the budget. As Cleveland argued in 1915, only the executive "could think in terms of the institution as a whole," and, therefore, he "is the only one who can be made responsible for leadership."[4]

The executive budget idea also took root in the administrative integration movement, and here was allied with such reforms as functional consolidation of agencies, elimination of independent boards and commissions, the short ballot, and strengthening the chief executive's appointive and removal powers. The chief executive often was likened to the general manager of a corporation, the Budget Bureau serving as his general staff.

Finally, the executive budget was intended to strengthen honesty and efficiency by restricting the discretion of administrators in this role. It was associated with such innovations as centralized purchasing and competitive bidding, civil service reform, uniform accounting procedures, and expenditure audits.

The Control Orientation

In the drive for executive budgeting, the various goals converged. There was a radical parting of the ways, however, in the conversion of the budget idea into an operational reality. Hard choices had to be made in the design of expenditure accounts and in the orientation of the budget office. On both counts, the control orientation was predominant.

In varying degrees of itemization, the expenditure classifications established during the first wave of reform were based on objects-of-expenditure, with detailed tabulations of the myriad items required to operate an administrative unit—personnel, fuel, rent, office supplies, and other inputs. On these "line-itemizations" were built technical routines for the compilation and review of estimates and the disbursement of funds. The leaders in the movement for executive budgeting, however, envisioned a system of functional classifications focusing on the work to be accomplished. They regarded objects-of-expenditure as subsidiary data to be included for informational purposes. Their preference for functional accounts derived from their conception of the budget as a planning instrument, their disdain for objects from the contemporary division between politics and administration.[5] The Taft Commission vigorously opposed object-of-expenditure appropriations and recommended that expenditures be classified by class of work, organizational unit, character of expense, and method of financing. In its model budget, the commission included several functional classifications.[6]

In the establishment of a budget system for New York City by the Bureau of Municipal Research, there was an historic confrontation between diverse conceptions of budgeting.

In evolving suitable techniques, the bureau soon faced a conflict between functional and object budgeting. Unlike almost all other budget systems which began on a control footing with object classifications, the bureau turned to control (and the itemization of objects) only after trial-and-error experimentation with program methods.

When confronted with an urgent need for effective control over administration, the bureau was compelled to conclude that this need was more critical than the need for a planning-functional emphasis. "Budget reform," Charles Beard once wrote, "bears the imprint of the age in which it originated."[7] In an age when personnel and purchasing controls were unrealiable, the first consideration was how to prevent administrative improprieties.

> In the opinion of those who were in charge of the development of a budget procedure, the most important service to be rendered was the establishing of central controls so that responsibility could be located and enforced through elected executives. . . . The view was, therefore, accepted, that questions of administration and niceties of adjustment must be left in abeyance until central control has been effectively established and the basis has been laid for careful scrutiny of departmental contracts and purchases as well as departmental work.[8]

Functional accounts had been designed to facilitate rational program decisions, not to deter officials from misfeasance. "The classification by 'functions' affords no protection; it only operates as a restriction on the use which may be made of the services."[9] The detailed itemization of objects was regarded as desirable not only "because it provides for the utilization of all the machinery of control which has been provided, but it also admits to a much higher degree of perfection than it has at present attained."[10]

With the introduction of object accounts, New York City had a threefold classification of expenditures: (1) by organizational units; (2) by functions; and (3) by objects. In a sense, the Bureau of Municipal Research was striving to develop a budget system that would serve the multiple purposes of budgeting simultaneously. To the bureau, the inclusion of more varied and detailed data in the budget was a salutary trend; all purposes would be served and the public would have a more complete picture of government spending. Thus the bureau "urged from the beginning a classification of costs in as many different ways as there are stories to be told."[11] But the bureau did not anticipate the practical difficulties which would ensue from the multiple classification scheme. In the 1913 appropriations acts

> there were 3992 distinct items of appropriation. . . . Each consti-tuted a distinct appropriation, besides which there was a further itemization of positions and salaries of personnel that multiplied this number several times, each of which operated as limitations on administrative discretion.[12]

This predicament confronted the bureau with a direct choice between the itemization of objects and a functional classification. As a solution, the bureau recommended retention of object accounts and the total "defunctionalization" of the budget; in other words, it gave priority to the objects and the control orientation they manifested. Once installed, object controls rapidly gained stature as an indispensable deterrent to administrative misbehavior. Amelioration of the adverse effects of mul-tiple classifications was to be accomplished in a different manner, one which would strengthen the planning and management processes. The bureau postulated a fundamental distinction between the purposes of budgets and appropriations, and between the types of classification suitable for each.

> An act of appropriation has a single purpose—that of putting a limitation on the amount of obligations which may be incurred and the amount of vouchers which may be drawn to pay for personal services, supplies, etc. The only significant classification of ap-propriation items, therefore, is according to persons to whom drawing accounts are given and the classes of things to be bought.[13]

Appropriations, in sum, were to be used as statutory controls on spending. In its "Next Steps" proposals, the bureau recommended that appropriations retain "exactly the same itemization so far as specifica-tions of positions and compensations are concerned and, therefore, the same protection."[14]

Budgets, on the other hand, were regarded as instruments of planning and publicity. They should include "all the details of the work plans and specifications of cost of work."[15] In addition to the regular object and organization classifications, the budget would report the "total cost incurred, classified by *functions*—for determining questions of policy having to do with service rendered as well as to be rendered, and laying a foundation for appraisal of results."[16] The bureau also recommended a new instrument, a *work program,* which would furnish "a detailed schedule or analysis of each function, activity, or process within each organization unit. This analysis would give the total cost and the unit cost wherever standards were established."[17]

Truly a far-sighted conception of budgeting! There would be three documents for the three basic functions of budgeting. Although the bureau did not use the analytic framework suggested above, it seems that the appropriations were intended for control purposes, the budget for planning purposes, and the work program for management purposes. Each of the three documents would have its specialized information scheme, but jointly they would comprise a multi-purpose budget system not very different from PPB, even though the language of crosswalking or systems analysis was not used.

Yet the plan failed, for in the end the bureau was left with object accounts pegged to a control orientation. The bureau's distinction between budgets and appropriations was not well understood, and the work-program idea was rejected by New York City on the ground that adequate accounting backup was lacking. The bureau had failed to recognize that the conceptual distinction between budgets and appropriations tends to break down under the stress of informational demands. If the legislature appropriates by objects, the budget very likely will be classified by objects. Conversely, if there are no functional accounts, the prospects for including such data in the budget are diminshed substantially. As has almost always been the case, the budget came to mirror the appropriations act; in each, objects were paramount. It remains to be seen whether PPB will be able to break this interlocking informational pattern.

By the early 1920s the basic functions of planning and management were overlooked by those who carried the gospel of budget reform across the nation. First generation budget workers concentrated on perfecting and spreading the widely approved object-of-expenditure approach, and budget writers settled into a nearly complete preoccupation with forms and with factual descriptions of actual and recommended procedures. Although ideas about the use of the budget for planning and management purposes were retained in Buck's catalogs of "approved" practices,[18] they did not have sufficient priority to challenge tradition.

From the start, federal budgeting was placed on a control, object-of-expenditure footing, the full flavor of which can be perceived in reading

Charles G. Dawes' documentary on *The First Year of the Budget of The United States*. According to Dawes,

> The Bureau of the Budget is concerned only with the humbler and routine business of Government. Unlike cabinet officers, it is concerned with no question of policy, save that of economy and efficiency.[19]

This distinction fitted neatly with object classifications that provided a firm accounting base for the routine conduct of government business, but no information on policy implications of public expenditures. Furthermore, in its first decade, the bureau's tiny staff (forty or fewer) had to coordinate a multitude of well-advertised economy drives which shaped the job of the examiner as being that of reviewing itemized estimates to pare them down. Although Section 209 of the Budget and Accounting Act had authorized the bureau to study and recommend improvements in the organization and administrative practices of federal agencies, the bureau was overwhelmingly preoccupied with the business of control.

The Management Orientation

Although no single action represents the shift from a control to a management orientation, the turning point in this evolution probably came with the New Deal's broadening perspective of government responsibilities.

During the 1920s and 1930s, occasional voices urged a return to the conceptions of budgeting advocated by the early reformers. In a notable 1924 article, Lent D. Upson argued vigorously that "budget procedure had stopped halfway in its development," and he proposed six modifications in the form of the budget, the net effect being a shift in emphasis from accounting control to functional accounting.[20] A similar position was taken a decade later by Wylie Kilpatrick who insisted that "the one fundamental basis of expenditure is functional, an accounting of payments for the services performed by government."[21]

Meanwhile, gradual changes were preparing the way for a reorientation of budgeting to a management mission. Many of the administrative abuses that had given rise to object controls were curbed by statutes and regulations and by a general upgrading of the public service. Reliable accounting systems were installed and personnel and purchasing reforms introduced, thereby freeing budgeting from some of its watchdog chores. The rapid growth of government activities and expenditures made it more difficult and costly for central officials to keep track of the myriad objects in the budget. With expansion, the bits and pieces into which the objects were itemized became less and less significant while the aggregate of activities performed became more significant. With expansion, there was heightened need for central management of the incohesive sprawl of administrative agencies.

The climb in activities and expenditures also signaled radical changes in the role of the budget system. As long as government was considered a "necessary evil," and there was little recognition of the social value of public expenditures, the main function of budgeting was to keep spending in check. Because the outputs were deemed to be of limited and fixed value, it made sense to use the budget for central control over inputs. However, as the work and accomplishments of public agencies came to be regarded as benefits, the task of budgeting was redefined as the effective marshaling of fiscal and organizational resources for the attainment of benefits. This new posture focused attention on the problems of managing large programs and organizations, and on the opportunities for using the budget to extend executive hegemony over the dispersed administrative structure.

All these factors converged in the New Deal years. Federal expenditures rose rapidly from $4.2 billion in 1932 to $10 billion in 1940. Keynesian economics (the full budgetary implications of which are emerging only now in PPB) stressed the relationship between public spending and the condition of the economy. The President's Committee on Administrative Management (1937) castigated the routinized, control-minded approach of the Bureau of the Budget and urged that budgeting be used to coordinate federal activities under presidential leadership. With its transfer in 1939 from the Treasury to the newly-created Executive Office of the President, the bureau was on its way to becoming the leading management arm of the federal government. The bureau's own staff was increased tenfold; it developed the administrative management and statistical coordination functions that it still possesses; and it installed apportionment procedures for budget execution. More and more, the bureau was staffed from the ranks of public administration rather than from accounting, and it was during the directorship of Harold D. Smith (1939–46) that the bureau substantially embraced the management orientation.[22] Executive Order 8248 placed the president's imprimatur on the management philosophy. It directed the bureau

> to keep the President informed of the progress of activities by agencies of the Government with respect to work proposed, work actually initiated, and work completed, together with the relative timing of work between the several agencies of the Government; all

to the end that the work programs of the several agencies of the executive branch of the Government may be coordinated and that the monies appropriated by the Congress may be expended in the most economical manner possible to prevent overlapping and duplication of effort.

Accompanying the growing management use of the budget process for the appraisal and improvement of administrative performance, and the scientific management movement with its historical linkage to public administration, were far more relevant applications of managerial cost accounting to governmental operations. Government agencies sought to devise performance standards and the rudimentary techniques of work measurement were introduced in several agencies including the Forest Service, the Census Bureau, and the Bureau of Reclamation.[23] Various professional associations developed grading systems to assess administrative performance as well as the need for public services. These crude and unscientific methods were the forerunners of more sophisticated and objective techniques. At the apogee of these efforts, Clarence Ridley and Herbert Simon published *Measuring Municipal Activities: A Survey of Suggested Criteria for Appraising Administration,* in which they identified five kinds of measurement—(1) needs, (2) results, (3) costs, (4) effort, and (5) performance—and surveyed the obstacles to the measurement of needs and results. The latter three categories they combined into a measure of administrative efficiency. This study provides an excellent inventory of the state of the technology prior to the breakthrough made by cost-benefit and systems analysis.

At the close of World War II, the management orientation was entrenched in all but one aspect of federal budgeting—the classification of expenditures. Except for isolated cases (such as TVA's activity accounts and the project structure in the Department of Agriculture), the traditional object accounts were retained though the control function had receded in importance. In 1949 the Hoover Commission called for alterations in budget classifications consonant with the management orientation. It recommended "that the whole budgetary concept of the Federal Government should be refashioned by the adoption of a budget based upon functions, activities, and projects."[24] To create a sense of novelty, the commission gave a new label—performance budgeting—to what had long been known as functional or activity budgeting. Because its task force had used still another term—program budgeting—there were two new terms to denote the budget innovations of that period. Among writers there was no uniformity in usage, some preferring the "program budgeting" label, others "performance budgeting," to describe the same things. The level of confusion has been increased recently by the association of the term "program budgeting" (also the title of the Rand publication edited by David Novick) with the PPB movement.

Although a variety of factors and expectations influenced the Hoover Commission, and the commission's proposals have been interpreted in many ways, including some that closely approximate the PPB concept, for purposes of clarity, and in accord with the control-management-planning framework, performance budgeting *as it was generally understood and applied* must be distinguished from the emergent PPB idea. The term "performance budgeting" is hereafter used in reference to reforms set in motion by the Hoover Commission and the term "program budgeting" is used in conjunction with PPB.

Performance budgeting is management-oriented; its principal thrust is to help administrators to assess the work-efficiency of operating units by (1) casting budget categories in functional terms, and (2) providing work-cost measurements to facilitate the efficient performance of prescribed activities. Generally, its method is particularistic, the reduction of work-cost data into discrete, measurable units. Program budgeting (PPB) is planning-oriented; its main goal is to rationalize policy-making by providing (1) data on the costs and benefits of alternative ways of attaining proposed public objectives, and (2) output measurements to facilitate the effective attainment of chosen objectives. As a policy device, program budgeting departs from simple engineering models of efficiency in which the objective is fixed and the quantity of inputs and outputs is adjusted to an optimal relationship. In PPB, the objective itself is variable; analysis may lead to a new statement of objectives. In order to enable budget-makers to evaluate the costs and benefits of alternative expenditure options, program budgeting focuses on expenditure aggregates; the details come into play only as they contribute to an analysis of the total (the system) or of marginal trade-offs among competing proposals. Thus, in this macroanalytic approach, the accent is on comprehensiveness and on grouping data into categories that allow comparisons among alternative expenditure mixes.

Performance budgeting derived its ethos and much of its technique from cost accounting and scientific management; program budgeting has drawn its core ideas from economics and systems analysis. In the performance budgeting literature, budgeting is described as a "tool of management" and the budget as a "work program." In PPB, budgeting is an allocative process among competing claims, and the budget is a statement of policy. Chronologically, there was a gap of several years between the bloom of performance budgeting and the first articulated conceptions of program budgeting. In the aftermath of the first Hoover report, and especially during the early 1950s, there was a plethora of writings on the administrative advantages of the performance budget. Substantial interest in program budgeting did not emerge until the mid-1950s when a number of economists (including Smithies, Novick, and McKean) began to urge reform of the federal budget system. What the economists had in mind was not the same thing as the Hoover Commission.

In line with its management perspective, the commission averred that "the all-important thing in budgeting is the work or service to be accomplished, and what that work or service will cost."[25] Mosher followed this view closely in writing that "the central idea of the performance budget . . . is that the budget process be focused upon programs and functions—that is, accomplishments to be achieved, work to be done."[26] But from the planning perspective, the all-important thing surely is not the work or service to be accomplished but the objectives or purposes to be fulfilled by the investment of public funds. Whereas in performance budgeting, work and activities are treated virtually as ends in themselves, in program budgeting work and services are regarded as intermediate aspects, the process of converting resources into outputs. Thus, in a 1954 Rand paper, Novick defined a program as "the sum of the steps or interdependent activities which enter into the attainment of a specified objective. The program, therefore, is the end objective and is developed or budgeted in terms of all the elements necessary to its execution."[27] Novick goes on to add, "this is not the sense in which the government budget now uses the term."

Because the evaluation of performance and the evaluation of program are distinct budget functions, they call for different methods of classification which serve as an intermediate layer between objects and organizations. The activities relate to the functions and work of a distinct operating unit; hence their classification ordinarily conforms to organizational lines. This is the type of classification most useful for an administrator who has to schedule the procurement and utilization of resources for the production of goods and services. Activity classifications gather under a single rubric all the expenditure data needed by a manager to run his unit. The evaluation of programs, however, requires an end-product classification that is oriented to the mission and purposes of government. This type of classification may not be very useful for the manager, but it is of great value to the budget-maker who has to decide how to allocate scarce funds among competing claims. Some of the difference between end-product and activity classifications can be gleaned by comparing the Coast Guard's existing activity schedule with the proposed program structure on the last page of Bulletin 66-3. The activity structure which was developed under the aegis of performance budgeting is geared to the operating responsibilities of the Coast Guard: Vessel Operations, Aviation Operations, Repair and Supply Facilities, and others. The proposed program structure is hinged to the large purposes sought through Coast Guard operations: Search and Rescue, Aids to Navigation, Law Enforcement, and so on.

It would be a mistake to assume that performance techniques presuppose program budgeting or that it is not possible to collect performance data without program classifications. Nevertheless, the view has gained hold that a program budget is "a transitional type of budget between the orthodox (traditional) character and object budget on the one hand and performance budget on the other."[28] Kammerer and Shadoan stress a similar connection. The former writes that "a *performance* budget carries the program budget one step further: into *unit costs*."[29] Shadoan "envisions 'performance budgeting' as an extension of . . . the program budget concept to which the element of unit work measurement has been added."[30] These writers ignore the divergent functions served by performance and program budgets. It is possible to devise and apply performance techniques without relating them to, or having the use of, larger program aggregates. A cost accountant or work measurement specialist can measure the cost or effort required to perform a repetitive task without probing into the purpose of the work or its relationship to the mission of the organization. Work measurement—"a method of establishing an equitable relationship between the volume of work performed and manpower utilized"—[31] is only distantly and indirectly related to the process of determining governmental policy at the higher levels. Program classifications are vitally linked to the making and implementation of policy through the allocation of public resources. As a general rule, performance budgeting is concerned with the *process of work* (what methods should be used) while program budgeting is concerned with the *purpose of work* (what activities should be authorized).

Perhaps the most reliable way to describe this difference is to show what was tried and accomplished under performance budgeting. First of all, performance budgeting led to the introduction of activity classifications, the management-orientation of which has already been discussed. Second, narrative descriptions of program and performance were added to the budget document. These statements give the budget reader a general picture of the work that will be done by the organizational unit requesting funds. But unlike the analytic documents currently being developed under PPB, the narratives have a descriptive and justificatory function; they do not provide an objective basis for evaluating the cost-utility of an expenditure. Indeed, there hardly is any evidence that the narratives have been used for decision-making; rather they seem best suited for giving the uninformed outsider some glimpses of what is going on inside.

Third, performance budgeting spawned a multitude of work-cost measurement explorations. Most used, but least useful, were the detailed workload statistics assembled by administrators to justify their requests for additional funds. On a higher level of sophistication were attempts to apply the techniques of scientific management and cost accounting to the development of work and productivity standards. In these efforts, the Bureau of the Budget had a long involvement, beginning with the issuance of the trilogy of work measurement handbooks in 1950 and reaching its highest development in the productivity-measurement studies that were published in 1964. All these applications were at a level of detail useful for managers with operating or supervisory responsibilities, but of scant usefulness for top-level officials who have to determine organizational objectives and goals. Does it really help top officials if they know that is cost $0.07 to wash a pound of laundry or that the average postal employee processes 289 items of mail per hour? These are the main fruits of performance measurements, and they have an important place in the management of an organization. They are of great value to the operating official who has the limited function of getting a job done, but they would put a crushing burden on the policy-maker whose function is to map the future course of action.

Finally, the management viewpoint led to significant departures from PPB's principle that the expenditure accounts should show total systems cost. The 1949 National Security Act (possibly the first concrete result of the Hoover report) directed the segregation of capital and operating costs in the defense budget. New York State's performance-budgeting experiment for TB hospitals separated expenditures into cost centers (a concept derived from managerial cost accounting) and within each center into fixed and variable costs. In most manpower and work measurements, labor has been isolated from other inputs. Most important, in many states and localities (and implicitly in federal budgeting) the cost of continuing existing programs has been separated from the cost of new or expanded programs. This separation is useful for managers who build up a budget in terms of increments and decrements from the base, but it is a violation of program budgeting's working assumption that all claims must be pitted against one another in the competition for funds. Likewise, the forms of separation previously mentioned make sense from the standpoint of the manager, but impair the planner's capability to compare expenditure alternatives.

The Planning Orientation

The foregoing has revealed some of the factors leading to the emergence of the planning orientation. Three important developments influenced the evolution from a management to a planning orientation.

(1) Economic analysis—macro and micro—has had an increasing part in the shaping of fiscal and budgetary policy.

(2) The development of new informational and decisional technologies has enlarged the applicability of objective analysis to policy making. And,

(3) There has been a gradual convergence of planning and budgetary processes.

Keynesian economics with its macroanalytic focus on the impact of governmental action on the private sector had its genesis in the underemployment economy of the Great Depression. In calling attention to the opportunities for attaining full employment by means of fiscal policy, the Keynesians set into motion a major restatement of the central budget function. From the utilization of fiscal policy to achieve economic objectives, it was but a few steps to the utilization of the budget process to achieve fiscal objectives. Nevertheless, between the emergence and the victory of the new economics, there was a lapse of a full generation, a delay due primarily to the entrenched balanced-budget ideology. But the full realization of the budget's economic potential was stymied on the revenue side by static tax policies and on the expenditure side by status-spending policies.

If the recent tax policy of the federal government is evidence that the new economics has come of age, it also offers evidence of the long-standing failure of public officials to use the taxing power as a variable constraint on the economy. Previously, during normal times, the tax structure was accepted as given, and the task of fiscal analysis was to forecast future tax yields so as to ascertain how much would be available for expenditure. The new approach treats taxes as variable, to be altered periodically in accord with national policy and economic conditions. Changes in tax rates are not to be determined (as they still are in virtually all states and localities) by how much is needed to cover expenditures but by the projected impact of alternative tax structures on the economy.

It is more than coincidental that the advent of PPB has followed on the heels of the explicit utilization of tax policy to guide the economy. In macroeconomics, taxes and expenditures are mirror images of one another; a tax cut and an expenditure increase have comparable impacts. Hence, the hinging of tax policy to economic considerations inevitably led to the similar treatment of expenditures. But there were (and remain) a number of obstacles to the utilization of the budget as a fiscal tool. For one thing, the conversion of the budget process to an economic orientation probably was slowed by the Full Employment Act of 1946, which established the Council of Economic Advisers and transferred the Budget Bureau's fiscal analysis function to the council. The institutional separation between the CEA and the BOB and between fiscal policy and budget-making was not compensated by cooperative work relationships. Economic analysis had only a slight impact on expenditure policy. It offered a few guidelines (for example, that spending should be increased during recessions) and a few ideas (such as a shelf of public works projects), but it did not feed into the regular channels of budgeting. The business of preparing the budget was foremost a matter of responding to agency spending pressures, not of responding to economic conditions.

Moreover, expenditures (like taxes) have been treated virtually as given, to be determined by the unconstrained claims of the spending units. In the absence of central policy instructions, the agencies have been allowed to vent their demands without prior restraints by central authorities and without an operational set of planning guidelines. By the time the bureau gets into the act, it is faced with the overriding task of bringing estimates into line with projected resources. In other words, the bureau has had a budget-cutting function, to reduce claims to an acceptable level. The President's role has been similarly restricted. He is the *gatekeeper* of federal budgeting. He directs the pace of spending increases by deciding which of the various expansions proposed by the agencies shall be included in the budget. But, as the gatekeeper, the President rarely has been able to look back at the items that have previously passed through the gate; his attention is riveted to those programs that are departures from the established base. In their limited roles, neither the bureau nor the President has been able to inject fiscal and policy objectives into the forefront of budget preparation.

It will not be easy to wean budgeting from its utilization as an administrative procedure for financing ongoing programs to a decisional process for determining the range and direction of public objectives and the government's involvement in the economy. In the transition to a planning emphasis, an important step was the 1963 hearings of the Joint Economic Committee on *The Federal Budget as an Economic Document*. These hearings and the pursuant report of the JEC explored the latent policy opportunities in budget-making. Another development was the expanded time horizons manifested by the multi-year expenditure projections introduced in the early 1960s. Something of a breakthrough was achieved via the revelation that the existing tax structure would yield cumulatively larger increments of uncommitted funds—estimated as much as $50 billion by 1970—which could be applied to a number of alternative uses. How much of the funds should be "returned" to the private sector through tax reductions and how much through expenditure increases? How much should go to the states and localities under a broadened system of federal grants? How much should be allocated to the rebuilding of cities, to the improvement of education, or to the eradication of racial injustices? The traditional budget system lacked the analytic tools to cope with these questions, though decisions ultimately would be made one way or another. The expansion of the time horizon from the single-year to a multi-year frame enhances the opportunity for planning and analysis to have an impact on future expenditure decisions. With a one-year perspective, almost all options have been foreclosed by previous commitments; analysis is effective only for the increments provided by self-generating revenue increases or to the extent that it is feasible to convert funds from one use to another. With a longer time span, however, many more options are open, and economic analysis can have a prominent part in determining which course of action to pursue.

So much for the macroeconomic trends in budget reform. On the microeconomic side, PPB traces its lineage to the attempts of welfare economists to construct a science of finance predicated on the principle of marginal utility. Such a science, it was hoped, would furnish objective criteria for determining the optimal allocation of public funds among competing uses. By appraising the marginal costs and benefits of alternatives (poor relief versus battleships in Pigou's classic example), it would be possible to determine which combination of expenditures afforded maximum utility. The quest for a welfare function provided the conceptual underpinning for a 1940 article on "The Lack of a Budgetary Theory" in which V. O. Key noted the absence of a theory which would determine whether "to allocate x dollars to activity A instead of B."[32] In terms of its direct contribution to budgetary practice, welfare economics has been a failure. It has not been possible to distill the conflicts and complexities of political life into a welfare criterion or homogeneous distribution formula. But stripped of its normative and formal overtones, its principles have been applied to budgeting by economists such as Arthur Smithies. Smithies has formulated a budget rule that "expenditure proposals should be considered in the light of the objectives they are intended to further, and in general final expenditure decisions should not be made until all claims on the budget can be considered."[33] PPB is the application of this rule to budget practice. By structuring expenditures so as to juxtapose substitutive elements within program categories, and by analyzing the costs and benefits of the various substitutes, PPB has opened the door to the use of marginal analysis in budgeting.

Actually, the door was opened somewhat by the development of new decisional and informational technologies, the second item on the list of influences in the evolution of the planning orientation. Without the availability of the decisional-informational capability provided by cost-benefit and systems analysis, it is doubtful that PPB would be part of the budgetary apparatus today. The new technologies make it possible to cope with the enormous informational and analytic burdens imposed by PPB. As aids to calculation, they furnish a methodology for the analysis of alternatives, thereby expanding the range of decision-making in budgeting.

Operations research, the oldest of these technologies, grew out of complex World War II conditions that required the optimal coordination of manpower, material, and equipment to achieve defense objectives, Operations research is most applicable to those repetitive operations where the opportunity for qualification is highest. Another technology, cost-benefit analysis, was intensively adapted during the 1950s to large-scale water resource investments, and subsequently to many other governmental functions. Systems analysis is the most global of these technologies. It involves the skillful analysis of the major factors that go into the attainment of an interconnected set of objectives. Systems analysis has been applied in DOD to the choice of weapons systems, the location of military bases, and the determination of sealift-airlift requirements. Although the extension of these technologies across-the-board to government was urged repeatedly by members of the Rand Corporation during the 1950s, it was DOD's experience that set the stage for the current ferment. It cannot be doubted that the coming of PPB has been pushed ahead several years or more by the "success story" in DOD.

The third stream of influence in the transformation of the budget function has been a closing of the gap between planning and budgeting. Institutionally and operationally, planning and budgeting have run along separate tracks. The national government has been reluctant to embrace central planning of any sort because of identification with socialist management of the economy. The closest thing we have had to a central planning agency was the National Resources Planning Board in the 1939—1943 period. Currently, the National Security Council and the Council of Economic Advisors have planning responsibilities in the defense and fiscal areas. As far as the Bureau of the Budget is concerned, it has eschewed the planning function in favor of control and management. In many states and localities, planning and budgeting are handled by separate organizational units: in the states, because limitations on debt financing have encouraged the separation of the capital and operating budgets and in the cities, because the professional autonomy and land-use preoccupations of the planners have set them apart from the budgeteers.

In all governments, the appropriations cycle, rather than the anticipation of future objectives, tends to dictate the pace and posture of budgeting. Into the repetitive, one-year span of the budget is wedged all financial decisions, including those that have multi-year implications. As a result, planning, if it is done at all, "occurs independently of budgeting and with little relation to it."[34] Budgeting and planning, moreover, invite disparate perspectives: the one is conservative and negativistic; the other, innovative and expansionist. As Mosher has noted, "budgeting and planning are apposite, if not opposite. In extreme form, the one means saving; the other, spending."[35]

Nevertheless, there has been some *rapprochement* of planning and budgeting. One factor is the long lead-time in the development and procurement of hardware and capital investments. The multi-year projections inaugurated several years ago were a partial response to this problem. Another factor has been the diversity of government agencies involved in related functions. This has given rise to various *ad hoc* coordinating devices, but it also has pointed to the need for permanent machinery to integrate dispersed activities. Still another factor has been the sheer growth of federal activities and expenditures and the need for a rational system of allocation. The operational code of planners contains three tenets relevant to these budgetary needs: (1) planning is future-oriented; it connects present decisions to the attainment of a desired future state of affairs; (2) planning, ideally, encompasses all resources involved in the attainment of future objectives. It strives for comprehensiveness. The *master plan* is the one that brings within its scope all relevant factors; (3) planning is means-ends oriented. The allocation of resources is strictly dictated by the ends that are to be accomplished. All this is to say that planning is an economizing process, though planners are more oriented to the future than economists. It is not surprising that planners have found the traditional budget system deficient,[36] nor that the major reforms entailed by PPB emphasize the planning function.

Having outlined the several trends in the emerging transition to a planning orientation, it remains to mention several qualifications. First, the planning emphasis is not predominant in federal budgeting at this time. Although PPB asserts the paramountcy of planning, PPB itself is not yet a truly operational part of the budget machinery. We are now at the dawn of a new era in budgeting; high noon is still a long way off. Second, this transition has not been preceded by a reorientation of the Bureau of the Budget. Unlike the earlier change-over from control to management in which the alteration of budgetary techniques *followed* the revision of the bureau's role, the conversion from management to planning is taking a different course—first, the installation of new techniques; afterwards, a reformulation of the bureau's mission. Whether this sequence will hinder reform efforts is a matter that cannot be predicted, but it should be noted that in the present instance the bureau cannot convert to a new mission by bringing in a wholly new staff, as was the case in the late 1930s and early 1940s.

What Difference Does It Make?

The starting point for the author was distinguishing the old from the new in budgeting. The interpretation has been framed in analytic terms, and budgeting has been viewed historically in three stages corresponding to the three basic functions of budgeting. In this analysis, an attempt has been made to identify the difference between the existing and the emerging as a difference between management and planning orientations.

In an operational sense, however, what difference does it make whether the central budget process is oriented toward planning rather than management? Does the change merely mean a new way of making decisions, or does it mean different decisions as well? These are not easy questions to answer, particularly since the budget system of the future will be a compound of all three functions. The case for PPB rests on the assumption that the form in which information is classified and used governs the actions of budget-makers, and, conversely, that alterations in form will produce desired changes in behavior. Take away the assumption that behavior follows form, and the movement for PPB is reduced to a trivial manipulation of techniques—form for form's sake without any significant bearing on the conduct of budgetary affairs.

Yet this assumed connection between roles and information is a relatively uncharted facet of the PPB literature. The behavioral side of the equation has been neglected. PPB implies that each participant will behave as a sort of "Budgetary Man," a counterpart of the classical "Economic Man" and Simon's "Administrative Man."[37] "Budgetary Man," whatever his station or role in the budget process, is assumed to be guided by an unwavering commitment to the rule of efficiency; in every instance he chooses that alternative that optimizes the allocation of public resources.

PPB probably takes an overly mechanistic view of the impact of form on behavior and underestimates the strategic and volitional aspects of budget-making. In the political arena, data are used to influence the "who gets what" in budgets and appropriations. If information influences behavior, the reverse also is true. Indeed, data are more tractable than roles; participants are more likely to seek and use data which suit their preferences than to alter their behavior automatically in response to formal changes.

All this constrains, rather than negates, the impact of budget form. The advocates of PPB, probably in awareness of the above limitations, have imported into budgeting men with professional commitments to the types of analysis and norms required by the new techniques, men with a background in economics and systems analysis, rather than with general administrative training.

PPB aspires to create a different environment for choice. Traditionally, budgeting has defined its mission in terms of identifying the existing base and proposed departures from it—"This is where we are; where do we go from here?" PPB defines its mission in terms of budgetary objectives and purposes—"Where do we want to go? What do we do to get there?" The environment of choice under traditional circumstances is *incremental;* in PPB it is *teletic.* Presumably, these different processes will lead to different budgetary outcomes.

A budgeting process which accepts the base and examines only the increments will produce decisions to transfer the present into the future with a few small variations. The curve of government activities will be continuous, with few zigzags or breaks. A budget-making process which begins with objectives will require the base to compete on an equal footing with new proposals. The decisions will be more radical than those made under incremental conditions. This does not mean that each year's budget will lack continuity with the past. There are sunk costs that have to be reckoned, and the benefits of radical changes will have to outweigh the costs of terminating prior commitments. Furthermore, the extended time span of PPB will mean that big investment decisions will be made for a number of years, with each year being a partial installment of the plan. Most important, the political manifestations of sunk costs—vested interests—will bias decisions away from radical departures. The conservatism of the political system, therefore, will tend to minimize the decisional differences between traditional and PPB approaches. However, the very availability of analytic data will cause a shift in the balance of economic and political forces that go into the making of a budget.

Teletic and incremental conditions of choice lead to still another distinction. In budgeting, which is committed to the established base, the flow of budgetary decisions is upward and aggregative. Traditionally, the first step in budgeting, in anticipation of the call for estimates, is for each department to issue its own call to prepare and to submit a set of estimates. This call reaches to the lowest level capable of assembling its own estimates. Lowest level estimates form the building blocks for the next level where they are aggregated and reviewed and transmitted upward until the highest level is reached and the totality constitutes a department-wide budget. Since budgeting is tied to a base, the building-up-from-below approach is sensible; each building block estimates the cost of what it is already doing plus the cost of the increments it wants. (The building blocks, then, are decisional elements, not simply informational elements as is often assumed.)

PPB reverses the informational and decisional flow. Before the call for estimates is issued, top policy has to be made, and this policy constrains the estimates prepared below. For each lower level, the relevant policy instructions are issued by the superior level prior to the preparation of estimates. Accordingly, the critical decisional process—that of deciding on purposes and plans—has a downward and disaggregative flow.

If the making of policy is to be antecedent to the costing of estimates, there will have to be a shift in the distribution of budget responsibilities. The main energies of the Bureau of the Budget are now devoted to budget preparation; under PPB these energies will be centered on what we may term *prepreparation*—the stage of budget-making that deals with policy and is prior to the preparation of the budget. One of the steps marking the advent of the planning orientation was the inauguration of the Spring Preview several years ago for the purpose of affording an advance look at departmental programs.

If budget-making is to be oriented to the planning function, there probably will be a centralization of policy-making, both within and among departments. The DOD experience offers some precedent for predicting that greater budgetary authority will be vested in department heads than heretofore, but there is no firm basis for predicting the degree of centralization that may derive from the relatedness of objectives pursued by many departments. It is possible that the mantle of central budgetary policy will be assumed by the bureau; indeed, this is the expectation in many agencies. On the other hand, the bureau gives little indication at this time that it is willing or prepared to take this comprehensive role.

Some Basic Differences Between Budget Orientations

Characteristic	Control	Management	Planning
Personnel skill	Accounting	Administration	Economics
Information focus	Objects	Activities	Purposes
Key budget stage (central)	Execution	Preparation	Pre-preparation
Breadth of measurement	Discrete	Discrete/ activities	Comprehensive
Role of budget agency	Fiduciary	Efficiency	Policy
Decisional-flow	Upward-aggregative	Upward-aggregative	Downward-disaggregative
Type of choice	Incremental	Incremental	Teletic
Control responsibility	Central	Operating	Operating
Management responsibility	Dispersed	Central	Supervisory
Planning responsibility	Dispersed	Dispersed	Central
Budget-appropriations classifications	Same	Same	Different
Appropriations-organizational link	Direct	Direct	Crosswalk

Conclusion

The various differences between the budgetary orientations are charted in the table presented here. All the differences may be summed up in the statement that the ethos of budgeting will shift from justification to analysis. To far greater extent than heretofore, budget decisions will be influenced by explicit statements of objectives and by a formal weighing of the costs and benefits of alternatives.

Notes

[1] New York Bureau of Municipal Research, *Making a Municipal Budget* (New York: 1907), pp. 9–10.

[2] Robert N. Anthony, *Planning and Control Systems: A Framework for Analysis* (Boston: 1965), pp. 16–18.

[3] Frederick A. Cleveland, "Evolution of the Budget Idea in the United States," *Annals of the American Academy of Political and Social Science*, 62 (1915), 16.

[4] *Ibid.*, p. 17.

[5] See Frank J. Goodnow, "The Limit of Budgetary Control," *Proceedings of the American Political Science Association* (Baltimore: 1913), p. 72; also William F. Willoughby, "Allotment of Funds by Executive Officials, An Essential Feature of Any Correct Budgetary System," *ibid.*, pp. 78–87.

[6] U. S., President's Commission on Economy and Efficiency, *The Need for a National Budget* (Washington: 1912), pp. 210–213.

[7] Charles A. Beard, "Prefatory Note," *ibid.*, p. vii.

[8] New York Bureau of Municipal Research, "Some Results and Limitations of Central Financial Control in New York City," *Municipal Research*, 81 (1917), 10.

[9] New York Bureau of Municipal Research, "Next Steps in the Development of a Budget Procedure for the City of Greater New York," *Municipal Research*, 57 (1915), 39.

[10] *Ibid.*, p. 67.

[11] "Some Results and Limitations . . .," p. 9.

[12] "Next Steps . . .," p. 35.

[13] *Ibid.*, p. 7.

[14] *Ibid.*, p. 39.

[15] "Some Results and Limitations . . .," p. 7.

[16] *Ibid.*, p. 9.

[17] "Next Steps . . .," p. 30.

[18] See A. E. Buck, *Public Budgeting* (New York: 1929), pp. 181–88.

[19] Charles G. Dawes, *The First Year of the Budget of the United States* (New York: 1923), preface, p. ii.

[20] Lent D. Upson, "Half-time Budget Methods," *The Annals of the American Academy of Political and Social Science*, 113 (1924), 72.

[21] Wylie Kilpatrick, "Classification and Measurement of Public Expenditure," *The Annals of the American Academy of Political and Social Science*, 183 (1936), 20.

[22] See Harold D. Smith, *The Management of Your Government* (New York: 1945).

[23] Public Administration Service, *The Work Unit in Federal Administration* (Chicago: 1937).

[24] U. S. Commission on Organization of the Executive Branch of the Government, *Budgeting and Accounting* (Washington: 1949), p. 8.

[25] *Ibid.*

[26] Frederick C. Mosher, *Program Budgeting: Theory and Practice* (Chicago: 1954), p. 79.

[27] David Novick, *Which Program Do We Mean in "Program Budgeting?"* (Santa Monica: 1954), p. 17.

[28] Lennex L. Meak and Kathryn W. Killian, *A Manual of Techniques for the Preparation, Consideration, Adoption, and Administration of Operating Budgets* (Chicago: 1963), p. 11.

[29] Gladys M. Kammerer, *Program Budgeting: An Aid to Understanding* (Gainesville: 1959), p. 6.

[30] Arlene Theuer Shadoan, *Preparation, Review, and Execution of the State Operating Budget* (Lexington: 1963), p. 13.

[31] U. S. Bureau of the Budget, *A Work Measurement System* (Washington: 1950), p. 2.

[32] V. O. Key, "The Lack of a Budgetary Theory," *The American Political Science Review*, 34 (1940), 1138.

[33] Arthur Smithies, *The Budgetary Process in the United States* (New York: 1955), p. 16.

[34] Mosher, *op. cit.*, p. 47–48.

[35] *Ibid.*, p. 48.

[36] See Edward C. Banfield, "Congress and the Budget: A Planner's Criticism," *The American Political Science Review*, 42 (1949), 1217–1227.

[37] Herbert A. Simon, *Administrative Behavior* (New York: 1957).

2

The Budget Process

DAVID J. OTT
ATTIAT F. OTT

Crucial to any discussion of budget policy—the setting of levels and composition of taxes and expenditures to achieve certain goals—is a knowledge of the administrative and political process through which expenditures and taxes are, in fact, determined. This chapter describes the process at the federal level and also indicates briefly the forces and individuals involved in making the many difficult decisions that go into the final budget.

Although budgeting is a continuing process, the term "budget cycle" is often used to emphasize its periodicity. There are clearly defined phases of budgeting in most budgetary systems. At the federal level in the United States, four phases can be identified: (1) executive preparation and submission, (2) legislative authorization and appropriation, (3) execution, and (4) audit.

Executive Preparation and Submission

Every year the executive branch of the federal government prepares the budget, which in January is submitted to the Congress by the President

Reprinted from *Federal Budget Policy*, rev. ed. (Washington, D.C.: the Brookings Institution, 1969), pp. 22–42, by permission of the authors and publisher. Figures have been renumbered. Copyright 1969 by the Brookings Institution.

FIGURE 1
Formulation of the Executive Budget

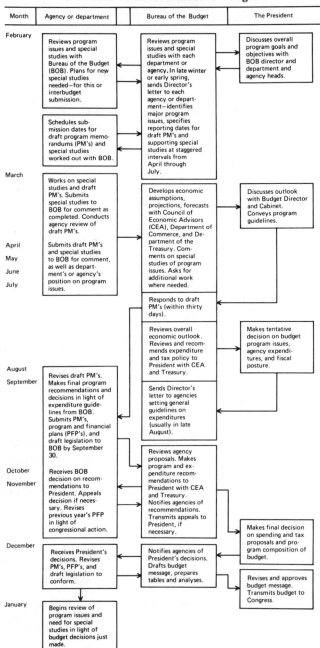

Month	Agency or department	Bureau of the Budget	The President
February	Reviews program issues and special studies with Bureau of the Budget (BOB). Plans for new special studies needed—for this or interbudget submission. Schedules submission dates for draft program memorandums (PM's) and special studies worked out with BOB.	Reviews program issues and special studies with each department or agency. In late winter or early spring, sends Director's letter to each agency or department—identifies major program issues, specifies reporting dates for draft PM's and supporting special studies at staggered intervals from April through July.	Discusses overall program goals and objectives with BOB director and department and agency heads.
March	Works on special studies and draft PM's. Submits special studies to BOB for comment as completed. Conducts agency review of draft PM's.	Develops economic assumptions, projections, forecasts with Council of Economic Advisors (CEA), Department of Commerce, and Department of the Treasury. Comments on special studies of program issues. Asks for additional work where needed.	Discusses outlook with Budget Director and Cabinet. Conveys program guidelines.
April May June July	Submits draft PM's and special studies to BOB for comment, as well as department's or agency's position on program issues.		
		Responds to draft PM's (within thirty days).	
		Reviews overall economic outlook. Reviews and recommends expenditure and tax policy to President with CEA and Treasury.	Makes tentative decision on budget program issues, agency expenditures, and fiscal posture.
August September	Revises draft PM's. Makes final program recommendations and decisions in light of expenditure guidelines from BOB. Submits PM's, program and financial plans (PFP's), and draft legislation to BOB by September 30.	Sends Director's letter to agencies setting general guidelines on expenditures (usually in late August).	
October November	Receives BOB decision on recommendations to President. Appeals decision if necessary. Revises previous year's PFP in light of congressional action.	Reviews agency proposals. Makes program and expenditure recommendations to President with CEA and Treasury. Notifies agencies of recommendations. Transmits appeals to President, if necessary.	Makes final decision on spending and tax proposals and program composition of budget.
December	Receives President's decisions. Revises PM's, PFP's, and draft legislation to conform.	Notifies agencies of President's decisions. Drafts budget message, prepares tables and analyses.	Revises and approves budget message. Transmits budget to Congress.
January	Begins review of program issues and need for special studies in light of budget decisions just made.		

with his budget message. This budget is for the fiscal year beginning on the first of July following transmittal of the budget message. However, the preparation of the budget begins long before January. Figure 1 shows the approximate time sequence of, and participants in, each stage of budget preparation by the executive branch. The timing suggested is only approximate since it may vary under different pressures or in different departments. Nevertheless, the chart does indicate the lead time required to prepare the executive's budget.

Figure 1 illustrates a basic characteristic of budgeting in the executive branch—the two-way flow of decisions, up from the departments and agencies and then back down from the Bureau of the Budget and the President.[1] The individual organizational units in the departments and agencies make early plans for their programs and expenditures, which are consolidated and reviewed by the budget offices in each agency. The budget offices provide the agency with information when, in May, June, and July, programs for the coming year are discussed with the Bureau of the Budget. The bureau then can advise the President about preliminary agency and department plans and goals. This information, together with projections of the economic outlook and revenue estimates from the Treasury, the Bureau of the Budget, and the Council of Economic Advisers (in June, July, or August), gives the President and his advisers the basis for tentative overall budget policy decisions—about total expenditures, revenues, and programs. Guidelines reflecting these policy decisions then flow back down through the Bureau of the Budget to the departments and agencies in the form of planning figures to guide the preparation of their eventual budget submissions in the fall. They must then either modify their programs to fit the guidelines or appeal to the Bureau of the Budget and possibly even to the executive for a reversal of a decision affecting their budgets.

Three facets of the budget-making process are apparent in Figure 1: (1) the program-issue orientation of most of the budget process through late September; (2) the fiscal policy decisions about total expenditures and taxes that become crucial in the late summer and early fall of each year; and (3) the meshing of these two facets of budget formulation in the final budget decisions in November and December.

PPBS AND PROGRAM-ORIENTATION IN THE BUDGET PROCESS

The orientation of executive budgeting toward program issues is a relatively new phenomenon. It began in an informal way under President Kennedy and, in August 1965, was formally introduced by President Johnson in the form of an integrated planning-programming-budgeting system (PPBS) in the executive branch, to be used initially during late

1965 and 1966 in the preparation of the budget that would be submitted in January 1967 (the fiscal year 1968 budget) and to be developed further thereafter. The adoption of PPBS has already had a considerable impact on the budget process (as Figure 1 shows) and will likely have an even greater effect in the longer run.

Under PPBS budgeting, the focus is on the *uses* of federal expenditures—on the *output* provided for—rather than on dollar amounts allocated by agency or department. The aim of PPBS is to specify (and where possible to quantify) the objectives, or "output," of federal spending programs and then to minimize the cost of achieving these objectives or to ascertain whether program benefits exceed costs. To do so requires the *systematic use of analysis* in connection with budget formulation and program development and evaluation (the "planning" in PPBS).

The hallmarks of PPBS, then, are (1) specification of the objectives to be achieved through federal spending, (2) investigation of alternative means of achieving the objectives, (3) minimization of the costs or comparison of costs and benefits (when the benefits can be quantified), and perhaps most important, (4) systematic use of analysis throughout the process. Specifying the objectives, or output, of the budget really begins with the President, according to a former Budget Bureau director, Kermit Gordon:

> for the budget is his plan, and the implied priorities are his priorities. . . . The budget is the President's budget, in a real as well as in a formal sense.[2]

Departments or agencies may vary in the extent to which they specify goals consistent with the "presidential perspective," as Gordon characterizes it.[3] Under PPBS, however, when department or agency objectives are inconsistent with the President's priorities, it is immediately obvious. The first step under PPBS is to reorganize the budget structures of departments and agencies, so that their activities are grouped under a relatively small number (five to ten) of major "program packages." These in turn are divided into subordinate categories, which are made up of a large number of "program elements." The next step is to develop indices or measures to indicate the level of accomplishment under each program (the output), how much the various program elements contribute to "output" under the program, and the cost of the elements. This step leads directly to the second and third features of PPBS—analysis of the alternative means of achieving program objectives, and choice of the least-cost combination of program elements to achieve a given output.

Three department or agency documents are critical in the budget process under PPBS: (1) the program memorandum (PM), (2) the program and financial plan (PFP), and (3) special analytic studies. The program memorandum provides an explicit statement of the objectives, goals, and strategy (program) of the agency; it shows the agency's choices of programs and program elements. In addition, it summarizes the analytic studies that have led to the choices and identifies major policy issues relating to each program.[4]

The program and financial plan is basically designed to present the future implications of current decisions. It presents pertinent data on output and costs for a five-year period (the current fiscal year plus at least four future fiscal years) for each program element, *based on current decisions.* It is *not* a projection of future activities and spending by the agency, since decisions may be made to enlarge, reduce, or eliminate programs in the future, but only an attempt to show the agency, the Budget Bureau, and the President the implications, in terms of outputs and costs, of current program decisions.

The special analytic studies, which are prepared by agency PPB specialists, provide the underlying analysis on which choices of programs and program elements are based. These may include rather elaborate efforts to compare costs and benefits of various programs, simply to define the goals and output of a program, or to analyze the "cost-effectiveness" of alternative programs (to see which achieves a given goal at least cost to the government).[5]

Since PPBS is relatively new, it is too early to evaluate and measure the results against the initial hopes and expectations. There is considerable variation in the extent to which the departments and agencies have embraced the system; some have shown considerable enthusiasm and have already gone far in developing program and program element categories and in undertaking the necessary analytic studies. Others have not been very responsive and will move in this direction only with considerable prodding from the Bureau of the Budget (and perhaps the President). However, the point is that at least formally the budget process is being focused on the *objectives* of federal programs and there is no longer a preoccupation with *inputs.* In addition, increasing emphasis is being placed on systematic program analysis and evaluation.

BUDGET REVIEW: THE DIRECTOR'S LETTER

The budget process from early February through the summer is referred to as the "budget preview." The first step in this part of the budget process is the development of a director's letter.[6]

During February, departments and agencies confer with the Bureau of the Budget on the coming budget. The most important aspect of this early consultation is to identify, for each department or agency, a set of "program issues"—decisions that must be made regarding the scope and size of the agency's programs and program elements. These partly reflect program issues left over from the previous year's budget process; new issues are also raised.

The program issues for each agency are the product of negotiations between the BOB and the agency, often at the highest levels. The director of the Budget Bureau discusses in general terms program priorities with the President and his White House staff; these are reflected in his and his staff's discussions with the departments and agencies. At this early stage, then, the program orientation of the budget process already reflects, in a broad sense, the presidential perspective.

The discussions and decisions on program issues lead rather naturally to simultaneous consideration of the special analytic studies needed from each agency. Since these studies often cannot be geared to an annual budget cycle, plans will be laid for studies over two- or three-year periods, as well as for interim studies to provide limited information for decision making in the current year.

By late winter or early spring, the Budget director sends a letter to each department or agency head. This letter formalizes the agreements reached on program issues and analytic studies for each agency. It also specifies the dates each agency is to submit a draft program memorandum, together with analytic studies, to the Budget Bureau. The reporting dates are scheduled at staggered intervals from April through the summer.

AGENCY BUDGET PREVIEW ACTIVITIES

After the director's letter has gone out, the budget process centers in the agencies and departments. The activities there focus on (1) initiation and completion of analytic studies needed to reach decisions on the program issues identified in the director's letter, (2) intra-agency budget reviews for which the analytic studies are used to make program decisions, and (3) preparation of draft PMs, PFPs, legislation, and analytic studies for submission to the Budget Bureau.

All federal agencies and departments have budget offices and officers. The organization of the offices may vary, but generally the budget officer serves as a member of the department or agency staff. Since the initiation of PPBS, all agencies and departments also have staffs or specialists in PPBS analysis, both at the top of the agency or department and down in the "line," or operating, agencies. In fiscal year 1968, some

685 PPBS professionals were located in 21 agencies or departments (not including the Department of Defense). About half represented new additions to staffs; the other half were previous employees redesignated or converted to PPBS analysis.[7]

These specialists undertake the analytic studies suggested by the director's letter. The studies are done at the operating level in many agencies and reviewed by other specialists at the agency or department level. In other agencies, much of the analytic work has thus far been centered in the agency or department staff.

Through the agency budgeting office and professional staffs flows the information on programs and costs needed by the administrator to decide on program issues raised in the director's letter as well as programs and costs not at issue in the current year's budget. Often it is impossible to conduct the needed analysis in the time provided, and program issues may have to be decided on rather diverse grounds, ranging from the political pressures that may be swirling around a program to the administrator's intuitive judgment. Many agency or department programs and much of their budgets may not be included in the program issues raised in the director's letter. Every program cannot be studied carefully every year, and some may coast along on their own impetus. Further, a large segment of budget expenditures is virtually outside the budget process and will not often be reflected in program issues. For the last few years, for example, such items as interest on the public debt, veterans' pensions, and agricultural price supports have accounted for over 60 percent of total nondefense budget expenses and for over 25 percent of total budget expenditures. The levels of expenditure for these items are determined by provisions written into legislation authorizing the programs and by other factors not readily subject to annual budgetary control. They are, however, subject to review, and occasionally, legislation is proposed to change them. The crucial budget decisions, then, relate primarily to programs subject to budgetary control and take the form of an evaluation of relatively small increases in costs and activities.

The focus of the budget preview process on program issues and the use of the analytical paraphernalia of PPBS should not obscure the fact that budget making is and always will be a *political* process, and the politics of budget making are important in several ways at the agency level. Agencies and their "line people" are expected to be advocates of increased appropriations. It is generally accepted as natural and inevitable by Congress and the Budget Bureau that agency budget offices will have a strong interest in justifying their program decisions and appropriation requests. After all, they are expected to believe in their work and be enthusiastic about it. In fact, Congress and the Bureau of the Budget would find their task much more difficult if the agencies refused to play the role of advocate; as advocates the agencies supply information crucial to congressional and Budget Bureau decisions—information Congress and the bureau would otherwise have to obtain for themselves.

On the other hand, agencies or departments rarely ask for all they feel they could use. If they did, the Bureau of the Budget or Congress would probably make substantial cuts; to have proposals cut sharply every year would set an unfortunate precedent, and in any case, some cuts are inevitable in an agency budget. As guardians of the public purse, the Budget Bureau and Congress are expected to be more economy-minded than agency heads, who are responsible for the execution rather than the financing of specific programs. Moreover, the bureau has the task of weighing budget requests across the whole range of federal activity—it must make recommendations to the President concerning the choices open to him.

So in making decisions on programs and expenditures, agencies cannot, for strategic reasons, aim too high or too low. Their decision making will reflect seeking out and receiving clues and hints from the executive branch, Congress, clientele groups, and their own organizations. In this way they are able in most cases to get a rough idea of what will prove acceptable to the Budget Bureau, the President and his advisers, and the appropriations subcommittees in Congress.[8]

Thus, from March through July, the agencies and departments prepare for submission of their draft budget proposals to the Budget Bureau. Prior to the submission date, the agency or department usually has its own preview, when internal drafts of PMs, PFPs, and analytical studies are submitted, criticized, and revised.

Once the department or agency head is satisfied, the PM, PFP, and analytical studies are submitted to the Budget Bureau. There they are studied by the bureau staff; comments are made and revisions suggested. The agency then turns to preparation of its final set of budget documents due on September 30. At this stage, the emphasis remains on *programs*, not dollar amounts.

THE FISCAL SIDE OF BUDGETING

Although the budget process from February-September is mostly concerned with program analysis and issues, there is a continuing and parallel interest in the fiscal implications of the developing budget. Beginning with President Kennedy's term of office and continuing through the Johnson administration, the agencies concerned with the overall budget and its impact on the economy—the Budget Bureau, the Treasury, and the Council of Economic Advisers—have submitted periodic memorandums to the President, reviewing the economic situation and recent budget trends and revising the budget totals when necessary. This informal group, known as the "Troika," is regarded as having an important influence on budget and fiscal decision making. The President has periodic discussions with the Troika, sometimes joined by the chairman of the Federal Reserve Board (the group then becomes the "Quadriad"), and receives frequent memorandums from them. Out of these discussions and memorandums comes the President's decision on tax and expenditure policy.

During the summer months, the director of the bureau and his staff deal directly with the President and his advisers on emerging problems, initial clearance on major program decisions, and the overall revenue and expenditure outlook. By late summer the administration's overall budget policy for the forthcoming fiscal year begins to take shape.

Next comes a meeting of the director with each of the major agency heads to discuss the economic outlook, revenue, the total budget picture, the President's overall budget objective, and the agency's major budget items. After these meetings and further discussions with the President, in late summer, a "policy letter" is usually sent by the director of the Bureau of the Budget to agency and department heads giving information on various policy aims. More important, the general budget policy is translated into budget planning figures for some twenty agencies. These are not ceiling figures. Rather, the bureau is informing the agency that, in view of the administration's program, it is likely that the agency's budget will be somewhere near a certain figure. Agencies can bring in estimates exceeding the planning figure, but if they do, they must indicate where they could make cuts if required to get back down to the planning figure. It is at this point that the program and fiscal aspects of the budget process come together.

THE REVIEW PROCESS

This is a crucial stage in the budget process. The agencies and departments conduct intensive examinations of their programs in light of the planning figures or budget directives that have been passed down to them and in light of the previous year's action by the appropriations committees of Congress. The agency or department that is well within its planning figure has no problems. (This is so rare as to be completely outside the experience of most career agency budget officers.) Most, however, face a difficult decision about where to cut (in the absence of specific directives), or whether to cut at all, or whether to fight it out by appealing to the Budget Bureau and, if necessary, the President himself.

Following the review within the department, estimates are submitted to the Bureau of the Budget, where they are reviewed by examiners and hearings are held, first with the agency official and then within the bureau, where the final decisions on recommendations to the President will be made. At these hearings, the department or agency presents and defends its programs and budget before the examiner and other staff members of the Budget Bureau.

Relations between agencies and the Budget Bureau are important at this stage, in particular the relation between each agency and the bureau's examiners assigned to it. On the one hand, the agency is reluctant to incur Budget Bureau disfavor, for the bureau's recommendations to the President do carry weight.[9] Congress usually exceeds the President's appropriations recommendations with some reluctance and more commonly cuts them. At the same time, the bureau cannot restrain the agencies too much, for "end runs" by agencies to Congress to get funds disapproved by the bureau are not unusual. So both parties are constrained, and the end result is usually somewhere between what each would prefer.

On the basis of the hearings and his knowledge of agency programs, operations, and overall policies, the Budget Bureau examiner submits his recommendations to the director of the bureau, usually after informal consultation with the bureau staff. At this stage, the examiner's recommendations are subjected to a relatively formal evaluation by the Bureau of the Budget, which is called the "director's review." This is conducted by top staff members of the bureau—the director, the deputy director, and other officials, with the director usually serving as chairman.

Concurrent with the director's review is the last stage of executive budget preparation—presidential review of the budget as it emerges from the bureau and preparation of the annual budget document. After the President's review, his program decisions and approved "allowances" are sent to each agency head, who may then accept them or appeal them to the bureau, to the White House, or to the President himself. Another hearing on some of the issues is thus sometimes obtained. Also at this very hectic time, final conclusions are drawn concerning the economic outlook and prospective revenue, and these, together with the emerging expenditure estimates of the bureau, make it possible for the bureau, the Council of Economic Advisers, and the Treasury to recommend last-minute changes that will affect the size of the budget surplus or deficit. These changes may stimulate final appeals from the departments and agencies on decisions affecting their budgets.

During the third week in January—somewhat miraculously, considering the coordination and effort involved—the budget document and message are transmitted to Congress.

Congressional Authorization

The distinctive feature of the congressional phase of the budget process in the United States is the separation of expenditures and taxes and their consideration by different committees; there is almost no consideration of the administration's budget as a unified proposal. As a matter of fact, the legislative phase of budgeting is usually thought of only in terms of appropriations; taxation is viewed as a separate problem.

TERMINOLOGY

Before we discuss the process by which the Congress affects the level of expenditures, the meaning of the terms "expenditure," "authorization," and "appropriation" must be clarified.

The budget document sets forth the President's proposals for the executive agencies regarding cash expenditures and new obligational authority during a fiscal year. The expenditures Congress finally approves reflect two separate stages of decision. First, it must approve the functions for which expenditures are to be made; this is called "authorization." That is, the Congress passes legislation authorizing specific activities, such as foreign aid and defense, but does not provide funds and sometimes does not even specify the amount of funds implied in the activity.[10] As a matter of custom, authorizing legislation must be enacted before funds are granted. Most federal programs now require *annual* authorization by Congress.

After a specific activity has been authorized, funds are provided in "appropriations"—legislation by Congress permitting a government agency or department to commit or obligate the government to certain expenditures, or what is commonly called "new obligational authority."[11] Since appropriations are not considered until authorizing legislation is passed, many agencies in recent years have received their appropriations late in the congressional session. When an agency does not receive its new appropriation before the old one lapses, it operates under a "continuing resolution" passed by Congress, which allows it to spend at the previous year's rate. Appropriations come in several forms, ranging from one-year appropriations, which allow an agency to incur obligations only during one fiscal year (the most common form) to no-year appropriations, which are available (for obligation and expenditure) until the purpose of the spending is accomplished. Generally, if the obligational authority is not used during the specified period, it lapses and is no longer available to the agency unless the Congress specifically reappropriates it.

Expenditures out of new obligational authority must be committed within a certain period but need not be actually paid within that period. Even in the case of one-year appropriations, the agency is given two more years to pay the bills (for example, after deliveries have been made).

Since new obligational authority may be granted for a period longer than the fiscal year, there is always a substantial carryover of obligational authority from previous years. There is also a carryover of unspent obligations from the previous year or two, that is, obligational authority

FIGURE 2
Outlays for 1969 Related to Budget Authority

Total obligational authority — $424.0 billion

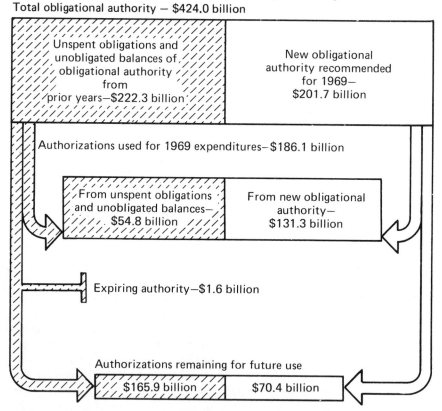

Source: *Budget for Fiscal 1969*, pp. 54–56.

that has been committed but under which no expenditures have actually been made. Thus the expenditure totals in a budget reflect expenditures expected to be made during the coming fiscal year out of uncommitted obligational authority—as well as unspent obligations—carried over from previous years and out of new obligational authority requested in the current budget, as is shown in Figure 2. Obligational authority and unspent obligations carried over from previous years were $222.3 billion as of July 1, 1968. The 1969 budget requested $201.7 billion of new obligational authority, making a total of $424.0 billion available to the agencies. Of this, some $186.1 billion was expected to be spent during fiscal year 1969, $54.8 billion was available from unspent obligations and unobligated balances carried over and $131.3 billion from new obligational authority. With authorizations for $1.6 billion expiring, about $236.3 billion of obligational authority and unspent obligations would remain for years after fiscal 1969.

Appropriations legislation, then, determines new obligational authority for the coming year. Congress does not vote on expenditures by department or agency; it only determines new obligational authority. In fact, in the debate on appropriation bills, Congress does not consider the effect that congressional changes in the amounts of new obligational authority requested by the President will have on expenditures in the next fiscal year.

CONGRESSIONAL CONSIDERATION OF APPROPRIATIONS

Tax legislation may be initiated only by the House, and in practice, it has been customary for the House also to initiate appropriations legislation. The Senate has typically acted later and has assumed the role of a liberal counterweight to generally conservative appropriation action by the House.[12]

In the House the content of appropriations measures generally reflects the decisions of the House Committee on Appropriations and, more specifically, its various subcommittees. The Appropriations Committee has fifty members—thirty from the majority and twenty from the minority. Its work is done largely in thirteen subcommittees of from five to eleven members each. Each subcommittee is responsible for reporting out one or, occasionally, two appropriations bills, of which there are thirteen or fourteen in each congressional session.

Tremendous power and authority rest with the various subcommittees and their chairmen. Each subcommittee holds hearings on requests from particular agencies for obligational authority. The hearings have been closed to the public for many years, but a record of what is said is kept and usually printed, except for those portions that relate to national security. Testimony is generally confined to agency and bureau heads and their budget officers.[13] After the hearings the subcommittee goes into executive session and decides on the recommendations it will make for appropriations and restrictions on activities. The recommendations are usually accompanied by reasons for the subcommittee's action and by comments on the agency's programs, efficiency, and personnel.[14]

The subcommittee's recommendations and report are then sent to the full committee for action. They are rarely discussed or even studied in detail; the full committee almost automatically approves the recommendations of the subcommittee and sends them on as a bill to the House, where they are debated with the House sitting as a committee of the whole. On the floor the chairman of the subcommittee acts as floor manager; extended debate is a rare occurrence, and the bill usually passes expeditiously.[15]

Formerly, the Senate did not begin hearings on an appropriations bill until the House bill neared passage. Now, however, the Senate sometimes begins hearings on the same subject even before the House bill is written. As in the House, the initial work is done in the subcommittees (of which there are twelve) of the Appropriations Committee. Also as in the House, they hold hearings, mark up the bill, and send it to the full committee; and here, too, the recommendations of the subcommittees are almost always accepted by the full committee.

When holding hearings, the Senate subcommittees often used to resemble courts of appeal. Agencies and departments often relied on the Senate to restore cuts made by the House. But since the Senate began holding some of its hearings before the writing of the House bill in the same area, the aura of an appeals court is less prevalent. Still, after the House has passed, or at least written, its bill, senatorial questioning tends to center on differences between the amounts of obligational authority recommended in the President's budget (or those currently being requested by the agency witnesses) and the amounts granted by the House. More often than not, the Senate subcommittees restore portions of cuts made in the House.

On the floor of the Senate, discussion of appropriations measures is more extensive than in the House because of the privilege of unlimited debate. The Senate as a whole tends to be more generous in appropriations than the House; the final Senate version of appropriations bills is typically higher.

Senate-House differences on appropriations are reconciled by a conference committee, which seeks to reach a middle figure—one that the conferees can recommend to their parent bodies. The conference committee draft is returned to the House and Senate for further consideration. Usually it is accepted, but occasionally one or the other house rejects it and sends it back to conference.

After final congressional approval the measure is then sent to the President for his signature or veto. Particular agencies and departments are consulted if their appropriations raise the question of a veto, but appropriations bills are rarely vetoed. The bill must be accepted or rejected as a whole; item veto is not provided for by the Constitution. Although the President may not like the bill, he usually signs it, expressing disapproval of certain portions. A veto of the whole bill might endanger the acceptable portions the next time through Congress. Where appropriations are considered by the executive branch to be too low, it can request changes in the next budget after collecting additional supporting evidence and mobilizing the force of public opinion. Where unwanted funds are voted, the President can refuse to spend them, though this is rare and somewhat difficult to do. After all the appropriations measures are passed (which is generally very late in the year since Congress acts on appropriations last), the Budget Bureau prepares a press release which summarizes the final data on appropriations and expenditures resulting from congressional action and updates the revenue estimates of the original budget.

Execution of the Budget

How is the obligational authority granted by Congress to an agency or department converted into expenditures?

APPORTIONMENT AND ALLOTMENT

When the appropriations bill is enacted, an appropriations warrant, drawn by the Treasury and countersigned by the General Accounting Office, is sent to the agency. The agency reviews and revises its budget in light of the appropriations bill and, within fifteen days of the appropriations bill's passage, submits to the Bureau of the Budget a request for apportionment. Apportionment basically means the rate at which the obligational authority can be used—the authority is usually apportioned by quarters over the period of the appropriation, both to insure that the obligational authority is not spent faster than Congress intended and to insure the most economical and effective use of the funds.

The Bureau of the Budget approves or revises the agency apportionment request; in effect, the bureau is the apportioning authority. The power of apportionment gives the executive some latitude in controlling the direction and timing of federal obligations, and it has on occasion been used to accelerate the rate of federal expenditure during a recession and to block programs the executive disapproves by refusing to use funds appropriated by Congress.[16]

Within the individual agencies, the use of the obligational authority apportioned by the bureau is controlled through a similar device. The breakdown of apportionment by organizational unit is called *allotment.*

OBLIGATIONS INCURRED AND EXPENDITURES

With minor exceptions, the various agencies actually incur obligations only after apportionment by the Bureau of the Budget.[17] Incurring obligations, however, does not necessarily mean immediate cash expenditures. In some cases, the expenditure of funds virtually coincides with the incurring of obligations; in others, the actual expenditure of funds may lag considerably behind.

In two kinds of commitment, the time lag between obligations and expenditures is very short. Expenditures for the purchase of existing assets (except land, where the lag may be considerable), social security benefits, veterans' pensions, public assistance grants to states, unemployment compensation, some farm subsidies, and other subsidies involving no use of productive resources typically coincide with, or are very close to, the incurring of the obligations. Government expenditures for services (in particular, those of government employees) also typically occur close to the time of commitment.

But when the federal government contracts with the private sector to employ resources on its behalf—that is, when the federal government buys good and services produced by the private sector—the lag of expenditures behind obligations may be substantial. This lag is both administrative and technological; it takes private producers time to draw plans, negotiate with subcontractors, and deliver the product.[18] Some of the economic impact on the private sector thus occurs long before actual delivery of goods and payment, since the producers must employ resources in order to produce goods.[19]

EXPENDITURES

When they occur, expenditures are generally made from Treasury deposits at the twelve Federal Reserve Banks, which are part of the "Account of the Treasurer of the United States." This account consists mostly of the Treasury checking accounts at the twelve Federal Reserve Banks and at commercial banks. Federal disbursing officers make payment by issuing checks against the Federal Reserve Bank accounts on the basis of vouchers approved by certifying officers of the various agencies; the amount that can be issued is set by the agency's obligational authority and the apportionment of it by the Bureau of the Budget. These checks are usually deposited in commercial banks, which then receive a credit to their Federal Reserve Bank accounts. The Federal Reserve Bank charges the Treasury account with the amount of the check and sends the check to the Treasury, where the checks that have been cashed are verified against the record of checks that have been issued.

It is the Treasury's responsibility to maintain adequate working balances at the Federal Reserve Banks to meet payments as they occur. For this purpose, amounts are funneled by the Treasury into Federal Reserve accounts from deposits at commercial banks made directly by district officers of the Internal Revenue Service and from receipts from debt issues.

Audit

The individual agencies and departments are responsible for insuring that the obligations they incur, and the resulting expenditures, are legal with respect to authorizing and appropriations legislation. The Congress, however, obtains an independent check through the General Accounting Office, which is headed by the comptroller general. The GAO audits the books of the administrative officers responsible for the custody and use of public funds. It has also played an important role in supervising the accounting systems of agencies and departments and in insuring that the methods of reporting result in full disclosure of the receipt and use of funds.

Three major types of audits are made by GAO. Recently, the *comprehensive audit* has become the most important. This audit concentrates on the accounting and reporting system used by a particular agency and checks transactions selectively. The *general audit* examines the accounts of agency disbursing and certifying officers to determine the legality of each transaction. If illegal or improper handling of receipts or expenditures is discovered, recovery procedures are instituted against the responsible officer. The *commercial audit* is applied to government corporations and enterprises. No recovery is possible in this case, but Congress is informed of questionable or improper practices.

The results of GAO audits are transmitted to Congress by the comptroller general. The results of special investigations of particular agencies and the annual report are referred to the House and Senate Committees on Government Operations.

Notes

[1] It should be noted that the budget of the Department of Defense is handled somewhat differently from those of other agencies. The Bureau of the Budget participates with the financial officers of the Defense Department in a review of the requests of the various services for budgetary allowances, but its role here is not quite the same as with other agencies. It acts more as an adviser to the Secretary of Defense than as an arbiter; more decisions in this agency must be left for presidential action. In addition, final Defense budgetary decisions are made later than those of other agencies; many of the crucial ones are held until late December.

[2] Kermit Gordon, "Reflections on Spending," *Public Policy*, Vol. 15 (1966) (Brookings Reprint 125), p. 11.

[3] *Ibid.*, p. 15.

[4] Since PPBS is relatively new, many decisions cannot be made on the basis of analytic studies, and in such cases only a brief statement of reasons for the choice is required.

[5] The interest here is in how cost-benefit and cost-effectiveness analysis are reflected in the budget process.

[6] The timetable and specific steps in the budget process reflected in this discussion are subject to adjustment and modification. PPBS is a new system and is undergoing change as experience is gained.

[7] Information from the Bureau of the Budget. In contrast, only some 15-20 members of the Budget Bureau staff are PPBS specialists. This illustrates a point worth noting, namely, PPBS is not a technique for building up the Budget Bureau's powers relative to the agencies but for giving the agencies devices to evaluate their own activities better.

[8] For further details of the motivations, aims, and policies of individual agencies, see Aaron Wildavsky, *The Politics of the Budgetary Process* (Little, Brown, 1964). Chap. 2.

[9] It is important to note that the Budget Bureau is an "arm of the President"; it is not itself a formulator of policy except insofar as the director influences presidential decisions. It is a *staff* agency. However, under the law the director of the Bureau of the Budget is specifically given the power to review federal statistical programs. Interestingly enough, the bureau has about the same number of personnel today that it had in 1948.

[10] However, authorizing legislation does specify a maximum amount for 30 percent of total funds in the administrative budget.

[11] Obligational authority is also provided in two other forms: (1) authorizations to expend from debt receipts and (2) contract authorizations. However, these account for only a very small proportion of new obligational authority and will not be discussed separately here. See U.S. Bureau of the Budget, *The Budget of the United States Government, Fiscal Year 1962* (1961), p. 114, and *The Federal Budget as an Economic Document,* Prepared for the Joint Economic Committee, 87 Cong., 2 sess. (1962), pp. 8–13.

[12] In 1962 a dispute broke into the open between the House and Senate over initiating appropriations legislation. The House felt that it alone could originate such legislation, but the Senate disagreed. Other issues, such as where Senate-House conference committees on appropriations should meet, were also involved. This dispute over powers of origination was not resolved, and the House has continued to originate such legislation.

[13]This is only because usually no one else asks to be heard. Subcommittees would schedule other witnesses advocating specific expenditure changes if they requested a hearing.

[14]The appropriations subcommittees have not reacted uniformly to PPBS. Further, the variation in their reaction has been reflected in no small degree in that of the agencies or departments that are dependent on them for appropriations. Where the subcommittee chairman is favorable to PPBS, agency use of it is encouraged and the subcommittee hearings will even be "program oriented." Attention will be focused on the program memorandum and analytic studies of the agency. Some subcommittee chairmen, however, have not fully accepted PPBS, and this has slowed their agencies' adoption of it and staffing for it.

[15]See Jesse Burkhead, *Government Budgeting* (Wiley, 1956), pp. 98–99.

[16]See "Federal Fiscal Behavior during the Recession of 1957–58," Bureau of the Budget Staff Report (multilithed; Jan. 13, 1967); statements of Walter Heller and David E. Bell in *January 1961 Economic Report of the President and the Economic Situation and Outlook*, Hearings before the Joint Economic Committee, 87 Cong., 1 sess. (1961); and *Economic Report of the President (1962)*.

[17]See *The Federal Budget as an Economic Document*, p. 14.

[18]See *The Federal Budget as an Economic Document*, pp. 18–21; and Murray Weidenbaum, "The Federal Government Spending Process," in Joint Economic Committee, *Federal Expenditure Policy for Economic Growth and Stability*, 85th Cong., 1 sess. (1957), p. A35. To the extent that there are progress payments or advance payments, the time lag is reduced. It should be noted that when the government buys goods offered for general sale to the public, which are generally quickly available from inventories, the lag is much less significant than when the government places an order for goods produced to its specifications.

[19]See Weidenbaum, "The Federal Government Spending Process," for a discussion of this point.

II

BUDGETING AND THE POLITICAL PROCESS

3

The Budget and Democratic Government

JESSE BURKHEAD

The growth in the size and complexity of the public sector in both developed and underdeveloped countries is undoubtedly one of the most important of recent political and economic changes. It is a phenomenon that has slowly altered the structures of economic systems and, of course, the distribution of economic power within these systems.

There are no signs of abatement. In the underdeveloped countries private entrepreneurship is often lacking and nationalized enterprise expands to take its place. Central governments not only assume responsibility for traditional governmental programs and for social welfare, but also for resource planning and allocation, all in the interests of economic growth. In the developed countries the public sector continues to increase, relatively and absolutely, in response to the forces of urbanization, with the increased specialization and interdependence that accompanies and contributes to an increase in urban economic activity. The public sector also grows because some public activities complement private, as

Reprinted from Roscoe C. Martin (ed.), *Public Administration and Democracy* (Syracuse, N.Y.: Syracuse University Press, 1965), pp. 85–99, by permission of the author and publisher.

The author is indebted to his colleagues Jerry Miner and Douglas Price for their helpful comments on an earlier draft of this manuscript.

with highways, and because there is at least some income elasticity in the demand for public goods. A portion of increases in income will be directed toward more affluent levels of community services.

The inevitable increase in the size of the public sector is not, of course, accomplished without the greatest of frictions in almost every country. This country, in particular, is marked by heated controversies over the level and scope of government programs. In some sense this is not surprising, since resources devoted to public purposes cannot be devoted to private purposes and the control of resources is a most contentious matter in any society. In addition, our system of fiscal federalism imparts some further elements of contention over the level of government that shall control public resources—shall government be "close to the people" or shall "the superior resources of the federal government" be devoted to what were once regarded as wholly state and local functions?

Unfortunately, much of the contemporary controversy in this country has an aura of unreality. Federal government expenditures, defense and nondefense combined, have not increased as a proportion of gross national product in the past ten years. In this country the increases in governmental activity have come at the state and local levels, where expenditures increased 23 percent in relation to GNP between 1955 and 1962. Moreover, those antagonistic to the growth of government seem often to be unaware that an increasing portion of expenditures at all levels in such areas as health, education, and research and development add substantially to the productivity of the private sector.

The growth of the public sector has a great many consequences. For one thing, it gives rise to theorizing, particularly on the part of economists and political scientists, about the processes by which decisions are or ought to be made concerning the size and composition of public programs. Academics undertake research projects on public decision-making. Practitioners become more conscious of the bases on which their decisions are made. Ancient and honorable concepts, such as the "public interest," are reexamined. Organization theory comes to the forefront as an effort to conceptualize complex arrangements. And all of this becomes more difficult as the traditional lines between "public" and "private" break down.

The involvement of colleges and universities in public affairs, the increased use of government contracts to private agencies rather than the conduct of "in-house" activities, the intertwining of government with business firms in research and development, and communications and information systems—these and other developments suggest that "public" versus "private" is an increasingly fuzzy dichotomy. Nonetheless, the distinction must be preserved for many analytical and operational purposes. However vague the line of demarcation, there are still important differences between the "public sector" and the "private sector."

The growth of government has had the further consequence of placing considerable strain on traditional management processes. New technologies intended to provide greater efficiency have become the major obsession of the traditional organization and management specialist in government. Personnel problems and morale become acute in the frenzied competition among government, industry, and the universities for the highly skilled and competent. New systems of financial management must be introduced to cope with increased size and complexity. And, of course, the traditional responsibilities of budget officers grow and change, and new budget techniques must be devised.

Twenty years ago, when these developments were under way after World War II, Paul Appleby did not view the increased size and complexity of government with any considerable alarm. In fact his first major work, *Big Democracy*, took quite the contrary view. For Appleby the task of government must remain very much the same, regardless of changes in size and complexity. This task is to assure that government continue to be responsive and responsible. The budget function is important for this purpose, but is only one of the processes of government intended to assure such responsiveness and responsibility.

Recent attempts to theorize about the nature of public decision-making, on the part of both economists and political scientists, has its counterpart in recent experience in budgetary practice. Not surprisingly, the conceptual difficulties in the theory are matched by operational problems encountered by the practitioners. These developments will be examined in turn.

Fiscal Theory

For almost two hundred years economic theorists have devoted considerable attention to resource allocation decisions in private markets. Out of these efforts has come a vast body of literature and a widely accepted theory that is thought to be reasonably useful in understanding and evaluating private market behavior.

In this framework the starting point is the preference of households (consumers) for goods and services. The distribution of income is assumed to be given at any moment in time. Business firms, with knowledge of their production possibilities and the costs of factors of production, will seek to maximize their profit positions. In so doing their decisions about price and output will maximize consumer satisfactions. There are many difficulties in the application of this (over-simplified) model to the market conditions of the real world. Knowledge may be imperfect; the mobility of factors may be limited; the distribution of income among households may not be ideal. Nevertheless, and with all its difficulties, the traditional theory of private markets has been useful in evaluating private behavior.

A theory of choice for the public sector, to provide an explanation of and guidelines for the selection of the levels and composition of government output, is of much more recent origin. Although some efforts were made by economists at the end of the last century, usually in terms of marginal utility economics, it was not until very recently that a complete attempt at elaboration was undertaken. Paul A. Samuelson made major contributions to this effort; a more complete framework appeared in 1959 with the publication of *The Theory of Public Finance* by Richard A. Musgrave.[1]

Musgrave proposes that the public sector be viewed as comprised of three branches or "budgets." The first he terms the allocations branch, which embraces decisions about the provision of government goods and services for such purposes as national defense, highways, public health, education, and the like. The second branch embraces decisions about economic stabilization, with the utilization of taxes and expenditures to control the total volume of economic activity. The third is the distribution branch, where decisions are made about the size and composition of income among households, and among groups and regions.

Decisions in the stabilization and distribution branches are social decisions, made collectively to reflect community consensus about the appropriate level of economic activity and about the distribution of societal rewards. But decisions in the allocations branch are (or should be) nonnormative efficiency judgments. They do (or should) reflect the underlying preference patterns of the citizenry for public goods, and their choices between public and private goods. Consumers cannot be expected to reveal directly their preferences for public goods, since individual taxpayers, regardless of who pays for the public good, cannot be excluded from the enjoyment of the collectively provided service. Since price tags cannot be attached to specific units of general government goods and services, it becomes the task of the political process to ascertain the underlying preference patterns of the citizenry and to translate these into decisions about the size and scope of government programs. Voting solutions will not yield determinate results since voters may favor either a low budget or a high budget but not one in between. Political decision-makers must attempt to ascertain the incidence of benefits of government programs. With decisions in hand on the distribution of income and the proper level of stabilization, taxes for the allocations branch should be imposed on a benefit basis; this will approximate a market solution. In the allocations branch the prices of commonly provided public goods will differ among taxpayers in accordance with their subjective evaluations of benefits. This is in contrast to private markets where prices are identical for all buyers.

This approach to the public sector provides a kind of general field theory that unites the public and the private sector. For both private markets and government programs, the consumer is sovereign. An "efficient" solution is one that maximizes consumer welfare with respect to both private and public goods. Musgrave specifically rejects any social determination for the allocations branch as authoritarian and undemocratic.

The three-branch approach is a substantial contribution to clarity in thinking about the economic responsibilities of government and hence about budget determination. There *are* important conceptual differences in programs for the provision of goods and services, for stabilization, and for income distribution. In so far as possible these considerations ought to be separated in decisions about the budget. And, of course, any effort to provide a general theory of the public and private sectors ought to be applauded; this approach has, at minimum, provoked systematic thinking about the economic characteristics of public and private activity. For example, one refreshing conclusion emerges from the consumer choice approach. It is that there are no arbitrary limits to the size of the public sector vis-à-vis the private. If consumers prefer more public goods and fewer private goods, an efficient solution requires that their demands be satisfied. There is no *economic* reason for restricting the public sector to 20 percent, 25 percent or any other arbitrary proportion of the total.

Unfortunately, there are difficulties with this framework. Indeed, it would be rather surprising to discover that a market efficiency solution could be applied with clarity and ease to the public sector at a time when there appears to be a cumulative drift away from a generally effective private market system.[2]

One of the most serious difficulties with the economic choice approach to the allocations branch is the inadequate attention paid to externalities or spillovers—the third party or neighborhood effects that are so characteristic of all government transactions.

In private markets there are, of course, spillovers as well. The housewife's purchases of food from the grocer are of particular concern to the housewife and her family and to the grocer (and his suppliers). But the community at large, in an imprecise kind of way, derives some benefit from the fact that the housewife's family is well fed and nourished. Indeed, it is difficult to find any economic transaction that does not carry with it some volume, however small, of third party benefits.

In the private sector it is customary to think that the proportion of external benefits to internal benefits is relatively small, and that external benefits do not affect preferences for specific commodities. But in the public sector the situation would appear to be reversed. Activities come to be "affected with a public interest," to use the old public utility phrase, as the proportion of external benefits is large in relation to the internal benefits, and as these are taken into account in demands for public goods. The immediate beneficiaries of a youth recreation program may be the children themselves, and the benefits may be roughly measurable in terms of their improved health and welfare. But externalities may be widespread. Taxpayers may benefit from reduced expenditures for police protection and public health. Employers and stockholders may benefit at some time in the future as their employees are more productive. And so it goes.

In fact, a case can be made for the proposition that activities come to be public in character simply because the proportion of externalities is high and these externalities are widely diffused. One economist has suggested that this condition—the remoteness of benefits from government programs—tends to hold down the size of the government budget below its true optimum; budgets are "incorrect" because of a lack of information about external benefits.[3]

If this is the case it follows that there is no way to attain an efficiency solution for the allocations branch. The citizenry cannot be expected to support government programs whose benefits are not perceptible. Even if citizens were to vote directly on budgets for the allocations branch in an effort to express their preferences, optimal solutions would not obtain.[4]

A further difficulty arises in the allocations branch because government programs are not always directed to the benefit of consumers. Producer groups benefit as well, sometimes from the end product, sometimes because they participate in public programs as suppliers. A forty-foot channel is constructed on the Delaware River and the major beneficiary is a single steel producer; the company's stockholders may benefit, but a consumer benefit is most elusive. The producers of cement and road construction machinery are important supporters of highway programs because of their expected profits from contracts with government agencies, not because of their interest as consumers in the use of the highway. Comparable situations exist in the private sector where motivations may run in terms of power, prestige, and possession and not in terms of the maximization of consumer satisfaction. Unfortunately, in these circumstances there is no simple conceptual framework by which these varieties of demands for public or private goods can be aggregated into a preference schedule that reflects the wishes of consumers.

In addition to the foregoing difficulties with the allocations branch there is a series of operational problems. In the policy-making arena the branches are not, of course, independent of one another. Distributional considerations are not examined separately from allocations decisions. On the contrary, goods and services expenditures directly affect the distribution of private incomes as between the rich and the poor—public health, public housing and recreation, for example—and the distribution of incomes among regions, as with resource development projects. Executives and legislatures may make reasonably direct and clear-cut decisions about the distribution of income as tax measures are proposed, modified, and adopted, but the expenditure side of the budget has its effect on income distribution in a nonexplicit fashion. The consequences are there, but they are seldom specified. [5]

Stabilization considerations are similarly intertwined with allocations and distributive concerns. If incomes are to be increased in the interests of moving to a higher level of economic activity for the economy as a whole, there will be some persons and groups whose incomes are increased more than others; stabilization programs are not neutral with respect to the distribution of income. Some of the distributional consequences may be intended; others may be largely unintended.

Rational choice solutions for the allocations branch also require a unitary budget, that is, all decisions about government goods and services expenditures must be brought together as a comprehensive decision-making process. This, of course, is very far from attainment in any government. In this country the federal government budget does not comprehend the growing volume of activity in the trust funds, and state and local budgets are fragmented almost unbelievably by special funds and earmarked revenues. Moreover, the very nature of a federal system means that unified budgetary consideration is basically unattainable. With the exception of international affairs, there is no government program which is not in some way or other conducted by at least two levels of government. The economists' ideal of a comprehensive allocations branch budget that reflects consumer choices between public and private goods is clearly beyond realization in practice.

Most of the conceptual and operational difficulties in the economic theory of the allocations branch lie in the starting point—the consumer approach to public resource allocation. The best framework for analysis may not be a unified theory but one of two economies—a market economy where consumer preferences may be used as a starting point for analysis—and a budget economy where consumer preferences as such play little part.[6] Social welfare functions and social preferences are very elusive concepts and economists' efforts to impart some reality to them have not been successful. But it may be that, vague and fuzzy as these constructs are, they come closer to describing real-world conditions of budgetary decision-making than the conceptually neater approach through consumer preferences.

The Role of Measurement

The world of budgetary theory and practice is divided in two. There are those who feel that budget decisions should be governed by a maximum of calculations and marginal comparisons of costs and outcomes, and there are those who feel that budget decisions are or should be governed by considerations of strategy and bargaining. In the first group there are none who feel that value judgments are or should be eliminated from the budgetary process but major emphasis, it is contended, must be placed on the quantification of the costs and benefits of government programs. Only in this way can value judgments be made explicit. In the second group there are none who contend that measurements are useless, and it is generally argued that wherever possible measurement techniques should be extended. But the essential rationality of budgeting, it is urged, is and must continue to be a political rationality, expressive of the conflicting values of interest groups, legislators, and administrators.

Generally speaking, most economists, whether academic or budget practitioners, are in the first group. Economists by nature are quantifiers and for the last ten or fifteen years have demonstrated a lively interest in extending the limits of measurement in public decision-making. As a rule, most political scientists, public administrators, and budget practitioners are nonquantifiers, or at least continually express doubts about the value of efforts to measure government costs and output.

The most forceful protagonists of the nonquantified view of budget decision-making are Charles E. Lindblom, an economist, and hence an exception to the foregoing generalization, and Aaron Wildavsky, a political scientist.[7] Lindblom's thesis in brief is that in budget decisions (and in most other public policy areas) a rational means-ends calculus is not possible, and indeed its pursuit would be unrealistic. The synoptic (means-ends) ideal calls for a sharp separation of values and goals from the techniques of implementation. But in the real world it is beyond human ability to consider the complete range of policies and means alternatives that are available. Means and ends are continuously intermingled, as are long-range values and short-range choices. The processes of partisan mutual adjustment require that there be agreement on means, but not on ends. An economic efficiency rationality is not possible; decisions on public policy are always made at the margin; a comprehensive budget policy is unattainable. Disjointed incrementalism best describes the technique of decision-making both with respect to the budget and with respect to other matters of public policy. Lindblom is not opposed to comprehensive or synoptic analysis, such as the measurement of budget costs and benefits where it is possible, but he is convinced that the area where such techniques are appropriate is not large, and may not be expanding.

Wildavsky is concerned to emphasize that government budgets are not solely devices for resource allocation, as economists would have it. A budget is, or may be "an expectation, an aspiration, a strategy, a communications network, or a precedent."[8] Budgeting is always incremental, never a total review of resource allocation. The decision process in the federal government is dominated by the strategies employed and the conflicts that arise among the participants: clientele groups, agencies, departments, the Bureau of the Budget, the President, congressional subcommittees and their parent committees. The conflicts give rise to definable strategies that require such things as the cultivation (on the part of an agency) of an active clientele, the development of confidence among other government officials, and skill in following tactics that exploit temporary opportunities. Budget strategies differ in accordance with whether the agency is attempting to hold the line on its existing program, expand the existing program, or add a new program. Budgeting is fragmented; it is repetitive—not every problem has to be resolved this year; and it is sequential—each problem is dealt with in turn, in partial isolation from all other budgetary problems. The reasonably stable roles that are played by major participants makes the process manageable. Comprehensive budgeting, complete budget calculations, and formal coordination by a single person or agency are unfeasible, undesirable, or both.

Wildavsky argues that there is a high degree of coordination in the process, but that it is informal coordination in anticipation of what others are likely to do. A very wide range of interests is thus considered. Paul Appleby once expressed something like this point of view as follows:

> The budget is not made merely by technical processes; it is made on a field where mighty forces contend over it. It is not made in a public arena, but the public is somehow well represented. This is one of the most mystifying of government phenomena.[9]

There would appear to be no reconciling Musgrave's fiscal theory of public sector choices with the pragmatic and descriptive system of

Lindblom and Wildavsky. This is not a difference between "theory" and "practice," but a difference between the starting points of analysis. In the Musgrave view the citizen must be viewed as an individual consumer of government services. To Lindblom and Wildavsky the citizen must be viewed as a part of a social decision process.

The Progress of Practitioners

Since the end of World War II there has been a large number of efforts to reform and strengthen the practice of budgeting in governments at all levels in the United States. A great many of these have come under the rubric of what is customarily described as performance or program budgeting. The federal government has engaged in such efforts in the name of cost-type budgets. A number of states and a very large number of municipal governments have reformed their budget classifications in the name of "performance."[10]

In its ideal form performance budgeting costs out the end products of government activity—the goods and services that are produced. It thus permits comparisons over time of the relationships between inputs and outputs and facilitates budget decisions in terms of agency accomplishment and efficiency. Performance budgeting thus (ideally) provides much of the information necessary for arriving at an optimum budget for separate programs in the allocations branch. But even in its ideal form it does not provide information for making comparisons among programs.

No thorough survey of experiences with performance budgeting has been undertaken, so that appraisals of the varied and sometimes conflicting results are most difficult. The greatest benefits would appear to lie at the agency management level, where this approach encourages attention to new ways of looking at programs, with emphasis on accomplishment and technological efficiency in securing that accomplishment. Performance budgeting is probably less useful at departmental, central budget office, or executive review levels, where choices among programs depend more on social, political, and economic judgments as to the "worth" of a program. Performance budgeting has not been generally popular with legislators, who find it easier to "control" the administration by attention to the traditional framework of obligations and the details of personnel and other projects of expenditure.

The challenge of the performance approach lies in the difficulties encountered in the measurement of government output—difficulties that are inherent in the conceptual scheme of economists who write about fiscal theory and also in the day-to-day work of the agency budget officer who is trying to measure end products with precision. The same range of problems is encountered, naturally enough, in efforts to measure productivity in government.[11] It is easy enough to measure the things that government buys; it is generally possible to measure the activities of government, although ingenuity is occasionally required here; it is perennially difficult to measure government output except for repetitive discrete products such as postal service. But in spite of the perhaps insuperable difficulties in some areas of government output, measurement efforts will continue and they will be useful, sometimes more for their by-products than for their direct results. In an increasingly quantified society it is hardly to be expected that the public sector shall remain isolated from measurement efforts.

The recent sweeping changes in programming and budgeting in the U.S. Department of Defense are illustrative of both the possibilities and limitations in budget quantification.[12] Since 1961 the defense budget has been organized in terms of nine basic programs: (1) strategic retaliatory forces, (2) continental air and missile defense forces, (3) general purpose forces, (4) airlift and sealift forces, (5) reserve and guard forces, (6) research and development, (7) general support, (8) civil defense, and (9) military assistance. Each program is subdivided into program elements, such as a specific missile or aircraft type. The program elements are costed in terms of research and development, initial investment, and annual operating expenses with five-year projections of each element. Costs are continually studied in relation to effectiveness for each weapons system. The result is an attempt to unify military planning and budgeting, with the linkage between the two established in terms of the program elements. The program structure, however, is used primarily for internal Department of Defense purposes. The budget presentation to the Congress is in traditional categories centering on procurement and personnel.

The DOD budget system appears to have enjoyed the same kinds of general advantages that are characteristic of other, more modest efforts at performance budgeting. Marginal costs and marginal effectiveness are under continuous review; alternative defense systems are continuously scrutinized; the relationship between investment and operational costs is specified.

But, as Assistant Secretary Hitch has made clear on a number of occasions, program budgeting for the Department of Defense does not resolve the value judgments about the appropriate level of defense expenditures. It has certainly centralized decision-making authority in the hands of the Secretary of Defense, as against the separate services, to permit better-informed judgments. It may provide some insight on whether as a nation we are "better defended" this year than last, although this is doubtful. But program budgeting cannot yield a computerized answer to the question: should we spend another $5 billion on defense?

In one of the few detailed studies available on budget decision processes—an examination of the defense budget for fiscal 1950—Schilling observed:

> The defense budget, while susceptible to rational analysis, remains a matter of political resolution. Choices of this order can be made in only one place: the political arena. There the relative importance of values can be decided by the relative power brought to bear on their behalf. There the distribution of power can decide matters that the distribution of fact and insight cannot. [13]

Paul Appleby once put the point succinctly: "There are few problems for which there are single right answers simply and clearly revealed by technical analysis." [14]

The Budget and the General Interest

The efforts of economists in recent years to construct a general theory of public finance with resource allocation principles to guide both the public and the private sector have been stimulating and provocative, but they fall short of providing operational guides to budget decisions. The efforts of budget practitioners to measure government performance have been useful and have certainly tended to improve the efficiency of some government operations, but they cannot be applied in important areas and in any event do not assure that proper choices will be made among programs or with respect to program levels. Nevertheless, the efforts of both the fiscal theorists and the performance budget practitioners have been very much worthwhile. Fiscal theory has provided a systematic way of looking at the economic functions of government; performance budgeting has integrated costs and outcomes in some decision processes.

The difficult problem that remains for performance budgeting is the determination of its area of applicability. We may be able to "muddle through" a great many decisions without attempting to measure costs and outcomes, but there is no assurance that incremental decisions will provide for the effective use of public resources just because they are incremental. A great many urban transportation systems which were constructed incrementally stand today as magnificent monuments to inefficient resource allocation. Even if one is persuaded that Lindblom and Wildavsky have done an excellent job of describing the reality of public decision processes, it should still be possible to add some economic calculations here and there that will help to guide the next incremental decision. Moreover, efforts to quantify will change the terms of trade on which decisions that are essentially political will be made. Measurement efforts no matter how imperfect will, at minimum, discipline and structure political decision processes.

There is no reason for an all-or-nothing attitude toward decisions systems, or for an all-or-nothing attitude toward performance measurements. It is not necessary to make a general choice between incrementalism and a rational means-ends calculus. Some governmental programs permit one and some permit the other. A multiplicity of approaches is possible. One would hope that the operations of the Post Office Department, for example, would be subject to the continuous application of operations research techniques.

Larger questions about the size and scope of government programs and the relative division of resources between the public and the private sector are now and will probably remain unanswered, either by fiscal theory or by the work of the practitioners. At one time, perhaps as recently as ten years ago, it was possible to discuss these questions in terms of "the public interest" or "the public welfare," but these notions have been so strongly attacked that they no longer seem to contain any systematic content.[15] We have also discovered that the "public interest state" can have some seriously adverse effects on the civil liberties of individuals.[16]

What we have left are some old-fashioned notions about the importance of a budget organization that, hopefully, provides a center of executive responsibility so that elected officials may ultimately be held responsible. We must rely on a budget procedure that is in the process of continued improvement with respect to the flow of information and the interrelatedness of programs.

Budgeting is and must remain a political process. If it is to be a democratic process those who are vitally affected must have an opportunity to be heard. The costs and benefits of government programs thus come to be reflected in the expressed feelings of persons and interest groups in terms of the intensity of demand for public programs and sensitivity to their costs.

There are some grounds for moderate optimism with respect to the ability of budget procedures to handle the larger issues. As society becomes increasingly urbanized, interdependent, and complex the volume of externalities for both public and private activity increases. Persons and groups affected by such external effects press their claims as budget decisions are made. The growing volume of externalities would appear to be the principal causal factor in the growth of the public (nondefense) sector. As long as political processes remain open to influence by affected persons and groups, and as long as concentrations of market power can be held reasonably in check, we should be able to assure an increasing measure of procedural due process in budgetary decisions. But there is no way by which we can determine whether we have achieved an economically efficient optimum between the public and the private sector.

Notes

[1] Richard A. Musgrave, *The Theory of Public Finance* (New York: McGraw-Hill).

[2] See, for example, Ewald T. Grether, "Consistency in Public Economic Policy with respect to Private Unregulated Industries," *American Economic Review*, 53, no. 2 (May 1964), 26–37.

[3] Anthony Downs, "Why the Government Budget is Too Small in a Democracy," *World Politics*, 12, no. 4 (July 1960), 541–63.

[4] The conceptual difficulties with voting solutions were first explored by Kenneth S. Arrow in *Social Choice and Individual Values* (New York: John Wiley & Sons, 1951), and are discussed in Musgrave, *op. cit.*, pp. 116–35.

[5] Musgrave attempts to deal with this problem as a special case within the allocations branch in terms of "merit wants." However, almost all public goods and services have "merit" or income distribution effects.

[6] See Gerhard Colm's elaboration of this viewpoint in *Essays in Public Finance and Fiscal Policy* (New York: Oxford University Press, 1955), pp. 258–86. Musgrave discusses and rejects this approach; *op. cit.*, pp. 86–89.

[7] Lindblom's major contributions are contained in "The Science of Muddling Through," *Public Administration Review*, 19, no. 2 (Spring 1959); "Decision-Making in Taxation and Expenditures," in National Bureau of Economic Research, *Public Finances: Needs, Sources, and Utilization* (Princeton: Princeton University Press, 1961), pp. 295–329; with David Braybrooke, *A Strategy of Decision* (New York: Free Press of Glencoe, 1963). The *Public Administration Review*, 24, no. 3 (September 1964) has an interesting symposium on Lindblom's system (pp. 153–65). Wildavsky's views are set forth in "Political Implications of Budgetary Reform," *Public Administration Review* 21, no. 4 (Autumn 1961), 183–90 and *The Politics of the Budgetary Process* (Boston: Little Brown, 1964).

[8] *The Politics of the Budgetary Process*, pp. 3–4.

[9] "The Influence of the Political Order," *American Political Science Review* 42, no. 2 (April 1948), 281.

[10] For an excellent review of this and other recent developments at the state level see the report on a survey of fourteen state budget administrations by Arlene Theuer Shadoan, "Developments in State Budget Administration," *Public Administration Review*, 23, no. 4 (December 1963), 227–31.

[11] See John W. Kendrick, "Exploring Productivity Measurement in Government," *Public Administration Review*, 23, no. 2 (June 1963), 59–66; U.S. Bureau of the Budget, *Measuring Productivity of Federal Government Organizations* (Washington, D.C.: U.S. Government Printing Office, 1964).

[12] Much of this development is associated with the work of Charles J. Hitch, Assistant Secretary of Defense. The economic theory underlying the DOD budget system is set forth in *The Economics of Defense in the Nuclear Age*, with Roland N. McKean (Cambridge: Harvard University Press, 1960). See also "Management of the Defense Dollar," *The Federal Accountant*, 11, no. 4 (June 1962), 33–44; David Novick, "Costing Tomorrow's Weapons System," *Quarterly Review of Economics and Business*, 3, no. 1 (Spring 1963), 33–40; Alain C. Enthoven, "Economic Analysis in the Department of Defense," *American Economic Review*, 53, no. 2 (May 1964), 413–23. Hitch has described the system in testimony before a Subcommittee of the Committee on Government Operations, House of Representatives, *Systems Development and Management*, Part 2, 87th Cong., 2nd Sess., 1962, pp. 513–47.

[13] Warren R. Schilling, Paul Y. Hammond, Glenn H. Snyder, *Strategy, Politics, and Defense Budgets* (New York: Columbia University Press, 1962), p. 15.

[14] Paul Appleby, "The Budget Division," *Public Administration Review*, 17, no. 3 (Summer 1957), 156.

[15] See, for example, Glendon A. Schubert, Jr., "'The Public Interest' in Administrative Decision-Making: Theorem, Theosophy, or Theory," *American Political Science Review*, 51, no. 2 (June 1957), 356–68; Frank J. Sorauf, "The Public Interest Reconsidered," *Journal of Politics*, 19, no. 4 (November 1957), 616–39.

[16] See Charles A. Reich, "The New Property," *Yale Law Journal*, 73, no. 5 (April 1964), 733–87.

4

Systems Politics and Systems Budgeting

ALLEN SCHICK

Change in budgeting means change in politics. Any doubts on this score ought to have been dispelled by Aaron Wildavsky's *The Politics of the Budgetary Process.* This implies that the arrival of planning-programming-budgeting, however brief its current run, heralds or reflects transformations in American political life. The politico-budgetary world is much different from what it was in 1965 when PPB was launched, and it probably will not be the same again. While PPB cannot claim parentage for many of the changes, neither can it be divorced from the ferments now sweeping the domestic political scene. Uniting the emergent changes in politics and budgeting is one of the popular metaphors of our times.[1] The central metaphor of the old politics and budgeting was *process;* the key metaphor of the new politics and budgeting is *systems.*[2]

With the process-systems dichotomy as the pivot, I will try to: (1) identify the distinctive and contrasting elements of old and new; (2) analyze the persistence of process politics and the challenge of systems politics; (3) assess the preparedness of politics and budgeting for the systems view; and (4) develop a taxonomy of political process deficiencies.

Reprinted from the *Public Administration Review*, 29, No. 2 (March/April 1969): 137-151, by permission of the author and publisher.

Process and System

The salient feature of process politics is the activity by which bargains are struck and allocations negotiated—the so-called rules of the game and the strategies of the contestants. There is a presumption that if the process is working properly, the outcome will be favorable. Hence, there is no need for an explicit examination of outcomes; one can evaluate the process itself to determine its performance and desirability. The *sine qua non* of systems politics is the outcome, not the activity, but what results from it. Take away this component and you do not have a system.[3] In systems politics allocations are formally related to preferred outcomes or objectives. Its assumption is exactly contrary to that which undergirds the process approach: unless outcomes are evaluated specifically, the results will be suboptimal or undersirable.

In systems budgeting the distinctive element is the analysis of alternative opportunities, while in process budgeting it is the bargaining apparatus for determining public actions. (To avert a possible misunderstanding, let me note that process and system are portrayed in pure form. In the hybrid world, analysis and bargaining coexist.[4]) Contrary to some interpretations, neither approach requires or rejects a zero-based determination of government programs. Systems politics does not force an all-or-nothing choice. The alternatives are always at the margins, and the margins, like the increments in process politics, can be large or small—a one percent increase in the appropriation for a bureau or a billion dollars for a new Medicaid program.[5] The critical difference is that the increments are negotiated in bargains that neglect the outcomes, while the systems margins are determined via an analysis of outcomes. Nor does systems politics require that every program be compared to all others; programs can be divided into parts for the purpose of analysis and choice. This is the familiar methodology of suboptimization. But unlike the fragmented and piecemeal tactics of process politics in which the part stands alone, in a systems view the part always is viewed in some relation to the whole. Systems politics does not require that everything be decided all at once or once and for all. Systems analysis is both serial and remedial, with iterative feeding back from means to ends.

In process politics the contestants tend to view the options from the perspectives of their established positions (existing legislation, last year's budget, the "base," etc.). Theirs is a retrospective bias. Budgeting is treated as the process of financing existing commitments and of creating some new commitments (the increments). Systems politics tends to have a prospective bias; budgeting is regarded as the allocation of money to attain some future value (the outcome or objective). This year's budget, in systems terms, is an installment in buying that future.

Because of its future orientation, systems budgeting is likely to induce somewhat larger annual budget shifts than might derive under process rules. But this does not mean a zigzag course of events, each successive budget disowning the previous allocations. All political life, whether process or systems, must achieve stability and continuity. Process politics accomplishes these through a chain of incremental adjustments; systems politics by embracing a large number of years and values within its analytic frame.

In process politics the strategy is that of mobilizing interests, and in process budgeting of mobilizing funds. In systems politics and budgeting it is the allocation and rationing of values and resources among competing powers and claimants. Process politics (and budgeting), therefore, tends to favor the partisans such as agencies, bureaus, and interest groups, while systems politics (and budgeting) tends to favor the central allocators, especially the chief executive and the budget agency. Systems politics also can be used to bolster certain officials who have mixed mobilizing-rationing roles. A few department heads such as Robert McNamara have used systems budgeting in this fashion. But this is likely to occur only when top officials have mobilizing values that diverge from those of their subordinates.

Systems politics takes a relatively holistic view of objectives compared to the partial view associated with process politics. As many pluralists have asserted, the group process produces public objectives as derivatives or aggregates of the special, limited interests of the groups. Systems politics encompasses a broader range of public purposes, including some which cannot be extracted from or negotiated via the usual group interactions. But it would be erroneous to attribute to systems politics a global concern with objectives. That would tax the political system with an overload of calculation and conflict management. All politics has to work with limits on cognition and with the realities of multiple and conflicting objectives. To cope with these constraints, systems politics relies on the indispensable division of analytic and political labors furnished by group bargaining. Systems politics, in short, does not eschew group objectives, but it certainly is not confined to them.

The important facts of process budgeting have been portrayed in Aaron Wildavsky's *The Politics of the Budgetary Process*. Process budgeting is "incremental, fragmented, nonprogrammatic, and sequential."[6] There is a tendency to accept last year's budget as the base for next year's and to use an array of nonanalytic tactics to reduce the complexities and conflicts of budget making and to strengthen the opportunities of agencies to obtain funds. These tactics have stabilized into the rules and role of bargaining that govern the incremental budget process. Although

Wildavsky has underestimated the program content of traditional budgeting, he correctly observes that there is little explicit consideration of objectives and policies and almost no search for alternatives. The line-item method is one technical manifestation of process budgeting.

Systems budgeting is represented by the planning-programming-budgeting systems now being established in many government jurisdictions. While there are many versions of PPB and PPB is not the only appropriate expression of systems in budgeting, all PPB systems direct allocative choice to future outcomes, to the costs of achieving public objectives, and to alternative means of pursuit. The technology of PPB—the program memoranda, program and financial plans, and other federal documentation or the variant methods used in other jurisdictions—are of considerable relevance in the conversion of the systems idea into practice, but it is the concept of systems budgeting that overrides and ultimately must determine the techniques.

The Dominance of Process

The process school dominated American politics from the early 1950s through the mid-1960s. From David Truman's *The Governmental Process* (1951) through Wildavsky's justly praised budget study (1964) there prevailed the confidence that pluralist politics—particularly transactions among interest groups—produces favorable outcomes. For the most part, the politics of the period was practiced as described by the pluralists and incrementalists. The emphasis was on consensus and stability, on limiting the scope and intensity of conflict by allocating to each group its quota of public satisfactions. Change was gradual and piecemeal, with departures from the status quo limited by established rules and by the actions of the "partisan mutual adjusters" who orchestrated the group process.[7] Despite their slavish lip service to Lasswell's formulation of politics as "who gets what, when, how," the pluralists gave scant attention to the outcomes of group interactions. One can search the vast pluralist literature and locate only scatterings of concern with "who gets what" from the power distribution in a community or from the established government policies. The pluralists were deterred from looking into such questions by their own focus on process.

Wildavsky's study is an excellent illustration of the pluralist methodology. After two lengthy chapters on "Calculations" and "Strategies" devoted to the partisan process of budget making, and with hardly a word about outcomes,[8] Wildavsky opens the next chapter with a strong rebuke to budget reformers:

There is little or no realization among the reformers, however, that any effective change in budgetary relationships must necessarily alter the outcomes of the budgetary process. . . . proposed reforms inevitably contain important implications for the political system; that is, for the "who gets what" of governmental decisions.[9]

Yet nowhere in *The Politics* does the author evaluate "who gets what" from traditional budgeting. Instead, there is a *deus ex machina* faith in the goodness of the pluralist process:

The process we have developed for dealing with interpersonal comparisons in government is not economic but political. Conflicts are resolved (under agreed upon rules) by translating different preferences through the political system into units called votes or into types of authority like a veto power.[10]

Why have the pluralists neglected to study the outcomes of their process? What inspired their awesome respect for the ability of that process to deliver the right results time and again? There are a number of explanations which manifest the potency and attractiveness of the pluralist view.

American political science is habituated to confidence in the formal relations among power holders. Just as the Constitution makers believed that government would be good (nontyrannical) if power were divided among the several branches, the pluralists have argued that government is good (responsible) because power is shared by many groups. A social checks and balances system has replaced the legal checks and balances as the "democratizing" process of government. The pluralists also have been swayed by the market model of economic competition. In the same way that the unseen hand of the market effectively and fairly regulates supply and demand, the interactions of competing groups yields the desired supply of political goods, and at the right price. Moreover, the proper functioning of both private and public markets hinges on the partisanship of the contestants. Social welfare is maximized by the self-interest of buyers and sellers, not by an attempt to calculate the general welfare. If either economic man or political man abandoned his partisan role, the expected result would be a misallocation of resources.

The pluralists were impressed by their "discovery" of interest groups. In the pluralist mind, not only do groups supplement the electoral process by providing additional channels of influence and information, they also compensate for some of the limitations of electoral politics, notably its inability to transmit unambiguous policy preferences (mandates) from voters to public officials or to accommodate differentials in the intensity of preferences. By virtue of the overlapping pattern of group identifications, interest groups also were esteemed as effective brakes on socioeconomic conflict. Accordingly, the pluralists came to regard the group process as the cornerstone of modern democratic government, possessing a representative capability superior to the voting process.

According to this pluralist interpretation, government is sometimes a representative of special interests (for example, a bureau advocating the interests of its clientele), and sometimes an arbiter of interests (for example, the budget bureau allocating the shares among the various agencies). But its role is not that of promoting some overarching public interest. Its job is to keep the process going, not to maximize some consistent set of policy objectives. Bureaucracies were considered faithful reflectors of group preferences; consequently, their growth to enormous power was not deemed a threat to norms of representation.

Once they were sold on the efficacy of interest groups, the pluralists stopped worrying about the ends of government. They were persuaded by a tautological, but nonetheless alluring, proof that the outcomes of the group process are satisfactory. If the bargain were not the right one, it would not have been made. Since it was made, it must be the right one. Unlike many economists who have become cognizant that market imperfections and limitations, such as external costs and benefits or imperfect competition, can produce unfavorable outcomes, most pluralists stayed solidly convinced group competition has no major defects.

The process approach offered a convenient escape from difficult value questions. A decisional system that focuses on the outcomes and objectives of public policy cannot avoid controversy over the ends of government, the definition of the public interest, and the allocation of core values such as power, wealth, and status. But the pluralists bypassed their matters by concentrating on the structure and rules for choice, not on the choices themselves. They purported to describe the political world as it is, neglecting the important normative implications of their model. The pluralists scrupulously avoided interpersonal comparisons and the equally troublesome question of whose values shall prevail. Instead, they took the actual distribution of values (and money) as Pareto optimal, that is, as the best that could be achieved without disadvantaging at least one group.

These political scientists, along with many others, assumed that politics is a giant positive sum game in which almost everyone comes out ahead. This perspective was inspired by the affluent mood of the period and by the "out of sight, out of mind" predicament of the poor. It had a powerful analog in the Keynesian model of economic growth and stabilization; if everyone benefits from economic development, it is hard to ask the question "development for what?" For verification of their interpretation, the pluralists resorted to a "failsafe" tautology. If there were any losers, surely they would have joined into groups to protect their interests. If a disadvantaged group had a great deal at stake, it would have been able to veto the proposed bargain or to demand compensation for its losses. The affluence, everyone wins presumptions removed any compulsion for an evaluation of policy outcomes; satisficing solutions would do. (Pareto solutions are, by definition, satisficing conditions, *modus vivendi* worked out to the satisfaction of those groups whose interests are involved.) Satisficing became a way of political life and a justification for the status quo, not merely a means of cutting down the cost of choice.[11] "Second best" became the preferred solution because the best would have required some agonizing reappraisal of policy and purpose, along with a renegotiation of delicate group relationships. More than a decade ago Robert C. Wood explained why America was doing little to reconstruct her cities despite the warnings of reformers:

> Despite our predictions, disaster has not struck: urban government has continued to function, not well perhaps, but at least well enough to forestall catastrophe. Traffic continues to circulate; streets and sewers are built; water is provided; schools keep their doors open; and law and order generally prevail.[12]

It is only at the point of crisis that satisficing no longer is good enough and governments are compelled to reexamine what they are doing and where they are heading. But the crises that surround our public institutions today were remote, or at least underground, a few years ago.

Affluence enables winning groups to compensate their competitors. For this reason, log-rolling among interests was viewed as an efficient mechanism for negotiating side-payments. The quality of the "pork," in terms of some public interest criterion, was not taken into account—only the success of the groups in obtaining agreement. The fact that the groups consented to the exchange was taken as sufficient evidence of its utility. It is easy to understand that under conditions of scarcity the quality of the exchange would more likely be subjected to scrutiny. But these were not perceived as times of scarcity.

The pluralists emphasized the remedial features of incrementalism. A decision made today is provisional; it can be modified tomorrow. If this year's budget is deficient, corrections can be made next year. One need not search for the optimal outcome, nor need one attempt to take all factors into account before deciding. Some pluralists argued that better results can be achieved through a series of partial adjustments than through a systematic canvass of alternatives. The serial and remedial aspects of incremental politics were regarded as especially helpful in reducing the complexities and controversies involved in the negotiation of a $185 billion national budget.

The pluralists were impressed by the ability of the budgetary process to limit political and bureaucratic conflict. The annual competition over billions of dollars has the potential of generating explosive and divisive conflicts. The fact that this competition usually is waged peacefully and leaves few scars attests to the effectiveness of the traditional process. The pluralists tend to view anything that might broaden the scope of intensity of conflict as undesirable, and they believe that an explicit and systematic evaluation of public objectives, accompanied by emphasis on alternatives, trade-offs, and the outcomes of competitive resource allocations, will increase the level of conflict.

Finally, the pluralists looked at the American political scene and liked what they saw—abundance, growth, consensus, stability, satisfaction with the American way. (It should be remembered that the pluralist age followed a great depression and a great war.) Given these "success indicators," the pluralists readily assumed that the shares were being divided equitably and to the satisfaction of the citizenry. They saw no need to quicken the pace of change or to effect radical redistributions in political values. And, of course, they saw no need to question the entrenched politico-budgetary process or to reexamine the outcomes of that process.

In many ways, the political life of the times was a faithful image of the pluralist view. Political practice was geared to consensus, an avoidance of the big ideological issues. The economy was buoyant, the mood optimistic. Writing of "The Politics of Consensus in an Age of Affluence." Robert Lane identified this mood as a key to understanding the political behavior of the common man:

> Since everyone is "doing better" year by year, though with different rates of improvement, the stakes are not so much in terms of gain or loss, but in terms of size of gain—giving government more clearly the image of a rewarding rather than a punishing instrument. [13]

It was not a time for thinking about purposes or worrying about priorities. Perspectives did not extend much beyond this year and the next. There was great confidence in the capability of the political process to produce the right results. Muddling through was canonized as the American virtue. It was a time of governmental immobilism, capable neither of disowning the New Deal legacy nor of forging new directions in economic and social life. If there was an industrial-military-political cartel, it was outside the range of pluralist inquiry, above the middling levels of politics. If there were nonvoters, or apathetic voters, or uninformed voters, that all was good, for it cooled the level of political excitement and demonstrated the basic satisfactions with the process. If there were losers in American politics, there was no need for concern, for they, too, could look to a better tomorrow when they would share in the political bargains.

The politicians practiced what the pluralists described.

The Systems Challenge

It is well known that the main impetus for PPB came from the new decisional technologies associated with economic and systems analysis, not from public administration or political science. Accordingly, it was possible for the governmentwide introduction of PPB to occur at the time that the pluralist's bargaining model had reached its academic apogee, approximately one year after the publication of major works by Lindblom and Wildavsky. Yet a full appreciation of the sources and implications of systems politics and budgeting must take into account a wider range of influences and ferments. To move from process to systems requires at least the following: (1) dissatisfaction with the outcomes resulting from the established process and (2) confidence that better outcomes can be obtained via the systems approach.

The entry of economists into positions of political influence was important on both counts. Economists, unlike their political science brethren, were not committed to the established process. As they applied their specialized norms and perspectives to the political world, many economists became convinced that the process was inefficient and inequitable.[14] Moreover, economists already possessed sophisticated methodologies for examining outcomes: the positivist input-output models and the normative welfare economics concepts.

However, few political scientists qualified for the systems approach during the 1950s and 1960s. Rather than show concern about political outcomes, they were preoccupied with celebrating an *ancien regime* that exhibited few signs of the traumas developing within.[15] There were some stirrings by men of prominence, but their work was premature or too late. David Easton did his first work on systems politics, but only in recent years have his input-output categories been filled with useful data.[16] On the normative side, Lasswell's call for a policy science to "enable the most efficient use of the manpower, facilities, and resources of the American people,"[17] evoked a feeble response from his colleagues. (After all, if someone is convinced of the efficacy of the ongoing process, what incentive does he have to examine its outcomes?) A major methodological development has been the comparative study of state politics. Some scholars have taken advantage of the opportunities for multijurisdictional comparisons to correlate policy outcomes with certain economic and political characteristics.[18] Several of these studies call into question the pluralist assumption that the group process produces representative and desirable outcomes. Where these first methodological steps will lead is difficult to anticipate. Yet if it is true that researchers tend to follow their methodologies, the development of new systems techniques will have an impact on future conceptions of political reality. We might expect novel efforts to evaluate the performance of political systems and the quality of public policies. This is the forecast issued by Gabriel Almond in his 1968 Benedict Lectures at Boston University.[19] It is likely that when political scientists begin to probe policy outcomes, many will cast off the pretense of neutrality and take explicitly normative positions in evaluating the outcomes.[20]

More influential than the methods will be the level of dissatisfaction with political life. As more scholars become sensitive to politics in which there are losers and to a political world beset by scarcities, there will be a growing unwillingness to accept the process and its outcomes as givens. In this connection Michael Harrington's *The Other America* warrants notice because of the actions it provoked. For so many, the book was a revelation, bringing into sight and mind what long had been obscured by the pluralists' decision-making models. Its message was forthright: not everyone is protected and represented by the group mechanism. Not everyone benefits from the way politics works in the United States. There are unfavorable outcomes, and some of them are the results of the very processes and policies that have been established over the past 35 years. Once the spotlight was turned on outcomes, the weaknesses of the old processes became more conspicuous. Hence the search for new processes: community action, "maximum feasible participation," income guarantees, neighborhood cooperations, taking to the streets.

The systems mood became political reality when the President decided to "go public" with PPB. Viewed from the White House, what might have been some of the attrative features of PPB? During the initial part of his presidency, Lyndon Johnson displayed two characteristics that might have induced dissatisfaction with the pluralist processes: (1) a desire for involvement and initiative in program development and (2) an insistence on scrutinizing existing programs. Both characteristics required some modification in the rules of incremental choice; the first because it meant presidential rather than bureau leadership in program development; the second because it meant presidential rejection of the "preferred position" of last year's budget.

The traditional budget processes are unsuited for an active presidential role. In the usual bureaucratic pattern, budgetary power is located at the lower echelons, with successively higher levels having declining power and less involvement. By the time the budget reaches the President, most of the decisions have been made for him in the form of existing programs and incremental bureau claims. Barring unusual exertion, the President's impact is marginal, cutting some requests and adding some items of his own. PPB may have been perceived as a means of establishing the presidency earlier and more effectively in the making of budgetary and program policy. (No claim is made here that the President saw PPB as a vitalizer of his budgetary power or in a systems context. But the very arrival of PPB is strong evidence of high-level dissatisfaction with the status quo processes.)

Dissatisfaction is not enough to sway political leaders to underwrite an innovation. They also must have confidence that the new way is workable and desirable. This optimism was fueled by the Great Society mood. There was confidence in the ability of government to eradicate hard-core social and human problems, and in its ability to specify and reach long-range objectives. A few years earlier President Kennedy had predicted a moon landing in this decade; why not set concrete targets for a wide range of social endeavors? PPB was perceived as an effective apparatus for identifying legitimate national objectives and for measuring progress toward their attainment. PPB's objectives would be operational and reachable, politically appealing yet based on socioeconomic analysis, not just the expedients of politicians or the dreams of futurists. PPB's objectives would be presidential, marking the accomplishments of his administration.

The legislative explosion of the first Johnson years may have supplied another incentive. A President who was intensely concerned with building a program and legislative record was impelled to become an administrative innovator. This pattern parallels the course of New Deal politics. Following his unsurpassed legislative accomplishments, President Roosevelt appointed his Committee on Administrative Management and embarked on a battle for reorganization that was to culminate in the establishment of the Executive Office of the President and the growth of the budget function to its contemporary status. In both the New Deal and the Great Society, basic changes in program goals aggravated and exposed the organizational deficiencies rooted in the bureau-congressional committee-interest group axis that dominates the pluralists processes. There is reason to believe that the President viewed PPB as an opening prong in a major overhaul of federal organization, an expectation that was aborted by the Vietnam situation.

While economists and analysts have been credited and debited for PPB's debut, many hands and influences have been involved. One can even go back to the waning years of the Eisenhower Administration, to the commissions on national goals and purpose. These quests reflected disenchantment with the drift of the period, the lack of purpose or progression. As one expression of this temper, PPB has attracted both conservative and liberal sponsorship. The conservative version is based on the conviction that public outputs are not worth the private cost and that multiyear projections would disclose the ominous growth in government spending implicit in current policies. The motives of the liberals are more complex. They are confident that public objectives are worth the cost, but they also feel that existing programs are not producing optimal outcomes.[21]

Political Process Deficiencies

If systems politics is in step with the times, it is because the political process has been found wanting. The imperfections have produced unsatisfactory outcomes. But it would be senseless to discard the process because it is deficient: we can compensate for its weaknesses. This is what economists have done with the market.

The pluralist process is based on competition among interest groups. Its archetype is the economic model of competition among buyers and sellers. But the economists have come to reject a total reliance on the market's capability to allocate all resources efficiently or equitably. They have identified several classes of market limitations, the most important of which pertain to public goods and external costs and benefits. They also have identified certain characteristics of imperfect markets, in which competition is restricted, supply and demand are controlled or manipulated, and prices are administered. The pluralists still are in their *laissez faire* period. They attribute few faults to their political market. But the economic market supplies useful analogs for the appraisal of the political process. It is reasonable to expect that a political process which is modeled on market competition will exhibit many of the deficiencies of the economic market itself. Yet for many of the market defects and limitations, economists have looked to government for corrective action. Accordingly, the political process might reinforce rather than combat market inadequacies. As a first step toward conceiving a political process that is free of market-like defects, I propose to develop a taxonomy of political process deficiencies.

PUBLIC GOODS

Goods that are available to all consumers, whether or not they pay for them, cannot be supplied efficiently by the private economy. For such public goods, nonmarket institutions, usually but not exclusively governmental, are used for determining how much should be provided.

In transferring the case of public goods from the private sector to the polity, economists assume that collective values will prevail. But the political process, as conceived by the pluralists, operates via competition. Is the process of political competition superior to, or different from, the process of market competition in deciding public goods issues? If government were to provide public goods on the basis of some public interest determinant—in terms of systems criteria—it might be superior to the market, for there would be a means of evaluating the social costs and benefits to the whole polity of an investment in national defense, space exploration, or other public goods. But when private group influences prevail, the result is that public goods are produced and distributed on the basis of private calculations. Perversely, something which economists regard as a public good, our pluralists regard as a private good. Take the case of defense. An economist would argue that we all receive, more or less, the same benefits. The pluralists would have to argue, however, that we do not benefit equally, for the defense establishment and military contractors get more out of defense spending than the rest of us do. Thus, while each of us is equally defended, we do not equally benefit from the production of defense.

Whether the supply of public goods will be distorted by the polity depends on the shape of group politics. When an influential group gains disproportionately from a public good, society may produce too much of it. Since we all gain some benefit from defense, we do not have the usual checks and balances that operate in the case of private goods. A swollen or misallocated defense budget may result. When the public good is promoted by a weak group, too little of the good might be produced. Perhaps this is what has hobbled the national movement for pure air. (Some pluralists now speak of two polities, one with the ordinary interplay of group interests, the other where the group process is subordinate.[22] The latter sector consists mainly of the national security and foreign policy areas which consume a huge portion of our public wealth and deal with the survival of this nation and the world.)

EXTERNALITIES

A second class of allocative decisions which cannot be entrusted completely to the competitive market pertains to external costs and benefits. A classic case of an external cost is the discharge of pollutants into the air; the pollutor does not pay for the social cost he engenders. An external benefit results when the beneficiary does not have to pay for another's largess. Some economists regard education as such a benefit because society benefits but does not pay for the investments I make in my own education. While the market can supply goods that carry external costs or benefits, it is not capable of producing them in the optimal quality or quantity. It would tend to overproduce goods that have external costs, and to underproduce those that provide external benefits.

Because of this market disability, the public sector gets the call. In the case of an external cost such as air pollution, the job of government would be to make the pollutor pay (through taxation, regulation, fines, or some other mode) so that his cost equals the social cost. For an external benefit such as education, government would require all members of the community to pay some share of the cost. But in a competitive polity, the group process might stimulate rather than inhibit the production of goods with external costs. After all, one of the aims of an interest group is to get others to pay for your benefits or to avoid paying your share of the costs. As a result, government can and does play Robin Hood in reverse, taking from the poor and giving to the rich. Urban renewal is a case in point. Government's fiscal and legal powers were used by developers to impose all sorts of costs on residents and shopkeepers in the renewal area. Sometimes powerful interests can engineer public policy to obtain rewards for imposing costs on the community. Thus we hear proposals to award tax credits to air pollutors in order to motivate them to cease their harmful activity. Where there are external benefits, powerful beneficiaries may refuse to tax themselves for their gain.

Why doesn't the unseen hand of group competition keep everyone honest, making the pollutor pay for the costs he imposes and society for the benefits it receives? The obvious answer is that not all interests are equally powerful. Pollutors probably have better lobbies than city residents who breathe the air. And they use their political power to ratify, not to countermand, the edict of the market.

INCOME DISTRIBUTION

Left to its own wills, the market will produce a distribution of income in which some have very much and some have very little. In a capitalist polity, we tend not to regard the possession of wealth as an evil, but we have become concerned about those who are poor. Hence the array of welfare programs that have grown over the past 35 years. Certainly these programs have resulted in a net redistribution of income in favor of low-income groups. But the results are not one-sided, as indicated by the regressive Social Security tax structure, the welfare problems, and some of the housing programs.

But the basic income distribution established by the market has not been greatly affected by public micropolicy. (Macropolicy, the stimulation of economic growth, definitely has had considerable impact on the numbers of people living below the poverty line.) The poor subsist under welfare; they also subsisted under the poor laws. Often the poor are denied the bootstraps that might enable them to rise above the poverty level. We rarely redistribute wealth by giving the poor money; instead we give them benefits in kind. These are woefully inefficient from an economic point of view (as the conservatives tell us) and woefully inadequate from a social viewpoint (as the liberals have discovered). Somehow, however, they are efficient and desirable from a political standpoint. There are several explanations for this anomaly (see the paragraphs below on imperfect competition and ideology). The main reason is that the poor lack not only money but political power as well. They cannot compete fully in political life because they lack money, status, self-confidence, political skill, and group and bureaucratic representation. Perhaps there can be no effective redistribution of income unless there is a concomitant redistribution of political power. But the established group structure is committed to the prevailing distribution of power because it is advantaged by that distribution, just as those who are economically potent tend to approve the market distribution of incomes. In order to achieve a meaningful redistribution of political resources, it might be necessary to challenge the group norms that undergird the political process, that is, to contest the legitimacy of the process itself.

IMPERFECT COMPETITION

A market with few buyers and sellers will not produce the right outcomes; neither will a polity which is itself oligopolistic. The political process possesses the same tendencies toward concentration that drive competition from the market. In both instances there are advantages in bigness and in the ability to control resources. We have the Big Three in automobile production and the Big Two in political parties. While they are not interchangeable players, the robber baron and the boss had much in common, and so do the contemporary elites in business and government.[23] Powerful men have not been known to favor competition when competition does not favor them. In pluralist politics there is a special kind of market imperfection. Four-fifths of the population, according to most reckonings, is fairly affluent. When we speak of 30 or 40 million poor people, we tend to forget the political implications of the 160 or 170 million who are not poor. It is of great ideological import that the rise of pluralist politics coincided with the emergence of an advantaged majority and disadvantaged minority. At the very time the pluralists were celebrating minorities rule,[24] we had become a homogeneous majority of affluents. Under the guise of consensus, we had a new kind of tyranny of the majority. Not a deliberate or invidious tyranny, but one of political incapability to deal with the interests of the minority. John K. Galbraith spelled out the economic and social implications in *The Affluent Society*.[25] As Mills argued, what passed for political competition were petty family quarrels, but the big issues went unchallenged.

How then have things begun to change in the cities and the ghettos? I would not leave altruism out of the answer, nor the efforts of activists and analysts who have warred against the established process and its stark outcomes. But the number one factor is that the poor and the blacks are becoming majorities in our inner cities, those strategic centers of communications and commerce that remain vital to suburban interests.

Not only did the affluence of the period create a new set of majority interests, it also turned would-be competitors into allies. As Galbraith has pointed out, countervailing power (which he carefully differentiates from pluralist competition) does not function well "when there is inflation or inflationary pressure on markets."[26] Unions can conspire with management to gain higher wages and to pass the cost on to consumers. In the political arena, interests can logroll and pass the cost on to taxpayers. Only under conditions of scarcity is competition an efficient allocator of resources. This is one important reason why systems politics converges with the politics of scarcity.

IDEOLOGY

According to the principles of competition, both economic man and political man know their own interests and fight for them against the competing interests of others. But one of the things a political process can do is to make people not know their own interests. In the market it is somewhat difficult to misdirect people; there is the profit motive and the relatively unambiguous price mechanism. In politics it's a lot easier; you use ideology to do the job. Any successful mode of political inquiry becomes a set of biases, encumbering its practitioners from viewing the world from some alternative perspective. Pluralism, more and more of us are willing to concede, became a statement of the way politics ought to be, not merely a descriptive summing up of the way it is. As political reality began to move from group pluralism to group conflict, many political scientists were debarred by their concepts from recognizing the changes that were occurring. Only the cumulative hammerings of urban, racial, fiscal, diplomatic, and military crises have uprooted growing numbers from their pluralists anchorage.

To study the workings of political interests, the pluralists refined the art and science of public opinion polling, asking citizens about every conceivable issue and reporting the results with statistical fidelity. They also studied power to communities to determine who participates in the making of decisions and which interests get their way. Both techniques assume that there are no ideological impediments to interest formation and expression. Two very different scholars, C. Wright Mills and Joseph Schumpeter, argued to the contrary. The Marxist thread in Mills leads to this statement:

> What men are interested in is not always what is to their interest; the troubles they are aware of are not always the ones that beset them . . . it is not only that men can be unconscious of their situations; they are often falsely conscious of them.[27]

Schumpeter took the view that the conditions of modern politics inevitably dull man's capacity to form a political will:

> Thus the typical citizen drops to a lower level of mental performance as soon as he enters the political field. He argues and analyzes in a way which he would readily recognize as infantile within the sphere of his real interests. . . . the will of the people is the product and not the motive power of the political process.[28]

Schumpeter anticipates and rejects the pluralist response that groups act as surrogates for individual interests, converting the ignorance of the voter into a powerful political asset, and possessing a collective intelligence that compensates for the citizen's lack of knowledge. But rather than serving as representatives of individual interests, groups "are able to fashion and, within very wide limits, even to create the will of the people. What we are confronted with in the analysis of political processes is largely not a genuine but a manufactured will."[29]

The community power studies often were exhaustive in their coverage, but they covered very little. Banfield was able to find only six controversies of citywide importance in the Chicago of 1957 and 1958, and none of them dealt with the guts of living in a mass urban environment. Apparently the political process already had dried up the wells of conflict, relegating the important things to what Bachrach and Baratz aptly termed "nondecisions." It is the "mobilization of biases," E. E. Schattschneider wrote in his last antipluralist work, that determines the scope of political conflict.[30]

Ideology is one critical reason why people do not always know their own interests, why there are so few controversies. The political process socializes its citizens to accept certain norms and rules as legitimate, not to be challenged or questioned. The myopics who have climbed the political socialization bandwagon (the successor to community power studies) look at the small things like who is Democratic and who is Republican, as if Tweddledee and Tweedledum made much difference, and all the time they neglect the big questions of the citizens' linkage to the polity.

"My chief objection," Christian Bay has said, "is not to a pluralist society but to a pluralist political theory." This theory "does not jibe with what political scientists *know* about the power of elites or the techniques of mass manipulation."[31] Under the cover of pluralism elites flourished, but they were given new, deceptive titles: the active minority, opinion leaders, decision makers. Rarely were they identified in terms of the power they wielded or in terms of the gaps between mass and elite, powerful and powerless, manipulator and manipulated. All were given statistical equality and anonymity in the opinion polls.

The pluralists thought that their age was "The End of Ideology." Looking backward, we can see it as the triumph of an ideology—the ideology of pluralism. For pluralism became more a norm than a fact, the glorification of the bargain and the status quo, the sanctification of consensus and stability. Elite interests benefited from these norms; minority interests were constrained by them.

IMMOBILITY OF RESOURCES

Unlike water, economic resources such as labor and capital do not always flow to the right place. There can be barriers to their mobility. Unemployed miners remain in Appalachia and subsistence farmers on their farms. Bankers put their money downtown, not in Harlem where the interest rates are higher. One responsibility of government is to stimulate mobility via subsidies, loans, and regulatory devices.

There also can be immobility of political resources, by which I mean the failure of the political process to behave in response to numbers. For in a democratic polity, numbers (weighted for intensity of interest) is the key resource. Over the long run, this political resource tends to attract power. If Negroes move into a city and come to outnumber the whites, they ultimately will take over the elective offices, much as the Irish displaced the Yankees. But there are at least two kinds of impediments to the free flow of numbers—structural and ideological. All sorts of structural roadblocks stand in the way of interests which have the votes and want the power. Legislative apportionment, the committee system, parliamentary rules, seniority, federalism, the balkanization of metropolitan regions, bureaucratic patterns, election laws—whatever justification they may have, these structures have the potential of depriving interests of their just political fruits. Sometimes the structures are contrived for this purpose (gerrymandering, for instance); sometimes they evolve over many years of inaction (urban sprawl); sometimes they are abolished (as in the case of legislative malapportionment).

The second factor is a product of the incremental character of political choice. What economics writes off as sunk cost, politics rewards as a vested interest. The incremental ideology has the effect of immobilizing numbers because it protects status quo interests. Each incremental move forecloses additional opportunities, with the consequence that the iron grip of the past is tightened with each successive decision. Of the $180 billions in the budget, only a tiny fragment is actionable. A President who would war on poverty today has fewer options than Franklin Roosevelt had in his time. By the time the pluralist process reached its zenith, the political world was almost immobilized by the accumulation of previous commitments. (In his study of state expenditures, Ira Sharkansky shows that previous expenditures are an excellent predictor of current spending. For selected years between 1913 and 1965 he was computed the deviation between actual and incrementally predicted spending. For the years prior to 1957, an average of 22 states had a deviation of at least 15 percent. But for the years between 1957 and 1965, only seven states had a 15 percent deviation of actual from predicted spending.) [32] Lindblom was right. You can move far with incrementalism, but only in the direction in which you started. [33]

It is not surprising that Pareto norms became popular to some sophisticated pluralists. The economists' justification of the status quo had more appeal than their own "veto group" concept. By 1965 politics was a massive Pareto optimum. In politics the optimum almost always is what is; at least one person (or group) would be displeased by any proposed change. Every moment of the Vietnam war has been Pareto optimal; regardless of the political or military conditions, every moment was justifiable in terms of any alternative. [34]

REPRESENTATION

There is one kind of imperfection in the political process that has no market analogy. While the market is impelled by hidden levers, the polity is dependent on a representative mechanism, whether electoral, bureaucratic, or group. There is no other way to convert numbers and preferences democratically into policy. Many have written on the inadequacies of representation; the structural impediments mentioned above; the ignorance of the electorate and its limited "yes-no" vocabulary; the under- or over-representation of group interests; the tendency of group leaders to represent themselves rather than their members; the conspiratorial relationship between bureaucracies and their clienteles. The research of Nelson Polsby has added one more to this formidable inventory: the "institutionalization" of the House of Representatives (and, I suspect, of many other legislative bodies.)[35]

It would take papers the length of this one to map all the blockages between citizens and their representatives. The sociopsychological studies of mass and elite call into question many critical aspects of voting and interest group theory. In sum, regarding all the modern institutions of representation, one can apply the characterization of Erich Fromm concerning the voting process:

> Between the act of voting and the most momentous high-level political decisions is a connection which is mysterious. One cannot say that there is none at all, nor can one say that the final decision is an outcome of the voter's will.[36]

The Status of Systems Budgeting

Just as the process strategies described by Wildavsky suited the politics of its times, so the systems vistas of PPB are in tune with the politics of its times. PPB is part of a larger movement of revision in political study and adjustment in political practice. But just as upheavals in political life have produced disorder and confusion, the new wave in budgeting has generated a good deal of costly disruption and obfuscation.

PPB has had a rough time these past few years. Confusion is widespread; results are meager. The publicity has outdistanced the performance by a wide margin. In the name of analysis, bureaus have produced reams of unsupported, irrelevant justification and description. As Schumpeter said of Marxism: it is preaching in the garb of analysis. Plans have been formulated without serious attention to objectives, resource constraints, and alternative opportunities. PPB's first years have been an exercise in technique. There have been the bulletins and the staffings, the program memoranda, and the program and financial plans. Those who have been apprehensive over possible threats to cherished political values can find no support for their fears in what has happened during these years. Those who had hoped that PPB would not succumb to the tyranny of technique can find much disappointment in what has happened. PPB's products have become its end-products. For so many practitioners, PPB is not some majestic scrutiny of objectives and opportunities, but going through the motions of doing a program structure, writing a program memorandum, of filling in the columns of a program and financial plan.

It is tempting to attribute PPB's difficulties to the manner in which it was introduced, for the implementation strategy has been faulty. But the decisive factor has been the prematurity of PPB.

The conceptual side of PPB presents something of a paradox. The important ideas are few in number and easy to understand. But they happen to run counter to the way American budgeting has been practiced for more than half a century. The concepts which took root in economics and planning will have to undergo considerable mutation before they can be successfully transplanted on political soil. PPB is an idea whose time has not quite come. It was introduced governmentwide before the requisite concepts, organizational capability, political conditions, informational resources, and techniques were adequately developed.[37] A decade ago, PPB was beyond reach; a decade or two hence, it, or some updated version, might be one of the conventions of budgeting. For the present, PPB must make do in a world it did not create and has not yet mastered.

It is hard to foretell PPB's exact course of development. Certainly there will be many PPB's arising out of the diverse roots and images of systems politics and budgeting, and also out of the diverse perceptions of budget participants and the diverse capabilities of governments. In a technical and methodological sense, there will be continual upgrading in the sophistication of systems budgeting. But there will be no revolutionary overthrow of process in politics. There is an understandable tendency in politics to rely on stable, consensual processes. The pluralists were right about many of their claims for the existing process, the way it reduces conflict and complexity. One can make much the same case for any established process which governs the relationships among competing interests. A permanent systems politics might mean permanent crisis, constant struggle over public ends and means.

I have indicated that the systems ferment is grounded in the conviction that the existing process produces unfavorable outcomes. If systems people had confidence in the process, it would make little sense to go through the costly and possibly divisive reappraisals involved in a systems analysis of objectives and alternatives. How, then, can we reconcile the tendency toward process equilibrium with the challenges to the established process? I think the answer is that systems politics will induce a revision in the process. The systems approach enables us to ascertain why the process yields imperfect outcomes. But like the market, we need not throw out the political process because it is deficient; we can compensate for its weaknesses. The task of systems politics is to correct for the defects by making adjustments in the process and by creating new institutions of power and choice. Optimally, the political process should have some gyroscopic capability to assess its outcomes rather than accept them on blind faith as the pluralists have. Budgeting will have a leading role in this readjustment because it is the closest thing politics has to a system for choice. The hybrid process that will emerge will be more responsive and efficient by virtue of the feedback from outcome to process.

Notes

[1] See Martin Landau, "On the Use of Metaphor in Political Analysis," 28 *Social Research*, 1961.

[2] Of course, there are other ways to view the changes currently unfolding. I use the systems concept because it unites study and practice and politics and budgeting.

[3] It should be noted that systems politics and systems analysis are of much more modest proportions than "general systems theory" defined by Kenneth Boulding as the quest "for a body of systematic theoretical constructs which will discuss the general relationships of the empirical world." See Walter Buckley (ed.), *Modern Systems Research for the Behavioral Scientist* (Chicago: Aldine Publishing Company, 1968).

[4] See William M. Capron, "The Impact of Analysis on Bargaining in Government," presented to the 1966 Annual Meeting of the American Political Science Association.

[5] A hint of the closing of the gap between incrementalism and systems analysis is implicit in the latest version of Wildavsky's views, "Toward a Radical Incrementalism: A Proposal to Aid Congress in Reform of the Budgetary Process," in Alfred deGrazia (ed.), *Congress: The First Branch of Government* (Garden City, N.Y.: Doubleday Anchor Books, 1967).

[6] Aaron Wildavsky, *The Politics of the Budgetary Process* (Boston: Little, Brown and Company, 1964), p. 136.

[7] The best statement of pluralist process for purposes of this paper is Charles E. Lindblom, *The Intelligence of Democracy* (New York: The Free Press, 1965).

[8] While his work contains numerous illustrations and anecdotes, Wildavsky does not deal explicitly with which interests win or lose as a consequence of the budget process, or with the outcomes of the process, for example, with the question of whether people are well or poorly housed.

[9] Aaron Wildavsky, *The Politics of the Budgetary Process*, p. 127.

[10] *Ibid.*, p. 130.

[11] When he introduced the concept, Simon's argument was "that men satisfice because they have not the wits to maximize. . . . If you have the wits to maximize, it is silly to satisfice." Herbert A. Simon, "The Decision-Making Schema: A Reply," *Public Administration Review*, Winter 1958.

[12] Robert C. Wood, "Metropolitan Government, 1975: An Extrapolation of Trends," 52 *American Political Science Review*, March 1958, p. 112.

[13] Robert E. Lane, "The Politics of Consensus in an Age of Affluence," 59

American Political Science Review, December 1965, p. 893. For a fuller picture on the optimism of the common man in the 1950s, see Robert E. Lane, *Political Ideology: Why the American Common Man Believes What He Does* (New York: the Free Press, 1962).

[14]More than anything else, this skeptical view of public spending prodded economists to be the leading sponsors of PPB.

[15]See Leo Strauss, "An Epilogue," in Herbert J. Storing (ed.), *Essays on the Scientific Study of Politics* (New York: Holt, Rinehart and Winston, 1962), p. 327. This caustic yet penetrating critique of the pluralist method was "buried" by the establishment.

[16]David Easton, *The Political System* (New York: Alfred A. Knopf Inc., 1953). See, also, his *A Systems Analysis of Political Life* (New York: John Wiley & Sons, 1965).

[17]Harold D. Lasswell, "The Policy Orientation," in Daniel Lerner and Harold D. Lasswell (eds.), *The Policy Sciences* (Stanford: Stanford University Press, 1951), p. 3. The call for policy or systems analysis often is coupled with a comment on resource scarcity and the need for optimization.

[18]Thomas R. Dye, *Politics, Economics, and the Public: Policy Outcomes in the American States* (Chicago: Rand McNally, 1966); and Ira Sharkansky, *Spending in the American States* (Chicago: Rand McNally, 1968).

[19]Gabriel Almond, *Perspectives on Political Development*, Benedict Lectures on Political Philosophy, March 18-20, 1968, Boston University.

[20]In explaining why behavioral political scientists have emphasized process over content, Austin Ranney observes that many scholars "think that focusing on content is likely to lead to evaluations of present policies and exhortations for new ones," "The Study of Policy Content: A Framework for Choice," in *Items* (Washington, D. C.: Social Science Research Council, September 1968).

[21]Thus Governor Reagan has emphasized multi-year projections in his application of PPB in California government. A liberal's concept of PPB is suggested in Michael Harrington's *Toward A New Democratic Left* (New York: Macmillan, 1968).

[22]E.g., Aaron Wildavsky, "The Two Presidencies," *Trans*-Action, December 1966, pp. 7–14.

[23]It is not necessary, however, to accept Mills' view of interlocking military-industrial-political directorates to acknowledge the affinities in their behavior.

[24]The "minorities rule" phrase along with its theoretical elaboration is in Robert A. Dahl, *A Preface to Democratic Theory* (Chicago: University of Chicago Press, 1956).

[25]Much of Galbraith's thesis was misunderstood, and especially his comments on poverty.

[26]John Kenneth Galbraith, *American Capitalism* (Boston: Houghton Mifflin Company, Sentry Edition, 1962), p. 128 ff.

[27]C. Wright Mills, *White Collar* (New York: Galaxy Books, 1956), p. xix.

[28]Joseph A. Schumpeter, *Capitalism, Socialism and Democracy*, Third Edition (New York: Harper Torchbooks, 1962), pp. 262–263.

[29]*Ibid.*, p. 263.

[30]E. E. Schattschneider, *The Semisovereign People* (New York: Holt, Rinehart & Winston, 1960).

[31] Christian Bay, "Needs, Wants, and Political Legitimacy," *Canadian Journal of Political Science*, September 1968, p. 252.

[32] Ira Sharkansky, *op. cit.*, Table III-8.

[33] See Charles E. Lindblom, *A Strategy of Decision* (New York: The Free Press, 1963).

[34] In this light, it is understandable why public opinion polls fluctuated with Administration policy in Vietnam before the Tet crisis. Tet revealed some of the true outcomes of the war.

[35] See Nelson Polsby, "The Institutionalization of the U.S. House of Representatives," *American Political Science Review*, March 1968.

[36] Erich Fromm, *The Sane Society* (New York: Holt, Rinehart & Winston, Inc., 1955), p. 191.

[37] These prematurities have been examined in Allen Schick, "PPB's First Years: Premature and Maturing," Washington, D.C.: U.S. Bureau of the Budget, September 1968, mimeo.

5

Information Change and Congressional Behavior: a Caveat for PPB Reformers

JAMES E. JERNBERG

The history of budgeting in the United States is a history of reform. Throughout this century attempts have been made to alter either the participants, their roles, and their relations with one another, or the informational inputs, methods of decision making, and likely outputs of the existing budget system.[1] PPB, the planning-programming-budgeting system, is the most recent, most widely heralded, and most controversial package in the lengthy reform series. Essentially PPB calls for a change in focus from inputs to outputs, with outputs clearly reflecting choices related to goals. Participants are expected to consider a time-horizon consequence beyond the single year, to five years (program period) and even to twenty years (planning period). The actual budget choices are to be the products of cost-benefit, cost-utility, or cost-effectiveness studies within a systems-analysis framework.

Reprinted from the *Journal of Politics*, 33, No. 3 (August 1969): 722–40, by permission of the author and publisher.

The concept has generated as many interpretations and embellishments during the 1960s as it has camps of devotees and detractors. In recent years the dialogue appears to have produced a change in the "posture" of the parties interested in this particular reform concerning information in decision making. Initially, open advocacy encountered hostility and skepticism. Claims by some of the recent origin and distinctive features of the reform[2] were countered by the assertions of others that no differences existed between the current conception and similar attempts in the past.[3] Charges that the existing budget process was not conducive to rational or efficient decision making, but that program budgeting would reverse this unfortunate situation,[4] were parried by defenses of the existing process and critiques of the expectations of rationality and efficiency espoused by the devotees of reform.[5]

An apparent consequence of the dialogue has been a modification in claims and somewhat more modest statements of expectations expressed by at least the official proponents of the PPB creed.[6] One might say that the concept of program budgeting (PPB) was itself subjected to systems analysis and synthesized, and that it now appears more likely to be intellectually acceptable to both original advocates and skeptics.

As the intellectual fervor subsides and the thrust of August 25, 1965, extends beyond domestic national agencies to state and local governments, either by choice or as spin-offs of financial federalism, certain unanswered questions persist. Wildavsky's demand for systematic studies supporting the claims (better decision making) of the advocates of PPB in Defense has not yet received a public response, apart from statements and assertions in testimony that such studies exist and that they do support the case.[7] We have, in addition, a set of questions that is both practically and theoretically significant. Senator Henry Jackson asked: "How has the introduction of PPB in Defense affected Congressional consideration of the defense budget?"[8] In a more general view Allen Schick raised the basic question that must be asked of any reform, namely "what difference does it make?" He then elaborated his point:

> The case for PPB rests on the assumption that the form in which information is classified and used governs the actions of budget makers, and conversely, that alterations in form will produce desired changes in behavior. Take away the assumption that behavior follows form, and the movement for PPB is reduced to a trivial manipulation of techniques. . . .
>
> Yet this assumed connection between roles and information is a relatively uncharted facet of the PPB literature. The behavioral side of the equation has been neglected. . . .
>
> PPB probably takes an overly mechanistic view of the impact of

form on behavior and underestimates and strategic and volitional aspects of budget making. In the political arena, data are used to influence "who gets what" in budgets and appropriations. If information influences behavior, the reverse is also true. Indeed data are more tractable than roles; participants are more likely to seek and use data which suit their preferences than to alter behavior automatically in response to formal changes.[9]

This paper reports some research that may provide insights into both Jackson's and Schick's concerns. Senator Jackson's special interest in defense may now be broadened to include all federal government budgets developed under PPB. At this juncture the answer necessarily must be that PPB has not affected Congressional consideration of the budget because the decision system has been limited internally to the Executive branch. Congress continues to receive the "traditional" budget-document information. Thus, we can broaden the question beyond defense, but we must translate it into a more speculative form: "How would the introduction of PPB affect Congressional consideration of the budget?" Schick's broader theoretical concern can be translated into the following questions: Does a change in information produce a change in behavior? How can we explain the discrepancy between assumed behavior and observed behavior following the introduction of a reform? Finally, under what conditions may we expect observed behavior to resemble expected behavior?

Conveniently for these purposes the Hoover Commission[10] recommended in 1949 an information reform similar to PPB in the broad, general sense of the concept, if not in its technical sophistication.[11] The plaudits and publicity accorded the Hoover version as a truly innovative budget-decision-making measure were comparable to those received by PPB in recent years.[12] Furthermore, Congress was the intended user and beneficiary of the Hoover Commission's program budgeting. We therefore can ask how and why Congress responded as it did to the information reform sponsored by the Hoover Commission. The answers may suggest insights into the revised version of Jackson's precise question and may provide empirical evidence relevant to Schick's commentary.

Beginning with fiscal year 1951, budgets of the U.S. government differed markedly in information and format from those presented previously. Executive participants clearly responded to the recommendations of the Hoover Commission by presenting the budget in a form that permitted Congress to review requests in program or activity terms.[13] The task of this paper is to inquire whether Congressional behavior was influenced by this change in information.

Research Design and Methods

Many recent studies have enhanced our understanding of Congressional behavior in the budget process.[14] We have learned that when we speak of the *Congress* in the budget process, we really mean the Appropriations Committees of the two houses. We know that the House is more thorough in its work than the Senate, relying exclusively upon executive rather than public hearings and "mark-up" sessions. The economics of research suggests that the present study focus on the House Appropriations Committee because of its greater importance and dedication, but the exclusiveness of the committee's decision-making process bars direct observation of member behavior.

In this study one aspect of the House Appropriations Committee's decision process, the hearing, has been selected to test the influence of reform on behavior. The hearing is the single structured situation in which the researcher has data readily accessible for analysis. Although the hearings are held in executive session, the committee prepares a public record of the action.[15] This investigation of House appropriations hearings specifically seeks to determine whether there is a relationship between the use of program terms in the presentation of budgets and supplementary information and the types of questions asked of agency representatives in the hearing. The Hoover Commission asserted that participants in the process were input-oriented because of the manner in which information was presented, and they assumed that providing program information would result in an output orientation. (This assumption parallels the outlines of the PPB reformers' assumptions today.) It thus seems reasonable to expect that the types of questions asked by a committee will reflect their information orientation. This study focuses on the kinds of questions members ask, and whether inquiry and interest differ in the pre- and post-reform periods.

A cursory reading of a few years' hearings reveals a wide range of inquiry types rather than a dichotomous input-output alternative. A committee member is not limited but asks any question that suits his particular interests.[16] To make manageable the wide range of possible questions that committee members ask of agency representatives, content analysis was applied to the hearings. Content analysis is a useful technique for the classification of communications.[17] While it has been used primarily in studies of international communications, at least one previous study of appropriations behavior utilized content analysis.[18] Apart from meeting the requirements of objectivity, systematic coverage, and quantification, there is the added need to establish meaningful operational categories into which all questions or themes of inquiry could be placed. For the purposes of this study, an original cumbersome set of thirty-seven categories has been collapsed into four major categories: [19]

Program: All inquiry focusing on agency outputs was placed into this category. Outputs were pre-identified as the activities shown in the agency budget document. Inquiry could range from performance (e.g., "How many immigrants were processed into this country last year?") to finance (e.g., "How much are you spending on soil moisture conservation this year?"). This was the type of inquiry advocated by the Hoover Commission, and the kind they expected would develop with the change in information.

Objects of Expenditure: This category includes all inquiry focusing on agency budget inputs. The inputs were pre-coded according to the classification in the budget document. Inquiry could range from costs of employee housing, numbers of personnel, types of automobiles being purchased, to amount of fence purchases. According to the Hoover Commission, this was the traditional type of inquiry that occurred.

Oversight of Administration (Supervision): It is often stated that appropriations committees combine spending with oversight of adminis- tration. [20] To anticipate and accommodate this type of inquiry, a major category of supervision of "Oversight" was established. This includes all inquiry focusing on internal agency-management matters. Inquiry would range from types of training given employees, proper number of regions, methods of cashing checks, desirable ratios of central to field personnel, etc. These are questions that appear to be designed to increase committee supervision over the agency.

Other: Included here are the miscellaneous kinds of inquiry that arise out of the wide variety of members' interests. Subcategories include: (1) Size of budget—this has to do with neither program nor objects of expenditure, yet it is clearly a budgetary question; (2) relations with Congress, other agencies, the public; (3) other non-budgetary, non- oversight inquiry.

After the hearings were analyzed, members of the appropriations subcommittees and their staff directors were interviewed to seek informa- tion that would help interpret the findings of the content analysis.

Research Sample

Given the restrictions of time and resources, the sample was limited to appropriations hearings for five agencies that appeared before three different House Appropriations subcommittees. The agencies and their corresponding subcommittees are as follows:

Agency	Subcommittee
U.S. Forest Service	Interior
National Park Service	Interior
Federal Prison System	State, Justice, Commerce, Judiciary (SJCJ)
Immigration and Naturalization Service	State, Justice, Commerce, Judiciary (SJCJ)
Internal Revenue Service	Treasury—Post Office

The agencies have certain common characteristics: they are domestic in nature, they have central headquarters with field operations, they are line- or operating-type agencies, and they all existed prior to the impact of the Hoover Commission reform in fiscal year 1951. Only the last characteristic is actually crucial to the study, while the first three provide a sense of consistency. No claim is made that the five agencies or the three subcommittees constitute a representative sample of all federal agencies or of all subcommittees, but their use is justified in that findings bearing comparative analysis may yield more meaningful results than might otherwise be expected.

TABLE 1
Committee Distribution of Attention by Type of Inquiry
(Two-Year Mean)
1949–1950

	Program	Objects of expenditure	Supervision (oversight)	Other	Total	N
Federal Prison System (FPS) (SJCJ Subcommittee)	53.2%	22.3	6.4	18.1	100.0	94
Immigration and Naturalization Service (I&NS) (SJCJ Subcommittee)	46.3%	27.8	3.7	22.2	100.0	54
Internal Revenue Service (IRS) (T-PO Subcommittee)	28.6%	24.6	35.9	10.9	100.0	192
Forest Service (FS) (Interior Subcommittee)	50.3%	14.7	1.6	33.4	100.0	191
National Park Service (NPS) (Interior Subcommittee)	40.3%	24.6	17.9	17.2	100.0	134

Content analysis was applied to hearing of these five agencies for the period of fiscal years 1949–1964, and for 1968, a total of seventeen years and eighty-five hearings. In total 3,614 separate themes of inquiry were assigned to the four major categories.[21]

Evidence

In the distribution of inquiry for the hearings of each agency three periods are distinguished: (1) 1949–1950, the most recent years prior to the change in information; (2) 1951–1952, a similar period following the information change; and (3) 1951–1964, a fourteen-year consecutive period since the introduction of program information. The data are presented initially in percentage terms, utilizing the two-year mean for 1949–1950 and 1951–1952, and a fourteen-year mean for 1951–1964.

The most obvious initial conclusion is that no hearing can be characterized as solely of one type. The scope of inquiry and interest is broad, covering all categories constructed for this study. A review of the 1949–1950 data does not confirm the assertion made by the Hoover Commission that Congress assumed an input orientation.[22] Indeed, with the exception of the Internal Revenue Service (IRS) hearings by Treasury-Post Office (T-PO), inquiry concerning agency programs and activities exceeded 40 percent, whereas input questions constituted less than 30 percent of the total. This finding does not refute the Commission's case for program budgeting, but it clearly does not provide an empirical base for its assumptions about the behavior and frames of reference of Congressional decision makers.

A more important question, however, is whether the behavior of committee members changed, and in the tended direction, following the change in information. Table 2 identifies the committees' mean distribution of inquiry for the immediate reform period 1951–1952.

The behavior change between the two periods is mixed. Both the T-PO (NPS) and the Interior (FS, NPS) subcommittees asked more questions about programs and fewer questions about objects of expenditure in the two-year period. On the other hand, the SJCJ subcommittee (FPS, I and NS) demonstrated a reverse inclination toward program information, resorting to more objects-of-expenditure or other inquiries than they did prior to the change.[23] The data are persuasive enough to reject the hypothesis that the change in information would produce a change in behavior directed toward program information. Participants shifted in both directions and, perhaps more importantly, the participants did not limit themselves to the categories of program and objects-of-expenditure, but rather covered a wide range of inquiry.

TABLE 2
Committee Distribution of Attention by Type of Inquiry
(Two-Year Mean)
1951–1952

	Program	Objects of expenditure	Supervision (oversight)	Other	Total	N
Federal Prison System (FPS) (SJCJ Subcommittee)	51.6%	30.6	1.7	16.1	100.0	62
Immigration and Naturalization Service (I&NS) (SJCJ Subcommittee)	39.2%	24.9	11.5	24.4	100.0	94
Internal Revenue Service (IRS) (T-PO Subcommittee)	53.9%	21.4	17.9	6.8	100.0	63
Forest Service (FS) (Interior Subcommittee)	59.4%	8.2	6.8	25.6	100.0	98
National Park Service (NPS) (Interior Subcommittee)	70.3%	9.2	13.0	7.5	100.0	54

After taking into account the "shock" effect of the new information and its publicity upon the committees, the investigation was extended to cover a fourteen-year period (1951–1964) in an attempt to detect evidence of increased growth or decline in program inquiry. While it is noteworthy that all committees decreased their proportion of program inquiry in the succeeding years the data suggested a more interesting question, viz., how to account for the overall inquiry behavior of the committee.

Broadening the focus of attention to all categories in Table 3, we find that a number of interesting patterns emerge. Committees differ markedly, relatively speaking, in the emphasis they place upon each category of inquiry. The Interior subcommittee, for example, relies upon program inquiry to a greater extent (FS, 57.3 percent; NPS, 55.2 percent) than do the SJCJ (FPS, 38.8 percent; I and N, 32.9 percent) and the Treasury-PO (IRS, 39.6 percent). The objects-of-expenditure category reveals the seemingly disproportionate emphasis placed upon that type of inquiry by the SJCJ subcommittee as compared with the other subcommittees (Prison, 37.7 percent and I and N Service, 34.9 percent, contrasted to IRS, 16.3 percent, FS, 11.3 percent and NPS, 18.3 percent). Finally, while all subcommittees ask some supervisory or oversight questions, the Treasury-PO subcommittee appears to place much greater relative emphasis on that concern than do other subcommittees.

TABLE 3
Committee Distribution of Attention by Type of Inquiry
(Fourteen-Year Mean)
1951–1964

	Program	Objects of expenditure	Supervision (oversight)	Other	Total	14-Yr. N
Prison system (SJCJ)	38.8%	37.7	2.5	21.0	100.0	361
I and N Service (SJCJ)	32.9%	34.9	11.8	20.4	100.0	289
IRS (Treasury-PO)	39.6%	16.3	24.7	19.4	100.0	653
Forest Service (Interior)	57.3%	11.3	12.0	19.4	100.0	674
Park Service (Interior)	55.2%	18.3	9.2	17.3	100.0	665

In order to determine whether the findings represented by the data in Table 3 reflect chance occurrences or distinct differences in the information orientation of the inquiry, the data have been translated into observed-expected frequency distributions, and calculations between the two have been made and presented in Table 4 below.

We are interested in comparative differences, and Table 4 confirms that differences among the three subcommittees do exist. The two Interior

TABLE 4
Ratio Between Observed-Expected Frequencies of Hearings Inquiry*
1951–1964

	Program	Objects of expenditure	Supervision (oversight)	Other
Prison System (SJCJ)	.825	1.824	.191	1.101
I and N Service (SJCJ)	.693	1.712	.895	1.073
IRS (Treasury-PO)	.841	.791	1.872	1.008
Forest Service (Interior)	1.214	.551	.932	1.000
Park Service (Interior)	1.169	.904	.690	.906

*An expected frequency was computed for each cell on the basis of row and column (marginals) totals for the observed frequencies from which the percentages in Table 3 were derived. This is essentially the expected value used in computing chi square. The ratio of observed to expected frequencies in each cell was then computed. Any ratio less than 1.0 indicates that the observed cell frequencies are less than would be expected by chance, while a ratio exceeding 1.0 indicates that the cell frequencies are greater than would be expected by chance.

hearings are not only more program-oriented than the other subcommittee hearings, but more than would be expected by chance. The Treasury-PO-Internal Revenue hearing displays a distinctive emphasis on supervision or oversight just as the other subcommittees emphasize their particular interests. We find no special subcommittee emphasis on the "other" category. Comparatively and relatively the three subcommittees can be distinguished as follows:

Interior—Program Oriented
SJCJ—Objects of Expenditure Oriented
Treasury-PO—Supervision or Oversight Oriented

Interpretation

The evidence identifying inquiry-distribution differences gives rise to the question why these differences exist. The information provided all subcommittees in the President's budget is similar in that all agencies conform to procedural and content guidelines established by the Bureau of the Budget. What is the basis for the differences in subcommittee behavior? Preliminary, yet basic, to answering these comparative questions is an understanding of the hearing itself. What purpose does it serve for the participants, principally the subcommittee members?

Interviews with participants in the study[24] produced a consensual notion that the primary purpose of the appropriations hearings is to serve the subcommittee's search for *confidence* in the agency and in their own predispositions.[25] The subcommittee's need is to feel assured that either the amount requested is the appropriate amount to be granted, or that their previous patterns of behavior (e.g., cut a little, grant request, or increase request) should prevail. In short, they seek faith and trust in the agency and in themselves.

Limited time and the complexity of budget considerations make it difficult, if not impossible, for a subcommittee to determine objectively that $595.3 million, for example, is precisely the correct amount to grant an agency. Subcommittees have therefore devised an alternative subjective system, which places the initial burden of calculation upon the agency (actually the entire executive "side") and which then demands that the agency defend its calculation by responding to the questions of the subcommittee members. How well the agency performs in this structured situation determines the level or degree of confidence established.[26] This search for confidence brings some meaning, order, coherence, and rationality to what often appears to outside observers as a series of unnecessary, irrelevant, or petty questions and exchanges, with far too few really probing questions on budgetary policy.

While all subcommittees engage in this search for confidence, they search differently.[27] One may seek confidence or assurance in the capability of the agency representatives and in the reliability of the data presented by the agency, both in the budget document and in supporting materials (e.g., justification sheets). A concentrated reading of the SJCJ (Rooney) hearings suggests this to be their approach. If the director can answer a detailed question about an object of expenditure, e.g., the cost or justification of a new fence or flagpole, without hesitation or assistance (a question we might not "expect" a director to know without staff assistance), the committee members are likely to feel he can probably answer the more general questions and justify the broader request. To be wrong on figures or to require assistance or additional time in providing information, may cost the agency the subcommittee's confidence.[28]

Another subcommittee may be seeking assurance that the agencies before them are impartially and honestly executing the law. This appears to be the approach followed by the Treasury-PO subcommittee as they ask numerous supervisory or oversight questions. Integrity, internal communications, and control are at the heart of the inquiry. Committee members seek assurance that the tax laws are impartially administered (with annually recurring questions about notorious tax cases), that fraud is prevented, and that privacy is preserved in both postal and money operations. Treasury-PO agencies operate in personally highly sensitive areas and the subcommittee seeks reassurance that internal operations are strictly aboveboard.

This study produced yet a third approach to the search for confidence—confidence that the agencies are carrying out their programs satisfactorily, that they are living up to the performance expectations of the subcommittee. This appears to be the approach followed by the Interior subcommittee. "How many new recreation areas have you opened up?" "How many campsites?" "What is the progress on Mission 66?"

A preliminary typology of hearings in terms of their orientation to inquiry and their mode of searching for confidence might take the following form:

Subcommittee	Inquiry orientation	Confidence search mode
SJCJ	Objects of expenditure	Capability-reliability
Treasury-PO	Supervision (oversight)	Integrity
Interior	Program	Performance expectation

Conclusions

This typology, while not exhaustive,[29] is useful in suggesting the relation between the types of questions committee members ask and their reasons for asking them. In the hearings—admittedly only a part of the budget process—this dimension was overlooked by the Hoover Commission. As events developed, budget information on a particular program was only part of a system of open information flows, in which program information had to compete with information from other sources and in which its use and influence depended upon the particular needs of the committee members. Committee members neither uniformly embraced nor rejected the new information. Instead, they eclectically selected and used information that met their preferences and needs. For some, program information met these preferences, but for others, it did not.

Apart from verifying the Schick contention, what insights do the evidence and interpretation bring to the pragmatic concerns of the Jackson Committee, viz., "How would the introduction of PPB affect Congressional consideration of the budget?" Without imposing any rule change that would prohibit other forms of information,[30] an initial requirement would be to effect changes in the degree of search satisfaction with nonprogram information.[31] As long as participants continue to have their informational needs satisfied by nonprogram information, the likelihood of voluntary reliance exclusively on program information, or upon other combinations of information appears remote. Congressional participants have thus established patterns of searching for information and have not expressed discontent with the existing sources.[32]

The likelihood of continued satisfaction with nonprogram information remains high because of the function of the hearing and the established patterns of decision making in each subcommittee. Members have over time come to feel that these "are the types of questions one asks at an appropriations hearing." It is noteworthy that distinctive inter-subcommittee differences persist in 1968, despite the "shock" effect of the introduction of PPB among the agencies and despite the curiosity and skepticism its publicity may have generated for committee members. (See Table 5.)

A prediction, based upon the findings and in the context of this study, is that PPB, to have an effect, would first have to be deemed acceptable to the Appropriations committees as "available additional" information.

It appears doubtful that Congress, i.e., the House committee, would permit the wholesale changeover from current traditional information to PPB information. If it were attempted, we might expect Congressman Rooney, for one, to reintroduce the "foisting" charge made in 1951.

TABLE 5
Committee Distribution of Attention by Type of Inquiry
1968

	Program	OExp.	Super.	Other	Total	N
FPS	56.5%	30.4	0.0	13.1	100.0	23
I and NS	44.4%	44.4	0.0	11.2	100.0	9
IRS	40.8%	13.2	18.4	27.6	100.0	76
FS	75.4%	11.9	3.4	9.3	100.0	101
NPS	55.8%	23.4	6.3	14.5	100.0	111

Once PPB information is available and competing with others, its effect, at least insofar as it relates to the limited scope of this study (the hearing), depends upon its attractiveness to the users. Some participants, predictably the Interior subcommittee, may unequivocally endorse it; others may remain hostile or skeptical. Senator Jackson's question, however, delves much deeper and is more encompassing, for PPB implies more than changing the language and conversation orientation of participants. It also implies making hard comparative choices, considering and selecting a certain policy, program element or package from among alternatives; in a word, it implies conflict.

For this more fundamental aspect of PPB to become effective, it would require, by inference, a change in the recruitment and retention patterns and operating norms of the Appropriations committee. Both Wildavsky's[33] and Fenno's[34] brilliant analyses of PPB and committee goals and decision-making processes suggest that PPB and Congress are incompatible under existing conditions. Wildavsky suggests that traditional budgeting increases agreement among members while at the same time it reduces the burden of calculation for them by not raising the specter of comparative choice that most decision makers prefer to avoid. The House committee has consciously recruited members who easily adopt the prevailing norms of minimal partisanship, compromise, and reciprocity. Fenno found that adherence to these norms produces agreement among members. This agreement not only serves to meet House expectations that the committee (1) develop consensus-building procedures, and (2) avoid the jurisdictional domain of substantive committees, i.e., policy, but also provides the key to committee influence in the House. Disagreement within the committee leading to disagreement among committee members on the House floor is an open invitation to non-committee members to consider an appropriations bill vulnerable to change. Agreement produces unity, and unity is their banner of influence. Thus, for the committee to "do PPB" would result in both subcommittee and committee disintegration, and a subsequent loss of committee power before the entire House. PPB implies a development that Appropriations committees have long sought and taken great pains to avoid.

Notes

[1] See Allen Schick, "The Road to PPB: The Stages of Budget Reform," *Public Administration Review*, 26 (December 1966), 243–258. Hereafter referred to as *PAR*.

[2] See David Novick, "Origin and History of Program Budgeting," *RAND Corporation Paper No. P-3427* (October 1966) reprinted in U.S., Congress, Senate, Subcommittee on National Security and International Operations of the Committee on Government Operations, *Planning-Programming-Budgeting, Selected Comment*, July 26, 1967. Hereafter all references to publications by this subcommittee (Henry M. Jackson, chairman) shall be termed the Jackson Committee. See also Werner Z. Hirsch, "Toward Federal Program Budgeting," *PAR*, 26 (December 1966), 259–269.

[3] See, for example, Frederick C. Mosher, "PPBS: Two Questions," a letter to the editor-in-chief of *PAR*, 27 (March 1967). Also reprinted in a Jackson Committee print, *Selected Comment*, 23–28. That this type of disagreement can develop is quite understandable in light of the conceptual problems associated with program budgeting as it is identified and discussed by Roland N. McKean and Melvin Anshen, *Program Budgeting* (Washington, D.C.: Government Printing Office, 1964), pp. 219–223.

[4] See Hirsch, "Program Budgeting," as an example of those least restrained in their enthusiasm over the expectations of PPB.

[5] See A. Wildavsky, "The Political Economy of Efficiency: Cost-Benefit Analysis, Systems Analysis, and Program Budgeting," *PAR*, 26 (December 1966), 292–310, for the most elaborate and forceful statement by the "skeptics" group. This article is also found in somewhat modified form in *The Public Interest*, 8 (Summer 1967), 30–48.

[6] Support for this assessment is evident in the hearings testimony by Charles L. Schultze (Part 1, August 23, 1967) and Alain C. Enthoven (Part 2, September 27 and October 18, 1967) before the Jackson Committee.

[7] The skeptic should perhaps not be denied the right to require that the same standards be applied in arriving at assertions about the performance of PPB as the advocates established when calling for its adoption.

[8] Jackson Committee print, "Initial Memorandum," August 11, 1967, 5.

[9] Schick, "Stages of Budget Reform," *PAR*, 26 (December 1966), 257.

[10] The official title of the commission was The Commission on Organization of the Executive Branch of the Government, and the late President Herbert C. Hoover was chairman. Throughout this study, we refer to the group as the Hoover Commission.

[11] The introduction to the Budget and Accounting section of the Commission report stated in part: "Present budgeting . . . procedures confuse the Congress and the public. . . . With this unfortunate situation in mind, this Commission proposes a radical revision in the Federal Government's budgetary presentation. . . . Under performance budgeting, attention is centered on the function or activity—on the accomplishment of the purpose—instead of on lists of employees or authorizations of purchases. In reality this method of budgeting concentrates Congressional action . . . on the scope and magnitude of the different Federal activities. It places both accomplishment and cost in a clear light before the Congress and the public." *The Hoover Commission Report*, (New York: McGraw-Hill, 1949), pp. 33, 36. The Commission used the terms performance and program interchangeably. We elect to use program to establish the similarity of the two information reforms.

[12] For examples of publicity see A. E. Buck, "Performance Budgeting for the Federal Government," *Tax Review,* 10 (July 1949); Daniel Borth, "Hoover Commission Recommendations on Budgeting and Accounting," *Current Economic Comment,* 12 (Fall 1950); D. S. Burrows, "A Program Approach to Federal Budgeting," *Harvard Business Review,* 27 (May 1949); "What Hoover Would Do to the Government: Better Organization and Better Budgeting are the Hard Core of the Hoover Commission's Recommendations," *Business Week* (March 19, 1949), 26; Douglass Cater, "The Power of the Purse and the Congressmen's Plight," *Reporter,* 5 (December 11, 1951); E. D. Lindley, "New Style Budget," *Newsweek,* 35 (January 16, 1950); *New York Times,* August 4, 1949, 2–4; December 5, 1949, 34–36.

[13] For a more careful demonstration of the development of program information in the President's budget, see James E. Jernberg, "Program Budgeting: The Influence, Effects, and Implications of Reform" (PhD dissertation, University of Wisconsin, 1966), ch. 2.

[14] See, for example, Richard F. Fenno, Jr., *The Power of the Purse* (Boston: Little, Brown, 1966); A. Wildavsky, *The Politics of the Budgetary Process* (Boston: Little, Brown, 1964); Ralph K. Huitt, "Congressional Organization and Operations in the Field of Money and Credit," in *Fiscal and Debt Management Policies* (Englewood Cliffs, N.J.: Prentice-Hall, 1963).

[15] Admittedly the published record of hearings is an edited version in which both committee members and agency witnesses have the opportunity to elaborate or eliminate and to clarify or correct their testimony. Further, the observer will also note instances in which the dialogue goes "off the record," suggesting that perhaps the most interesting or important exchanges are beyond public scrutiny. Granting the lessened value of the hearings as a result of these practices, I nonetheless submit that, on the basis of interviews with agency representatives and committee members, the exclusions or revisions are not sufficiently compelling to alter the results and conclusions of this research. Finally, the usual plea can be made that it is imprudent to deny the usefulness of all data on the grounds that a minute portion may be beyond grasp.

[16] See the exchange between the then director of USIA, Arthur Larson, and Senator Johnson on this point as reported in Huitt, *Management Policies,* 439.

[17] For a complete discussion of content analysis, its uses, development, and objectives, see Harold D. Lasswell, Daniel Lerner, Ithiel de Sola Pool, *The Comparative Study of Symbols: An Introduction,* Hoover Institute Studies (Stanford: Stanford University Press, 1952); Bernard Berelson, "Content Analysis" in *Handbook of Social Psychology,* ed. by Gardner Lindzey, I (Cambridge: Addison-Wesley Publishing Co., 1954); Harold D. Lasswell, Nathan Leites and Associates, *Language of Politics* (New York: George W. Steward Publisher Inc., 1949); Claire Selltiz, Marie Jahoda, Morton Deutsch, Stuart W. Cook, *Research Methods in Social Relations* (New York: Holt, Rinehart, and Winston, 1962), pp. 335–342. See Selltiz et al. for further references, p. 335.

[18] Ira Sharkansky, "An Appropriations Subcommittee and Its Client Agencies: A Comparative Study of Supervision and Control," *American Political Science Review,* 59 (September 1965), 622–628.

[19] Decisions concerning the determination of meaningful categories and the means for making them operational are important initial considerations. Provision had to be made in advance to include all possible lines of inquiry. This is

especially difficult given the wide scope of inquiry permissible for a committee member and his propensity to extend that scope. A reading of at least one year's hearings aided in determining the range of categories that could be expected. Understandably the purpose of the research determines the categories selected. Other studies focusing on such variables as (1) ease-difficulty, (2) justification-projection, or (3) hostility-friendliness, etc., would require different categories. These variables, of course, are not incompatible with those developed for this study. The process of collecting and recording the data was relatively primitive. Initially, data were recorded by year from the published hearings on prepared worksheets; the actual inquiry was recorded (the theme or summary, not the verbatim exchange) with the source (Congressman), intensity, and classification of the inquiry. The data were then transferred to code sheets and punched cards, and processed to facilitate analysis.

[20] See, for example, Huitt, *Management Policies*, 436.

[21] A theme of inquiry includes the initial question and all subsequent questions or utterances related to the original question. A committee member may ask a single question and then leave that area of inquiry, presumably satisfied with the response, or he may pursue the initial question with another, or others. By limiting our recordings to the total theme we thereby avoid the problem of biasing the distribution in favor of those areas where a line of inquiry is pursued with greater intensity. The question of intensity by category is a matter of separate interest.

[22] To take the Commission's statements at face value, of course, subjects one to charges of naivete. It may be said that a gross indictment is necessary to create the desired impact on more lethargic decision-makers. Sacrificing accuracy to establish a position, however, can have the consequences of reducing one's credibility. See F. C. Mosher's letter to the Editor-in-Chief, *PAR*, 27 (March 1967), 68, relating to Hirsch's article, "Program Budgeting," 260, and/or generating retaliatory evidence proving exceptions to the charge: see W. A. Carlson, "The Planning-Programming-Budgeting System in the U.S. Department of Agriculture" (Paper given during a seminar on Executive Orientation on PPBS, conducted for Forest Service Region 9 personnel, Milwaukee, Wisconsin, February 1, 1968).

[23] Behavior changes cannot be attributed to changes in committee membership, for these subcommittees evidence member stability; the same men serve as chairmen during the entire period of the study, except for the 1954-55 Republican years. J. Vaughn Gary chaired the Treasury-PO subcommittee and asked 48.3 percent of all questions; Michael J. Kirwan chaired Interior and asked 53.9 percent of Park Service questions, and 42.0 percent of Forest Service inquiry. John Rooney chaired SJCJ and asked 72.3 percent of all I&N Service questions, and 73.4 percent of all questions asked of the Prison System. It is tempting to speculate that Rooney's "anti-program" inquiry behavior stems from a basic distrust of the intended purpose of the new information, as witnessed in the following exchange:

Mr. Rooney: Incidentally, who prepares these justifications, Mr. Bennett? Do you have any part in foisting upon us these new justifications?

Mr. Bennett: No sir, Mr. Chairman. The budget this year, as I understand, all through, has been completely reorganized, and put on a so-called program budget basis, a performance basis, rather than by institutions. By presenting all costs of a program together and describing the work to be done and objectives to be accomplished it is believed, I understand, that Congress can more clearly pass on the cost of each activity.

Mr. Rooney: Is this new system designed to get by an Appropriations committee faster or more safely?

Mr. Andretta: It grew out of the Hoover Commission report. In their report they indicated that the public did not know what the money was being spent for.

Mr. Rooney: The Appropriations committee, I think, knew more of what the money was being spent for than it will under this system. FPS, 1951 hearings, 347.

[24] Fourteen of the seventeen subcommittee members, the staff director for each subcommittee, and relevant representatives of each agency, i.e., those appearing at appropriations committee hearings.

[25] For elaborations of the concept of confidence, see Wildavsky, *Budgetary Process,* 74–84, and R. F., Fenno, *The Power of the Purse* (Boston: Little, Brown, 1966) esp. pp. 288–303. By emphasizing the gaining and creation of and the search for confidence as the objective of the hearing, we do not intend to imply that inquiry has no other specific purposes. Committees, in their words, seek to make an appraisal of the agency to find out what it did, what it is doing, and what it expects to do. And as one clerk stated: "The hearing serves two purposes; it is used as a basis for budget decisions (confidence operates here) and as a record to support the chairman when he manages the bill on the floor." See also Elias Huzar, *The Purse and the Sword* (Ithaca: Cornell University Press, 1950) for a discussion of other functions of the hearing. We also do not mean to imply that the establishment of confidence alone will determine the level of appropriations for an agency. It could very well be that a committee will grant an agency's request or even increase it at a time when committed to the agency programs. Conversely, if a committee does not favor the program requests, the most solid hearing performance may not influence the committee to grant all that was requested. Committee interests and objectives are important factors determining appropriations levels. They may be more important than the confidence developed or lost at the hearing. The relative importance of these non-hearings' variables to the appropriation is beyond the scope of the present report, though by no means less important. The author is indebted to Rufus Browning for making this distinction between confidence and the other variables that together form the basis for the appropriations decision.

[26] The ease or difficulty in attaining the desired agency performance is conditioned by many variables under the strategic control of both the subcommittee and the agency, and they are not cited here. This equally interesting topic is treated in another study in preparation by the author.

[27] Searching differently corresponds with Fenno's notion of "sampling." See Fenno, *Power of the Purse*, pp. 286–290. Actually the findings of this study serve as added empirical support to Fenno's analysis of confidence and sampling.

[28] Empirical support for the hypothesis about a capability-reliability search by the Rooney subcommittee can be found in D. E. Kenyon, "The Effect of Four Selective Criteria on Confidence in Agency Budget Requests before House Appropriations Subcommittees" (Undergraduate major paper, Department of Political Science, University of Minnesota, June 1966).

[29] There are nine other subcommittees, and we do not presume that they would necessarily fall neatly into the established categories of inquiry and modes of search.

[30]The most severe rule change, of course, would be that committee members be permitted to accept and use only PPB information. Thus far, no single authority has emerged in our political system with the capacity to determine what the informational requirements of both executive and Congressional participants shall be, and how these requirements shall be imposed. The existing rules were well stated during the colloquy between Senator H. Jackson and then Director of the Budget David Bell during a hearing on the budget and the policy process:

Mr. Bell: . . . at the same time you will recognize, much of the form of the budget has been determined by past actions of the Congress and they have indicated very clearly, the committees that are concerned—certain requirements which they want us to follow.

Sen. Jackson: They indicate to you how they would like to have it presented?

Mr. Bell: Exactly. A great portion of the detail that is now in the budget is there because the committees want it there. I am not arguing about this, they surely know what it is they want.

Subcommittee on National Policy Machinery of Senate Government Operations Committee, *Hearings Vol. 1, Organizing for National Security, The Budget and the Policy Process*, 1961, 1169.

[31]Search and satisfaction are basic concepts in organization theory. See J. March and H. Simon, *Organizations* (New York: John Wiley & Co., 1958), 48 ff., also R. Cyert and J. March, *A Behavioral Theory of the Firm* (Englewood Cliffs, N.J.: Prentice-Hall, 1963), pp. 52ff. A. Downs, *Inside Bureaucracy* (Boston: Little, Brown, 1967), chs. 14–15.

[32]These findings could perhaps have been predicted from a reading of the legislative history relating to the Budget and Accounting Procedures Act, 1950, which permitted the inclusion of Hoover Commission-type program information. At that time House Appropriations Committee members, especially the leadership (Rep. John Taber), were not unwilling to permit the inclusion of the new information, but were insistent on preserving the flow and receipt of previously satisfying information. See, *Congressional Record* (August 29, 1950), 13770–13776. John Rooney's comments to the director of the Prison System in footnote 23 are also instructive here in terms of satisfaction.

[33]Wildavsky, *Budgetary Process*, pp. 135–142.

[34]Fenno, *Power of the Purse*, chs. 3–5.

III

THE PROGRAM PLANNING-EVALUATION BASE OF PPB

6

Strategic Planning

CHARLES M. MOTTLEY

Introduction

The possibility of being caught unprepared always haunts a responsible manager. The risk is increasing as the tempo of technological change accelerates, as populations "explode" and the demands for certain materials threaten to exhaust the supplies or increase prices. Disruptive events, like the Mid-East war and the recurring Congo crises, which disturb patterns of supply, production, and distribution, make the task of estimating future needs even more formidable. If the past is a reliable guide to the future, we shall continue to be faced somewhere in the world with twenty or more such conflict situations each year. The difficulties of preparing for these emergencies are further compounded by the long lead times required either to get ready in advance or to make adjustments after the event.

Consider, for example, the problem of preparing for the future management of our natural resources. This is a mission of stewardship which poses unique difficulties and requires a high degree of diagnostic

Reprinted from *Management Highlights,* release No. 56, Office of Management Research, U.S. Dept. of the Interior (September 1967), by permission of the author.

and planning skill. The importance of the stewardship of our mineral resources is illustrated, for example, by the fact that, although the mining industry represents less than 3 percent of the United States gross national product (GNP), its material output is the basis for the products of other industries that comprise 75 percent of the GNP. There are also at least twenty industrially and strategically significant mineral commodities for which we are largely dependent on imports. A failure to provide for the efficient management, conservation, and development of supplies of such resources, i.e. a failure in stewardship, could have serious repercussions in the national economy. Because of the time required to make industrial adjustments, strategic foresight must be exercised to develop appropriate alternatives.

How, then, can we visualize the needs of the future, identify the important issues, and initiate timely and appropriate courses of action in order to keep the risks of being caught unprepared to a minimum?

Before we explore this question, it seems advisable to set the stage by defining certain basic management concepts.

Management Concepts

First, the steward or manager of an enterprise, public or private, must be acutely aware of "what business he is in," i.e. his mission.

Second, whatever his mission, he is responsible for detecting and defining the foreseeable issues, setting the organization's objectives—being able to say which ones are the most important—charting the course of action and seeing that the right resources are provided at the right place and time, with the right quality, in the right quantity.

Third, he is responsible for using the available resources in the right way, whenever changing circumstances, or contingencies, require a change of course.

Fourth, he must prepare for contingencies long enough ahead to allow the necessary amount of time and maneuvering room for decisions and preparations. The longer lead times inherent in modern management situations place a premium on competent planning. These activities require an input of accurate information, analysis, and understanding to provide guidance for the contemplated steps into the future.

PLANNING

If the manager wishes to make properly planned steps into the unknown, he must first make them in the mind and visualize the important events, or milestones, and possible sources of interference, or barriers, on the way to the desired goals. To do this he must have an appropriate conceptual framework—a concept of his mission—around which to organize and guide systematic information gathering and analysis. In the face of uncertainty, it is not enough to trust that random observations and unplanned activities will accomplish his purposes; nor can past and present experience be uncritically projected into the future. In summary, planning is essentially a management function concerned with visualizing future situations, making estimates concerning them, identifying the issues, needs and potential danger points, analyzing and evaluating the alternative ways and means for reaching desired goals according to a certain schedule, estimating the necessary funds and resources to do the work, and initiating action in time to prepare what may be needed to cope with changing conditions and contingent events.

STRATEGIC PLANNING

The specialized branch of the planning activity which is concerned with anticipating events, making diagnoses and shaping appropriate courses of action, so that an organization can be in the best position, ready and capable, to respond effectively to contingencies, is called *strategic planning*. Activities like research and engineering which usually must be initiated a long time in advance of the application of their results are particularly affected by the quality and pertinence of strategic planning. Competent strategic planning is also essential for the efficient stewardship of the natural resources—normally a long-range endeavor. Unfortunately, the value of it is not always appreciated by management, both public and private. Emergencies and crises are the mark of our times because we do not exercise strategic foresight in time either to prevent them or ameliorate their impact.

POLICY FORMULATION

Strategic planning is closely related to long-range policy formulation. It should be emphasized, however, that the word "policy" is frequently used ambiguously. Often it means the way things are being done at a given time. In this sense it is descriptive of a present state of affairs which has been arrived at, not by the exercise of strategic foresight, but by "muddling through" and hoping for the best. Contemporary positions are frequently used as policy guides for the future. This is a short-range procedure resembling the probing advance of the ameba, which has a very limited capability to sense conditions beyond those which lie immediately around it. The term "policy" as used in relation to strategic planning has a distinctly different meaning. A strategic policy for minerals, for example, would be one shaped by considering long-range future needs to guide the operations of exploration, mining, processing, use, and reuse of mineral substances.

Policy is essentially an agreement, however arrived at—whether by a vote, a decree, a consensus, or even better, by a meeting of the minds after examining the alternatives. It is an agreement with regard to the objectives of action, and the ways and the means of achieving those objectives. It implies: an accurate diagnosis of the needs of future situations, a definition of the issues involved, a capability to act, the will to act, and timeliness of the action. The agreement with regard to both the explicit and implicit elements of policy is what unifies it and permits its transformation into a course of action.

The strategic planning concepts discussed in the preceding paragraphs are shown schematically in Figure 1. However, before leaving the topic of management concepts in relation to strategic planning, it seems advisable to draw attention briefly to certain distinctions between strategic analysis and systems analysis because there is a tendency to assume that systems analysis is all that is needed.

FIGURE 1
Strategic Planning Concepts

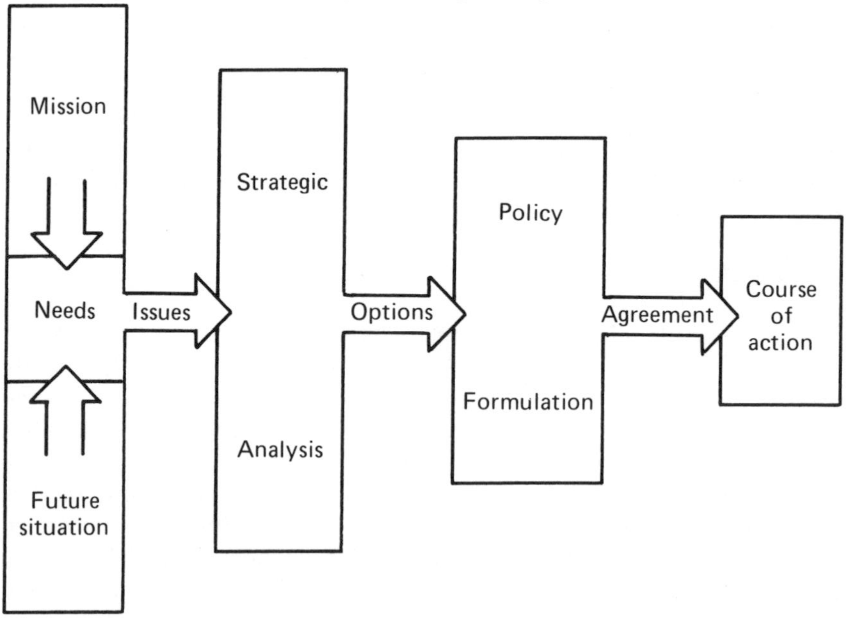

STRATEGIC ANALYSIS VS. SYSTEMS ANALYSIS

The first point is that strategic analysis should precede systems analysis. The latter technique has an important place in the realm of management but it should be used in its proper role to evaluate proposed means for a course of action. Systems analysis was developed in the 1950s by the Rand Corporation and applied by the U.S. Air Force to the problem of evaluating alternative weapons systems proposed to carry out its missions. Since then the technique has been popularized by the Department of Defense and "exported" to other agencies of the federal government, to state and foreign governments and to industry, especially in support of program and budget planning. However, the necessity for strategic analysis as the basis for policy formulation and as the logical predecessor to systems analysis seems to be either inadequately understood or neglected by the importing agencies. This may be so because the analysts of the Rand Corporation originally had very little involvement in strategic planning, especially at the joint or DOD level. The more ardent proponents of the systems analysis technique today are economists who generally have a descriptive outlook on national affairs and rarely take a direct part in setting goals or shaping the action. Furthermore, the strategic planning activities as well as the strategic plans which are generated in DOD are highly classified and are not open to public inspection. It is not surprising, therefore, that the "steering wheel" for program and budget planning was left out when the vehicle was imported by the non-DOD agencies.

The second distinction between the two techniques is related to the fact that systems analysis is primarily concerned with such questions as: "which system (hardware) will give the best performance for the investment," "what would be the best trade-off," "what to buy" or "what program should be authorized." In order to make such decisions the systems under consideration have to be costed in advance. To do this the system and its components should have passed the concept phase and reached the hardware or engineering development stage. However, at that point the ends and ways of policy are often frozen by the very nature of the proposed means and the decision maker is locked in because he has no other choices. Unless ample opportunity has been given to examine the implications of alternative means in advance, the objectives and strategy are necessarily determined by the available means. Frequently, even in DOD, what is available as potential hardware results from considerations other than those generated by strategic analysis. Only too often the decision maker is faced with the "tools" which an industrial producer is anxious to sell or with the existing capabilities of an on-going program for

FIGURE 2
The Relation Between Ends, Ways, and Means

Serial arrangements		Order		
		First	Second	Third
	1.	Ends ⟶	Ways ⟶	Means
	2.	Ends ⟶	Means ⟶	Ways
	3.	Ways ⟶	Means ⟶	Ends
	4.	Ways ⟶	Ends ⟶	Means
	5.	Means ⟶	Ways ⟶	Ends
	6.	Means ⟶	Ends ⟶	Ways

Coordinate arrangement

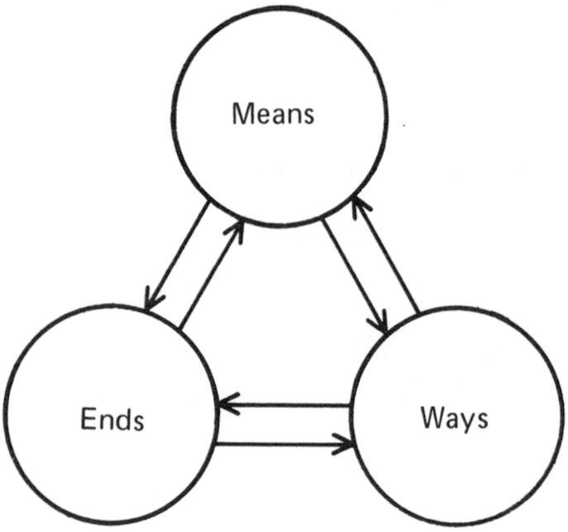

which an agency wishes to obtain continued funding support. The real needs, objectives, and strategies thus become overshadowed or even altered by the *availability* of the means and have little opportunity to shape the means.

The third distinction is more subtle. Although systems analysis is said to be used to support cost-effectiveness evaluations, in reality what is usually being evaluated is the *performance* of a system or its components, not its effectiveness in the strategic sense. The output measures which are used in cost-benefit studies to support budget requests are often not true measures of an organization's effectiveness in meeting its objectives or in executing its policies. Effectiveness can only be evaluated in relation to the six interactions between desired objectives and the ways and means proposed to achieve those objectives. Instead of evaluating the three strategic elements one at a time in a serial arrangement, a coordinate arrangement, as suggested in Figure 2, is preferable. However, if there is no stated policy, or if it is fuzzy, there is a natural tendency to turn to the means proposed and judge the cost of its technical performance. In the case of weapons systems, or water, power, and mining systems, performance is usually evaluated in terms of engineering, technical, or performance objectives. Rarely are such cost-benefit measurements ever related to the accomplishment of an organization's mission or the attainment of strategic objectives. However, one of the facts of life which a strategic planner in government or industry must face is that long-range policy and objectives are seldom openly expressed, except in very broad terms, e.g., "to make a profit," "uphold the Constitution," or "in compliance with the Act." The most difficult task is to obtain explicit statements of objectives to serve as a guide for strategic analysis. However, in the absence of such guidelines, the substitution of the techniques of systems analysis will not turn out to be a very effective procedure in the long run.

THE PPB SYSTEM

A word is also needed regarding the planning-programming-budgeting system (PPBS) which the President directed in 1965 to be installed in the non-DOD agencies of the federal government. The "planning" part of this system is essentially a programming and budgeting activity. An attempt has been made to fill the strategic planning vacuum by means of "program memoranda," but these have turned out to be budget justification documents which lack the force of an officially approved strategic plan. In the DOD the program and budget decisions are normally preceded by the preparation of two documents called the Joint Strategic Objectives Plan (JSOP) and the Joint Long-Range Strategic Study (JLRSS). In addition to these, numerous special studies are performed which attempt to weigh the effectiveness of alternative policies. Hopefully they do exert a significant influence on national security policy and on the ultimate effectiveness of our military posture.

It should be noted that there are no plans or studies comparable to the JLRSS and JSOP to guide the PPB activities of the non-DOD agencies. Although long-range policy agreement, in the sense being used in this paper, is difficult to achieve in the much more open arena of public discussion which is characteristic of non-defense planning, nevertheless it is essential for efficient management. In its absence, program and project objectives which are much easier to agree to are usually substituted for strategic objectives. It would be interesting to explore what would happen to the effectiveness of the management of government operations if there were officially approved strategic plans comparable to the national security documents, i.e. the JLRSS and JSOP, to guide the PPB system for such things as food, health, urban affairs, transportation, natural resources, and commerce.

Strategic Planning Techniques

The central problem stated in the introduction was: how can a manager minimize his risks of being caught unprepared? The recommended solution is pictured in Figure 1. Essentially this model says to him: "relate your mission to estimates of future situations; diagnose your needs; identify the issues, being especially sensitive to lead time; conduct strategic analyses and studies to help define alternative courses of action or options; agree upon an appropriate policy, then transform it into a preferred course of action and embark on it."

If the manager has done his homework carefully and has made astute decisions he should be as well prepared to meet the uncertainties of the future as it is humanly possible to do. There is no magic formula to aid travelers into the unknown, but there are certain techniques which, if systematically applied, can help to reduce the risks. A full treatment of the subject obviously would require a lengthy treatise. All that will be attempted here is to describe some of the techniques applicable to the steps shown in Figure 1.

MISSION ANALYSIS

The manager's first task is to develop a concept of his mission in relation to the situations expected to be encountered in the future. The basic mission of the Director of the Bureau of Mines, for example, is to make the necessary inquiries and produce the information needed in the public interest to assure an adequate, dependable flow of mineral materials to meet defense, industrial, economic and social needs at reasonable costs. In accordance with the phrase, "in the public interest," the Director prepared and presented this year's briefings to the appropriate committees of the House and Senate which are concerned with the stewardship of the Nation's mineral resources. The testimony presented to the House Committee on Interior and Insular Affairs [1] was in essence a statement of the Director's concept of his mission. The comments of the members of the committee suggested certain amendments and additions, but in general they appreciated and endorsed the Director's analysis of the needs and the identification of the important issues. The statement should be studied as an example of the application of the general techniques of mission analysis.

NEEDS AND ISSUES

The bituminous coal situation affords an excellent example of the application of the techniques of diagnosis in relation to mission analysis. There appears to be no serious problem regarding the total supply of energy materials over the next twenty or thirty years; it has been forecast to be adequate to meet our needs.[2] However, the issues arise from the competitive "mix" of the different energy-producing materials and other sources, like hydropower.

With full awareness of the risk of oversimplification, let us examine some of the salient features of the bituminous coal situation and the Bureau of Mines' mission in relation to it. Coal's share of the total energy production in the United States slipped from about 70 percent in 1900 to 23 percent in 1965. It lost the transportation market to oil and now faces the prospect of losing its *growth share* of the electric utility market to nuclear power and eventually the prospect of obsolescence. Besides this competitive threat, coal now must conform to stringent air pollution regulations to reduce the amount of sulfur oxides emitted by burning into the atmosphere of our largest cities. In the time frame being considered, up to thirty years ahead, the domestic natural gas and oil reserves are expected to diminish because of decreased exploration. These points are cited to illustrate some of the uncertainty with which a strategic planner must cope.

Without going too deeply into the matter, let us assume that it is in the public interest—for socioeconomic reasons—to keep a viable coal industry in being and that it is not desired that coal should be allowed to go into another serious decline for the lack of advanced technology to utilize the vast coal reserves as a source of power at reasonable costs. The first step is to construct a model of the future situation, in this case a series of future conditional energy balances is required. Let us assume that we are interested in the year 1980. The techniques of the traditional econometric forecast methodology are used to project the trends of the major components of energy consumption by source and form (e.g., coal, oil, gas, shale oil, nuclear), within the various markets or consuming sectors. The effects of several contingent factors, such as different rates of economic and population growth are also introduced.

The purpose of this procedure is not to "predict" in the usual sense, but to discover contingent boundary conditions. For example, a model used by the Bureau of Mines[3] indicated that the consumption of coal in 1980 might be as high as 950 million tons or as low as 650 million tons (the consumption in 1965 was about 500 million tons). The swing in the estimates of future consumption depends on investment decisions in the next few years, which are conditioned by such things as whether or not a successful nuclear breeder reactor becomes operational, whether nuclear power can compete economically with the smaller coal-fired electric utility plants, and whether coal can be transformed economically to more convenient forms. In the case of the upper boundary of 950 million tons, the issue would appear to be how to meet the increased demand: possibly by expanding coal mining operations, or increasing productivity through mine mechanization and evolutionary technology. In the case of the threat of the lower boundary of 650 million tons, the slower growth rate might be cushioned by expanding export markets and by improved technology which would reduce the cost of production thus keeping coal in a pacesetter position leading the other forms of *energy in keeping costs down.* Furthermore, new technology which would permit the transformation of coal to more convenient liquid and gaseous forms at competitive costs might allow the coal industry to recapture markets dependent on automobile gas tanks and fuel transmission systems with their heavy investments in pipelines. It is, of course, assumed that the air pollution abatement needs will be solved by advances in technology. Each of these expressed contingent needs and issues provides an opportunity for generating new ideas to overcome the technical barriers. Then the necessary research resources may be programed to achieve the desired technical objectives. Thus, the approach of the strategic planner is to examine future potential situations, and diagnose the needs as the basis for delineating the issues and deciding what courses of action should be initiated.

Let us examine another situation which illustrates the complexity of issue delineation. A panel of the President's Science Advisory Committee on the world food supply indicated that there is a need to double food production in developing countries during the next twenty years. Assuming that the United States will continue to help alleviate the shortages, consider some of the issues. We could increase domestic production of foodstuffs and ship the products overseas. Our surplus supplies are immediately available. We could increase the manufacture of fertilizers and ship the materials; this would take at least a crop year, assuming that the recipients have the land and know how to use the fertilizers. We could export the technology of fertilizer production and build plants but it would take several years to bring them into production. It would take many more years, perhaps a generation, to teach the people the agricultural techniques to make full use of the fertilizers. From the standpoint of costs, food worth $1 million will feed approximately 70,000 people for a year, but fertilizer worth the same amount would provide food for 200,000 people and also help the development of the economy of the country. The courses of action chosen to deal with these issues obviously have a very important bearing on the stewardship of fertilizer mineral resources.

A further note is in order regarding the technique of diagnosis as applied to issue delineation. There is a constellation of interlocking elements which are present in every issue. The components are shown in Figure 3, clustered around the central element of purpose or intention. The diagnostic interrogatives listed below are keyed to the numbers shown in the figure. A competent strategic diagnostician seeks answers to the questions and combinations of questions in a systematic way. If he finds that one or more of the questions cannot be answered satisfactorily,

FIGURE 3
Constellation of Strategic Elements

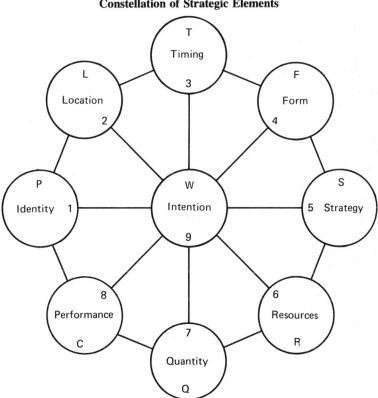

then he raises the appropriate issue. Problems raised in this way invariably generate one or more possible courses of action to solve them. The manager's problem is to reduce the number to a preferred course of action. This process is facilitated by the technique of strategic analysis.

Diagnostic Interrogatives
1. What is the subject? (e.g. coal, aluminum, mining, processing)
2. Where is it located or to be located?
3. When is it to take place?
4. What form of action is to be taken?
5. How is it to be done?
6. How much investment is needed?
7. How many units are needed?
8. What performance is necessary for each unit?
9. What is the purpose or intention of the course of action?

STRATEGIC ANALYSIS

Strategic analysis is primarily concerned with a phenomenon or unit called the "course of action." The special field of interest here is the method of selecting courses of action in support of the mission of stewardship of our natural resources. The term, option, is used to denote those defined courses of action which have been subjected to a formal selection procedure and judged by competent authority to be suitable, feasible and acceptable. The options are, therefore, the set of choices open to the judgment of decision makers who are responsible for formulating policy and selecting a preferred course of action.

The principles of selection were treated in a document first published by the U.S. Naval War College in 1936.[4] However, the text is rather vague as to how the criteria of suitability, feasibility, and acceptability are to be applied in actual practice. Certain advances have been made in analytical and evaluative techniques since the publication of the treatise, which now permit a more systematic and objective treatment of the process of selecting a preferred course of action. The process is shown as a flow diagram in Figure 4. It should be noted that the flow does not always take place in the one direction as shown in the diagram; in practice there will be a considerable amount of feedback and recycling. In the interest of simplicity this phase has not been included. An important feature of the diagram is the screening or sorting gate which is controlled by selection criteria. This technique is discussed below.

In order to visualize how the techniques of strategic analysis are to be applied and the selections are made, the reader might keep an example

FIGURE 4
The Selection Process for Deriving a Preferred Course of Action

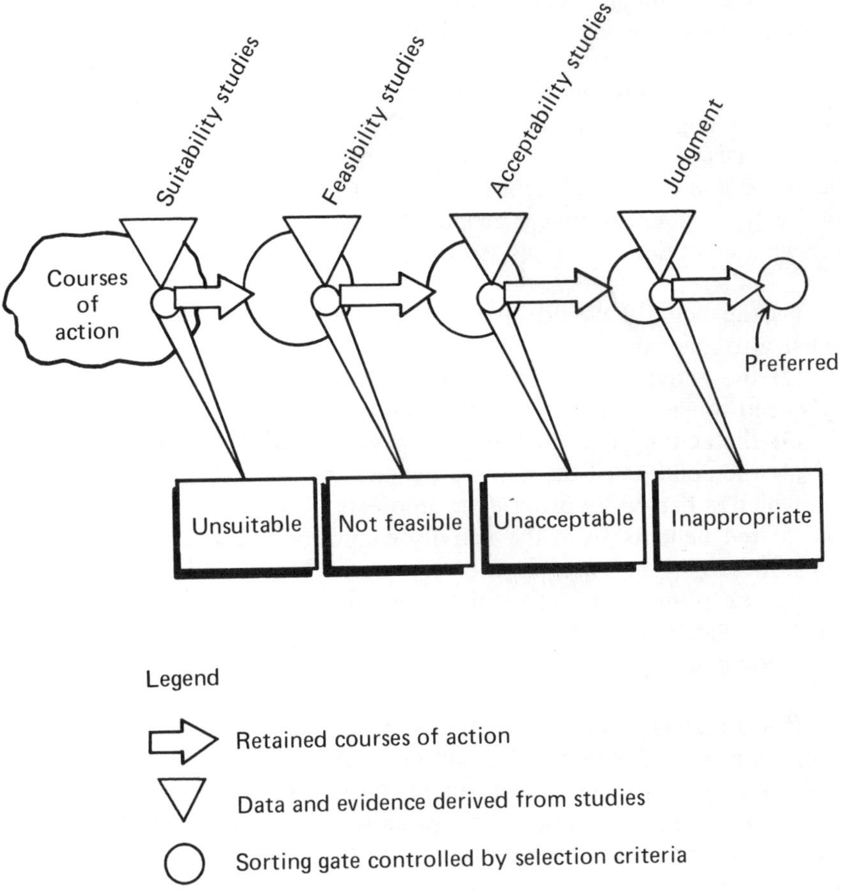

Legend

Retained courses of action

Data and evidence derived from studies

Sorting gate controlled by selection criteria

in mind, e.g. the issue of air pollution abatement with particular reference to the control of the emissions of sulfur oxides by the burning of fuel in electric utility and other plants. There is a long history of research and engineering activity directed toward the control of such emissions from smelters and many possible courses of action have been conceived, proposed, and used. The problem is to arrive at an effective course of action to meet the strict standards now being imposed on fuel-burning plants by some of the large cities.

Given a set of possible courses of action the number is reduced in the following way:

SUITABILITY

First the number of candidates is reduced in accordance with general policy guidance, mission responsibilities, and assumptions. In practice several sets of criteria will have to be applied. For example, a generally accepted guideline is that it is unsuitable for the government to engage in an activity, if private enterprise could do it better and is willing to do so. On the basis of this assumption certain criteria might be used to sort out the unsuitable courses of action. It would be considered to be unsuitable for the government to take a proposed action unless one or more of the following conditions were judged to apply:

(1) the activity would be too broad in scope or too complex for industry to manage,

(2) the activity is too long-range to be justified, considering industry's need to show a relatively early return on its investment,

(3) the activity is too large for a single company to finance,

(4) the conduct of the activity depends on an exchange of information which is barred by proprietary interests,

(5) the benefits from the activity cannot be realized by those who invest in it,

(6) the primary objective of the activity is to achieve broad social benefits, such as improving the quality of the environment, for which no single company can, or is willing to, assume the responsibility.

If, for instance, one of the proposed actions was the development of a certain process for removal of sulfur oxides from the stack gases, not only would it have broad social benefits (criterion No. 6), but criteria No. 3 and No. 5 would also apply. The proposed action would, therefore, be retained under these criteria as a *suitable* course of action for the government to undertake. Presumably, there could also be several other alternatives which would also be considered and retained.

FEASIBILITY

The retained, suitable courses of action are subjected next to feasibility studies to provide the basis for ruling out the infeasible alternatives. Feasibility studies include the appraisal of the effects of a number of factors considered separately and together. For example, the feasibility of the proposed courses of action for pollution abatement would be judged on the basis of the extent to which the systems would meet such things as, (1) the required standards (i.e. the operational requirements), (2) the conditions of the operational environment, (3) the restrictions imposed by the state of the art (i.e. the status of the applicable science and technology), and (4) limitations on the resources required (e.g. funding, facilities, operating costs and skills). A factorial path technique for making feasibility appraisals is suggested in Figure 4. Two paths are shown. In the upper one the feasibility is judged in relation to the operational requirements (A). Next, the effects of the conditions of the operational environment are considered (AB), the state of the art is introduced (ABC), and, finally, the feasibility of supplying the required resources is considered (ABCD). If the proposed course of action meets all of the criteria it is retained as a feasible alternative. The lower zig-zag path is one that starts with a new opportunity or an advance in the state of the art (C), after which its feasibility in terms of the operational requirements (AC), the resources required (BCD), and the operational environment (ABCD) are appraised in succession. Any course of action which is judged to be not feasible at any of the steps in the path would be ruled out.

ACCEPTABILITY

The retained courses of action, i.e. those judged to be suitable and feasible, are then subjected to analytic evaluations to provide the basis for ruling out the unacceptable courses of action. Four principal factors taken together enter into these evaluations as illustrated in Figure 5. The purpose of acceptability studies is to judge the *strategic* effectiveness of the proposed courses of action. To do this the factors of timing— including contingent events—the performance of the proposed means employed in different ways, and gross cost estimates are examined by varying the parameters and relating their effects in sensitivity analyses. Families of curves showing the various relationships, sensitivities, and tradeoffs are usually displayed graphically to aid in making judgements of strategic effectiveness. The techniques used for these evaluations are similar to those employed in systems analysis. However, in strategic analysis, *assumptions* regarding contingent events, timing, cost and performance are employed to a much greater extent. In strategic analysis the techniques are used to explore boundary conditions, to reveal important interfaces, and to find critical tradeoffs among the factors. The output from such evaluations is a set of acceptable alternatives which then become the candidates or options for policy formulation and decision. The inappropriate alternatives are either discarded or set aside for future reference in case the need should arise.

FIGURE 5
Factorial Path Technique for Feasibility Studies
Interactions

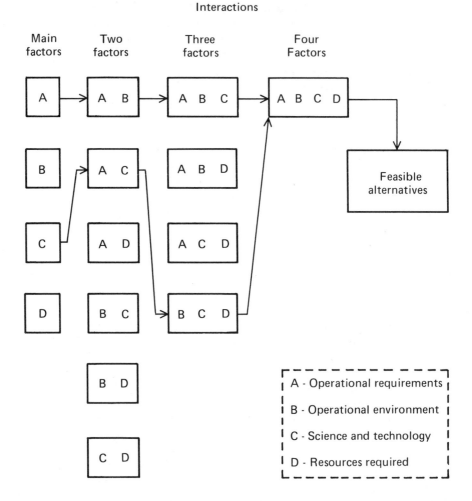

Strategic Plans

It may be concluded from the discussion that the concept of strategic planning which has been presented places primary emphasis on reaching agreement in a series of steps. Under this procedure agreement is required at each step in the planning operations before the planner can proceed satisfactorily to the next. The sequence has been described as follows:

(1) diagnosis of needs,

(2) identification and delineation of the issues,

(3) formulation of proposed courses of action to settle the issues,

(4) elimination of inappropriate proposals and retention of the suitable, the feasible and the acceptable,

(5) preparation of the retained alternatives as options for a policy decision,

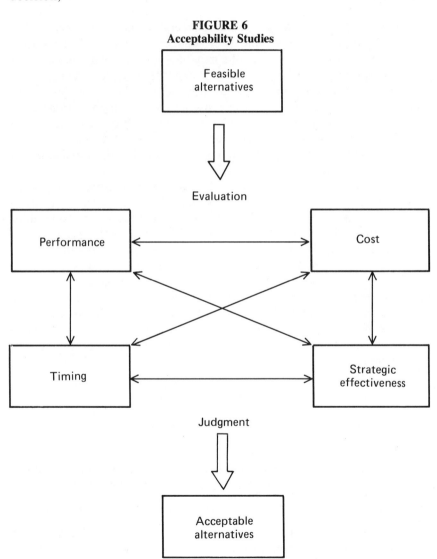

FIGURE 6
Acceptability Studies

(6) agreement regarding policy, i.e. the objectives, ways and means of action,

(7) transformation of the policy into a preferred course of action as the basis for program and budget planning.

Summary

Certain principles of strategic planning emerge from the discussion. The prudent manager must be able to visualize the needs of the future, identify the important issues that he may have to face, and initiate timely and appropriate action in order to keep the risks of being caught unprepared to a minimum. To do this he should be supported by competent strategic plans to guide his actions. Today's actions must necessarily be designed and timed to meet future needs and contingencies. Strategic planning requires a high degree of diagnostic skill to provide insight regarding future situations, and also the application of exceptional foresight to discern what may be encountered on the way to desired goals, i.e. the opportunities, the constraints, the barriers, and the contingencies. The techniques of mission analysis and strategic analysis help provide the requisite insight and foresight, but these techniques must not be confused with systems analysis which is a useful program and budget planning tool. Agreement reached by a systematic identification of the issues, definition, and selection of the alternatives, and evaluation of the options is recommended as an appropriate way to meet the strategic planning needs of a prudent manager. It is strongly suggested that strategic plans and the requisite policy agreements should be reached in order to make the programing and budgeting system a truly effective instrument of management in the non-DOD agencies of the federal government.

Notes

[1] Hearings before the Committee on Interior and Insular Affairs, House of Representatives, 90th Congress. Briefing session with the Director and staff of the Bureau of Mines. February 7, 1967.

[2] "Energy R & D and National Progress." Interdepartmental Study, Sept. 1966. (A. B. Cambel et al.)

[3] "Simulation of the 1980 Energy Model." A working paper by Warren E. Morrison. Division of Economic Analysis, U.S. Bureau of Mines, March 1967.

[4] "Sound Military Decision." U.S. Naval War College, Newport, R.I. 1942.

7

Evaluation of Program Effectiveness and Program Efficiency

O. LYNN DENISTON
IRWIN M. ROSENSTOCK
WILLIAM WELCH
V. A. GETTING

A systematic, comprehensive approach is needed to evaluate the effectiveness of programs in public health. Our approach is based on the assumption that all programs in public health can be viewed as consisting of a combination of resources, activities, and objectives of several kinds. We maintain that each program is characterized by one or more program "objectives," which represent the desired end result of program activities, and that each objective implies one or more necessary conditions, termed "subobjectives," which must be accomplished in order that the program objective may be accomplished. "Activities" are performed to achieve each subobjective and consequently the program objectives. "Resources" are expended to support the performance of activities. A

Reprinted, with portions omitted, from *Public Health Reports,* where this material appeared as two separate articles: "Evaluation of Program Effectiveness," 83, No. 4 (April 1968): 323–35, and "Evaluation of Program Efficiency," 83, No. 7 (July 1968): 608–10, by permission of the authors. Numbers enclosed in parentheses refer to references.

141

sharp distinction is made between activities, which imply the performance of work, and objectives, which refer to conditions of people or of the
environment deemed desirable. Every program plan, whether written or
not, makes three kinds of assumptions: *(a)* the expenditure of resources
as planned will result in the performance of planned activity, *(b)* each
activity, if properly performed, will result in the attainment of the
subobjective with which it is linked, and *(c)* each subobjective must
necessarily be accomplished before the next one can be achieved and, if
all subobjectives are attained, the program objective will be attained.

In evaluating the effectiveness of programs, specific measures of
accomplishment of each subobjective and the program objectives are set
up, and data on attainment of each are collected systematically, following
accepted principles of research design. In addition, data are collected on
the extent to which each activity is performed as planned and on the
extent to which resources are used as planned. Findings from the several
sets of data are used to strengthen subsequent program planning.

Kinds of Evaluative Questions

The evaluative questions that program directors ask most frequently can
be grouped into four categories.

APPROPRIATENESS

Questions on appropriateness concern the importance of the specific
problems selected for programing and the relative emphasis or priority
accorded to each. Program directors are concerned with appropriateness
when they ask, "Are our program objectives worthwhile and do they have
a higher priority than other possible objectives of this or other programs?"

ADEQUACY

Ideally, objectives are oriented toward elimination of the problem
which gave rise to the program, but various constraints may necessitate
reducing the scope of an objective from focus on complete solution of a
problem to the more modest scope of reducing a problem by a specific
amount or limiting an objective to a portion of a population experiencing
the problem rather than trying to reach all those at risk. Questions
concerning how much of the entire problem the program is directed
toward overcoming refer to the adequacy of program objectives.

EFFECTIVENESS

Programs may differ in their effectiveness; that is, in the extent to which preestablished objectives are attained as a result of activity. Effectiveness in attaining objectives is distinct from program appropriateness and adequacy.

EFFICIENCY

Program efficiency is defined as the cost in resources of attaining objectives. The efficiency of a program may be unrelated to its effectiveness, adequacy, and appropriateness.

These four kinds of evaluative questions may be asked before a program begins or at some point after it has been in operation. Applied beforehand, the questions are an evaluation of the planning process. They can then be phrased as asking whether the proposed program has important objectives, whether it is aimed at overcoming a large proportion of the problem, whether the activities proposed are likely to attain the objectives, and whether the unit cost of attaining objectives is likely to be acceptably low.

When these four questions are asked about an operating program, they constitute an evaluation of performance. The questions then focus on (a) whether the program has in fact been directed toward important problems, (b) how much of the total problem has been controlled, (c) the extent to which the predetermined program objectives have been attained, and (d) the actual costs of attaining objectives.

Our proposed model for evaluation is applicable only to assessing performance of a program and not the planning of a program. Furthermore, the model does not deal with appropriateness. Our model is applicable to adequacy only when all the dimensions of a problem can be specified. We can determine the extent to which a home health care program solved a specified set of problems in a specified sample of a population. But we cannot determine how adequately it solved the entire range of health problems in the whole population unless we are able to identify in advance the total range of health problems in the total population affected. If such information is available, the measurement of program adequacy can be computed simply from the measure of program effectiveness.

Our model is intended to answer two questions: (a) to what extent were objectives attained as the result of activities (program effectiveness) and (b) at what cost (program efficiency)? The model builds upon a number of contributions to program evaluation, especially those of Paul

(1), MacMahon and co-workers (2), Hutchinson (3), Freeman (4), and James (5). If there is anything unique in our model, it is the attempt to be comprehensive, uniform, and consistent in our definitions and logic and in the application of the definitions and logic to health programs.

Model to Evaluate Program Effectiveness

Our model for evaluating effectiveness requires systematic description and measurement of each variable of a program, that is, resources, activities, and objectives. If a variable or portion of a variable cannot be measured, the model cannot be fully applied. However, even partial application of the model will provide information useful to subsequent planning; in addition, it will show the evaluator precisely where additional measurements are needed.

The model is intended primarily for use by program personnel to evaluate certain aspects of their own performance. However, an outside evaluator can also use it. Regardless of who performs the evaluation, it should be remembered that the purpose of evaluation is improvement. Therefore, the evaluation should be endorsed, if not performed, by those who have the authority to make changes.

As a final constraint, the model does not offer a systematic procedure for assessing any unplanned impact of activities, although activities performed for a specific purpose may indeed have side effects. We recommend that program personnel attempt to assess side effects on a subjective, impressionistic basis until a more systematic way of measuring them is developed.

DEFINITION OF TERMS

The model uses terms that are familiar but have not always been used consistently. First, therefore, these terms will be defined.

Program. An organized response to reduce or eliminate one or more problems. This response includes (*a*) specification of one or more objectives, (*b*) selection and performance of one or more activities, and (*c*) acquisition and use of resources. Although the term "program" probably suggests similar concepts to most health workers, two ambiguities are common. First, for many workers, human ailments or hazardous environmental conditions constitute the only legitimate focus for a program. Thus, concern with tuberculosis or water pollution is a program, but disease casefinding or food handler training is not. Such workers frequently classify casefinding, food handler training, and similar concerns as a "subprogram," "component," "project," or "technique."

To simplify terminology and logic, any area or scope of concern may be considered a program for the purpose of evaluation of performance. Thus, disease casefinding, food handler training, and professional education can be evaluated, although their immediate objectives do not have direct impact on a human ailment or environmental hazard.

A second common ambiguity results when the word "program" is further specified by adding a content area, such as "school health program." To some workers, a school health program means correction of defects; to others, measurement of height and weight or immunization; and to yet others, school health may connote certain areas of instruction.

Both sources of ambiguity may be removed by stating the objectives of the program and listing the activities performed and resources used. If this is done, the result is a statement that the program consists of resources a, b, c, used to perform activities d, e, f, which, in turn, are designed to attain objectives g and h. This definition therefore, permits widely varying scopes of work to be defined properly as programs.

Objective. A situation or condition of people or of the environment which responsible program personnel consider desirable to attain. To permit subsequent evaluation, the statement of an objective must specify (*a*) what—the nature of the situation or condition to be attained, (*b*) extent—the quantity or amount of the situation or condition to be attained, (*c*) who—the particular group of people or portion of the environment in which attainment is desired, (*d*) where—the geographic area of the program, and (*e*) when—the time at or by which the desired situation or condition is intended to exist.

Within the framework of our definition are three kinds of objectives, each meeting the basic definition.

1. Ultimate objective. A condition which is desired in and of itself according to the value system of those responsible for the program. Reductions in morbidity and mortality are examples of conditions that are typically regarded as inherently desirable.

2. Program objective. A statement of that particular situation or condition which is intended to result from the sum of program efforts. It may or may not be considered inherently desirable, that is, an ultimate objective.

3. Subobjective. A subordinate or subobjective is an objective which must be attained before the program objective may be obtained. A subobjective is seldom inherently desirable.

Most programs have several subobjectives. All subobjectives are related in time to each other and to the program objective; that is, the program planner believes they must be accomplished in a particular order. Frequently, two or more subobjectives must be attained simultaneously.

In some programs subobjective 1 must be accomplished before subobjectives 2, 3, and 4 may be accomplished, and 2, 3, and 4 may have to be accomplished simultaneously in order that subobjective 5 may be obtained, and so on. Other writers have used such terms as "intermediate objectives" or "activity goals" to describe subobjectives.

There is a commonly used distinction between long-range and short-range objectives. The phrases are not recommended because they can be ambiguous, as the following examples illustrate.

In some circumstances long range refers to a program objective and short range to a subobjective. Thus the long-range (program) objective might be a 90 percent reduction in the prevalence of tuberculosis after five years and one short-range (sub) objective might be that all people with tuberculosis know how to follow a prescribed chemotherapeutic regimen.

In other instances long range and short range refer to amounts of the program objective that can be expected at any given stage. The long-range objective might be a 90 percent reduction in the prevalence of tuberculosis after five years and the short-range objective might be its reduction by 20 percent after one year.

The meanings of the concepts are different in these two examples. In the first, the short term objective is actually a subobjective which might be wholly attained and still not imply any attainment of the program objective. In the second, the short-range objective represents partial attainment of the program objective. The distinctions used in this paper make it possible to describe plans and outcomes without differentiating between long-range and short-range objectives.

Activity. Work performed by program personnel and equipment in the service of an objective. Activity as we use it does not imply any fixed amount or scope of work; it may be applied with equal validity to such diverse efforts as writing a letter or providing comprehensive health care. An activity can usually be subdivided into more specific activities. Providing comprehensive health care, for example, could be subdivided into providing curative health care and providing preventive health care; these, in turn, are capable of further subdivision and specification.

Probably the greatest cause of confusion and difficulty in both planning and evaluating health programs is lack of a clear and consistent distinction between an activity and an objective. James (5a) has made the distinction in terms of an analogy to a bird—the activity is flapping wings, the objective is being at some desired place. Activities consume program time and resources whereas objectives do not.

The distinction between objectives and activities may be further clarified by an analogy between the logic of an experiment and the logic of a program plan. In an experiment, the investigator asks whether a cause-effect relationship can be demonstrated. He performs some procedures on a group of subjects (cause) and predicts that a specific result will or will not occur (effect). The experimental procedure is linked to the expected outcome by an hypothesis. The hypothesis can be stated in an "if . . . then" form; that it, if treatment A is provided, then effect B will result. Program planning parallels the logic of an experiment. After identification and analysis of needs or problems, a program objective is established and decisions are made about the activities to be undertaken. A program objective is parallel to the experimenter's expected result or effect, and the program activities are parallel to the experimental procedure or cause. The planner hypothesizes that a given method or set of activities will lead to the attainment of the objective; if a certain activity is performed, then the desired objective will be achieved. The hypothesis can be tested only by evaluation.

Resource. Personnel, funds, materials, and facilities available to support the performance of activity. Resources, like activities, may be described with varying levels of specificity.

Program assumption. An hypothesis concerning the nature of relationships among the various aspects of a program. Every program plan includes three major kinds of assumptions.

1. The assumption that use of resources as planned will result in the performance of planned activity.

2. The assumption that performing planned activity will result in the attainment of the desired objectives. Similar assumptions link subdivisions of program resources to the subset of activities they support and, in turn, to the program subobjective they are intended to establish.

3. The assumption that each subobjective must necessarily be attained before the program objective can be attained and that attainment of all subobjectives will result in attainment of the program objective.

A PROGRAM OVERVIEW

It is helpful at this point to describe the logical planning of a program if such limiting factors as financial and technical constraints could be ignored. Assume that a program objective as we have defined it has been established; that is, a statement has been formulated that the program is intended to attain a given situation or condition in a particular group of people or portion of the environment, in a given geographic area, by a particular time, and to a particular extent. Ideally, the planners, having specified the objective of a program, would then specify the conditions that would have to occur before the objective could be attained. Each of these necessary conditions is a subobjective.

The planner then identifies alternative activities which might be effective in attaining the objectives. He considers the anticipated costs and effectiveness of each alternative. Finally, the planner selects the best alternatives in terms of his assessments of program appropriateness, adequacy, effectiveness, and efficiency. Current approaches to selecting objectives and activities include planning-programing-budgeting, cost-benefit analysis, systems analysis, and operations research.

The final phase of planning is assignment of resources to support the activity selected.

It has already been indicated that the total program plan contains many assumptions about the relationships among resources, activities, and objectives. In a very real sense, evaluation of effectiveness is the determination of the extent to which these assumptions are true; evaluation assesses (a) whether the expenditure of resources did lead to the performance of planned activity, (b) whether each activity did attain its intended outcome or subobjective, (c) whether each subobjective was necessary to attain the next higher subobjective, and (d) whether attainment of all subobjectives was sufficient to accomplish the program objective.

Application of the Model

To conduct an evaluation of program effectiveness using the model proposed involves a series of actions. The process is divided arbitrarily into three steps.

STEP 1. DESCRIBING THE PROGRAM

The program description consists of naming the program to be evaluated and specifying the program objective or objectives, subobjectives, activities, and resources. If these things have already been done in the planning phase, this step in evaluation is relatively simple and may require only copying them from the program plan. However, it is rare in current health practice to find written program plans with objectives spelled out in sufficient detail and precision to permit evaluation of effectiveness.

Specification of objectives. Specification of the program objective or objectives and subobjectives may prove especially troublesome if these concepts are new to health workers. Drawing up a sequence of objectives may improve understanding.

The time sequence of objectives may be placed on a horizontal line, with an ultimate objective at the extreme right. At left is the initial condition or subobjective that, in the opinion of program planners, must exist if the ultimate objective is to be attained. Other planners might formulate a still earlier subobjective. The initial subobjective is arbitrarily chosen to represent the first new condition that the planner believes must be attained before the succeeding conditions can occur. Everything to the left of the initial subobjective is taken as a given, that is, it is assumed to take place without program intervention.

Between the initial subobjective and the ultimate objective are the intervening subobjectives or necessary conditions. Many subobjectives are possible if each is stated specifically, or all subobjectives can be grouped under two or three general headings (Figure 1). There are disadvantages, however, in specifying either a very small or very large number of subobjectives.

The first task in describing a program to be evaluated is to state its objective. The program objective may or may not be an ultimate objective from a health professional's point of view. A program may encompass an entire line, or any portion of such a line. Nevertheless, the program objective is an arbitrary point on a line that is expected to culminate in an ultimate health objective. Thus one program might include only the portion of the line that includes the first three intervening subobjectives (Figure 1).

An evaluation of program effectiveness must include measurement of the condition that is specified in the program objective. In addition, it should include measurement of as many subobjectives as available time and resources permit. In general, we recommend that several subobjectives be measured in order to locate the source of trouble if a program is less effective than desired. Measurement of a large number of subobjec-

FIGURE 1
Time Sequence of Objectives
Subobjectives stated very specifically

Initial subobjective ———————— Intervening subobjectives ———————— Ultimate objective

Subobjectives stated generally

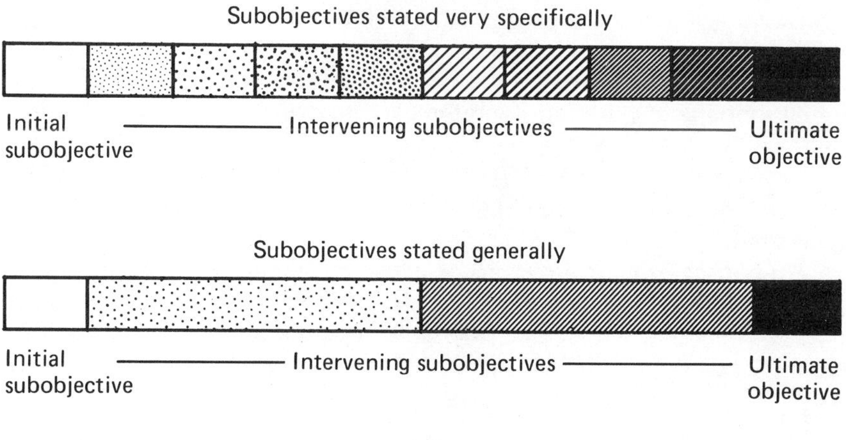

Initial subobjective ———————— Intervening subobjectives ———————— Ultimate objective

tives can consume great quantities of time and possibly of other resources. Should an administrator wish to evaluate the effectiveness of several programs and have limited resources for evaluation, he may prefer to measure attainment of program objectives only for all programs, returning to measure subobjectives for those programs manifesting lowest effectiveness.

No dictum can yet be given as to the optimal number of subobjectives since an infinite number of previous conditions (subobjectives) are necessary for a given condition (objective) to occur. Suppose sanitarians are attempting to increase restaurant operators' knowledge of defects in their operations. One necessary condition (subobjective) for acquisition of information is that the operator understand the sanitarian's vocabulary. But a necessary condition for the operator to understand is that he pay some attention to what is being said, and a necessary condition for his paying attention is that he be physically exposed to the message (he be physically present and capable of hearing, seeing, and thinking). The ability to perceive and think, in turn, is contingent upon the functioning of nervous tissue which, in turn, is contingent upon more basic biochemical balances. Biochemical function is contingent upon atomic motion which is dependent on subatomic motion and so on.

Although this is reduction to absurdity, it is clear that a somewhat arbitrary division will be needed to determine the number of subobjectives to be measured. The cutoff point would seem to be the point where the apparent disadvantages of expending further resources on measurements would about equal the apparent disadvantages of assuming that doubtful conditions will in fact be realized. Specifying too many subobjectives may make the evaluation too costly and detailed; specifying too few may yield insufficient information about weak aspects of the program. Most administrators assume that restaurant operators are not deaf, blind, and mentally defective, but many will be unwilling to assume that operators will automatically pay attention to what the sanitarian says. In that instance, the adequate functioning of sense organs would be accepted as a given rather than as a subobjective and would be to the left of the initial subobjective, but the operator's attentiveness would be a subobjective.

The nature of ultimate objectives, program objectives, and subobjectives is illustrated by combining examples from Hutchinson (3) and Knutson (6).

In a discussion of programs of early casefinding, Hutchinson cites a program with an ultimate objective. He considers that alteration of the natural course of disease in a favorable direction is intrinsically valuable from the point of view of the medical profession—although it may be only an intermediate or subobjective for such professions as theology and philosophy. On the other hand, a number of subobjectives (which he terms intermediate) are crucial to program effectiveness but are not in and of themselves intrinsically valuable, such as (*a*) that people come for screening, (*b*) that cases of illness are detected, and (*c*) that persons with the disease follow prescribed treatment. Subobjectives a, b, and c are desired not because of their inherent value but because the ultimate objective cannot be attained unless each of them is attained.

Knutson refers to a hypothetical health education program, whose objective is some desired behavior of people to whom the program is directed. He lists a number of subobjectives for his program which he, like Hutchinson, terms intermediate objectives: (*a*) the people must be exposed to the material, (*b*) they must give the material their attention, and (*c*) they must understand the words and concepts. If the objective (behavior of target audience) referred to by Knutson were that people come for screening, that objective would be identical with initial subobjective specified by Hutchinson. The subobjectives specified by Knutson, then, occupy a portion of the program line to the left of Hutchinson's initial objective (Figure 2).

The program objective for Knutson's health education program is the initial subobjective of Hutchinson's broader disease control program. Knutson's subobjectives are taken as givens in the Hutchinson example.

The importance of correctly stating the program objective may be illustrated by another example. Assume that the health education program within a larger disease control program is to be evaluated. The true

FIGURE 2
Relationship of Knutson and Hutchinson Program Lines

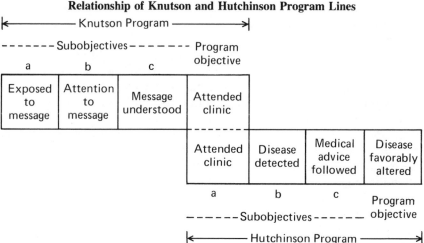

objective is that all members of a particular group residing in a given area come to a clinic for a particular screening test on a specified date. Figure 2 shows that the adjacent objectives, in elaborated form, are that all members of the group understand the words and concepts of the educational material and that all positive cases of disease in the group are detected.

If either adjacent objective were mistakenly stated as the program objective, the results of subsequent evaluation would be misleading. In the first instance, the program would be judged as more effective than it actually was, since many people may indeed have understood the words and concepts, but nevertheless failed to attend the clinic—failed, that is, to take the desired action. In the second instance the program would be judged as less effective than it actually was, since failures of diagnosis would incorrectly be attributed to the health education program. There-fore, it is essential to state as the objective of the program the precise outcome that is desired and expected to result from the activities to be evaluated.

To illustrate further the usefulness of measuring attainment of subobjectives, consider a program similar to the health education pro-gram discussed previously. The true objective was that stated in the previous example, and 50 percent of the specified group attended the clinic. Although that finding is important, it does not provide a clue as to why the program failed with half its intended audience. Such knowledge can be acquired, however, by measuring attainment of the program's subobjectives. In addition to the program objective, the following four subobjectives may have been specified: (a) all eligibles are exposed to the educational material, (b) all eligibles attend to (read, listen, and so forth) the material, (c) all eligibles understand the point of the communication, and (d) all eligibles be interested in early detection of the disease in question.

Recalling that 50 percent of the eligibles came in for screening, evaluative results can be arbitrarily assigned to each subobjective. A sample survey might show that for each 100 eligibles: 95 were exposed to the material; of those, 90 paid attention to it; of those, 65 adequately understood the point of the communication; and of those, 35 were interested in detecting disease early. Finally, all 35 satisfying all four subobjectives came in for screening. Thus, the first two subobjectives were attained with a total loss of 10 percent of the eligibles. Some attention might be given to reducing this loss. However, more important is the additional loss of 55 percent (25 and 30 percent respectively) that occurred in attaining the third and fourth subobjectives. Thus, of all 90 people attending to the program material, more than 60 percent (55 of 90) failed to understand the message and to become interested in early detection. Clearly, activities to accomplish these two subobjectives need to be strengthened.

It may be noted that 50 percent came in for screening, but only 35 percent were interested in early detection. This suggests that personal interest is important but not absolutely necessary to obtain participation. Perhaps further study would show that some people came in because of the influence of relatives or friends. The planners might wish to build on such a finding in subsequent programs.

The preceding discussion and examples have implied an objective that is identical for each person in the program population. However, for some programs, the objective for each member of the target group may be different as those in mental health and home care programs.

In these, it would be more appropriate to state a separate objective (and subobjectives) for each person to be served. In such programs the attending physician may establish a unique objective for each patient; for example, by the end of some time period, Mr. A will return to work. Mr. B will bathe and dress himself. The program objective can then be summarized as all, or some proportion of, program clientele will attain their unique objectives within specified periods.

Thus far, the discussion of objectives has focused on only one kind of content objective associated with programs. However, two other kinds of objectives need to be recognized.

Each health worker in a program will have personal objectives, such as advancement in rank or title, a higher salary, respect of his peers, popularity, and so forth. These may or may not be consistent with program objectives.

In addition to these personal objectives, every agency or organization has what may be called survival programs—a set of activities undertaken to insure the stability and continued existence of the agency. Certain public relations and public service activities are examples of survival programs.

Concern with personal satisfaction and organizational survival will act as constraints in planning programs, in the setting of priorities, and in the selection of objectives and activities. In this sense, they do not interfere with evaluation of program performance although knowledge of constraints may be useful in interpreting evaluation results. If desired, however, our model could be applied to the evaluation of employee morale or organization survival "programs."

The attention given to program objectives is deemed necessary because rarely have objectives been stated clearly when evaluation is desired and because it is difficult but extremely important to distinguish between objectives, subobjectives, and activities.

Some reasons for lack of predetermined objectives have been described by Selznick (7).

> Once an organization becomes a "going concern," with many forces working to keep it alive, the people who run it can readily escape the task of defining its purposes. This evasion stems partly from the hard intellectual labor involved, a labor that often seems but to increase the burden of already onerous daily operations. In part, there is the wish to avoid conflicts with those in and out of the organization who would be threatened by a sharp definition of purpose, with its attendant claims and responsibilities.

The threat engendered by making program objectives explicit becomes intensified when one seriously proposes measuring attainment (8–10). We do not see any ready way to eliminate all threatening aspects of evaluating program effectiveness, but we do believe that the threat can often be overcome if the benefits can be perceived as outweighing the costs.

Specification of activities. When the program objectives and subobjectives have been stated, the next task in step 1 is to specify all program activities, linking each to the objective or subobjective it is intended to accomplish. There are two reasons to do this. First, making activities explicit can serve as a check on the adequacy and completeness of stated objectives. If a planned or continuing activity cannot be linked to any stated objective or subobjective, either a necessary objective or subobjective has been omitted, or the activity is unnecessary. Conversely, if a stated objective or subobjective has no activity linked to it, either an essential activity is not being planned or performed or the stated objective or subobjective is not necessary to the program.

The second reason for including activities in the program description is to determine the extent to which they were performed as intended. For this purpose, activity must be carefully specified—what is to be done, by whom it is to be done, and when and where it is to be done.

If an objective or subobjective is not attained, either an activity was not performed as planned or the assumption linking the activity and the objective or subobjective was not valid. Of course, if the activity was not performed or not performed properly, the linking assumption must remain untested.

Specification of program resources. The final task in step 1, specification of program resources, makes it possible to determine if resources were used as planned. If planned activities were not performed, knowledge of whether resources were used will allow determination of the validity of assumptions linking resources and activities made in the planning process.

In summary then, the first step in evaluating program effectiveness requires a clear statement of the program objectives, the specification of a reasonable number of subobjectives, specification of program activities, and a description of program resources.

STEP 2. MEASUREMENT

A complete treatment of steps 2 and 3 is not possible in this paper. The interested reader is referred to standard texts which cover the material in detail (11–14). In addition, consultation from experts such as statisticians and behavioral scientists will often be helpful in completing steps 2 and 3.

Step 1 outlined a method for describing programs to permit evaluation of program effectiveness. Step 2 requires identification of the kinds of evidence needed to determine that an objective or subobjective has or has not been achieved.

In general, valid and reliable measures of program accomplishment are needed. Briefly, validity of a measure is the extent that an obtained score measures the characteristic that it is intended to measure. The terms "sensitivity" and "specificity" applied to diagnostic tests are components of validity. Reliability of evidence is the consistency or repeatability of a score.

We are concerned with validity and reliability because test scores do not always measure consistently what they are intended to measure. Suppose a series of measures are obtained on a group of persons or restaurants or on samples of water. A range of scores will be obtained. Differences in scores may reflect true differences in the characteristic being measured, but different scores may reflect other factors. If the measure is of people, responses may not only reflect the item being measured but also such transitory factors as mood or fatigue. In measures of the physical environment, factors such as variations in the administration of a test and the care with which instruments are read will also affect scores.

Another possible source of variation in scores exists in measurements of complex concepts such as health status, morbidity, or cleanliness. Such concepts are composed of many specific subconcepts. For example, good health might include almost an infinite number of measurements of the functions of various organ systems. It is unlikely that any one test will measure all functions. A test of two or three functions applied to a group of people might show that some are healthier than others without giving recognition to the fact that had tests been made of other functions, results might have been different.

Because test scores are determined not only by true differences in what is being measured but also by other causes, it is never completely safe to accept a test score at face value. When possible, evidence should be obtained that the test is valid (it measures what it is intended to measure) and that it is reliable (successive administrations of the test or administration by different persons yield similar scores).

In selecting a measure of accomplishment, the evaluator may know of valid and reliable measures or he may search the literature for relevant measures that others have used. If he fails to locate an acceptable measure, he may have to develop a unique measure which satisfies the basic criteria of measuring instruments. However, if his resources do not permit the development of a measure for certain objectives, he may be forced to omit some measures from the evaluation, thus reducing the resultant amount of information bearing on the success of a program.

When to measure. The program objectives and subobjectives state the time period in which the measures are to be applied. Although one tends to think of evaluation as being conducted over a relatively short period, evaluation will be most valuable if it is conceived as a more nearly continuous process. Since attainment of subobjectives occurs in a time sequence, attainment of each should be measured soon after attainment is expected.

How to measure. In deciding how to make the needed measurements, two problems are particularly important: how to avoid bias and the problem of sampling.

The possibility of bias is great if one evaluates his own work. This possibility is especially great if observational rather than physical measures are used, such as reporting the cleanliness of an object or the satisfaction of a patient. Bias can be reduced by using physical measures when possible, or if observation or judgment is necessary, by having more than one person judge.

Sampling procedures are often used in evaluating a program since it is rarely feasible to measure the attainment of objectives in every person in the target group or at every location. In such cases, a probability sample which accurately represents the total population must be selected.

The size of the sample required depends on such technical considerations as variance in the distribution of the quality being measured, the amount of change expected as a result of program activity, and the level of certainty desired when inferring that what is true of the sample is also true of the population from which it was drawn.

Collecting the data. Data on the attainment of objectives and subobjectives as well as on the performance of activities and use of resources must be collected at times indicated in the program description.

STEP 3. DETERMINING EFFECTIVENESS

In evaluating effectiveness the question is not merely were the program objectives accomplished but to what extent can achievement of the objective be attributed to the activities of the program?

Analysis of program effectiveness can be simplified by using a set of ratios involving the three program variables: resources, activities, and objectives.

Simplest is the ratio of actual resources to planned use of resources, *AR/PR.*

Slightly more complicated is the ratio of actual program activities performed to planned activities, *AA/PA.*

The ratio that indicates attainment of objectives is still more complex. We denote this ratio as *AO/PO.* *AO* is the net attainment of the objective attributable to program activity and *PO* is the attainment desired less the status that would have existed in the absence of the program. It might be imagined that the proper comparison would be between actual status of the objective when evaluation is performed and the status of the objective that had been planned. However, such a comparison is not valid since it does not take account of effects on the program of activities and events outside it. Evaluation should assess the extent to which achievement of the objective can be attributed to activities performed in the program.

Therefore, it is necessary to find a way of comparing the net accomplishment attributable to the program with the accomplishment intended for the program. One way of doing this is to determine the status of the objective at the time of evaluation and then to subtract from it an estimate of what the status would have been had the program not been undertaken. For example, if a program operator finds that 90 percent of a group of clients are immune to a disease following the conduct of a program, he cannot properly take credit for all 90 percent, but only for those who would not be immune had his program not been undertaken.

What is true for the actual status of the objective, the numerator, is also true for planned attainment, the denominator. One must subtract from planned attainment that portion of the desired status that would have occurred in the absence of the program. For example, suppose it was desired that 90 percent of a population be immune to a disease. Evaluation shows that 80 percent actually became immune but that half, 40 percent, became immune through activity outside the program (visits to physicians and so forth). Program effectiveness would then be

$$\frac{80 - 40}{90 - 40} = \frac{40}{50} = 80 \text{ percent.}$$

Another example based on actual data will show how the ratio may be computed. In a food service sanitation program consisting of inspections, a rating system was used as the measure both of the problem and the objective. The objective was that the average sanitation rating of food establishments in the county will be at lease as high as 90 by July 1, 1966. On July 1, 1966, the average rating was 85.7.

Additional data showed that the average rating in an uninspected section of the county was 81 on July 1, 1966. If we use the rating of 81 as an estimate of what the countywide rating would have been without the program, the program effectiveness ratio becomes

$$\frac{85.7 - 81}{90 - 81} = \frac{4.7}{9} = 52.2 \text{ percent.}$$

How is it possible to estimate the status of the objective in the absence of the program? The most certain way is to use a control or comparison group similar to the one exposed to the program. The control group procedure maximizes confidence in judging the results that may be properly attributed to the program.

Control groups are not always feasible in evaluations of health programs, but they could be employed more often than they currently are. For example, when a new program cannot be initiated throughout a jurisdiction, it may be possible to begin it in several places selected at random and to use the remaining areas as controls. Or alternate procedures to accomplish objectives might be applied systematically in different parts of the jurisdiction, as is done in clinical field trials to test whether one procedure is superior to another.

However, if a strict control group is not feasible, a control group can be approximated by comparing community status before and after the program with information about nearby communities not exposed to the program. While this is not an ideal procedure, it may provide guidance as to the impact of the program.

A major danger in using natural groups as comparisons or controls is that an available group, within or outside the community, may not be similar to the study group in crucial respects. The laboratory practice for minimizing this danger is to assign subjects randomly to treatment and control procedures. Sometimes this practice can be used in evaluating health programs, but often it will be impossible because treatment must be given to or withheld from whole groups.

Baseline measures are helpful when random assignments to experimental (program) and control groups cannot be made. If baseline measures show that the program and comparison groups were similar at the beginning of the program, one may be more confident that the status of the comparison group at evaluation represents what would probably have occurred in the program group without the program. If the groups differ at the beginning, one should be much less confident.

Where no comparison group can be devised, it may still be possible to obtain information on the probable impact of program activity on the objective. One can, for example, formulate alternative explanations for the outcome of the program and see whether available facts support the alternative explanations. Suppose, for example, one wishes to determine whether a decline in the incidence of tuberculosis in a community can properly be attributed to an ongoing tuberculosis control program, but the community in question cannot be compared with another.

The operator might examine other possible explanations for the falling incidence. He might consider improved nutrition and improved housing as two possible alternative explanations and investigate whether nutrition and housing indeed improved over the period being considered. If neither improved substantially, he could with greater confidence attribute the reduced incidence of tuberculosis to his program. If one or both alternative hypotheses were borne out by evidence, he could not attribute the outcome to his program. At that point he could, however, use the analysis of cross-tabulations to study the interrelationships among the alternative explanations and thus throw more light on the relative contribution of each explanation to the program objectives that were attained (14).

The conclusion that program activities caused program outcomes requires a judgment that can never be made with absolute certainty. After using control groups or testing alternative hypotheses, however, one can make a more confident judgment than would be legitimate without the use of such procedures.

Evaluation of Efficiency

If the attainment of objectives were considered desirable regardless of cost and if unlimited resources were available for health programs, efficiency would not be of great concern to administrators. Since neither of these conditions obtains, however, efficiency must be a concern in program operation.

A definition of efficiency in public health programs may be formulated by referring to the classical definition of physical efficiency—the ratio between the energy output of a machine and the energy input supplied to it. In public health programs, efficiency may be defined as the ratio between an output (net attainment of program objectives) and an input (program resources expended), or AO:AR. The inverse of this ratio, which would be AR:AO, yields a measure of average cost. Clearly it matters little in public health programing whether one examines efficiency or average costs, since the same relationship will emerge. However, it is sometimes more meaningful to look at one than the other. For example, it is easier to understand that it costs $10,000 to locate and cure one case of a particular disease than that 1/10,000 of a case was located and cured for $1. (This situation is not true in physics since the units of comparison—energy—are the same in both the numerator and the denominator, and maximum efficiency cannot exceed 100 percent because of the law of the conservation of energy. In instances, however, in which the numerator and denominator consist of different units, for example, of objectives and resources, there is no theoretical basis for estimating maximum possible efficiency, and the terms can be either numerator or denominator.)

The measure of overall program efficiency AO:AR or AR:AO may be interpreted by examining two intermediate efficiency measures, namely, the relationship of activities to objectives and resources. Specifically, efficiency studies may answer questions about the relationship (a) between the extent of attainment of objectives and the resources expended, (b) between the extent of attainment of objectives and the number and kind of activities conducted, and (c) between the number and kind of activities conducted and the resources expended.

The ratio of program effectiveness, as indicated earlier, reflects the relationship beten two estimates of the attainment of program objectives—the planned attainment and the actual attainment. And each of the

---

KEY TO ABBREVIATIONS

AO—Attainment of objectives that can be attributed to the program activity
PO—Proposed objectives for attainment through the program activity
AA—Actual activities performed
PA—Planned activities to be performed
AR—Actual resource expenditure
PR—Planned resource expenditure

two subordinate ratios of effectiveness involves similar comparisons of activities and resources. Program efficiency, on the other hand, reflects the relationship between two different variables—objectives and resources. Two subordinate efficiency measures also compare combinations of different variables. Three efficiency, or average-cost, ratios can thus be stated as follows, one for each of the foregoing questions:

1. Objectives attained to resources expended = AO:AR or AR:AO.
2. Activities performed to resources expended = AA:AR or AR:AA.
3. Objectives attained to activities performed = AO:AA or AA:AO.

Of course, each ratio may also be computed for the portions of the program related to each subobjective. As is true for effectiveness, consideration, as the program progresses, of the efficiency with which the plan is being carried out may demonstrate a need for modification of the original plan.

Relation of Effectiveness to Efficiency

In the typical program setting, the administrator attempts to obtain an acceptably high level of attainment of objectives at minimum cost (that is, to maximize attainment at a fixed level of resource input or to minimize resource input at a fixed level of attainment). However, a proper interpretation of efficiency requires a measurement of activity so that two subordinate efficiency ratios, AO:AA and AA:AR can be computed. Consequently, as a comprehensive evaluation of performance, data should be obtained on all three components—use of resources, performance of activity, and attainment of objectives (including subobjectives). Measures of effectiveness must be obtained before measures of program efficiency can be interpreted meaningfully since, from the definition of efficiency, knowledge is required of effectiveness as well as of resources.

Unless the administrator is satisfied with effectiveness, studies of efficiency will be uninterpretable or misleading. A person cannot decide that a program with an efficiency ratio of two units of attainment per unit of resource is superior to a program with a ratio of one unit of attainment per unit of resource unless he has knowledge of the effectiveness of each program. For example, suppose that two programs have the same objective. Program A attains all of the objective at a given cost, whereas program B attains half of the objective at a quarter of the cost. Program A is thus twice as effective as program B, but only half as efficient. Which program is superior? A rational answer can only be based on knowledge of both the effectiveness and efficiency of each program.

The attainment of subobjectives and of the program objective cannot be measured, of course, until some time after a program has been in operation, but other valuable information can be collected earlier. It is always desirable to collect data periodically on progress to insure that a program is being carried out as planned. If it is not, adjustments can be made in the course of operating the program.

Typically, continuous evaluative measures can be obtained in the following sequence:

1. The extent to which resources are being expended as planned (AR:PR).

2. The extent to which activities are being performed in the quantity and quality planned (AA:PA) and the efficiency of resource expenditures (AA:AR).

3. The net attainment of selected subobjectives (AOsub:POsub) and the efficiency of subobjective attainment (Osub:Rsub) and (Osub:Asub).

4. Program effectiveness (AO:PO), program efficiency (AO:AR), and activity efficiency (AO:AA).

If data on the first three of these evaluative measures are obtained early in the program operation, these data can provide a rational basis for changes in the program that may materially improve its effectiveness and efficiency. The only true measure of the effectiveness of a program, however, is the ratio of attained objectives to planned objectives, and the only true measure of efficiency is the ratio of attained objectives to expended resources. Therefore, for a comprehensive evaluation, the fourth evaluative measure must be applied.

Special Measurement Problems

We gave considerable attention to the measurement of objectives and subobjectives earlier. Little was said about the measurement of activities and resources.

Since any program variable includes quantitative and qualitative components, we believe that measures of variables must reflect both dimensions. In most instances quantitative measures alone do not provide a sufficient basis for judging how adequately a program component has been implemented. Rarely are there no qualitative differences among a class of objects or actions. The dollar seems to be an exception since any one is equal to another in terms of a program's buying power at a single point in time. Similarly, constancy of quality is probably fairly closely approached by many standardized medications and vaccines, although mishaps occasionally occur. Few problems of measurement arise when we deal with highly standardized variables.

Generally, however, an assessment of quality as well as of quantity is desirable in program evaluation. When resources are described in terms of a given number of "qualified" physicians, nurses, or sanitarians or a given number of "adequate" clinic facilities, the extent to which the resources actually fulfilled the qualitative as well as quantitative requirements has to be determined. How many physicians, nurses, sanitarians, or clinics were provided and how qualified or adequate was each? When activities are described in terms of numbers of nursing visits, sanitation inspection, physical examinations, or educational efforts, the qualitative as well as the quantitative aspects must be specified and subsequently measured. We have to measure not only the number of activities but the extent to which each was performed on the desired level of expertness.

At present no ready procedures are available for developing and applying qualitative measures; we can only point out that qualitative measures are necessary. It is desirable for program personnel to bear in mind that effectiveness and efficiency are influenced as much by the quality of resources and activities as by the quantity. In some circumstances, the program administrator and his staff will be able to work out their own systematic measures of the quality of selected factors and will thus be in a better position to evaluate overall program performance.

Use of Data on Efficiency

The major concern of the administrator obviously is to attain a desired (usually high) level of accomplishment of objectives at a minimum cost. As indicated throughout this paper, a concern with program effectiveness logically precedes a concern with program efficiency. After the desired levels of accomplishment of objectives are attained or maintained, an assessment of the program's efficiency then becomes of prime concern. The administrator who knows how effective and efficient his program is can then judge whether its results are worth the cost.

We have implied that evaluation always entails comparison with a standard. In evaluations of program effectiveness, the standard for comparison most frequently selected is the attainment level that had been planned before program implementation began. A similar standard may be used for determining efficiency. One may ask whether the actual level of efficiency or the average costs are similar to what had been planned. It may have been planned that each unit of attainment would cost, say, $100. An evaluation of efficiency may show that, in fact, each unit of attainment cost $104. A program operator might then decide that the actual efficiency was so close to what had been planned that extra attention was not warranted. On the other hand, he might conclude that the disparity between the planned and the actual efficiency was great enough to require additional analysis. The operator could then ask whether the planned efficiency of the resources or of the activities had been in error, and he would then attempt to revise the program planning accordingly.

Frequently, no sound basis for estimating planned efficiency is available, for xample, in instances in which little or no evidence can be obtained about how many resources are required to support an activity or about the number and kinds of activities that will be required to attain an objective. In this situation, another standard for comparison needs to be selected. One that is frequently used, but a dangerous one, is the operation of the same program in an earlier year. Costs and circumstances may vary so from year to year that conclusions drawn from efficiency ratios obtained in two different years may be invalid. Nevertheless, with a knowledge of local circumstances and the costs of living, a person may be able to estimate from data obtained periodically whether efficiency is increasing or decreasing. The important point is that a comparison of the actual operation of a program with a reasonable standard permits a judgment as to whether the efficiency attained is satisfactory or unsatisfactory.

An administrator may be satisfied with the effectiveness of a program and still believe that its efficiency is unsatisfactory. Attempts to improve program efficiency require consideration of the subordinate efficiency measures A:R and O:A for each subobjective and for the program objective. For example, studies may be made of ways to improve resource efficiency (A:R) by obtaining more or better activity, or both, from a given expenditure of resources. This ratio is the one being considered in speaking about the cost of a nursing visit or a sanitation inspection.

Use of a multiple-antigen immunization material in a broad communicable disease control program may be an example of improving the efficiency of an activity (O:A). In this instance, an equal or greater attainment of objectives may be accomplished as a result of a given amount of activity (thus, immunity to several diseases may be brought about from one series of inoculations). Of course, in such circumstances, resource efficiency may increase.

When program effectiveness is lower than desired, the administrator has four choices. One possibility is to reduce the desired level of accomplishment to the level actually attained. This choice might be suggested by the belief, perhaps bolstered by new data, that the observed attainment, although less than that desired, is the most which can reasonably be achieved given existing constraints. When new program objectives are set at current levels of attainment, studies of efficiency will be more useful in planning for subsequent program operations.

A second choice available to the administrator who is dissatisfied with his attainment is to decide, on the basis of his evaluative data, that he needs to increase the number or improve the quality of the activities directed toward subobjectives and objectives. Any such change will have implications for resource allocation and may thus be planned more rationally with the help of information on efficiency, namely, on the current ratios between activity and cost and between objectives and activities.

A third possibility is that the administrator will maintain the original program objective but, on the basis of evaluative data, decide to make substantial revisions in his program theory, that is, he will specify, and work toward, some new subobjectives. In such an event, study of the efficiencies associated with the achievement of each subobjective to be retained in the new program will aid in planning the subsequent operation of the program.

A final choice might be to abandon the program, especially if evaluation shows that it is low in efficiency and if pressures are being generated internally or externally to allocate the existing resources to other programs.

Limitations of Measures of Efficiency

One limitation on the usefulness of efficiency studies is that efficiency may not be constant at different levels of program operation. Consider a program objective to eliminate all of a given community problem. If a given input of resources and activities has eliminated 60 percent of the problem, it is not certain what returns could be expected from different levels of input. At the upper limit, doubling the resources and activities could not eliminate more than 100 percent of the problem. On the other hand, allocating exactly half of the resources and activities probably would not eliminate exactly 30 percent of the problem, but rather might eliminate 20 or 40 percent. It seems reasonable, on the basis of experience, that the expenditure of very limited resources will have little impact (low efficiency); increasing the resources will have a proportionately greater impact (higher efficiency); and finally, greatly increasing the resources will result in only a little more gain (reduced efficiency). This notion is illustrated in Figure 3.

A leveling off in efficiency can be expected to occur when a program approaches complete attainment of its objective or when the greatest effectiveness possible from the types of activities performed has been attained. If the curve shown in Figure 3 were known for a particular program, then an efficiency curve such as the one in Figure 4 could be

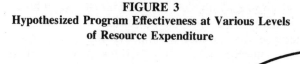

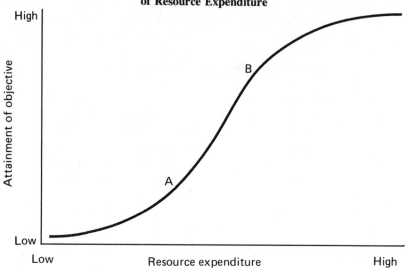

FIGURE 3
Hypothesized Program Effectiveness at Various Levels
of Resource Expenditure

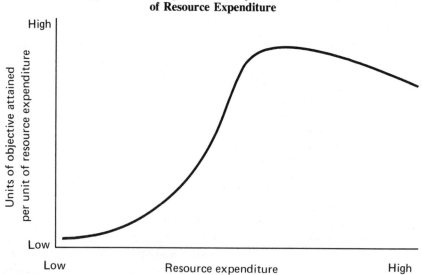

FIGURE 4
Hypothesized Program Efficiency at Various Levels
of Resource Expenditure

constructed. Thus, we would expect increasing efficiency with increased expenditures, but only up to a point; thereafter, the efficiency level would fall.

A single evaluation of program performance will not tell the administrator at what point on these curves his program lies. But, if the point could be determined, such knowledge would have important implications for the planning of subsequent programs. If an administrator knew what the correct shape of the curve in Figure 3 would be for a given program, he would know what proportion of the objectives could be attained with varying amounts of resource expenditures. If the current level of program attainment were at point B on the curve, obviously increased expenditures would not increase the attainment markedly; whereas increased expenditures for programs that begin at point A would have a great impact on the attainment of objectives. On the other hand, if the amount of resources that could be directed toward the program objectives were fixed, the administrator would know what proportion of the objectives might be attained and thus could judge whether the program was likely to be worth the effort. For example, if only enough appropriations were available to accomplish the objectives at point A in Figure 4, the administrator might decide to invest his resources in a different program in which the same financial allocation would permit greater attainment, or he might decide to go ahead with the original program if the problem being attacked was deemed to be worthy. In any event, knowledge of the efficiency curve would permit greater rationality in program planning.

Constructing Efficiency Curves

One way of constructing an efficiency curve would be for the administrator to subdivide the jurisdiction of the program and operate it at different levels of resource input in each sub-district. (Controls to assure that the subdistricts were similar would be essential.)

A second way of constructing efficiency curves would be for a state or the federal Government to arrange to operate, in similar communities, programs whose levels of operation are systematically varied. In such experiments, effects of previous program operation on the subsequent operation would be overcome. We would still be left, however, with the question of how far this knowledge would be applicable to future programs operating in constantly changing contexts.

How precise the prediction of future outcomes that will probably result from various resource inputs into a program will be depends in part on the composition of the target audience for the program. In some programs, the target audience changes from planning period to planning period; in others, it remains essentially the same. For example, consider a program directed toward increasing the proportion of seat belt users among the entire population of a community. The members of this population will change somewhat from year to year; all will age, some will migrate, some will die, new drivers will be added, but in large measure it will contain the same people from one year to the next. A seat belt program directed to the driver education courses would affect a new set of persons each year, except for the few students who might repeat the course.

For target populations that comprise essentially the same people from year to year (such as all people in a community, the mothers of school age children, restaurant operators), past programs may have considerable influence on the results of future operations. In programs like those represented in the first seat belt example, efforts expended in the first few years of their operation may succeed in influencing all members of the target population who are predisposed to act while most of the remaining members resist all the subsequent efforts undertaken to influence them.

In programs such as the second seat belt example, that is, those in which potential clients come from a "new" population each year, similar outcomes from similar inputs would be expected from one year to the next if allowance is made for changes in the costs of living and other variables whose effects can be estimated.

Application of Methods

Application of the methods described here to real program situations will be fairly simple in programs in which resources, activities, and outcomes can be readily quantified in reasonably meaningful terms and in which the measure of attainment is consequently fairly straightforward. For example, the meaning of regular use of a seat belt is conceptually clear, although ascertaining actual achievement might require considerable ingenuity.

Such simple situations, however, are not common; more often program objectives are lacking in conceptual clarity. When a program director thinks in terms of raising the level of health in a group, he is dealing with ideas that may have no common meaning among a group of experts. One director may think of the absence of certain symptoms, a second thinks of certain physical signs, a third of emotional stability, a fourth of physical vigor, and a fifth of individual productivity. Others will think in combinations of several or all of these ideas. Before the program director can prepare an index of accomplishment, he has to specify the objectives he is going to try to measure, and this task proves most difficult in many health programs.

Similarly, in most settings, the conceptual meaning of the performance of an activity as planned is unclear. What is really meant by a "nursing visit" or an "inspection"? How, specifically, is the nurse or sanitarian expected to behave? When a person's role is termed "educational," what precisely is meant by education? Until one can specify, first in terms of concepts and then in terms of measures of quantity and quality, how the professional should behave in a particular situation, evaluation cannot be comprehensive, and programs cannot be systematically improved.

Conclusions

The tools described in this paper for evaluating effectiveness and efficiency are most useful for programs in which (*a*) the objectives have been specified qualitatively and quantitatively and have been fixed in time to particular geographic areas and to particular target audiences, (*b*) the programs are described in sufficient detail to permit reliable observations of performance of planned activity, and (*c*) all the resources that are directed toward program activity are identified.

Thus, the first step in evaluating effectiveness and efficiency appears to be to attain clarity about what the program is and what it contains. Then evaluation becomes straightforward.

References

(1) Paul, B. D.: Social science in public health. American Journal of Public Health 46: 1390–1396, November 1956.
(2) MacMahon, B., et al.: Principles in the evaluation of community mental health programs. American Journal of Public Health 51: 963, July 1961.
(3) Hutchinson, G. B.: Evaluation of preventive services. Journal of Chronic Diseases 11: 497 (1960).
(4) Freeman, R. B.: Public health nursing practice. W. B. Saunders, Philadelphia, 1963, p. 289.
(5) James, G.: Administration of community health services. International City Managers Association, Chicago, 1961, ch. 6, pp. 114–134; (a) p. 118.
(6) Knutson, A.: Pretesting: a positive approach to evaluation. Public Health Rep 67: 699–703, July 1952.
(7) Selznick, P.: Leadership in administration, Row, Peterson, New York, 1957.

(8) Bergen, B. J.: Professional communities and the evaluation of demonstration projects in community mental health. American Journal of Public Health 55: 1057–1066, July 1965.

(9) Stanley, D. T.: Excellence in public service—how do you really know. Public Administration Review 24: 170–174, September 1964.

(10) Herzog, E.: Some guidelines for evaluative research. Children's Bureau Publication, No. 378, U.S. Department of Health, Education, and Welfare, 1959.

(11) Selltiz, C., Jahoda, M., Deutsch, M., and Cook, S.: Research methods in social relations. Henry Holt, New York, 1960.

(12) Cronbach, L. J.: Essentials of psychological testing. Ed. 2. Harper & Row, New York, 1960.

(13) Kerlinger, F. N.: Foundations of behavioral research, Holt, Rinehart and Winston, New York, 1966.

(14) Hyman, H.: Survey design and analysis. Free Press, Glencoe, Ill., 1955.

8

Relating Program Evaluation to Planning

O. LYNN DENISTON
IRWIN M. ROSENSTOCK

Evaluation, by definition, is value laden, requiring the selection of certain qualities, attributes, or conditions; measurement of these qualities; and comparison of results with the underlying value system (1). Differentiating among several different uses of the concept of evaluation is important.

Evaluation is likely to be performed at the initial contact between a patient and a physician. The physician will select and measure a set of qualities (for example, weight, temperature, pulse rate, blood pressure, color, and alertness) and will compare the scores obtained with a norm that reflects his beliefs about the preferred condition of the patient. Such a procedure meets the formal definition of evaluation although it does not seem to describe all that is usually meant by evaluation of a program.

What is Program Evaluation?

Before the evaluation of a program can be discussed seriously, some agreement is needed about what a program is. We use the word

Reprinted from *Public Health Reports*, 85, No. 9 (September 1970): 835–40, where it appeared under the title "Evaluating Health Programs," by permission of the authors. Numbers in parentheses refer to references.

"program" in many different ways (2). Neal (3) has suggested that people with a management science viewpoint seem to agree that a program is "a set of activities, a social enterprise, with certain inputs of resources and conditions, certain ways of organizing those resources and conditions and establishing relations among them and certain outputs with standards for evaluating them."

We prefer the following formal definition of a program: an organized response to eliminate or reduce one or more problems where the response includes one or more objectives, performance of one or more activities, and expenditure of resources (4). Neal's definition differs slightly from this one in that he does not allude directly to a problem whose elimination is valued. We, on the other hand, do not insist that standards for evaluating outputs (objectives) must exist in order for a program to exist.

What the two definitions have in common is that any size of enterprise or response could constitute a program. One could with equal validity label as a program this paper, this issue of *Public Health Reports,* the totality of the Public Health Service, or the work of a neighborhood health center.

Once agreement has been reached about what constitutes a program, the requirements for evaluation of the program can be specified. We believe that evaluation of a program should focus on the objectives (outputs, outcomes, goals) of the program in terms of their appropriateness, adequacy, effectiveness, efficiency, and side effects.

Appropriateness of the program is most directly related to value: the good-bad continuum. In evaluating appropriateness of the program, one asks if the objectives of the program are desirable. The decision depends on who answers the question and what his values are. Most people agree on certain values—peace is good, murder is bad—but considerable disagreement exists about other values: U.S. involvement in Vietnam, registration of guns, or keeping certain people biologically alive through heroic medical manipulations.

The dimension of appropriateness may be viewed in two ways. First, is the proposed program desirable or undesirable in an absolute sense? Second, and more difficult, is determining the degree of desirability or priority of a program in relation to other programs. Even if an objective is desirable, it is necessary to decide whether it is better than all other possible desirable objectives. Health workers probably agree that the eradication of measles, tuberculosis, and lung cancer are each desirable objectives, but they might disagree about which is the most important.

The critical question centers on who has the right to decide: the professional? the consumer? which professional or which consumer? Even if these questions were answered, additional answers would be required concerning the objective and who is able and willing to describe it. If all these questions could be answered satisfactorily and appropriateness of the program thought of as a simple dichotomy (that is, good or bad), the evaluation could be straightforward. If appropriateness is a matter of degree, however, we have difficulty because our ability to measure the degree of value is not well developed.

Effectiveness and adequacy of the program are related; we separate them more for psychological than logical reasons. Adequacy is concerned with the extent to which a problem has been prevented or eliminated, while effectiveness is concerned with the extent to which an intended amount of attainment has occurred. Thus a program with an objective that the incidence of lung cancer be reduced by 50 percent and which attained that objective would be 100 percent effective but only 50 percent adequate since half of the problem still remained.

We believe that objectives should specify both what is to be attained (the valued condition) and how much is to be attained. The objectives of most current programs either propose the eradication of an existing problem or reduction of the problem by an unspecified amount. Eradication is usually unrealistic in that few people really expect it—at least in the short run. The second is unusable because it provides no basis for comparison of attainment with any value or expectation.

Efficiency is concerned with the cost in resources of attaining the program's objectives. Knowledge of effectiveness is thus prerequisite to knowledge of efficiency. Therefore, the definition clearly prohibits such often-stated conclusions as "we don't know how effective we were, but we were very efficient."

Thus four kinds of evaluation (appropriateness, adequacy, effectiveness, and efficiency) focus on the objective—the intended effect of operating the program. Another kind of evaluation focuses on other or side effects of the operation. We can never be sure that the operation will lead only to the intended effects. Side effects, either good or bad, nearly always occur. The thalidomide experience is one of the most familiar examples of undesirable side effects. The recent discovery of a highly selective and effective raticide while testing cancer drugs is an example of a good side effect.

Other Bases for Evaluation

Not all judgments about programs are based directly on the objectives of the program. Many judgments are based on data concerning the resources and activities rather than the objectives. Stanley (5) has aptly termed this approach to evaluation "presumptive." The operators of a program often presume that if the budget is of a particular size, if the personnel possess certain credentials, and if certain activities are performed, the program has some degree of effectiveness. The presumptive approach to evaluation in public health is best illustrated by the logic of the several evaluation schedules, appraisal forms, and "Health Practice Indices" published by the American Public Health Association between 1925 and 1950 (6–8). We are now more aware of the dangers associated with presuming that resources and activities invariably lead to desired outcomes.

WHO EVALUATES THE PROGRAM?

Everyone with any knowledge of a program evaluates it. Each evaluation varies with the knowledge of the evaluator, the criteria he selects as signs of success, and the data he uses to measure the criteria. Several groups have or will evaluate this paper: the authors, the reviewers, the readers, and those who read only the title of the paper but not its content. If the evaluations differ, who can say which are correct?

Our approach to the evaluation of a program proposes that those people who decide that a program shall be created, or that one already in existence shall be continued, are the people who know the program's objectives. Thus we would say that evaluations based on objectives described by the operators of the program are correct. But many people who judge a program by the same objective frequently differ in their conclusions. Which of them are correct? It is not easy to decide.

Many times different conclusions are reached because of variations in the objectivity of the measures used. Objectivity means the extent to which clear-cut rules are formulated and followed for obtaining measures. In this sense, the procedures for performing laboratory tests are more objective than the procedures for making clinical judgments. We tend to accept the results of those who use the most objective measure, not because a high correlation always exists between objectivity and validity of measures but because we simply cannot say much about the validity of subjective measures.

Stanley (5) has suggested the terms "impressionistic" and "proven" to describe the ends of a continuum of objectivity. The act of measuring fever by placing the hand on the forehead tends toward the "impressionistic" or subjective end of the scale; when fever is measured by a certified thermometer, the "proven" or objective end is approached.

If we grant that all judgments are evaluations, there is no real lack of numbers of evaluations of programs. Rather, concern is with kind and quality of the evaluation. What is generally wanted is (a) clarity about the actual objectives of the program, (b) measures of attaining these objectives, rather than allocation of resources or performance of activities, and (*c*) measures that are more objective and more valid than the usual.

Evaluation of the program is usually thought to be an assessment of its operation. We believe that in evaluating its effectiveness, not only the operation but also the accuracy of planning should be assessed.

Once decisions have been made about what problem should be attacked, the ideal process for planning usually would begin by obtaining information about the current state of affairs, referred to as baseline data, which rarely are sufficient to lead the planners of the program into action. Rather, baseline data are used for estimating what the status of the problem would be during or at the end of some planning period if no program were undertaken. On the basis of knowledge and expert judgment, one might estimate that, if left unchecked, the problem would increase, would stay about the same, or would diminish. This prediction of the future forms the basis for planning. Frequently, the projection is only implicit, but it is necessary. No one would use resources to eliminate a problem that he expected to disappear as quickly without using these resources.

Having estimated what the course of a problem would be without a program, one would next estimate how the problem would be affected if a program were undertaken. With cost-benefit analyses, one might have different estimates concerning the impact of the program. Such estimates could be based on the use of alternative programs by considering various levels of resources or different approaches to the problem.

Regardless of how one estimates the future status of a problem if a program were undertaken, that estimate constitutes the objective of the program and may be viewed in two ways: first, that the status of the problem be at a desired level during a given period or by a given time and, second, that the program produce the desired amount of change.

If both estimates of future status are made while planning the program, it becomes feasible to evaluate both accuracy of the planning and effectiveness of the program. When we evaluate, we measure the actual status of the problem and estimate what the status would have been without the program, using a control group, if possible, to make the estimate.

Although accuracy in planning and effectiveness of the program are related, the concepts are quite different, and the differences should be understood. Effectiveness refers to the extent to which specified objectives are attained as a consequence of program activity. Accuracy in planning refers to degree of correspondence between two estimates of what would happen to the problem if no program were undertaken. The two estimates are made at different points in time: the first before, and the second after, operation of the program. We use baseline data and expert judgment to make the first estimate and, if possible, control groups for the second estimate.

Since decisions to undertake or not to undertake programs at various levels of resource allocations are always based on estimates of what would happen without a program, it is important that health planners progressively increase their accuracy in planning. This can only be done by specifying each estimate for the future during the planning stage, checking the estimates against reality during evaluation, and then feeding that information back into the planning process.

Let us consider a hypothetical example (see chart) to illustrate the relationship between planning and evaluation. The top portion of the chart depicts a planning period. Point A represents the baseline status of the problem, point B represents the estimate of what the size of the problem would be if no program were undertaken, and point C represents the anticipated status of the problem if a program were undertaken. At D and E the status of the problem is estimated, given different levels of resource allocations or approaches to the problem that may have emerged from cost-benefit analyses, a computer simulation, or some other quantitative analysis. Assume that point C has been selected as the objective of the program. This means both that we want the absolute level of C to be at a particular point and that we wish to reduce the problem by the amount B minus C.

The bottom portion of the chart shows the results of an actual evaluation. Point C is determined by measuring the group exposed to the program, and point B is estimated by measuring a control group not exposed to the program or by some other method, several of which will be mentioned later. It can be seen that the absolute size of the problem following the program is lower than anticipated, but it is also evident that less change was produced than had been desired. That is, the actual difference between B and C is less than the difference planned between B and C. Looking merely at the absolute attained level of C gives cause for celebration, but looking at the difference between B and C gives cause for concern. Planning was not very accurate. When it is possible to make these various estimates, evaluation can contribute most to subsequent planning.

The typical but incorrect norm in evaluating the program is a before-and-after analysis; conditions at the time of evaluation are compared with conditions existing before the program. These two measures say little about the effect of the program itself. As shown in the chart,

CHART
Hypothetical Example of Relationship Between
Planning and Evaluation

Planning estimates

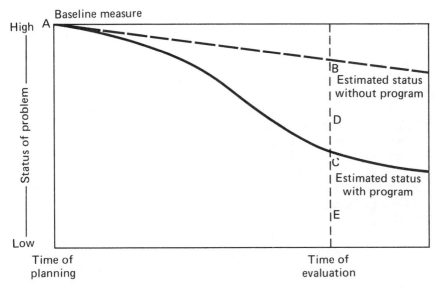

Evaluation findings

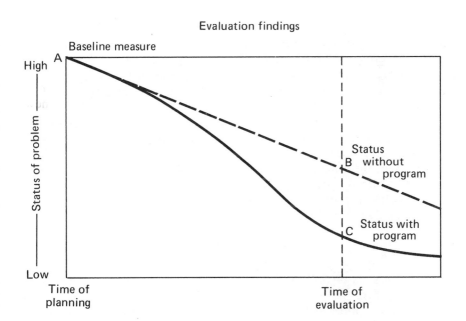

conditions might have improved without a program or they might have deteriorated. In one of our studies on food sanitation (9), conditions in restaurants that were inspected were worse at the end than at the beginning of a year; however, our analysis indicated considerable positive effect from the program. Without the program, conditions would have deteriorated far more than they did. A simple before-and-after analysis would have indicated a negative effect of the program.

Considerable attention has been given to estimating conditions at the time of evaluation had there been no program. We know that control groups provide the best estimates. Unfortunately, a classic experimental design often cannot be applied in real settings of programs; we cannot assign clients to treatment and nontreatment groups at random. Campbell and Stanley (10) have described a series of quasi-experimental designs that can be used for making this estimate. Most of these designs include measures of some group that is composed of persons not exposed to the program but who are believed to be similar in other important respects.

Circumstances often provide a basis for making this estimate even when none could be planned and built into the design for an evaluation. In the program for food sanitation, a staff vacancy that could not be filled and the subsequent lack of service to one district were the bases for estimating what would have happened without the program. In evaluating the housing for agricultural migrants (11), inadvertent failure to provide inspectional services to all housing areas during the first year of the program was the basis for the estimate.

Although the literature on research design devotes much attention to the problem of estimating how much of an apparent effect results from the procedures in the program rather than from other causes, not as much has been written about how one goes about estimating future status while planning. Where the data are available over a considerable span of time, trend analysis can be performed. This procedure is useful for new programs, but if a routine program has been operating for some time, trend analysis is of little help in estimating what the conditions would have been in the absence of a program.

Perhaps the attention now being given to formal planning in universities and planning agencies will develop techniques for making such estimates. Or, if program operators begin to use the concept of accuracy in planning, additional methodologies may be developed.

Summary

A program is an organized response to eliminate or reduce one or more problems where the response includes one or more objectives, performance of one or more activities, and expenditure of resources.

Five foci have been identified for evaluation of the program. For appropriateness, were the proper values used to select the problem? For effectiveness, to what extent were objectives attained? For adequacy, how much of the total problem was eliminated? For efficiency, at what costs were the objectives attained? And for side effects, what outcomes occurred that were not central to the objectives of the program?

Programs are always evaluated, but the evaluations vary as to whether the measures are presumptive or direct and the degree to which the measures are impressionistic or objective. Valid and objective measures of program goals make it possible to assess a program systematically. Ideally, we should compare the actual status at the time of the evaluation with the status that would have existed had there been no program.

In the process of setting objectives, one should not only specify the desired amount of change but also the absolute level expected. If both estimates are specified when the program is being planned, subsequent evaluation can reveal both the extent to which an intended amount of change has occurred and also the accuracy of the planning estimates. When the findings are fed back into the planning process they should have the effect of increasing both the effectiveness of the program and the accuracy of planning.

References

(1) Weekworth, E.: On evaluation: A tool or a tyranny. Presented at annual meeting of the American Public Health Association, Philadelphia, Nov. 12, 1969.

(2) Jackson, J.: Some issues in evaluating programs. Hospital and Community Psychiatry 18: 161–168, June 1967.

(3) Neal, F. W.: Doctors, dilemmas, data and decisions. Presented at a training institute on Program Evaluation in Mental Health Services, Portland, Oregon, Oct. 24, 1966. Mimeographed.

(4) Deniston, O. L., Rosenstock, I. M., and Getting, V. A.: Evaluation of program effectiveness. Public Health Reports 83: 323–335, April 1968.

(5) Stanley, D. T.: Excellence in the public service: How do you really know? Public Administration Review 24: 170–174, September 1964.

(6) Committee on Administrative Practice: Appraisal form for city health work. American Public Health Association, New York, 1925.

(7) Committee on Administrative Practice: Evaluation schedule for use in the study and appraisal of community health programs. American Public Health Association, New York, 1943.

(8) Committee on Administrative Practice: Grading standards for A.P.H.A. evaluation schedule. American Public Health Association, New York, 1950.

(9) Deniston, O. L., and Welch, W.: Evaluation of performance of a food sanitation program. Journal of Milk Food Technology 32: 115–121, April 1969.
(10) Campbell, D. T., and Stanley, J. C.: Experimental and quasi-experimental designs for research. In Handbook of research on teaching. Rand McNally, Chicago, 1963.
(11) Deniston, O. L.: Migrant camp conditions improved by inspection. Journal of Environmental Health 31: 338–346, January–February 1969.

IV

PROGRAM DESIGN: PPB STRUCTURE AND INFORMATION REQUIREMENTS

9

Establishing a Program Structure

PAUL L. BROWN

Purpose

One of the basic purposes underlying a PPB system is an attempt to furnish the most meaningful information to the decision-makers. This includes all people who must make decisions about how functions are carried out. Thus efforts should be made to build a structure that can provide the necessary information for internal administration and result in an improvement in the ability of the governor, the legislature, the press and the general public to understand the budget and the services provided.

An Approach to Classifying Programs

One of the characteristics of PPBS is that it is goal-oriented. It focuses on the fundamental purposes for which government should exist and then relates all activities to one of these fundamental purposes. One of the first

Excerpted from "An Operational Model for a Planning-Programming-Budgeting System," a paper presented to the Post Audit Seminar, Lexington, Kentucky (July 17, 1970), pp. 3–6, 12–24, by permission of the author.

problems that must be faced is how to define these fundamental purposes. Some advocate stating the broad governmental purpose first and then identifying all the efforts that should be undertaken to fulfill that purpose. Others propose to start at the bottom and group all existing activities by some functional arrangement until they are all accounted for in terms of some stated objectives. The proponents of the top-to-bottom approach express their concern that the "bubble-up" approach contains the inherent danger that each administrative subdivision will continue its traditional activities without challenge or change. This is a very real danger. However, I find some real problems of application in a methodology that works exclusively from the top down. For example, the Committee for Economic Development in its publication *Budgeting for National Objectives* recommends that the broad goals and objectives be stated and that agency activities be regularly subjected to a searching review to see that they conform to broad goals and government objectives. That committee developed definitions for several program levels. I tried working with some of the definitions and found it extremely difficult to arrive at very meaningful statements. For example, in Table 1 I have attempted to apply the definitions to the general area of education.

What disturbs me about this broad approach from the top down is that many of these definitions become almost truisms. They have to be refined through several levels before they become meaningful for im-

TABLE 1
Definitions of the Committee on Economic
Development Applied to Education

Definition	*Use for education*
1. Goal: Statements of highly desirable conditions toward which society should be directed.	1. Everyone should be given the opportunity to be educated to the highest level of their capability to learn.
2. Objectives: The stated purpose of an organization or individual capable of planning and taking action to gain intended ends.	2. To educate everyone to the highest level of their capability to learn.
3. Programs: Time-phased plans for allocating resources and for specifying the successive steps required to achieve the stated objectives.	3. Identify operations for elementary, secondary, vocational and higher education.
4. Program Objectives: The specific results to be attained by the planned commitment of resources.	4. To provide higher (or elementary or vocational as the particular program warrants) educational opportunities for all.

mediate budgetary or operational purposes. These immediate purposes are areas in which we must make decisions today. We do not have the luxury of declaring a moratorium for three to five years until a new structure can be developed and refined. Maybe it is more proper to speak in broader global terms on the national level, but many state programs are already homogeneous entities which just need proper identification for ease in categorization, and a workable program structure could be established. I see more of a payoff in concentrating initial attention at a lower level of activity than the goals and objectives of government.

I am not convinced that a proper description of the objective cannot be started at an intermediate level, be properly evaluated, measured, and combined with statements for higher levels to reach a unified goal which can then be evaluated and worked back down. In this way objectives and subobjectives could be formulated, and perhaps better measurements could be developed more rapidly. The measurements would be designed to answer such questions as what is to be accomplished, who is the target population, how much change is desired, when and where is the outcome expected, and what information must be generated to determine just how effectively the stated purpose for carrying on an activity is being fulfilled? I do not wish to imply that the broad goals and objectives should be ignored. Indeed, they should not be. I am merely offering an alternative approach which is more workable in the short run and should result in essentially the same structure in the long run. I think my approach has the added benefit of being able to utilize some of the PPBS methodology for today's decisions as we go along.

Thus, by way of getting started on the development of a PPB system, at least at the state level, I subscribe to starting an analysis at the departmental level rather than at the "role of government" level. The final application is going to take a number of years and there is little danger that the major activities of a department are going to be terminated in the near future. For example, workable alternatives to operating educational institutions and mental hospitals will have to be developed if indeed there are alternatives. Therefore, for the time being, I suggest a concentration of attention on the role these major programs play in meeting our society's needs, how effective they are in these roles, and the relationships of their programs to each other.

Developing the Rationale for Defining Programs

Identifying the basic programs carried on by the state and determining what operations should be included in the programs is no easy task. Operations can be structured many different ways. It is necessary to develop a systematic approach that can be easily understood and universally applied. To accomplish this project the director of the Office of Budget and Management released an analyst from all other duties, assigned him as project director to plan, coordinate and direct the conversion, and provided a full-time systems analyst to aid in the design and control of forms and their related data flow systems. The professional budget analysts in the Bureau were then made part of the team. This approach enabled the project to gain the advantage of the ideas of all the members of the staff and yet provided unity of direction and decision-making. With this organizational approach we found we were able to move very rapidly, converting the entire state to a program budget in less than a year.

The initial responsibility of this team was to study and define:

1. Just exactly what is program budgeting?
2. What are its objectives?
3. Can conversion be accomplished on a mass basis or must it be a gradual development over a period of years?

The purposes of program budgeting have been stated in a variety of ways. Perhaps the shortest, but probably one of the clearest, is that of Mosher in his book, *Program Budgeting: Theory and Practice with Particular Reference to the U.S. Department of the Army.* He states, "The program budget should be designed to furnish the most meaningful information for top administrative and political review" (p. 237).

Designing a program budget with this objective in mind makes the task one of analyzing the information needs of governmental decision-making. The underlying assumption behind this statement is that the way material is presented to the governor and the legislature significantly influences the kind of decisions they will make. It is assumed if we present detail they tend to make decisions on detail. If we present program data identifying major policy issues they tend to make decisions on policy. This no doubt seems overly obvious, yet most of the arguments we have received have been that no matter how well we develop the format, the decision-maker won't feel comfortable until he has gotten down to something small that he can understand more easily, and therefore, the whole concept of improving decision-making is fallacious. Certainly we cannot be 100 percent effective, for old habits and individual differences exist, but we feel we have improved the decision-making significantly.

Our view was that the first responsibility of the central budget office was to develop and present a synthesis of agency plans which would enable the constitutional intent of control of governmental activity by elected representatives to be implemented. We felt that all appropriations had to be built and all programs had to be defined with this end in mind. Convenience for agency administrators, the central budget office, or the central accounting agency should certainly be considered, but definitely, it should be subordinated to one of the basic needs of effective democratic government. We feel that one of those basic needs is the final determination of policy by elected representatives responsible to their electorate. This concept, that our budget format or synthesis should be a format which would best enable the governor and the legislature to make effective policy decisions on planned governmental programs, became our criterion for developing a program definition rationale.

The first thing we noted in developing a rationale for defining programs was that our appropriation structure did not conform to the general areas or units within which agencies planned their programs. The budget was not a formulation of agency plans, but rather a mechanical exercise in which the agencies took the dollar formulation of plans and recategorized the dollars according to the often meaningless appropriation accounts of the budget. The budget had become a reformulation of the dollars rather than a dollar formulation of the plans. The key policy decisions on planned programs were made prior and external to the budget formulation. As a result important policy decisions often lay buried in the mass of detail characteristic of the line-item budget.

Our solution to the problem was to attempt to find a program definition rationale which would define programs according to the categories and framework within which agencies planned. Appropriations could then be made to carry out these plans. We noted that agencies, especially the larger welfare and educational agencies, plan in two basic ways. They construct, sometimes very informally, long-range goals or plans based on growth, decline, or change in the nature of the population being served. Often cost per unit formulas are used to project the fiscal effect of change in the group to be served. It is here that many major policy issues are decided, that is, what groups or what percent of each group will be served, or what projections of growth, decline or change in the population will be assumed correct? It was important that our program structure would enable us to include and express these plans. We also noted, however, that these long-term program plans are translated into short- and long-range operational plans which correspond roughly to organizational units or subunits. Most of the remaining policy decisions are made here, that is, what will be the best administrative technique for serving this group, and what geographical area will we serve? We felt that our program definition should enable us to include and express these operational plans, for it is usually in these organizational units that the detail of a budget originates.

We also wanted our program definition to facilitate coordination and synthesis between programs of different agencies. We hoped to be able to prepare and present "policy plans" on the demand of the chief executive. For example, it would be much easier for the chief executive to prepare a synthesized package plan to eliminate water pollution if the budget were expressed in planned programs that could identify the overall efforts in water pollution abatement. In effect a plan could be based and constructed around a policy—the elimination of water pollution. We felt that ease of synthesis could only be achieved if we developed a common language for all programs which could be used by all.

Thus, our basic criterion for a program definition rationale was whether it enabled every agency to define its programs according to the categories and framework within which they planned. This would enable us to present to the governor and the legislature planned programs and the policies inherent in them translated into the language of dollars. Our subcriteria which implemented the above goal were that the definition rationale should:

1. Enable agencies to express the policies inherent in their long-range program plans based on projections of changes in the population to be served (numbers, composition, and the like).

2. Enable agencies to express the policies inherent in the operational, organizational plans.

3. Enable the budget office to synthesize plans of separate agencies into comprehensive programs or plans implementing a specific policy.

The basic rationale that was developed for defining programs centered attention on what service a legitimate state activity provides and who is to receive these services. The most important advantage of this rationale is the estimation of total impact of the services being provided for any particular clientele. Such an approach bridges the two basic orientations, the inner direct "what," with the outer directed "for whom." The concept, simple as it sounds, is an innovation in budgeting, making it conform to the realities of political allocation of resources.

Thus, we had developed a common language for program definition which we called the *what, for whom* and *how* program definition. Briefly, this definition involves taking an agency's operations and asking, "What are you doing?"; after this question has been answered, we ask, "For whom are you doing it?" This gave us a basic program definition, and one which was easy to follow.

After we had the basic program identified, we needed to get more specific and identify program sublevels. For the first sublevel we again used the same "what for whom" rationale, but added the ingredient of asking "what more specifically is done" or "for whom more specifically is it done?" After the "what for whom" had been answered for two levels of program operation, the next question was "how are you doing it?" For example, what administrative techniques or activities are performed to carry out the services? This original approach has now been refined to use a basic building block, the program element, which is described below.

The next determination that is prompted by the information on how you are doing something is "how well are you doing it?"—that is, how well are you performing each one of these activities of community services, institutional treatment, and so forth? We had to draw a practical line somewhere on the extent of our conversion. As I mentioned before, we decided to convert the entire state in one conversion process because the time was opportune. We wanted to go as far as necessary to get a program budget and to get an appropriation structure that conformed to the programs. But since there was the danger of such a major undertaking collapsing under its own weight, we decided to stop with "how" and not go immediately into "how well."

The distinction between "how" and "how well" is, in our own language, where program budgeting ends and performance budgeting begins. We felt that it was enough in the initial conversion phase to define the major services being provided and how they were carried out, and that later, following the conversion to program budgeting, we could more scientifically identify "how well they were doing something" by the development of performance information on how extensive, how efficient, or how effective a program was operated. We thought we had to make this distinction because "how they were doing something" involved the time-consuming task of identifying the units of accomplishment for all of the sometimes indeterminate programs in state government. As we all know, identifying workload units, identifying the cost, distinguishing the fixed from the variable costs that go into these work units, is a time consuming process. We felt that in using mass conversion techniques we had to postpone the performance element at this time and just define the major program areas.

Successful operation of a program budget requires a very careful definition of the programs and program sublevels carried out by a state agency. Programs are the basis for appropriations, and it is most important that programs and other breakdowns be defined so as to produce the most effective appropriation structure. All efforts put into a careful definition of programs will be rewarded with a successful appropriation structure in the years to come.

Wisconsin's Basic Program Structure

The basic concept of our program budget is to relate costs of government activity to services provided. This concept established our approach to grouping agency services. The Wisconsin program structure consists of a grouping of the basic units of governmental operations, starting with the most general and proceeding to the most specific. It includes the following general categories:

1. Functional Areas
2. Programs
3. Subprograms
4. Activities

Following is an explanation of these basic units with specific examples of how agency programs are classified in terms of these units.

1. *Functional Areas.* A program structure of state government should outline the basic purposes of state government and should be divided into program areas which are broadly encompassing and self-contained, yet easily definable in relation to each other. Each functional area has a purpose, goal or end product which is intrinsically different from those of other functional areas.

Wisconsin functions have been categorized as follows:

Commerce
Education
Environmental Resources
Human Relations and Resources
General Executive Functions

2. *Programs.* The major functional areas are in turn divided into programs carried out by state agencies. In the context of the program budget structure, programs are defined as: "A broad category of similar services for an identifiable group or segment of the population for a specific purpose." Programs are thus defined in terms of what services are provided for a group with similar disabilities, needs or attributes, or "What is done for whom?" For example, in our public instruction department one program we have identified is:

What	*For Whom*
Education and Related Services	Handicapped Children

3. *Subprograms.* Subprograms are defined as "A breakdown of the

program into units which identify more specific services or a more specific segment of the population."

Programs are thus categorized into subprograms to the point where the subprograms defined serve a more specific group because it has only one basic disability, attribute or need, or "What for whom more specifically." For example, in the major program of (What) Education and Related Services for (Whom) Handicapped Children, the term handicapped identifies a group with broadly similar attributes. However, this group can be divided into subprograms because there are meaningful groups served within the general category of handicapped children. They are distinguishable because they have a more specific disability or attribute than "handicapped." For example:

What	*For Whom*
Program I: Education and Related Services	Handicapped Children

What	*For Whom* *(more specifically)*
Subprogram A: Education and Related Services	Crippled Children
Subprogram B: Education and Related Services	Visually Handicapped Children
Subprogram C: Education and Related Services	Deaf Children

This identification of subprograms should make it possible to divide the program to the degree that the group served has a reasonably homogeneous disability or attribute. The decision-maker can now decide on the allocation of resources among competing groups.

Further categorization into subsubprograms is unnecessary. A further breakdown of Educational and Related Services for Visually Handicapped Children into services to the slightly blind, moderately blind, and totally blind is meaningless to those who are attempting to make a policy decision, for it would be based on the degree of disability not a kind of disability. The degree of disability does not identify an actually distinct interest group. More value will be gained by concentrating on the administrative techniques which accommodate the individual needs of the persons with the group which has a basic disability, such as being visually handicapped.

4. *Activities.* Activities have been defined as: "the administrative techniques employed to carry out the programs." Subprograms would, therefore, be broken down into the activities which illustrate *how* the service is performed for the group. For example:

What	*For Whom*
Program I. Education and Related Services	Handicapped Children

What	*For Whom* *(more specifically)*
Subprogram A. Education and Related Services	Crippled Children

How
Activity 1. Orthopedic Hospital Services
Activity 2. Financial Aids to Individuals
Activity 3. Aids to Orthopedic Schools
Activity 4. Transportation Aids

What	*For Whom* (more specifically)
Subprogram B. Education and Related Services	Visually Handicapped Children

How
Activity 1. Resident Instruction
Acitvity 2. Aids to Special Classes

MODIFICATIONS OF THE STRUCTURE

In the general approach and examples cited above, subprograms constitute a further clarification of the group (Whom), while the services (What) remained constant. This approach will be applicable to many programs, especially those in the health and welfare functions. In some cases, however, the group already constitutes a homogeneous group, and the most meaningful further breakdown would be a clarification of the type of service or the means by which it is accomplished. Following are some potential methods of developing meaningful breakdowns under these circumstances:

1. When a variety of related services is performed for one homogeneous group it may be more meaningful to define subprograms by more specific statements of "what" is done rather than more specific statements of "for whom" it is done. The Department of Administration is an example of meaningful subprograms being more specific breakdowns of "what is to be done." It might be classified as follows:

What	*For Whom*
Program I. Administrative Services	All State Agencies

What (more specifically)	*For Whom* (assumed the same)
Subprogram A. Accounting Services	

    B. Architectural and Engineering Services
    C. Budget and Management Services
    D. Data Processing Services
    E. Operational Services
    F. Personnel Services
    G. Printing Services
    H. Property Management
    I. Purchasing Services
    J. State Planning Services

2. In some circumstances, both the services (What) and the group for whom it is performed (Whom) already constitute a reasonably homogeneous unit. In these cases it may be most meaningful to break down the program immediately into activities, instead of further clarifying the services or the group. A good example is civil defense operations. It is a single type of service and it is performed for everyone in the state. Civil defense might, therefore, most meaningfully be divided into the "hows" (activities) of administrative techniques.

What   *For Whom*
Program I. Preparation for Disasters   (everyone implied)

How
Activities   A. Shelter Development
              B. Food and Clothing Storage
              C. Storage of Medicines
              D. Transportation Planning
              E. Communications Development
              F. Monitoring Radio Activity
              G. Training of Emergency Personnel
              H. Administration

Caution must be exercised in the use of this approach of immediately categorizing programs into activities instead of further clarifying the service or the group for whom the service is performed. Program budgets are aimed at assisting the governor and legislature in making policy decisions on the type of state services and the level to be provided for the recipient of the services. Seldom do the governor and legislature make policy decisions about the administrative means of providing services. This last approach of immediately categorizing programs by administrative techniques should be used only when it is clear that further clarification of the group or the service is completely without meaning to the governor and the legislature.

FURTHER BASIC CONSIDERATIONS

As an agency's operations are reviewed there is no uniform level of development which should be sought. In some cases, a program identification may be all that is desired. In other cases, it may be advisable to break out the activities into subclassifications. Basically we should be attempting to construct an overall structure that will enable us to identify and consider the lowest program sublevel that is presented as an autonomous building block that we can consider as a program element. Around this program element we should attempt to define the basic purpose of this element; determine what kind of performance indicators need to be developed to assess the adequacy of the program to carry out that basic purpose; and include this element as an identifiable entity in our accounting system, our reporting systems, our statistical systems, etc.

One of the primary advantages in the identification of these basic building blocks is the ability to develop a broader executive program budget which makes it possible to identify major problem areas and/or specific target groups served by related programs in separate agencies. An example of this type of executive program budget might be in the area of recreation. Today, we may not have any program which we would formally identify to focus on recreation. However, there are several activities which we are carrying on which pertain to recreation. Such activities appear, for example, under hunting and fishing, game management, parks, forests, and open-area development. We also might want to identify other areas of concern which we should be preparing to meet. An area to consider could be educating people on how to use an increased amount of leisure time that will develop through shorter working weeks, earlier retirement, and so forth.

A fully developed program structure should enable us to pull out all of these activities that are related to a specific executive program budget that we might want to develop; line them up; determine what basic purpose each of these activities is designed to serve; determine how effectively they are meeting this basic purpose; and determine whether or not the purposes of the various activities are in conflict or whether the administrative techniques used to carry out the activities are in conflict. If it is decided that the program is important enough to warrant making it a special program, we could then pull these basic building blocks out of the various programs and assign them to a new program. However, if we did not care to alter the program structure we could still pull them out for informational purposes to look at them in a different context or a different frame of reference. Consequently, our attention must be directed toward defining the rationale that will enable us to properly identify these program elements. Proper identification is necessary to insure that these elements are really the building blocks around which we want to concentrate our efforts in building our management information systems.

10

Criteria for Evaluation in Planning State and Local Programs

HARRY P. HATRY

Section I. The Criteria Problem

A major part of a program planning process is the attempt to estimate the contribution that each alternative program, or mix of programs, makes toward meeting fundamental governmental objectives. For the purpose of this paper, the terms "goals", "aims", "purposes", "missions", or "functions" may be substituted for "objectives." The need for evaluation criteria arises because funds and physical resources are scarce; there are not enough available to satisfy all needs and proposals. (The term "measures of effectiveness" is sometimes used by analysts instead of "criteria.") Thus the problem of choice arises, and evaluation of pro-

Reprinted from U.S., Congress, Senate, Subcommittee on Intergovernmental Relations of the Committee on Governmental Operations, *Criteria for Evaluation in Planning State and Local Programs* (Washington, D.C.: U.S. Government Printing Office, July 21, 1971), by permission of the author. Footnotes have been renumbered.

posals is needed to make the best use of available resources. To perform this evaluation, it is necessary to identify specific criteria that can be used to evaluate performance against the governmental objectives.[1]

For example, if a governmental objective such as "to reduce crime" was identified, then it would be appropriate to use crime rates as the major criterion (but not necessarily the only criterion) for evaluating activities aiming at these objectives. That is, in comparisons between various proposals, each proposal's effect upon the anticipated future crime rates would need to be estimated.

As the example indicates, the selection of criteria depends upon the objectives that are formulated. Also the process of selecting the criteria will often suggest the need for revision of the objectives. Thus, the establishing of objectives and criteria are interacting processes. In this paper, the emphasis is on criteria; objectives are discussed and presented only briefly. Ideally, a thorough discussion of state and local government objectives would be undertaken first.

An important characteristic of both "objectives" and "criteria" as used in this paper is that they are intended to be "end" oriented rather than "means" oriented. That is, they are intended to reflect what is ultimately desired to be accomplished and for whom, not ways to accomplish such objectives.

For example, the phrase, "to disperse cultural facilities rather than concentrating them in a single locality" is a means "to provide adequate cultural opportunities to all." Use of the former phrase as the statement of objective rather than the latter would lead to somewhat different criteria, such as "the number of cultural facilities." Program analysis would better compare dispersal programs with centralized programs as alternative means to providing adequate cultural opportunities.

Also, the concept of objectives as used in this paper avoids inclusion of specific numerical magnitudes. For example, a statement of objectives such as "to reduce crime rates 10 percent," should be avoided. For program analysis it is seldom appropriate to prespecify magnitudes. The specific amount of improvement that should be sought should generally not be determined until after the alternatives have been evaluated as to the costs and benefits of each and after these tradeoffs are understood.

The criteria for program analyses ideally should have the following general properties:

(1) Each criterion should be relevant and important to the specific problem for which it is to be used. (This will depend upon the fundamental objectives to be satisfied.)

(2) Together the criteria used for a specific problem should consider all major effects relative to the objectives. Enough criteria should be

evaluated to cover all major effects. The use of insufficient criteria can be very misleading.

For example, programs to improve housing conditions should in general consider not only the number of acres of slums removed but also the effects upon the persons removed (perhaps by including a second criterion: the number of persons still living in sub-standard dwelling units).

Although it would make the evaluation considerably easier to have only one criterion, or at least very few criteria, the important thing is to avoid excluding major considerations from an analysis.

As indicated in the previous example, probably any single objective if emphasized too much without considering other needs could lead to excesses and result in even worse conditions. Other examples are: sole consideration of safety in moving traffic could result in excessive trip delay times; in the law enforcement area, sole concentration on crime rates might lead to programs that result in excess control of individual movement.

With all the criteria expressed in terms of one unit (such as the dollar) or two units (such as the dollar and some nonmonetary unit), neat, analytically optimizable solutions would usually be possible. However, forcing the analysis into oversimplified forms may hide many major considerations. Use of multiple evaluation criteria seems, in general, to be unavoidable.

(3) Each of the criteria ideally should be capable of meaningful quantification. This involves two major problems. The first is the measurement of the current and historical magnitudes of each of the criteria. This measurement is needed to give a clear picture of the magnitudes of the problem, to determine how well the jurisdiction is actually doing toward meeting its objectives, and to provide a basis for making projections into the future.

For the housing example used above we would want to be able to measure how many acres of slums and how many people are living in substandard dwelling units there currently are, and how many were living in such units previously.

The second problem is the estimation of the future magnitudes for these criteria for each of the alternative programs being considered. Projecting into the future is always hazardous. One of the most, if not the most, difficult problems in program analysis is the estimation of the effects on the criteria of the various courses of action. Historical data are important both for measuring progress and for making inferences as to what has caused any changes that have occurred. This latter information is very important for preparing estimates of the effects of future courses of action.

In practice, it is very difficult, and probably impossible, to meet perfectly all three of these ideal properties of criteria. The list in section III is a first attempt to identify the major criteria that are likely to be pertinent for governmental programs. An explicit attempt has been made to make the list conform with the first two properties (that is, relevancy and coverage) given above for ideal criteria. However, the list is certainly far from definitive in either depth or coverage. It is also somewhat idealistic; the analysts' ability to estimate meaningfully the effects of alternative program upon the criteria (the third property given above) will undoubtedly be limited in many instances—particularly with current information systems.

On occasion, it may be necessary to utilize purely qualitative criteria, such as, "In reducing crime, alternative A is more effective than alternative B but less effective than C." This ranking procedure might be partially quantified by having experts apply their judgments to some type of ranking scale. This would result in such a result as, "In reducing crime, alternative A has a value of 80 on the specially prepared ranking scale, B has a value of 65 and C a value of 85."

Thus in practice, even though criteria are not completely capable of being satisfactorily quantified, criteria that have the other two properties may still be useful.

The list of criteria in section III is hoped to be a reasonable starting point from which individual governments would develop a sound set of criteria appropriate to their own specific problems and governmental objectives. Many of these criteria are already in use. For an individual problem, the analysts will need to determine the specific criteria appropriate to that problem. The list in section III may help to suggest the appropriate ones. Each interested reader is encouraged to think through and work out what he feels to be an improved list.

With few exceptions, only nonmonetary criteria are listed in this paper. It is assumed that, in general, all problems will need to consider the actual monetary effects of each alternative course of action proposed. That is, one objective in all problems will be to keep monetary costs as low as possible for any level of program effectiveness aimed for. However, it is a premise of this paper that in the past too much emphasis has been placed upon attempting to translate all program effects into dollar terms. It is true that if this could be done meaningfully, the evaluation of alternative and final program selection would be eased considerably since the quantitative evaluations would all be expressed in the same unit—the dollar.

Realistically most governmental problems involve the major objectives of a nondollar nature. Not only is it very difficult for analysts to assign dollar "values" to such nondollar objectives, but it is also questionable whether it would be desirable even if it could be done. Thus, questions of the value of such effects as reducing death rates, reducing illness incidences and severities, improving housing conditions, and increasing recreational opportunities should not become simply a problem of estimating the dollar values of these things. The analysts should rather concentrate upon the estimation and presentation, for each alternative, of full information as to the actual dollar effects and the effects upon the nonmonetary criteria. This is the primary function of program analysis— and of "cost effectiveness," "cost benefit," "cost utility," or "systems analysis," terms which for the purpose of this paper are all assumed to be equivalent. Attempts to force the criteria into commensurability are in most cases not worth much effort. It should be left to the decisionmakers to provide the value judgments needed to make the final program decisions.[2]

Section III. Illustrative List of Criteria for the Evaluation of Proposed Programs

I. PERSONAL SAFETY[3]

Objective: To reduce the amount and effects of external harm to individuals and in general to maintain an atmosphere of personal security from external events.

A. Law enforcement.
Objective: To reduce the amount and effects of crime and in general to maintain an atmosphere of personal security from criminal behavior. (To some persons the punishment of criminals may be an important objective in itself as well as a means to deter further crimes.)
1. Annual number of offenses for each major class of crime (or reduction from the base in the number of crimes).
2. Crime rates, as for example, the number per 1,000 inhabitants per year, for each major class of crime.
3. Crime rate index that includes all offenses of a particular type (e.g., "crimes of violence" or "crimes against property"), perhaps weighted as to seriousness of each class of offense.
4. Number and percent of populace committing "criminal" acts during the year. (This is a less common way to express the magnitude of the crime problem; it is criminal oriented rather than "crime oriented.")
5. Annual value of property lost (adjusted for price level changes).

This value might also be expressed as a percent of the total property value in the community.

6. An index of overall community "feeling of security" from crime, perhaps based on public opinion polls and/or opinions of experts.

7. Percent of reported crimes cleared by arrest and "assignment of guilt" by a court.

8. Average time between occurrence of a crime and the apprehension of the criminal.[4]

9. Number of apparently justified complaints of police excesses by private citizens, perhaps as adjudged by the police review board.

10. Number of persons subsequently found to be innocent who were punished and/or simply arrested.

Notes

(a) Criteria 1 through 6 are criteria for the evaluation of crime prevention programs. Criteria 7 and 8 are aimed at evaluating crime control after crimes have occurred (i.e., when crime prevention has failed). Criteria 9 and 10 and to some extent 6 aim at the avoidance of law-enforcement practices that themselves have an adverse effect upon personal safety. Criterion 6 and to some extent 8 aim at indicating the presence of a fearful, insecure atmosphere in the locality.

(b) Some argue that the primary function of criminal apprehension and punishment is to prevent future crimes; and, therefore, that criteria 7 and 8 would not be sufficiently "end oriented," but rather "means" oriented, and would not be included in the list.

(c) For many analyses it would probably be appropriate to distinguish crime activity by the type of criminal, including such characteristics as age, sex, family income, etc. (juvenile delinquency is an obvious subcategory).

B. Fire Prevention and Firefighting.

Objective: To reduce the number of fires and loss due to fires.

1. Annual number of fires of various magnitudes (to be defined).

2. Fire rates, for example, number per 10,000 inhabitants per year.

3. Annual dollar value of property loss due to fire (adjusted for price level changes).

4. Annual dollar value of property loss due to fire per $1 million of total property value in the locality.

5. Annual number of persons killed or injured to various degrees of seriousness due to fires.

6. Reduction in number of fires, in injuries, in lives lost, and in dollars of property loss from the base. (These are primarily different

forms of criteria 1, 3, and 5 and can be substituted for them.) This reduction might in part be obtained by, for example, drawing inferences from the number of fire code violations (by type) found.[5]

7. Average time required to put out fires from the time they were first observed, for various classes of fires.

Notes

(a) Criteria 1 through 6 are intended for evaluation of fire prevention programs. Criteria 7 and to some extent 3, 4, and 5 can reflect the results of programs which aim at the control of fires after they have started. Criterion 7 also is a proxy for the anxiety related to duration of fires.

(b) It may be appropriate to distinguish among geographical areas within the jurisdiction.

II. HEALTH

Objective: To provide for the physical and mental health of the citizenry, including reduction of the number, length, and severity of illnesses and disabilities.

1. Incidence of illness and prevalence (number and rates).[6] (Armed Forces rates of rejection for health reasons of persons from the jurisdiction could be used as a partial criterion.)

2. Annual mortality rates by major causes and for total population.[7]

3. Life expectancy by age groups.

4. Average number of days of restricted activity, bed confinement, and medically attended days per person per year. (Such terms as "restricted activity" need to be clearly and thoroughly defined. Also, probably more than one level of severity of illness should be identified.)

5. Average number of workdays per person lost due to illness per year.

6. Total and per capita number of school days lost owing to illness per year.

7. Number of illnesses prevented, deaths averted, and restricted-activity days averted per year as compared with the base. This is primarily a different form of such criteria as 1 through 6.

8. Average number of days of restricted activity, of bed confinement and of medically attended days per illness per year.

9. Number and percent of patients "cured" (of specific types of illnesses and various degrees of cure).

10. Some measure of the average degree of pain and suffering per illness. (Though there seems to be no such measure currently in use, some rough index of pain and suffering could probably be developed.)

11. Some measure, perhaps from a sampling of experts and of patients, as to the average amount of unpleasantness (including consideration of the environment in the care area) associated with the care and cure of illnesses.

12. Number or percent of persons with aftereffects, of different degrees, after "cure."

13. Number or percent of persons needing but unable to afford "appropriate health care"—both before receiving public assistance and after including any public assistance received.

14. Number or percent of persons needing but unable to receive "appropriate health care" because of insufficient facilities or services.

15. Some measure of the overall "vigor," the positive health, of the populace, rather than simply the absence of illness—such as "the average per capita energy capacity." Meaningful measures are needed.

Notes

(a) A number of subobjectives can be identified for this major program area. Those subobjectives and the criteria that attempt to measure each are as follows:

1. Prevention of illness—criteria 1 through 7.

2. "Cure" of patient when illness occurs including reduction of its duration—criteria 1 through 9.

3. Reduction of unpleasantness, suffering, anxiety, etc., associated with illness—criteria 10 and 11.

4. Reduction of aftereffects—criterion 12.

5. Making necessary health care available to the "needy"—criteria 13 and 14.

Note, however, that during consideration of the overall problem of health, these subobjectives will often compete with each other. For example, with limited funds, they might be applied to programs aimed primarily at preventing an illness or at reducing its severity (or at some mix of these programs). Also note that criteria 1 through 7 are affected by programs that are directed at curing illnesses as well as those directed at preventing them.

(b) The criteria can be defined to distinguish specific types of illnesses as well as to consider the aggregate effect on individuals of all possible illnesses. For certain problems the incidence of a specific disease may be of concern, whereas for other problems the incidence of illness per person per year, regardless of specific disease, might be the appropriate criterion. One such breakdown which is very likely to be desirable distinguishes mental health from physical health, though even here there will be interactions.

(c) Note that such common measures as "hospital-bed capacity" or "utilization rates of available medical facilities" are not included above since these are not fundamental indicators of the effectiveness of health programs.

(d) As with most of the major program areas, program analyses will need to consider the contributions of other sectors, including private institutions and activities undertaken by other jurisdictions.

(e) The role of governmental jurisdictions may emphasize health services for certain specific target groups such as the needy, and the very young. Therefore, it will frequently be appropriate to distinguish target groups by such characteristics as family income, race, family size, and age group.

(f) To further focus on the positive side of health, in addition to the use of criterion 15, such criteria as 4 might be replaced by such criteria as "average number of healthy days (appropriately defined) per person per year."

III. INTELLECTUAL DEVELOPMENT

Objective: To provide satisfactory opportunities for intellectual development to the citizenry. See also notes *(b)* and *(c)* below.

1. Annual number and percent of persons satisfactorily completing various numbers of years of schooling.

2. Annual number and percent of dropouts at various educational levels.

3. Annual number and percent of each age group enrolled in educational institutions.

4. "Intellectual development attainment" measures, such as performance on various standardized achievement tests at different ages and educational levels.[8] Major educational areas, for example, reading skills, reasoning skills, and general knowledge, might be measured.

5. Performance on the achievement tests indicated in criterion 4 as related to intelligence tests (to indicate attainment relative to capacity).

6. Annual number and percent of students continuing their education at post high-school educational institutions.

7. Participation in selected cultural and civic activities (and perhaps the number of persons who read newspapers, or at least certain parts of them).

Notes

(a) Criteria 1, 2, and 3 emphasize quantity of formal education received. Criteria 4, 5, 6, and 7 attempt to indicate the quality of education received. Since formal education is not the only means to intellectual development, criteria such as 4, 5, and 7 when various age groups are considered should be applied to persons regardless of whether they are in school or not or how much formal education they have had. Criterion 6 also provides some information as to the success of education to stimulate intellectual curiosity. None of the criteria provides much help in measuring the development of individual creativity if it can indeed be developed.

(b) Education not only affects intellectual development but also social development. The above criteria (with the minor exception of 7) fail to measure such things as "social adjustment," "responsible citizenship," and increased "personal pleasure." Such criteria as crime rates, juvenile delinquency rates, including school vandalism, etc., such as are used for major program area I, "personal safety," might be used to draw inferences on certain aspects of social adjustment.

(c) "Education" clearly may be a means to other ends (for example, to lower crime rates) as well as an end in itself. In fact some persons may consider education to be primarily a means to increase future dollar earnings and therefore would consider the above criteria solely as proxy measures for getting at earnings. If so, education programs would better be considered under major program area V, "economic satisfaction and satisfactory work opportunity for the individual." The perspective here is that education and, more broadly, intellectual development, has more than economic value to individuals and society, and is, therefore, an important end in itself. The objectives: to increase earnings, to increase job opportunities and job satisfaction, and to supply needed scarce skills are, in the categorization used in this paper, considered under major program area V. Education programs are some of the means to these ends and in this role would need to be considered in performing such program analyses.

(d) To estimate quality of formal education, frequently such "proxy" indicators are used as "annual expenditures per student," "professional-student ratios," "number of professionals with advanced degrees," "teacher salary levels," etc. These are less direct, lower level criteria than those given above, but nevertheless may be of some use if qualified sufficiently.

(e) The role of government in intellectual development varies considerably among jurisdictions.

(f) It will frequently be appropriate to distinguish target groups by such characteristics as: race, family income level, family size, and sex.

IV. SATISFACTORY HOME AND COMMUNITY ENVIRONMENT[9]

Objective: To provide opportunity for satisfactory living conditions.

A. *Satisfactory homes.*

Objective: To provide opportunities for satisfactory homes for the citizenry, including provision of a choice, at prices they can afford, of decent, safe, and sanitary dwellings in pleasant surroundings.

1. Number and percent of "substandard" dwelling units. More information would be provided by identifying more levels than just two. In any case, "substandard" should be fully defined; the definition should include consideration of crowding, physical deterioration, unsatisfactory sanitation, etc.

2. Number and percent of substandard units eliminated or prevented from becoming substandard. (This is essentially another form of 1.)

3. Acres of blighted areas eliminated and other areas prevented from becoming blighted areas.

4. Total number and percent of persons and families living in substandard dwelling units.

5. Number and percent of persons and families upgraded from one level of housing (for example, "substandard") to a higher level (for example, "standard") or prevented from degrading to a lower level. This is essentially another form of 4.

6. Measure of neighborhood physical attractiveness. (Perhaps *(a)* as indicated by the number of negative conditions estimated by neighborhood inspectors, including adverse physical appearance, excessive noise, lack of cleanliness, offensive odors, excessive traffic, etc.; or *(b)* an index based upon a public opinion poll of persons passing through the neighborhood and/or experts.

7. Measure of neighborhood psychological attractiveness. Perhaps an index based upon a public opinion survey of persons living in the neighborhood and/or experts.

8. Average, and distribution of, property values adjusted for price level changes. Expected changes, from year to year, in property values might also be used as a criterion.

9. Number of fires, other accidents, deaths, and injuries resulting from housing deficiencies.

Notes

(a) Important secondary effects (such as changes in crime and juvenile delinquency rates, in health conditions, in fire problems, and in job opportunities) are likely to result from changes in housing conditions and urban redevelopment. Criteria relating to these effects are included under the other major program areas.

(b) It will frequently be appropriate to distinguish target groups by such characteristics as family income, race, family size, and location.

(c) Criteria 1 through 5 aim at provision of housing, with 4 and 5 probably the most important, since they directly evaluate effects on people rather than things. Criteria 3 and 6 and probably 7 evaluate the physical attractiveness of the neighborhood. Criteria 7 and 8 are attempts at evaluating the overall quality of the housing and living conditions. Criterion 8 is included here rather than under major program area V, economic satisfaction, as a measure of the overall quality of the neighborhood; that is, property values are used as a proxy for the many features contributing to the attractiveness of the property. Criterion 9 measures the safeness of housing.

B. *Maintenance of a satisfactory water supply.*

Objective: To provide sufficient water in adequate quality where and when needed.

1. Water supply capability relative to average and to peak demand.

2. Number of days per year during which water shortages of various degrees occur. (Downtime for repairs should be included.)

3. Measure of "quality of water (e.g., biological oxygen demand and percent of solid waste removed) supplied to homes or businesses. (If waste water is not recycled, the quality of the effluent fed back into streambeds, etc., could be used as a criterion.)

4. Measures of taste, appearance, and odor of water—perhaps based upon such factors as amount of chlorination or upon opinion samplings of water users.

5. Measures of hardness and temperature of water.

6. Annual number of illnesses and other incidents due to low-quality water.

7. Annual number of complaints of water odors due to low-quality water.

Notes

(a) Criteria 1 and 2 are measures of the sufficiency of the quantity of water supplied. Criteria 3 through 7 are measures of the quality.

(b) Each of the quantity measures is also dependent upon the minimum quality level established. That is, more water can generally be supplied if the quality requirements are reduced. Program analysis will need to consider such tradeoffs.

(c) The seasonal and diurnal effects of water supply and demand has to be considered in the analysis.

(d) It may be appropriate to distinguish individual user needs such as water for home consumption, for industrial use, for recreational needs, for irrigation, etc., each of which will have its own quantity and quality characteristics.

V. ECONOMIC SATISFACTION AND SATISFACTORY WORK OPPORTUNITY FOR THE INDIVIDUAL

Objective: To permit each family and each person to meet basic economic-physical needs, while maintaining dignity and self-respect. To permit any employable person desiring employment to obtain satisfactory employment without loss of dignity and self-respect.

1. Annual number and percent of persons or families whose incomes before receiving public assistance placed them in the "poverty" class. More evaluation information. would be provided by identifying more levels than just "poverty" and "not poverty." In any case, "poverty" should be fully defined; the definition should probably take into consideration such factors as family size, ages of persons in the family, location, cost of living, etc. (Note that programs which reduce the cost of living are alternatives to programs which increase income.)

2. Average and distribution of per capita or per family income. (This criterion essentially supplements 1.)

3. Annual number and percent of persons or families whose incomes, considering any public assistance received, still places them in the "poverty" class.

4. Annual number and percent of persons or families whose economic condition is improved through public assistance (preferably further grouped by the amount of total public assistance per person or per family).

5. Some measure of the "standard of living" levels of all residents.

6. Number and percent of persons or families formerly in the "poverty" group that achieve self-sufficiency during the year.

7. Number and percent of persons in job market who are unemployed or underemployed (in terms of number of hours worked).

8. Number of persons previously "unemployed," or who would

become unemployed, who are placed in jobs during the year. (This is essentially another form of criterion 6.)

9. Index of individual job satisfaction, perhaps based upon a sampling of the employed and/or upon expert opinion. Another measure would be the number of persons whose jobs did not appear to match the workers "capacities." Both current capacity as well as "potential" probably should be considered.

Notes

(a) This major program area can be considered to include two major subcategories: "welfare" and "employment" programs. These subcategories are both complementary to and competitive with each other in meeting the objective to achieve overall "economic satisfaction." However, the human need for worthwhile activity is probably not met by welfare but can be by employment. In addition other types of programs, e.g., general education, can contribute to the objectives. (Vocational-oriented education and training are here considered as being one type of "employment" program.)

(b) Criteria 1 through 5 emphasize the evaluation of economic satisfaction (regardless of employment condition) whereas 6 through 9 are work opportunity oriented.

(c) Criterion 9 is needed to measure the extent to which individuals are matched to satisfying, rather than just any, jobs.

(D) It will frequently be appropriate to distinguish target groups by such characteristics as family size, race, and age.

VI. SATISFACTORY LEISURE-TIME OPPORTUNITIES

Objective: To provide year-around, leisure-time opportunities for the citizenry which are accessible, permit variety, are safe, physically attractive, avoid uncomfortable crowdedness, and are in general enjoyable.[10]

1. Number of acres of recreational land of various types per 1,000 population (perhaps as compared to "standards" that may be available). Or for indoor activities, some such measure as the number of square feet, or number of seats, per 1,000 population for each type of activity.

2. Number of percent of "potential users" within, say, one-half mile and/or a 10-minute walk of neighborhood recreational area (note that for some facilities such as large state parks, people who live farther away may account for more use of the facilities than persons living close by.)

3. Number of man-days usage per year for each public leisure-time activity (perhaps related to some usage standards).

4. Ratio of attendance to capacity, during specified critical periods for certain activities (both as a measure of attractiveness and "crowdedness" of the facilities).

5. Number of different leisure-time activities available.

6. Average waiting times, during specified key periods, for use of certain public facilities (such as golf, tennis, and boating) or average requests for attendance turned away such as at concerts, theater shows, etc.

7. Number of accidents in recreational areas related to usage, e.g., per 1,000 man-days usage per year.

8. Number of persons unable or unwilling to take advantage of available leisure-time opportunities who would if they could (categorized by the reason for their disuse of available opportunities).

9. Number of persons who would use currently unavailable leisure-time opportunities if made available.

10. Some measure of overall pleasurableness and sufficiency of leisure-time opportunities, perhaps based upon a public opinion poll sample.

Notes

(a) For many analyses, such criteria as 1, 2, and 5 will need to consider private leisure-time facilities as well as public facilities.

(b) Criteria 1 through 6 and 9 are indicators of whether leisure-time opportunities are provided in sufficient quantity. Criteria 3, 4, and 8 are indicators (unfortunately, indirect ones) of the quality of the opportunities. Criterion 5 aims at measuring the amount of variety available. Criterion 7 measures the safeness of the activities. Criteria 3, 8, and 9 are also indicators of the "pleasurableness" of the opportunities (such things as overcrowdedness are not included in the concept of the term "quality" as used above and therefore "pleasurableness" is also used). Criterion 10 is an overall measure that probably encompasses all of the attributes. Note that except for criterion 10 the criteria do not attempt to measure what is achieved from the leisure-time activities; the degree of pleasure that is derived from each type and quality of activity is not addressed in 1 through 9.

(c) Criteria 8, 9, and 10 will be particularly difficult to measure. Well constructed surveys and polls will probably be needed to provide meaningful information.

(d) Leisure-time opportunities in addition to being considered ends in themselves (to satisfy the human need for recreation and pleasure) are also means to meet other major program area problems such as physical and mental health (major program area II) and crime and delinquency (major program area I). Effects on the criteria in these other program areas, therefore, have to be considered when evaluating leisure time program alternatives.

(e) It may be appropriate to distinguish target groups by such characteristics as age, family income level. (For example, recreational opportunities for the aged, for the poor, and for youth are likely to be of particular concern.)

VII. TRANSPORTATION—COMMUNICATION—LOCATION
(SEE NOTE (a) FOR CLARIFICATION)

Objective: To transport needed amounts and types of "traffic" quickly, safely, and pleasurably.

1. Average time for performing specific tasks. The criterion "average trip time between selected locations" would be an appropriate form of this criteria if only physical transportation systems are being evaluated.

2. Average delay times at selected locations during selected parts of the day, week, and year.

3. Number of passenger miles transported per day and the passenger mile capacity of the system (probably categorized by the different types of transportation systems).

4. Number of transportation accidents, injuries, and deaths per year.

5. Transportation accident, injury and death rates, e.g., per so many passenger miles or per trip.

6. Some measure, or measures, of the overall pleasantness of the travel or of such individual characteristics as physical attractiveness, noise, crowdedness, convenience, and comfort, perhaps indexes based upon a public opinion poll of travelers or opinions of "experts." (A proxy measure such as the average number of trees per mile of road, or the percentage of roadway that is landscaped might be helpful but could be quite misleading if not carefully qualified.)

Notes

(a) This major program area is intended to include all types of systems including communications and locational programs as well as automobile, rail, water, mass transit, and pedestrian physical movement. The former affect the amount of physical transportation required. The term "traffic" is meant to convey the concept of transmission of "messages" as well as physical objects and people. Physical transportation systems may be specific means to transmit messages of certain types but are not the only solution. For example, the function of shopping might be supported by a lengthy transportation system, by originally locating the

shops near the users, or by audiovisual-telephone selection of goods with mass delivery provided by the shops. Thus, programs to avoid the need for physical movement of people or goods may be effective in reducing the overall problem.

(b) This major program area is not really an end in itself. Rather it is a means to satisfy other human needs, such as employment (commuter service), economic progress, accessibility to recreational areas, etc. However, because of its importance in most communities and the need to consider these "transport" systems in an integrated manner, identification as a separate major program area, with its own criteria, seems reasonable. In the evaluation of transport alternatives, however, these basic purposes of transport must be considered. For the same reason, such potential negative effects as air pollution and noise generation must also be considered.

(c) Criteria 1, 2, and 3, attempt to measure the adequacy of the transportation system to move needed traffic and to move it quickly enough. Criteria 4 and 5 measure the safety of the system. Criterion 6 attempts to indicate the pleasurableness content in the system.

(d) It may be appropriate to distinguish user target groups by such characteristics as geographical location; income level; whether the users are commuters, shoppers, leisure-time activity seekers, commercial users, etc.; and whether they are acting as pedestrians, drivers, or passengers, or in other roles.

Appendix

ILLUSTRATIVE PPB SYSTEM GOVERNMENT PROGRAM STRUCTURE

Summary.
  I. Personal safety.
 II. Health (physical and mental well-being).
III. Intellectual development and personal enrichment.
IV. Satisfactory home and community environment.
 V. Economic satisfaction and satisfactory work opportunities for the individual.
VI. Satisfactory leisure-time opportunities.
VII. Transportation-communication-location.
VIII. General administration and support.

Notes
1. This program structure is for illustrative purposes only. Its underlying framework is the identification of the needs of the individual citizen.

2. It is not a complete program structure. More detail is used in some areas than others; many categories have not been subcategorized sufficiently. Each individual government jurisdiction needs to specify the primary governmental objectives of its activities and based upon this formulate its own specific program structure. The lower level program categories particularly are difficult to structure without reference to the specific governmental jurisdiction and its problems.

3. It is highly desirable to have a statement of objectives, in as specific terms as possible, for each element of the program structure.

4. Such activities as planning, research, and experimentation should be included with the program structure category to which they apply. If applicable to a whole program area (i.e., I through VIII above) it might be included under an "unassignable" category as shown below.

5. Categories shown in brackets are those which seem to fall readily into more than one location of the program structure. The brackets indicate the "secondary" location for these categories to avoid double counting when grand totals are prepared.

6. In many cases, it will be appropriate to include subcategories which distinguish particular "target groups." For example, consideration should be given to identification of certain programs by age, race, income level, geographical location, type of disability, etc. One illustration is shown under category IV A. For the most part, however, this program structure does not identify target groups.

7. The lowest level categories, not illustrated here, should identify the specific programs or activities.

I. Personal safety (protection from personal harm and property loss):
   A. Law enforcement (i.e., crime prevention and control):[11]
      1. Crime prevention.
      2. Crime investigation.
      3. Judging and assignment of punishment.
      4. Punishment and safekeeping of criminals.
      5. Rehabilitation of criminals:
         (a) Probation.
         (b) Parole.
         (c) Rehabilitation while confined.
   B. Traffic safety:
      1. Control.
      2. Judging and punishment.
      3. Accident prevention.
   C. Fire prevention and firefighting:
      1. Prevention.
      2. Fighting.

D. Safety from animals.
E. Protection from and control of the natural and manmade disasters:
    1. Civil defense.
    2. Flood prevention and control.
    3. Miscellaneous emergencies/disaster control:
        (a) National Guard.
        (b) Emergency rescue squads.
        (c) Other.
F. Prevention of food and drug hazards, nonmotor vehicle accidents and occupational hazards.
G. Unassignable research and planning, personal safety.
H. Unassignable support, personal safety.
II. Health (physical and mental well-being):[12]
    A. Physical health:
        1. Preventive medical services:
            (a) Chronic diseases.
            (b) Communicable diseases.
            (c) Dental disorders.
            (d) Other.
        2. Treatment and rehabilitation:
            (a) Communicable diseases.
            (b) Dental disorders.
            (c) General.
            (d) Other.
    B. Mental health:
        1. Mental retardation:
            (a) Prevention.
            (b) Treatment and rehabilitation.
        2. Mental illness:
            (a) Prevention.
            (b) Treatment and rehabilitation.
    C. Drug and alcohol addiction prevention and control:
        1. Drug addiction:
            (a) Prevention.
            (b) Treatment and rehabilitation.
        2. Alcohol addiction:
            (a) Prevention.
            (b) Treatment and rehabilitation.
[D. Environmental health, included under IV C through G.]
    E. Other.
    F. Unassignable research and planning, health.
    G. Unassignable support, health.

III. Intellectual development and personal enrichment.[13]
    A. Preschool education.
    B. Primary education:
        1. Education for special groups:
            (a) Handicapped.
            (b) Culturally deprived:
                (1) Tutorial assistance.
                (2) Family orientation.
                (3) Mass media.
        2. General education.
    C. Secondary education.
    D. Higher education:
        1. Junior colleges.
        2. Liberal arts colleges.
        3. Universities.
        4. Specialized professional schools other than 5.
        [5. Medical and dental schools training functions, included under II].
    E. Adult education:
        1. General.
        [2. Adult vocational education, included under V B.]
    [F. Public libraries, included under VI C 2.]
    [G. Museums and historical sites, included under VI C1.]
    [H. Vocational education other than III E 2, included under V B.]
    I. Other.
    J. Unassignable research and planning, intellectual development and personal enrichment.
    K. Unassignable support, intellectual development and personal enrichment.
IV. Satisfactory home and community environment (creation of a livable and pleasant environment for the individual):
    A. Provision of satisfactory homes for dependent persons:
        1. For children.
        2. For youth.
        3. For the aged.
        4. Other dependent persons.
    B. Provision of satisfactory homes for others:
        1. Upgrading existing housing.
        2. Satisfactory supply of homes for low-income persons.
        3. Information and counseling to home dwellers.
        4. Enforcement of housing standards.

        5. Land-use regulation.
   C. Maintenance of a satisfactory water supply:
        1. Water supply.
        2. Water sanitation.
        3. Storm drainage (this category might also be included under I E 2).
   D. Solid waste collection and disposal:
        1. Garbage.
        2. Refuse.
   E. Maintenance of satisfactory air environment (including air pollution control).
   F. Pest control.
   G. Noise abatement.
   H. Local beautification.
    I. Intracommunity relations.
   J. Homemaking aid and information.
   K. Other.
   L. Unassignable research and planning, satisfactory home and community environment.
   M. Unassignable support, satisfactory home and community environment.
 V. Economic satisfaction and satisfactory work opportunities for the individual:
   A. Financial assistance to the needy (other than for homes. which is included in IV B and C):
        1. Aid to the blind.
        2. Aid to the disabled.
        3. Aid to the aged.
        4. Aid to families with dependent children.
        5. Aid to the unemployed (other than above).
        6. Programs to reduce the cost of living.
   B. Increased job opportunity:
        1. Job training.
        2. Employment services and counseling.
        3. Job creation.
        4. Combinations of 1, 2, and 3.
        5. Equal employment opportunity.
        6. Self-employment assistance.
   C. Protection of the individual as an employee.
   D. Aid to the individual as a businessman, including general economic development:
        1. Support for individual industries.

2. General community promotion.
E. Protection of the individual as a consumer of goods and services (other than food and drug hazards contained in II A 1 (c)).
F. Judicial activities for protection of consumers and business-men, alike.
G. Other.
H. Unassignable research and planning, economic satisfaction and satisfactory work opportunities for the individual.
I. Unassignable support, economic satisfaction and satisfactory work opportunities for the individual.
VI. Satisfactory leisure-time opportunities:
  A. Provision of outdoor recreational opportunities:
    1. Parks and open space.
    2. Athletics and playgrounds.
    3. Zoo.
    4. Other.
  B. Provision of indoor recreational opportunities:
    1. Recreation centers.
    2. Other.
  C. Cultural activities:
    1. Museums and historical sites.
    2. Public libraries.
    3. Theaters.
    4. Music activities.
    5. Other.
  D. Leisure time activities specifically for senior citizens.
  E. Other.
  F. Unassignable research and planning, leisure-time opportunities.
  G. Unassignable support, leisure-time opportunities.
VII. Transportation-communication-location[14]
  A. Motor vehicle transport:
    1. Highways.
    2. Streets.
    [3. Traffic safety, included under I B.]
    4. Parking.
  B. Urban transit system.
  C. Pedestrian.
  D. Water transport.
  E. Air transport.
  F. Location programs.

G. Communications substitutes for transportation.

H. Unassignable research and planning, transportation-communication-location.

I. Unassignable support, transportation-communication-location.

VIII. General administration and support:[15]

A. General government management.

B. Financial:

1. Expenditures.

2. Revenues.

3. General.

C. Unassignable purchasing and property management.

D. Personnel services for the government.

E. Unassignable EDP.

F. Legislative.

G. Legal.

H. Elections.

I. Other.

Notes

[1] The term "output measure" is also occasionally used instead of "criteria." However, when "output measure" is used, it often is used to encompass not only program evaluation criteria (the subject of this paper) but also indicators of the size of programs such as the number of cases handled, the number of fire stations, policemen, teachers, hospital beds, etc., which though of considerable interest are not major evaluation criteria in the sense used in this paper.

[2] However, if the analysts can uncover some clues as to the worth that the jurisdiction's public does assign to such nonmonetary criteria, this information should also be provided to the decisionmakers (but not substituted for the basic information on the nonmonetary effects) to assist them in making their judgments. For example, various surveys of the public might give some information as to the degree to which persons currently might be willing to exchange money for changes in the nonmonetary criteria magnitudes. Highway tolls, for example, do indicate that the persons still using the highway are willing to pay at least the price of the toll for the advantages provided by the highway over alternate routes.

[3] Criteria for personal safety are here presented for two subcategories: "Law Enforcement" and "Fire Prevention and Firefighting." Other subcategories could be identified such as "Traffic Safety" (in this paper relevant criteria for traffic issues are included under major program area VII) and "Protection From Natural and Manmade Disasters." The appendix illustrates the particular subcategories that might be included under this, as well as the other, major program areas.

[4] A major purpose of criterion 8 as used in this list is to reflect the psychological reduction in anxiety due to the length of this time period. Note that

it is not the purpose of this or any of these criteria to evaluate the efficiency of the police organization.

[5] From current data on the violations found, estimates could be prepared of the number of additional violations that would be found and corrected if more fire-code inspectors were added. However, the more important (that is, the higher level) criterion is not the number of violations found and corrected but the reduction in the number of fires and in the loss of lives and property. To get to this higher level criterion, estimates would have to be made of the consequences of not finding and correcting such violations. This footnote is included to indicate the kinds of inferences that are likely to be needed in program analyses. Similar situations can be identified for many of the other criteria presented in this list.

[6] Here and in the following material the term "illness" is also intended to cover disability and impairments.

[7] Suicide rates should be included; these are likely to provide some indication of the overall mental health of the community. Note that reducing mortality from certain causes would presumably increase mortality from other causes. Life expectancy, criterion 3, is thus a more important overall criterion.

[8] Armed Forces rejection rates—for intelligence reasons—of persons from the jurisdiction could be used to provide a partial measure.

[9] Two subcategories have been singled out for illustration: "Satisfactory homes" and "maintenance of a satisfactory water supply." Others such as "maintenance of satisfactory air environment," "noise abatement," and "sanitation," can also be identified as subcategories and require selection of appropriate criteria that also help to evaluate home and living conditions.

[10] Both in-door and out-door, and both active and inactive, type activities are to be covered by the criteria.

[11] In addition, programs for juveniles should probably be distinguished from programs for adults. Subcategories for major types of crime might also be appropriate.

[12] Subcategories distinguishing programs for various age groups and for specific diseases would be appropriate. Medical assistance welfare programs should probably be included here as well as under VA (and placed in brackets in one place or the other).

[13] In many cases, neither State, county, nor city governments will control the bulk of the programs and expenditure for education. However, these are of such importance, and interrelate with all other program areas, that it may be advisable to retain this complete category. The jurisdictions would focus upon those areas which they control and those which seem to be neglected and for which government encouragement can be given.

[14] The inclusion of the terms "communication" and "location" are to emphasize the need to consider the broader spatial relationships involved. Thus, the relative location of homes, jobs, and businesses, etc., will have a significant effect upon the transportation and communication systems needed. Such other categories as IV B 5 (land use regulation) will interact with this program area.

Transportation activities predominately concerned with one of the preceding program packages should be assigned to them. For example, park road activities would be included under VI A. Note: Transportation-communication-location is not really an end in itself but rather supports other objectives such as employment (commuter service), economic progress, recreation, etc. However, because of this importance in most communities and the need to consider transportation systems in an integrated manner, identification as a separate major program area seems justified. When evaluating alternatives, the fundamental purposes of transportation should be recognized.

[15]This category contains activities that cannot reasonably be assigned to the other major program areas. For example, the following should be assigned, to the extent possible, against the specific programs generating the need for these expenses: Research and planning, employment benefit expenses, maintenance of buildings and equipment, data processing costs, special purpose engineering, and associated capital costs.

V

PROGRAM DESIGN: ANALYTIC TECHNIQUES

11

Toward a Theory of Budgeting

VERNE B. LEWIS

The $64.00 question on the expenditure side of public budgeting is: On what basis shall it be decided to allocate X dollars to Activity A instead of allocating them to Activity B, or instead of allowing the taxpayer to use the money for his individual purposes? Over a decade ago V. O. Key called attention to the lack of a budgetary theory which would assist in arriving at an answer to this question.[1] Pointing out that budgeting is essentially a form of applied economics, since it requires the allocation of scarce resources among competing demands, Professor Key urged that this question be explored from the point of view of economic theory.

The purpose of this article is to analyze three propositions that are derived from economic theory[2] and appear to be applicable to public budgeting and to be appropriate building blocks for construction of an economic theory of budgeting. In brief, the three principles are:

1. Since resources are scarce in relation to demands, the basic economic test which must be applied is that the return from every expenditure must be worth its cost in terms of sacrificed alternatives.

Reprinted from *Public Administration Review*, 12, No. 1 (Winter 1952): 42–54, by permission of the author and publisher.

Budget analysis, therefore, is basically a comparison of the relative merits of alternative uses of funds.

2. Incremental analysis (that is, analysis of the additional values to be derived from an additional expenditure) is necessary because of the phenomenon of diminishing utility. Analysis of the increments is necessary and useful only at or near the margin; this is the point of balance at which an additional expenditure for any purpose would yield the same return.

3. Comparison of relative merits can be made only in terms of relative effectiveness in achieving a common objective.

Part I of this article will be devoted to consideration of these principles. In Part II a proposal, which will be called the alternative budget procedure, will be outlined and analyzed in terms of the three principles. Primary emphasis throughout will be placed on the applicability of concepts developed by the economists to methods of analyzing budget estimates. The discussion is pointed specifically at problems of the federal government; the general ideas, however, should be equally applicable to state and local governmental units.

I

RELATIVE VALUE

Budget decisions must be made on the basis of relative values. There is no absolute standard of value. It is not enough to say that an expenditure for a particular purpose is desirable or worth while. The results must be worth their cost. The results must be more valuable than they would be if the money were used for any other purpose.

Comparison of relative values to be obtained from alternative uses of funds is necessary because our resources are inadequate to do all the things we consider desirable and necessary. In fact, public budgeting is necessary only because our desires exceed our means. The desires of human beings are virtually unlimited. Although the supply of resources has been greatly expanded in recent decades, the supply is still short in relation to demands. It would be nice if we had enough to go around, but we do not. Some demands can be met only in part, some not at all.

Scarcity of resources in relation to demands confronts us at every level of public budgeting. Public services consume scarce materials and manpower which have alternative uses. If used for governmental activities, they cannot be used for private purposes. If used for Activity A of the government, they cannot be used for Activity B. Expressed in terms of money, the problem of scarcity arises in connection with appropriations. As individual taxpayers, we put pressures on Congress to hold down federal taxes so that a larger proportion of our already inadequate personal incomes will be available to satisfy our individual desires. In view of these pressures, Congress usually appropriates less than is requested by the President and interest groups. The President in turn usually requests the Congress to appropriate less than the total of the estimates submitted to him by agency heads. Rarely does an agency have sufficient funds to do all the things it would like to do or that it is requested to do by citizen groups.

Confronted with limited resources, congressmen and administrative officials must make choices. The available money will buy this *or* that, but not *both*. On what basis should the choice be made?

The economists, who specialize in problems of scarcity, have a general answer to this question. It is found in the doctrine of marginal utility. This doctrine, as applied to public budgeting, has been formulated by Professor Pigou as follows:

> As regards the distribution, as distinct from the aggregate cost, of optional government expenditure, it is clear that, just as an individual will get more satisfaction out of his income by maintaining a certain balance between different sorts of expenditure, so also will a community through its government. The principle of balance in both cases is provided by the postulate that resources should be so distributed among different uses that the marginal return of satisfaction is the same for all of them. . . . Expenditure should be distributed between battleships and poor relief in such wise that the last shilling devoted to each of them yields the same real return. We have here, so far as theory goes, a test by means of which the distribution of expenditure along different lines can be settled.[3]

Other aspects of the marginal utility concept will be considered in later sections; here we want to note that this concept poses the problem in terms of relative values rather than absolutes. To determine the distribution of funds between battleships and poor relief we must weigh the relative value of the results to be obtained from these alternative uses. Is it worth while to spend an additional $1,000,000 for battleships? We can answer "yes" only if we think we would get more valuable results than would be obtained by using that $1,000,000 for poor relief.

When the economists approach the problem in terms of costs rather than results they arrive at the same conclusion. Fundamentally, as the economists indicate in their "opportunity" or "displacement" concept of costs, "the cost of a thing is simply the amount of other things which has to be given up for its sake.''[4] If Robinson Crusoe finds he has time to build a house *or* catch some fish, but not *both,* the cost of the house is the fish he does not catch or vice versa. The cost of anything is therefore the result that would have been realized had the resources been used for an alternative purpose.

Of what significance from the point of view of budget analysis are these concepts of relative value and displacement costs? They indicate that the basic objective of budget analysis is the comparison of the relative value of results to be obtained from alternative uses of funds. If an analyst is convinced after reading the usual argument supporting a budget request that the activity in question is desirable and necessary, his task has just begun. To be justifiable in terms of making the most advantageous use of resources, the returns from an expenditure for any activity must be more desirable and more necessary than for any alternative use of the funds. On the other hand, a budget request for an activity cannot legitimately be turned down solely on the basis that the activity costs too much. Costs and results must be considered together. The costs must be judged in relation to the results and the results must be worth their costs in terms of alternative results that are foregone or displaced.

INCREMENTAL ANALYSIS

If the basic guide for budget analysis is that results must be worth their costs, budget analysis must include a comparison of relative values. How can such a comparison of values be made?

The marginal utility concept suggests a way of approaching the problem. The method, briefly, is to divide available resources into increments and consider which of the alternative uses of each increment would yield the greatest return. Analysis of increments is necessary because of the phenomenon of diminishing utility. This means, roughly, that as we acquire more and more units of anything, the additional units have less and less use value. If enough units are acquired, an added unit may be of no value at all and may even be objectionable. To illustrate, four tires on a car are essential, a fifth tire is less essential but is handy to have, whereas a sixth tire just gets in the way. Although a sixth tire will cost as much as any of the first five, it has considerably less use value. In deciding how many tires to buy, we must therefore consider the use value to be derived from each *additional* tire.

Because of the phenomenon of diminishing utility, there is no point in trying to determine the *total* or *average* benefits to be obtained from total expenditures for a particular commodity or function. We must analyze the benefits by increments. If one million bazookas make a valuable contribution toward winning a war, we cannot assume that the contribution would be doubled if we had two million. Perhaps there are not enough soldiers to use that many. No matter how valuable bazookas might be in winning a war, a point would be reached sometime on the diminishing scale of utility where additional expenditures for bazookas would be completely wasted. Since we do not have enough resources to do all the things we would like to do, we certainly should not produce anything that will not or cannot be used.

But we cannot assume that we would make the best use of resources even if we produced no more bazookas than could be used. Perhaps the manpower and materials consumed in producing the last thousand bazookas would serve a more valuable purpose if they were used for producing additional hand grenades or some other item. This reasoning leads us back to the basic criterion for deciding how much should be spent for each activity. We should allocate enough money for bazookas so that the last dollar spent for bazookas will serve as valuable a purpose as the last dollar for hand grenades or any other purpose. If more than this amount is spent for bazookas, we sacrifice a more valuable alternative use. Thus, as is suggested by the marginal utility theory, maximum returns can be obtained only if expenditures are distributed among different purposes in such a way that the last dollar spent for each yields the same real return.

The marginal utility concept also indicates that a comparison of incremental values is meaningful and necessary only at or near the margins. When analyzing the value of the returns by increments of expenditure near the margins we would ask: How much will be sacrificed if proposed expenditures for Function A are reduced by $1,000? Can efficiency be increased so that output will not have to be reduced? What would be the consequences of lowering standards of quality? Of reducing quantities? Of postponing some portion of the work?

When these issues are explored, the payoff question can be tackled. Would the sacrifices be greater or less if the $1,000 cut is applied to Function B rather than to Function A? This question brings up the most difficult and most critical problem. How can the values of unlike functions be compared? How can the value of an atom bomb and cancer research be compared? Or public roads and public schools? So far we have not indicated how this question can be answered. We have only narrowed the field by indicating that the value of functions must be compared by increments rather than in total and that the value of increments need only be compared near the marginal point of balance. Incremental analysis at the margins is just a tool, though a useful one, we believe. It does not supply the answers, but it helps to focus attention on the real points at issue.

The relative value of different things cannot be compared unless they have a common denominator. The common aspect of an atom bomb and cancer research, of public roads and public schools, is the broad purpose each is designed to serve. These items, as well as all other public and private activities, are undertaken to serve human needs and desires. We can only compare their values by evaluating their relative effectiveness in serving a common objective.

To revert to a previously used example, we do not make bazookas just for the sake of making bazookas. We make them because they help win wars. Although bazookas, hand grenades, and K-rations are unlike things, they serve a common military purpose. The relative values of these items can be weighed in terms of their relative effectiveness in fighting a war. We do not fight wars for their own sake either. They are fought for a larger purpose of national security. Economic aid to foreign countries also serves this purpose. Since they share a common objective, the relative value of military activities and economic aid can also be compared in terms of their effectiveness in achieving this objective.

Let us take a different type of case which is less general and more tangible than national security. Purchasing officers and engineers perform quite different functions. Yet, if they are working in an organization which does construction work, for example, they share the common objective of that organization. Operating within a ceiling on total expenditures, the head of the agency might be faced with this question: Would a part of the money allocated to the procurement section yield greater returns if transferred to the engineering section? This question involves value comparisons of unlike things, whether for a private firm or for a government agency. Moreover, the firm or the agency usually cannot express the contributions of procurement officers and engineers in terms of precise numbers. Nevertheless, reasonable men who are reasonably well informed arrive at substantially the same answer to such questions, provided the basic objective has been decided in advance. If the objective is to build a structure according to prescribed specifications in X months and at not to exceed Y dollars, this objective provides a common basis for evaluation. The answer will depend upon forecasts of facts and will also be influenced by relative need. For example, if design is on schedule but construction is being delayed because purchase orders are not being issued on schedule, additions to the procurement staff would probably yield greater returns than additions to the design staff. On the other hand, if design is behind schedule and, as a consequence, the procurement staff has no material requisitions to process, more design engineers would yield the greater return.

Evaluation in terms of relative effectiveness in achieving a common objective is, therefore, a second fundamental method of budget analysis.[5]

Evaluation in terms of common purposes is another way of saying that alternative means can be evaluated in terms of the end they are designed to achieve. That end can be considered, in turn, as a means of achieving a broader end. This process requires, of course, that the ultimate ends be somehow established. How can these fundamental decisions be made? In a democracy we are not so much concerned with how they are made as by whom they are made. The ideal of democracy is that the desires of the people, no matter how they are arrived at or how unwise they may be, should control the actions of the government. The representatives of the people in Congress make the fundamental decisions as to the ultimate aims of governmental services. These decisions, in the form of laws and appropriation acts, provide the basis for economic calculation by administrative agencies in the same way as consumer action in the marketplace provides the basis for decisions in the private economy.

We now have some basic elements of an economic theory of budgeting. The economic aim of budgeting is to achieve the best use of our resources. To meet this test, the benefits derived from any expenditure must be worth their cost in terms of sacrificed or displaced alternatives. As a first step in applying that test, we can use incremental analysis at the margins as a means of concentrating attention at the areas where comparison of values is necessary and meaningful. These values can be compared by determining their relative effectiveness in achieving a common purpose. Analysis in terms of common purposes requires a set of basic premises which are found in the ultimate ends or purposes established by Congress, acting for the people. This means that Congress is charged by the people with the basic responsibility for deciding what constitutes the "best use of resources," so far as the federal government is concerned.

PRACTICAL LIMITATIONS

Although the propositions outlined above concerning relative value, incremental analysis, and relative effectiveness constitute, in a sense, a formula for budget analysis which appears to be theoretically sound, the formula is not always easy to apply. Precise numbers to use in the equations are frequently unavailable. Although the formula will work in a theoretically valid manner, even if one has to guess the numbers to put into the equation, the practical usefulness of the answers will depend upon the accuracy of the numbers.

One area where firm numbers are hard to get involves forecasts of future needs and conditions. As we have noted, value is a function of need and need changes from time to time. In comparing the relative value of guns and butter, for example, we will strike a balance between them at different points at different times depending upon whether we are engaged in a hot war, a cold war, or no war at all. The balance between public health and police will be struck at one point if communicable diseases are rampant at a time when the traffic accident rate is low. The balance will be struck at a different point if the state of public health is good but the accident rate is alarming.

Budgetary decisions have to be based not only on relative needs as they are today but also on forecasts of what the needs will be tomorrow, next year, or in the next decade. The point is illustrated most dramatically by the decision made by the federal government during World War II to try to develop an atomic bomb. At the time, no one knew whether a bomb could be made, or if it could be made in time to help win the war. Hence, the government in deciding to divert tremendous quantities of scarce resources to this purpose had to take a calculated risk. Its decision was based not on firm facts but on forecasts and hopes as to the values to be realized.

There are probably as many budget arguments over forecasts of needs as there are over the relative merits of the expenditures which are proposed to meet those needs.

Not only must budget decisions be based, in some cases, on sheer guesses as to future needs and future accomplishments, but often the nature of governmental activities is such that accomplishments in relation to costs cannot be precisely measured even after the fact. How can one tell, for example, how much fire damage was prevented for each $1,000 spent by the fire department for fire prevention?

Perhaps it was the frequent difficulty in obtaining precise numbers that led Professor Key to question the applicability of the marginal utility theory to public budgeting. He concluded:

> The doctrine of marginal utility, developed most finely in the analysis of the market economy, has a ring of unreality when applied to public expenditures. The most advantageous utilization of public funds resolves itself into a matter of value preferences between ends lacking a common denominator. As such, the question is a problem of political philosophy.[6]

Whether firm numbers are available or not, judgments and decisions have to be made. The lack of precise numbers does not invalidate the basic principles or methods of calculation which we have outlined. The methods have to be judged on the basis of whether or not they lead to proper conclusions *if* it is assumed that the numbers used in the equations are the right ones. Obtaining the right numbers, though a fundamental and difficult problem, is separate and distinct from the problem of developing methods of calculation.

On the other hand, Professor Key may have been questioning the basic principle. It is perfectly true, as Key points out, that budgeting involves questions of value preferences which must be based on philosophy rather than science or logic. We agree that it is a problem for philosophers, but not exclusively, since the methods of the economists can also be applied. The problem of value has long been one of the central topics on the agenda of the economists. They do not approach the problem from the point of view of trying to develop an absolute standard of value or from the point of view of trying to prescribe which ends, goals, or objectives men should strive for. Rather they concentrate on methods to be used to achieve the most valuable use of scarce resources as judged by whatever standard of value men embrace. While the philosopher helps us to decide which goals we should strive for, the economist helps us achieve those goals most efficiently. Thus, I believe, the economists' approach to the problem of value as expressed in the marginal utility theory can be accepted as a useful approach for public budgeting.

The views outlined in this article concerning the applicability of the methods of the economists to public budgeting run sharply counter to the views of some economists. Ludwig von Mises, for example, contends, in his book, *Bureaucracy*,[7] that there is no method of economic calculation which can be applied to government. It can be shown, I think, that the problem in government, so far as it exists, arises out of the lack of firm numbers rather than out of the lack of a method.

Dr. Mises' central argument is that bureaucrats have no means of calculating the relative usefulness of governmental activities because these activities have no price in the marketplace. Therefore, he contends, government agencies have no criterion of value to apply. In private business, he points out (p. 26), "the ultimate basis of economic calculation is the valuation of all consumers' goods on the part of all the people" in the marketplace. Further, "economic calculation makes it possible for business to adjust production to the demands of the consumers" (p. 27). On the other hand, he argues, "if a public enterprise is to be operated without regard to profits, the behavior of the public no longer provides a criterion of its usefulness" (p. 61). Therefore, he concludes, "the problem of bureaucratic management is precisely the absence of such a method of calculation" (p. 49).

We can agree with the part of his argument that says market prices provide a criterion of value which serves as a basis for economic calculation in private business; but we cannot agree that government agencies are completely lacking in such a criterion. As has been noted, appropriations, like market prices, indicate in quantitative terms how much the representatives of the people are willing to pay for goods and services rendered by the government. In appropriating funds, congressmen express their attitudes concerning the usefulness of governmental activities as definitely as individuals do when they buy bread at the corner bakery. Congressmen, in effect, are serving as purchasing agents for the American people.

What function does the market price criterion serve in determining whether an activity is worth its cost? One function is to provide the numbers necessary for determining how the cost of doing a particular job can be reduced to a minimum. Nothing, of course, is worth its cost if the same result can somehow be achieved at a lower cost. Market prices are as useful in government as they are in business in this regard. In constructing a road, a building, or a dam—even in running an office—the government has to pay market prices for the raw material and manpower it uses just as a private businessman does. If the guide to economic calculation is the market price, the government engineer has numbers to put into his equations just as his engineering brother in private industry has. Market prices provide the data he needs to calculate which combination of available materials, men, and machines will be least costly.

After all corners have been cut and the cost of doing a job has been reduced to the minimum, we face a broader question. Is the job worth doing? Dr. Mises undoubtedly would answer that a job is worth doing in private business if it yields a profit. In attempting to calculate whether a given activity will yield a profit, a businessman, however, faces some of the problems faced by government. He has to forecast market conditions. The numbers he forecasts may or may not be right. Likewise, a businessman cannot always determine even after the fact whether an individual activity has been profitable or not. No method has yet been found, for example, of measuring precisely how much of a company's profit or loss results from such activities as advertising, research, and employee welfare programs. Moreover, a businessman, if he wants to maximize profits, cannot engage in an activity just because it is profitable. It must be more profitable than alternative activities open to him. Thus, he is faced with the same problem of relative value as is the government official. Suppose it costs $1.00 a pound to recover scrap materials in a private factory and that the scrap can be sold on the market for $1.10 a pound, thereby yielding a profit of 10 percent. Does it automatically follow that the scrap should be recovered? Not at all, since the firm might make a profit of 20 percent if the men and materials were used instead for making new products.

The method of calculation by a government agency for a similar situation would be exactly the same. In fact, if government appropriations specified precisely the quantities, quality, standards, and maximum permissible unit prices for each government service, the problem of economic calculation would not only be exactly the same but the answer could be expressed in terms of a profit equivalent. If the agency could produce at a lower unit cost than specified by Congress, the funds saved would be comparable to profit and would be returned to the Treasury as a dividend to the taxpayers.

In many cases, however, government services are of such a nature that Congress cannot enact precise specifications. For example, the production of plutonium by the Atomic Energy Commission has not yet reached the stage where such specifications can be written. Congress, in effect, tells the commission to produce as much plutonium as it can, according to specifications deemed most suitable by the commission, with a total expenditure not to exceed X million dollars. The commission then has no basis for knowing exactly what dollar value is placed on a pound of plutonium by the Congress. Nevertheless, the commission is not without means of making economic decisions. The problem might be to decide whether it is worth spending Y dollars to recover scrap plutonium which accumulates during the manufacturing process. The decision can be made on the basis of comparison of alternative means of accomplishing a common objective. This objective is to produce the maximum amount of usable plutonium during a specified period within the limits of available funds and other resources. In the light of this objective the commission can afford to spend as much per pound for recovery as it has to spend to produce a pound of new plutonium. If it spent either more or less than this amount, the total usable quantity of plutonium produced during a period would be less than the potential maximum. Faced with this kind of problem, a private business would calculate in precisely the same way. The common objective of new production and recovery operations might be expressed in terms of dollars of profit rather than pounds of product, but the answer would be the same.

When the problem facing the government involves activities such as education, foreign relations, and public recreation where the goals are less tangible, where the results are less subject to measurement, and where the amount of results arising from an increment of expenditures is more difficult to determine, the numbers used in the equations will be less firm. Even so, we conclude, Dr. Mises' arguments notwithstanding, that the differences between business and government in economic calculation lie not so much in the methods of calculation as in the availability of precise numbers with which to calculate.

II

In the foregoing analysis of economic ideas in relation to public budgeting, we have stressed the importance of looking upon budgeting as a problem of relative values and have examined the applicability of two methods—incremental analysis and evaluation of relative effectiveness—in achieving a common objective to budget analysis.

On the administrative implications of these ideas, Professor Key has said, "Perhaps the approach toward the practical working out of the issue lies in canalizing of decisions through the governmental machinery so as to place alternatives in juxtaposition and compel consideration of relative values."[8]

The budget machinery of the federal government does accomplish this purpose. The federal budget forces a simultaneous, or nearly simultaneous, consideration of all the competing claims by the President and the Congress. Moreover, at each level in the administrative hierarchy, the budget forces consideration of the relative merits of competing claims within each jurisdiction.[9]

Budget estimates and justifications are rarely prepared in a manner, however, which makes it easy to compare relative merits. We shall, therefore, now outline a budget system designed to facilitate such comparisons and to apply other ideas derived from the preceding economic analysis. After outlining this system, we shall compare it with other budget methods now being used.

The system to be described will be called the alternative budget system. Under this procedure, each administrative official who prepares a budget estimate, either as a basis for an appropriation request or an allotment request after the appropriation is made, would be required to prepare a basic budget estimate supplemented by skeleton plans for alternative amounts. If the amount of the basic estimate equals 100, the alternatives might represent, respectively, 80, 90, 110, and 120 percent of that amount. The number of alternatives might vary with the situation. Ordinarily, three alternatives would seem to secure a sufficient range of possibilities. In the interest of providing a safety valve, each subordinate might be permitted to prepare one or more additional alternative budgets totaling more than the top figure prescribed by his superior. In order to focus attention on problems near the margins, the amounts of the alternative budgets should range from a little less than the lowest amount that is likely to be approved to a little more than the recommended amount. Increments of 10 percent might be appropriate in some cases; larger or smaller increments might be required in others.

The establishment of the alternative levels would have to start with the President. He would select alternative levels of overall governmental expenditure, and he would establish corresponding alternative levels for each department or agency. The head of each department or agency would, in turn, establish alternative levels for each of his subordinates which would be consistent with the prescribed departmental levels.

In preparing the alternative budgets, the subordinate official would first indicate, as he does under present procedures, the nature, quantity, and quality of services his agency could render the taxpayers if the amount of the basic budget were approved. In addition, he would indicate the recommended revisions in the plan of service for each of the alternative amounts and the benefits or sacrifices which would result.

At each superior level the responsible official would review the alternative proposals submitted by his several subordinates and select from them the features that would be, in his opinion, the most advantageous to the taxpayers for each alternative amount set for him by the next highest organization level. Finally, the President would submit alternative budgets to the Congress. At this level the alternatives would reflect the major issues involved in determining the work program for the entire government.

The advantages of the alternative budget procedure will be brought out by comparing it with other budget methods and techniques now in use. For convenience, the other techniques will be labeled (a) open-end budgeting, (b) fixed-ceiling budgeting, (c) work measurement and unit costing, (d) increase-decrease analysis, (e) priority listings, and (f) item-by-item control. These methods are not mutually exclusive; some of them could very well be incorporated as features of the alternative budget plan. Some are used primarily in budget estimating, others in budget control.

OPEN-END BUDGETING

Some agencies of the federal government (and in some years the Bureau of the Budget) permit subordinate officials to submit a single budget estimate for whatever amount the subordinate decides to recommend. This method has been used not only for preparing requests for appropriations but also for submission of allotment requests to agency heads after the appropriations have been made. This single estimate represents, by and large, the official's judgment as to optimum program for his agency for the ensuing year, tempered perhaps by his judgment as to what the traffic will bear in view of the general political and economic climate existing at the time. No restrictions are placed on him; the sky is the limit so far as the amount he can request is concerned. For this reason, we have selected the short title "open-end budgeting" as being descriptive of this method.

In justification for such a budget estimate, the official, in effect, says, "I think it is desirable (or important, or essential) that the taxpayers be given the services outlined in this budget. Such a program will cost X dollars. Any reductions in the amount requested will deprive the public of exceedingly valuable services." While such general statements are, of course, backed up by more or less specific facts and figures, the information provided leaves many gaps from the point of view of what the superior official needs in order to weigh the importance of each dollar requested by one subordinate against each dollar requested by other subordinates.

Statements which merely prove that a program is desirable do not fulfill the needs of a superior who is faced with the necessity of reducing the total amount requested by the subordinates, not because he thinks the requests are for undesirable or unnecessary purposes, but simply because the pattern is too big for the cloth. The subordinate's budget estimates and justifications, submitted to him under the open-end procedure, are deficient because they do not indicate specifically how plans would be changed if a smaller amount were available or specifically the subordinate's judgment as to the consequences of such a change in plans. Almost the entire burden, then, of ascertaining where the reductions can be made with the least harmful consequences is placed on the superior official, who naturally is less well informed on the details than are his subordinates.

In what way would the assistance rendered by the subordinate to his superior be enhanced if the alternative budget method were used? Under any circumstances the contribution of a subordinate official is limited by the fact that he is concerned with a segment rather than with the whole. His advice as to how much should be appropriated for his particular sphere of activities obviously cannot be accepted without careful scrutiny. He lacks information about other activities which would be necessary to make a comparison of relative importance. Even if he had complete information, he would be quite unique if he did not place a higher valuation on his own activities than others do. This generalization is borne out by the fact that the aggregate of requests from subordinate officials is invariably more than the public, acting through Congress, is willing to devote to public services.

The subordinate administrative official can be expected, however, to make a substantial contribution in advising the Congress and the Preident on the relative merits of competing demands within his own jurisdiction, even though he cannot be expected to weigh those demands against demands in other jurisdictions. The subordinate official can perform an indispensable service by comparing the relative effectiveness of each activity in achieving the goals of his agency and by indicating how he thinks any specified amount of money can best be distributed among the programs of his agency. His service in this respect is valuable not only because considerable technical knowledge and experience usually is required as a basis for arriving at such judgments, but also because the pressure of time may force the President and the Congress to rely greatly on his judgment.

This phase of the contribution of the subordinate official to budget-making is comparable to services I can get from an architect if I should decide to build a house. The architect's advice as to whether I should spend eight, twelve, or sixteen thousand dollars for a house is not very helpful. On the other hand, the architect can be very helpful in advising me as to how I can get the most of what I want in a house for any given sum I choose to spend.

Another way in which a subordinate can be of service is in advising his superiors on probable gains or losses from appropriating more or less for his portion of the government's work. This kind of contribution is comparable to the assistance an architect can render by analyzing the additional features in a house which can be obtained for each increment of cost, and by indicating the features that would have to be sacrificed if costs were reduced by specified amounts.

Alternative budgets prepared by subordinates would take advantage of both of these types of assistance. The subordinate would indicate his judgment as to the best way of using several alternative amounts and in addition he would analyze the benefits to be gained by each increment of funds.

FIXED-CEILING BUDGETING

If the open-end procedure is one extreme, the fixed-ceiling method represents the opposite pole. Under this plan, a fixed ceiling is established in advance which the subordinate's budget estimate cannot exceed. Such a ceiling creates for the subordinate a situation similar to that facing the President if he should decide to recommend a balanced budget. Then the amount of anticipated revenues constitutes the ceiling on the amount of expenditures he can recommend.

Whatever the merits, or lack thereof, of allowing revenues to determine the total amount to be spent by the government, working to a set ceiling does have the advantage of forcing consideration, at the presidential level, of relative merits to a greater extent than is likely to prevail under open-end budgeting. In open-end budgeting, it is easy to keep adding items that appear to be desirable and thereby pass the buck to the next level of review in the event the total cost of the "desirable" items exceeds an acceptable figure. But prescribing a single fixed ceiling in advance for subordinate levels of the executive branch involves the danger of judging a case before the evidence is heard. The basic reason for requiring estimates from subordinate officials is that higher officials do not have enough detailed information, time, or specialized skill to prepare the plans themselves. How can these officials judge the merits of the experts' plans before they are submitted? In setting the ceiling figures in advance, how can one be sure that the ceiling for one function is not set too high and the ceiling for another too low?

The alternative budget plan, like the fixed-ceiling practice, forces consideration of relative merits within a given amount at each organization level, but the final decision as to amount does not have to be made by the superior until the evidence is in.

WORK LOAD MEASUREMENT AND UNIT COSTING

Increasing emphasis has been placed in recent years on work load measurement and unit costing for budgetary purposes. The ultimate goal is to devise units of work and to determine unit costs wherever possible so that budget requests can be stated in this fashion: "It costs X dollars to perform each unit of this type of work. If you want us to perform 100 units, the cost will be 100 times X dollars. If you want only fifty units the cost will be fifty times X dollars."

This approach is useful for budgeting in many situations. It supplies some of the numbers needed for the economic calculation discussed in Part I. Precise, quantitative measures, if pertinent and feasible, are better than vague generalities. Some budget questions cannot be answered, however, in terms of work load and unit cost data. These data will show how many units are being done, but not how many should be done. They show what unit costs are, but not what they should be. They may or may not give an indication of the quality of the work, but they leave unanswered the question of the proper quality standards.

A further limitation on use of work load measurement is that the end product of many agencies is not measurable by any means yet devised. In other cases, the amount of work performed is not a measure of its significance or value. Some work is standby in character. Some facilities, for example, are maintained to meet emergencies if and when they arise. In such cases the less work there is to be done the better. Much of the work of military agencies and fire fighters is of this type. In other cases, too, the amount of work performed is inadequate as an index of results. This is true with respect to many research projects and enforcement activities. In the case of research, it is the final result that counts, not the amount of work required to achieve the result. In enforcement work, the number of infractions dealt with is not an adequate measure since the ideal would be to have no infractions at all.

Lacking an adequate way of measuring or even identifying the end product in precise terms, it is still possible in many cases to develop significant measures of work load of subsidiary activities that contribute to the end product. Examples are number of letters typed, miles patrolled, or purchase orders processed. Detailed data of this type are useful in budgeting but their use is largely confined to the lower organization levels. The sheer mass of such data precludes their extensive use at higher levels.

The alternative budget proposal would permit use of work load and unit cost data to the extent feasible in each case. Under each alternative total figure, the number of units of work that could be performed, the quality standards, and unit costs could be shown. Thus the benefits to be derived from work load measurement would be fully utilized under the alternative budget procedure. In addition, the judgment of subordinates would be obtained on questions which cannot be answered by work load data alone. Such questions involve, for example, the gains or losses of performing alternative amounts of work, the achievement of alternative quality standards, and the effects of spending more or less per unit of work.

INCREASE-DECREASE ANALYSIS

A common technique in the federal government is to require in budget estimates identification of the items representing increases and decreases as compared with the prior year's budget. Special explanations are required for the increases. Budget reviewers are frequently criticized for concentrating on the increases and giving too little attention to items in the base amount. This criticism is justified in part because the amount appropriated last year is not necessarily appropriate for this year and the activities carried on last year are not necessarily appropriate for this year. However, the sheer mass of work involved in reviewing budget estimates precludes examination of every detail every year. Even if it were possible, it would not be necessary, for conditions do not change so fast that every issue has to be rehashed every year.

The basic fault of the increase-decrease method is the fact that it does not require comparison of the relative values of the old and the new. While the proposed increase may be for an eminently desirable purpose, it does not necessarily follow that the appropriation of the agency should be increased. Perhaps other programs of the agency should be cut back enough, or more, to make room for the new. The alternative budget approach has all the advantages of the increase-decrease method without having this basic fault. It would require agencies to weigh the relative merits of all proposals, whether old or new, and thus would reflect the agency's evaluation of the importance of the proposed additions to the spending program in relation to the items composing the base.

PRIORITY LISTINGS

Subordinates are required, in some cases, to indicate priorities of items included in their budget estimates or allotment requests to assist reviewers in determining where cutbacks should be made. Budgets for construction of physical facilities, for example, might contain a listing in priority order of the facilities proposed. The assumption underlying this method is that a budget reduction would be met by eliminating enough projects at the lower end of the list to bring the estimates down to the desired level. When that is the case priority listings are useful. Elimination of the lowest priority items, however, is only one of several means of reducing estimates. Some of the other types of adjustments are as follows: cheaper materials may be used in some or all of the facilities; the size, strength, or durability of the facilities may be decreased; or certain features may be eliminated or postponed until a later date. All of these types of adjustments can be reflected in alternative budgets since they all affect dollar requirements. The priority approach reflects only the one kind of adjustment.

ITEM-BY-ITEM CONTROL

Approval of individual items of expenditure by higher authority is a common budgetary control technique. Equipment purchases, additions to staff, travel, expensive types of communications as well as entire projects, are frequently subjected to this type of control. An actual case will illustrate the problems involved. During World War II, the Secretary of the Navy was concerned about the expansion of the physical plant of the Navy in the continental United States. In an effort to assure that no facilities would be built unless vitally needed for war purposes and that costs and use of scarce materials would be minimized, the Secretary of the Navy required that all proposed construction projects should be subject to his approval. Prior to this approval they had to be screened at several different levels in the Navy Department. The projects were reviewed by officials in the sponsoring bureau, by the Bureau of Yards and Docks (to insure conformity to wartime engineering standards), by the Chief of Naval Operations (to determine their military necessity), and by a special committee in the Secretary's office composed mainly of civilian businessmen (to determine their overall justification). Even with this series of reviews, the Secretary apparently was not convinced that outlays for facilities were being held down as much as they should be. The process was something less than satisfactory to subordinate officials, too, but for different reasons. They complained of the delays involved in getting a decision and of the amount of time and effort required to justify and rejustify each proposal at the several screening points.

The root of the difficulty, if the thesis of this article is sound, is that controls of individual items do not require or facilitate systematic consideration of relative desirability. Item-by-item control poses the problem at each level of review in these terms: Is the proposal desirable, or essential, or justified? A more pertinent question is: Is the proposal more essential than any alternative use of the funds?

The alternative budget procedure could be applied to this situation in the following manner: bureau chiefs, as well as officials at lower levels, if desired, would be asked to prepare alternative programs for construction of facilities for the period in question. The bureau chiefs in presenting these alternatives would, in effect, tell the Chief of Naval Operations and the Secretary, "If only X dollars are available, I recommend using the money this way . . .; if two X dollars are available, I think the money should be used this way. . . . The advantages and disadvantages of each plan are as follows: . . ." Having an opportunity to see the picture as a whole, having before him alternatives from which to choose, and having the judgment of his subordinates as to gains and losses resulting from each alternative, the Secretary, it would seem, would be able to make his decision fairly readily and with assurance. It is unlikely that he would have to spend as much time reviewing details as is necessary under the item-by-item approach. He would be in a better position to exercise his responsibilities while the subordinates would be freed from the delays, burdens, and irritations invariably involved in piece-by-piece screening processes.

In addition to the specific points discussed above, the alternative budget plan appears to have certain general advantages. It would, we believe, make budgeting a little more palatable to the technically minded operating official who must prepare and justify budgets. His role will be less that of a special pleader for *the* plan he thinks should be accepted and more that of an expert adviser. He will be less like an architect who tries to sell a client on a single plan costing a certain sum and more like an architect advising the client on the relative merits of several house plans and suggesting how the client can get the most for his money regardless of the amount he decides to spend.

Budget analysts under this plan would have a frame of reference which would enable them to operate more effectively. At present, much of their effort is directed toward determining desirability or necessity and not enough attention is given to issues of relative desirability. Under the plan suggested here, the primary job of the budget analyst would be to assist his superior in weighing the relative value of alternative uses of each increment of funds as a step in developing the alternatives to be submitted to the next higher level in the organization. Another aspect of his work would be to explore some of the many possible variations and combinations of features that could not be reflected in the limited number of alternatives formally submitted by the lower officials. Moreover, the analyst would have to check for accuracy, objectivity, and general adequacy the subordinate official's statements of the advantages and disadvantages of the alternatives submitted.

Another significant advantage of the alternative budget proposal is that it would make budgeting somewhat less authoritarian. It would make the budget recommendations of administrative officials less final without weakening in any way their usefulness.

At present, an item screened out of a budget by any administrative official even though it is of major importance is not considered at later stages unless it is brought to the attention of higher executive officials or the Congress by some method which is prohibited by the prevailing rules. To put it mildly, quite definite steps are taken to discourage later consideration. A bureau chief, for example, would be considered out of bounds if he appealed to the President for consideration of an item screened out of his budget by his departmental head. Any administrative officer is prohibited from recommending congressional consideration of any alternatives to the single proposal contained in the President's budget unless specifically requested to do so by a member of Congress. Publication of requests submitted by the departments to the President is also banned.

It is not at all unlikely that superior administrative officials or the Congress would want to adopt some of these screened-out items if they had an opportunity to consider them. Since Congress, in our form of government, is largely responsible for deciding what shall or shall not be done by the executive agencies, the wisdom of such strict censoring of proposals submitted for consideration by Congress seems questionable. Since the President's budget estimates are only recommendations, there would seem to be no disadvantage in his outlining the major alternatives from which he made his selection. In this way the views of subordinates who may have an honest difference of opinion with the President could be submitted to Congress for consideration openly and without subterfuge. After considering the evidence pertaining to each alternative, Congress could then take its choice. Since the making of such choices is involved in exercising congressional control over the purse strings—a control which historically and currently is a basic cornerstone of democratic government—the provision of information which will assist Congress in evaluating the major alternative courses is of vital importance.[10]

In general, the alternative budget plan is designed to emphasize throughout the budget process the economic ideas discussed in Part I of this article. Its purpose is to pose budget questions at every level in terms of relative value. It also is designed to make maximum use of the expert knowledge and judgment of officials at the lower organization levels by having them analyze, incrementally, the estimates of their agencies and evaluate the relative effectiveness of their several activities in achieving the goals of their organizations.

In proposing this system, I am not particularly concerned with detailed mechanics. There are undoubtedly other ways of accomplishing substantially the same results as this plan is designed to achieve. More important than the precise mechanics is the way of looking at budget problems, the approach to budget analysis and control which this plan reflects.

How practical is the alternative budget plan? How well will it work in practice? The answers to these questions depend in large measure on the relationships between superior and subordinate and between the administration and the Congress. Neither this system nor any other can work satisfactorily if the relations are strained, if the reviewer lacks confidence in the integrity or judgment of the official who is submitting the estimate, or if those who prepare the estimates are not sincerely interested in providing information which the reviewers need to form an intelligent judgment on the merits of the issues.

Perhaps undue faith in the rationality of man underlies the approach to budgeting outlined in this article. In real life, budget decisions are undoubtedly influenced to a greater or lesser extent by such noneconomic and non-rational factors as pride and prejudice, provincialism and politics. These aspects deserve consideration, but they lie beyond the scope of this article. My primary purpose herein has been to stimulate further consideration of the economic aspects of budgeting.[11]

Notes

[1] V. O. Key, Jr., "The Lack of a Budgetary Theory," *American Political Science Review,* 34 (December, 1940), 1137–44.

[2] Ideas derived from Herbert A. Simon's works concerning the applicability of economic concepts to administration have been particularly useful for this purpose. See his *Administrative Behavior* (New York: Macmillan, 1947).

[3] As quoted by Key, *op.cit.,* p. 1139.

[4] L. M. Fraser, *Economic Thought and Language* (A. and C. Black Ltd., 1937), p. 103.

[5] This method, as it applies to public administration in general, has been extensively analyzed by Herbert A. Simon under the heading of the "criterion of efficiency," *op. cit.,* pp. 172–97.

[6] Key, *op. cit.,* p. 1143.

[7] Ludwig von Mises, *Bureaucracy* (New Haven: Yale University Press, 1944), p. 47.

[8] *Op. cit.,* p. 1142.

[9] See also, Simon, *op. cit.,* p. 214.

[10] Simon also has recommended submission of alternative budget plans to legislatures for substantially the same reason. *Op. cit.,* p. 195.

[11] Note on relation to a performance budget. A performance budget, as proposed by the Hoover Commission, would give primary emphasis to the result or end product to be obtained with the money spent by the government. The commission wisely critized budget presentations that deal only with the ingredients that are required to produce the end product. Certainly first attention should be given to what is to be accomplished rather than to the people who have to be employed, or the materials which have to be bought, in order to accomplish the basic purpose.

Emphasizing performance or end results does not require us to ignore the ingredients or the means to the ends. It should not lead to that result. Important budget issues often involve only the means. While there may be agreement about purpose, the methods may be in dispute. For example, a conservation agency may be responsible for inducing producer-conservation of some natural resource. Should the objective be accomplished by an educational program, by regulatory action, or by subsidy?

The alternative budget plan is flexible enough to be adapted to the situation. Alternative purposes as well as alternative methods could and should be reflected in the alternative budget estimates. Whether greater emphasis would be placed on purposes than on methods would depend upon the nature of the problem.

12

Systems Analysis Techniques for Planning–Programming–Budgeting

E. S. QUADE

Introduction

Broadly speaking, any orderly analytic study designed to help a decision-maker identify a preferred course of action from among possible alternatives might be termed a systems analysis. As commonly used in the defense community, the phrase "systems analysis" refers to formal inquiries intended to advise a decision-maker on the policy choices involved in such matters as weapon development, force posture design, or the determination of strategic objectives. A typical analysis might tackle

Reprinted from "Systems Analysis Techniques for Planning-Programming-Budgeting," Report P-3322 (Santa Monica, California: The Rand Corporation, March 1966), by permission of the author and publisher.

Any views expressed in this paper are those of the author. They should not be interpreted as reflecting the views of the Rand Corporation or the official opinion or policy of any of its governmental or private research sponsors. Papers are reproduced by the Rand Corporation as a courtesy to the members of its staff.

A condensed version of this paper was presented in the course Executive Orientation in Planning, Programming, and Budgeting sponsored by the U.S. Bureau of the Budget and the U.S. Civil Service Commission, Washington, D.C., February 24–5, 1966.

the question of what might be the possible characteristics of a new strategic bomber and whether one should be developed; whether tactical air wings, carrier task forces, or neither could be substituted for United States ground divisions in Europe; or whether we should modify the test-ban treaty now that the Chinese Communists have nuclear weapons and, if so, how. Systems analysis represents an approach to, or way of looking at, complex problems of choice under uncertainty that should have utility in the Planning–Programming–Budgeting (PPB) process. Our purpose is to discuss the question of extending military systems analysis to the civilian activities of the government, to point out some of the limitations of analysis in this role, and to call attention to techniques that seem likely to be particularly useful. I will interpret the term "technique" broadly enough to range from proven mathematical algorithms to certain broad principles that often seem to be associated with successful analysis.

Some fifteen years ago a similar extension raised quite some doubt. When weapons system analysts (particularly those at The Rand Corporation) began to include the formulation of national security policy and strategy as part of their field of interest, experienced "military analysts" in the Pentagon and elsewhere were not encouraging. They held that the tools, techniques, and concepts of operations analysis, as practiced in World War II, or of weapons system optimization and selection—in which analysts had been reasonably successful—would not carry over, that strategy and policy planning were arts and would remain so.

Fortunately, these skeptics were only partially right. It is true that additional concepts and methodologies significantly different from those of earlier analysis had to be developed. But there has been substantial progress, and the years since 1961 have seen a marked increase in the extent to which analyses of policy and strategy have influenced decisionmakers on the broadest issues of national defense.

Today's contemplated extension to PPB is long overdue and possibly even more radical. Systems analysis has barely entered the domain of the social sciences. Here, in urban planning, in education, in welfare, and in other nonmilitary activities, as Olaf Helmer remarks in his perceptive essay:

> We are faced with an abundance of challenges: how to keep the peace, how to alleviate the hardships of social change, how to provide food and comfort for the inaffluent, how to improve the social institutions and the values of the affluent, how to cope with revolutionary innovations, and so on. [1]

Since systems analysis represents an approach to, or way of looking at, any problem of choice under uncertainty, it should be able to help with these problems.

Actually, systematic analysis of *routine* operations is widespread throughout the civil government as well as in commerce, industry, and the military. Here analysis takes its most mathematical form and, in a certain sense, its most fruitful role. For example, it may help to determine how Post Office pickup trucks should be routed to collect mail from deposit boxes, or whether computers should be rented or purchased to handle warehouse inventories, or what type of all-weather landing system should be installed in new commercial aircraft. Such problems are typically an attempt to increase the efficiency of a man-machine system in a situation where it is clear what "more efficient" means. The analysis can often be reduced to the application of a well understood mathematical discipline such as linear programming or queuing theory to a generic "model," which, by a specification of its parameters, can be made to fit a wide variety of operations. An "optimum" solution is then obtained by means of a systematic computational routine. The queuing model, for example, is relevant to many aspects of the operations of the Post Office, airports, service facilities, maintenance shops, and so on. In many instances such models may actually tell the client what his decision or plan ought to be. Analysis of this type is usually called operations research or management science rather than systems analysis, however.

There are, however, other decisions or problems, civilian as well as military, where computational techniques can help only with sub-problems. Typical decisions of this latter type might be the determination of how much of the federal budget should be allocated to economic development and what fraction of that should be spent on South America; or whether the needs of interstate transportation are better served by improved high-speed rail transport or by higher performance highway turnpikes; or if there is some legislative action that might end the growth of juvenile delinquency. Such problems will normally involve more than the efficient allocation of resources among alternative uses; they are not "solvable" in the same sense as efficiency problems in which one can maximize some "payoff" function that clearly expresses what one is trying to accomplish. Here, rather, the objectives or goals of the action to be taken must be determined first. Decision problems associated with program budgeting are mainly of this type—where the difficulty lies in deciding what ought to be done as well as in how to do it, where it is not clear what "more efficient" means, and where many of the factors in the problem elude quantification. The final program recommendation will thus remain in part a matter of faith and judgment. Studies to help with these problems are systems analyses rather than operations research.[2]

Every systems analysis involves, at one stage, a comparison of alternative courses of action in terms of their costs and their effectiveness in attaining a specified objective. Usually this comparison takes the form of an attempt to designate the alternative that will minimize the costs, subject to some fixed performance requirement (something like reduce unemployment to less than 2 percent in two years, or add a certain number of miles to the interstate highway system); or conversely, it is an attempt to maximize some physical measure of performance subject to a budget constraint. Such evaluations are called cost-effectiveness analyses.[3] Since they often receive the lion's share of attention, the entire study also is frequently called a cost-effectiveness analysis. But this label puts too much emphasis on just one aspect of the decision process. In analyses designed to furnish broad policy advice, other facets of the problem are of greater significance than the comparison of alternatives: the specification of sensible objectives, the determination of a satisfactory way to measure performance, the influence of considerations that cannot be quantified, or the design of better alternatives.

The Essence of the Method

What is there about the analytic approach that makes it better or more useful than other ways to furnish advice—than, say, an expert or a committee? In areas such as urban redevelopment or welfare planning, where there is no accepted theoretical foundation, advice obtained from experts working individually or as a committee must depend largely on judgment and intuition. *So must the advice from systems analysis.* But the virtue of such analysis is that it permits the judgment and intuition of the experts in relevant fields to be combined systematically and efficiently. The essence of the method is to construct and operate within a "model," a simplified abstraction of the real situation appropriate to the question. Such a model, which may take such varied forms as a computer simulation, an operational game, or even a purely verbal "scenario," introduces a precise structure and terminology that serve primarily as an effective means of communication, enabling the participants in the study to exercise their judgment and intuition in a concrete context and in proper relation to others. Moreover, through feedback from the model (the results of computation, the countermoves in the game, or the critique of the scenario), the experts have a chance to revise early judgments and thus arrive at a clearer understanding of the problem and its context, and perhaps of their subject matter.[4]

THE PROCESS OF ANALYSIS

The fundamental importance of the model is seen in its relation to the other elements of analysis.[5] There are five all told, and each is present in every analysis of choice and should always be explicitly identified.

1. *The objective (or objectives).* Systems analysis is undertaken primarily to help choose a policy or course of action. The first and most important task of the analyst is to discover what the decision-maker's objectives are (or should be) and then how to measure the extent to which these objectives are, in fact, attained by various choices. This done, strategies, policies, or possible actions can be examined, compared, and recommended on the basis of how well and how cheaply they can accomplish these objectives.

2. *The alternatives.* The alternatives are the means by which it is hoped the objectives can be attained. They may be policies or strategies or specific actions or instrumentalities and they need not be obvious substitutes for each other or perform the same specific function. Thus, education, anti-poverty measures, police protection, and slum clearance may all be alternatives in combating juvenile delinquency.

3. *The costs.* The choice of a particular alternative for accomplishing the objectives implies that certain specific resources can no longer be used for other purposes. These are the costs. For a future time period, most costs can be measured in money, but their true measure is in terms of the opportunities they preclude. Thus, if the goal is to lower traffic fatalities, the irritation and delay caused to motorists by schemes that lower automobile speed in a particular location must be considered as costs, for such irritation and delay may cause more speeding elsewhere.

4. *A model (or models).* A model is a simplified, stylized representation of the real world that abstracts the cause-and-effect relationships essential to the question studied. The means of representation may range from a set of mathematical equations or a computer program to a purely verbal description of the situation, in which intuition alone is used to predict the consequences of various choices. In systems analysis, or any analysis of choice, the role of the model (or models, for it may be inappropriate or absurd to attempt to incorporate all the aspects of a problem in a single formulation) is to estimate for each alternative the costs that would be incurred and the extent to which the objectives would be attained.

5. *A criterion.* A criterion is a rule or standard by which to rank the alternatives in order of desirability. It provides a means for weighing cost against effectiveness.

The process of analysis takes place in three overlapping stages. In the first, the formulation stage, the issues are clarified, the extent of the inquiry limited, and the elements identified. In the second, the search stage, information is gathered and alternatives generated. The third stage is evaluation.

To start the process of evaluation or comparison (see Figure 1), the various *alternatives* (which may have to be discovered or invented as part of the analysis) are examined by means of the *models.* The models tell us what consequences or outcomes can be expected to follow from each alternative; that is, what the *costs* are and the extent to which each *objective* is attained. A *criterion* can then be used to weigh the costs against performance, and thus the alternatives can be arranged in the order of preference.

Unfortunately, things are seldom tidy: too often the objectives are multiple, conflicting, and obscure; alternatives are not adequate to attain the objectives; the measures of effectiveness do not really measure the extent to which the objectives are attained; the predictions from the model are full of uncertainties; and other criteria that look almost as plausible as the one chosen may lead to a different order of preference. When this happens, we must take another approach. A single attempt or pass at a problem is seldom enough. (See Figure 2.) The key of successful analysis is a continuous cycle of formulating the problem, selecting objectives, designing alternatives, collecting data, building models, weighing cost against performance, testing for sensitivity, questioning assumptions and data, re-examining the objectives, opening new alternatives, building better models, and so on, until satisfaction is obtained or time or money force a cut-off.

In brief, a systems analysis attempts to look at the entire problem and look at it in its proper context. Characteristically, it will involve a systematic investigation of the decision-maker's objectives and of the relevant criteria; a comparison—quantitative insofar as possible—of the

FIGURE 1
The Structure of Analysis

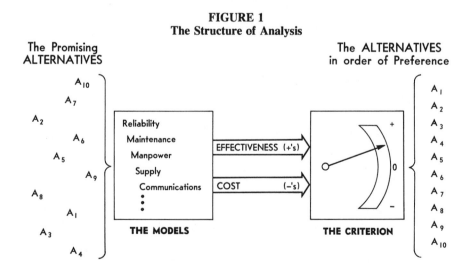

FIGURE 2
The Key to Analysis

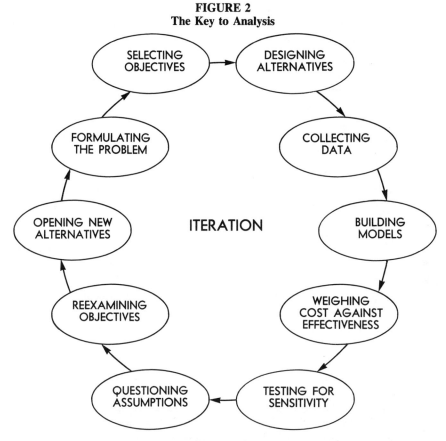

cost, effectiveness, risk, and timing associated with each alternative policy or strategy for achieving the objectives; and an attempt to design better alternatives and select other goals if those examined are found wanting.

Note that there is nothing really new about the procedures I have just sketched. They have been used, more or less successfully, by managers throughout government and industry since ancient times. The need for considering cost relative to performance must have occurred to the earliest planner. Systems analysis is thus not a catchword to suggest we are doing something new; at most, we are doing something better. What may be novel though, is that this sort of analysis is an attempt to look at the entire problem systematically with emphasis on explicitness, on quantification, and on the recognition of uncertainty. Also novel are the schemes or models used to explore the consequences of various choices and to eliminate inferior action in situations where the relationships cannot be represented adequately by a mathematical model.

Note that there is nothing in these procedures that guarantees the advice from the analysis to be good. They do not preclude the possibility that we are addressing the wrong problem or have allowed our personal biases to bar a better solution from consideration. When a study is a poor one it is rarely because the computer was not powerful enough or because the methods of optimization were not sufficiently sophisticated, but because it had the wrong objective or poor criteria. There are some characteristics of a study, however, that seem to be associated with good analysis. Let me identify some of these.

PRINCIPLES OF GOOD ANALYSIS

1. It is all important to tackle the "right" problem. A large part of the investigators' efforts must be invested in thinking about the problem, exploring its proper breadth, and trying to discover the appropriate objectives and to search out good criteria for choice. If we have not chosen the best set of alternatives to compare we will not discover the best solution. But if we have chosen the wrong objective then we might find a solution to the wrong problem. Getting an accurate answer to the wrong question is likely to be far less helpful than an incomplete answer to the right question.

2. The analysis must be systems oriented. Rather than isolating a part of the problem by neglecting its interactions with other parts, an effort should be made to extend the boundaries of the inquiry as far as required for the problem at hand, to find what interdependencies are important, and to study the entire complex system. This should be done even if it requires the use of purely intuitive judgment.

An interdisciplinary team of persons having a variety of knowledge and skills is helpful here. This is not so merely because a complex problem is likely to involve many diverse factors that cannot be handled by a single discipline. More importantly, a problem looks different to an economist, an engineer, a political scientist, or a professional bureaucrat, and their different approaches may contribute to finding a solution.

3. The presence of uncertainty should be recognized, and an attempt made to take it into account. Most important decisions are fraught with uncertainty. In planning urban redevelopment we are uncertain about city growth patterns, about the extent to which freeways or rapid transit systems will be used, about costs, about tax revenues, about the demand for services. For many of these things, there is no way to say with confidence that a given estimate is correct. The analyst attempts to

identify these uncertainties and evaluate their impact. Often he can say the value of a parameter will be more than A but less than B. Sometimes it is possible to indicate how the uncertainty can be reduced by further testing and how long that will take. Most important, the analysis should determine the effect of uncertainty on the answers. This is done by a sensitivity analysis that shows the answers change in response to changes in assumptions and estimates.[6]

The study report should include the presentation of a contingency table showing the effectiveness and cost associated with each significant alternative for various future environments and for each set of assumptions about the uncertainties.

4. The analysis attempts to discover new alternatives as well as to improve the obvious ones. The invention of new alternatives can be much more valuable than an exhaustive comparison of given alternatives, none of which may be very satisfactory.

5. While in problems of public policy or national security, the scientific method of controlled repeated experiment cannot be used, the analysis should strive to attain the standards traditional to science. These are (1) intersubjectivity: results obtained by processes that can be duplicated by others to attain the same results; (2) explicitness: use of calculations, assumptions, data, and judgments that are subject to checking, criticism, and disagreement; and (3) objectivity: conclusions do not depend on personalities, reputations, or vested interests; where possible these conclusions should be in quantitative and experimental terms.

The Models

As mentioned earlier, systems analysis is flexible in the models it uses. Indeed, it has to be. Mathematics and computing machines, while extremely useful, are limited in the aid they can give in broad policy questions. If the important aspects of the problem can be completely formulated mathematically or represented numerically, techniques such as dynamic programming, game theory, queuing theory, or computer simulation may be the means of providing the best solution. But in most policy analyses, computations and computers are often more valuable for the aid they provide to intuition and understanding, rather than for the results they supply.

While a computer can solve only the problems that the analyst knows conceptually how to solve himself, it can help with many others. The objection that one cannot use results which depend on many uncertain parameters represents a lack of understanding of how systems analysis can help a decision-maker. For a study to be useful it must indicate the *relative* merit of the various alternatives and identify the critical parameters. The great advantage of a computerized model is that it gives the analyst the capability to do numerous excursions, parametric investigations, and sensitivity analyses and thus to investigate the ranking of alternatives under a host of assumptions. This may be of more practical value to the decision-maker than the ability to say with high confidence that a given alternative will have such and such a rank in a very narrowly defined situation.

The type of model appropriate to a problem depends on the problem and what we know or think we know about it.

For example, suppose we are concerned with long-range economic forecasting or decisions about the development of a national economy. The type of model to use will depend on the particular economy and on the kind of questions that must be answered. If the questions were about the United States, the model might be mathematical and possibly programmed for a computer because of its size and complexity. (By a mathematical model I mean one in which the relationships between the variables and parameters are represented by mathematical equations.) In the case of the United States, because of the vast amount of data available in the form of economic and demographic time series regarding just about every conceivable aspect of economic life, numerous mathematical and computer models have been formulated and used with more or less success.

If we are not able to abstract the situation to a series of equations or a mathematical model, some other way to represent the consequences that follow from particular choices must be found. Simulation may work. Here, instead of describing the situation directly, each element making up the real situation may be simulated by a physical object or, most often, by a digital computer using sets of random numbers, and its behavior analyzed by operating with the representation. For example, we might use computer simulation to study the economy of some Latin American country. The distinction between a computer simulation and the use of a computer to analyze a mathematical model is often a fuzzy one, but the fundamental difference is that in simulation the overall behavior of the model is studied through a case-by-case approach.

For studying the economy of a newly emerging nation such as is found in Africa, where the situation is even more poorly structured and where we have little firm knowledge of existing facts and relationships, a possible approach would be through the direct involvement of experts who have knowledge of the problem.

Ordinarily, we would like to have the judgment of more than one expert, even though their advice usually differs. There are several ways to try for a consensus; the traditional way has been to assemble the experts in one place, to let them discuss the problem freely, and to require that they arrive at a joint answer. They could also be put to work individually, letting others seek methods for the best combined use of their findings. Or they could be asked to work in a group exercise—ranging from a simple structured discussion to a sophisticated simulation or an "operational game"—to obtain judgments from the group as a whole.

This latter approach is a laboratory simulation involving role-playing by human subjects who simulate real-world decision-makers. To study the economy of an underdeveloped country the various sectors of the economy might be simulated by specialized experts.[7] They would be expected, in acting out their roles, not so much to play a competitive game against one another, but to use their intuition as experts to simulate as best they could the attitudes and consequent decisions of their real-life counterparts. For instance, a player simulating a goods-producing sector of the economy might, within constraints, shut down or expand manufacturing facilities, modernize, change raw material and labor inputs, vary prices and so on. There would also need to be government players who could introduce new fiscal or monetary policies and regulations (taxes, subsidies, tariffs, price ceilings, etc.) as well as social and political innovations with only indirect economic implications (social security, education, appeals to patriotism, universal military service, etc.). In laying down the rules governing the players' options and constraints and the actions taken within these rules, expert judgment is essential. It is also clear that for this problem political and sociological experts will be needed, as well as economists.

There is, of course, no guarantee that the projections obtained from such a model would be reliable. But the participating experts might gain a great deal of insight. Here the game structure—again a model—furnishes the participants with an artificial, simulated environment within which they can jointly and simultaneously experiment, acquiring through feedback the insights necessary to make successful predictions within the gaming context and thus indirectly about the real world.

Another useful technique is one that military systems analysts call "scenario writing." This is an effort to show how, starting with the present, a future state might evolve out of the present one. The idea is to show how this might happen plausibly by exhibiting a reasonable chain of events. A scenario is thus a primitive model. A collection of scenarios provides an insight on how future trends can depend on factors under our control and suggests policy options to us.

Another type of group action, somewhat less structured than the operational game, attempts to improve the panel or committee approach by subjecting the views of individual experts to each other's criticism without actual confrontation and its possible psychological shortcomings. In this approach, called the Delphi method, direct debate is replaced by the interchange of information and opinion through a carefully designed sequence of questionnaires. At each successive interrogation, the participants are given new refined information, and opinion feedback is derived by computing consensus from the earlier part of the program. The process continues until either a consensus is reached, or the conflicting views are documented fully. [8]

It should be emphasized that in many important problems it is not possible to build really quantitative models. The primary function of a model is "explanatory," to organize our thinking. As I have already stated, the essence of systems analysis is not mathematical techniques or procedures, and its recommendations need not follow from computation. What counts is the effort to compare alternatives systematically, in quantitative terms when possible, using a logical sequence of steps that can be retraced and verified by others.

THE VIRTUES

In spite of many limitations, the decision-makers who have made use of systems analysis find it extremely useful. In fact, for some questions of national defense, analysis is essential. Without calculation there is no way to discover how many missiles may be needed to destroy a target system, or how arms control may affect security. It may be essential in other areas also; one cannot experiment radically with the national economy or even change the traffic patterns in a large city without running the risk of chaos. Analysis offers an alternative to "muddling through" or to settling national problems by yielding to the strongest pressure group. It forces the devotees of a program to make explicit their lines of argument, to calculate the resources their programs will require as well as the advantages they might produce.

It is easy, unfortunately, to exaggerate the degree of assistance that systems analysis can offer the policy-maker. At most, it can help him understand the relevant alternatives and the key interactions by providing an estimate of the costs, risks, payoffs and the time span associated with each course of action. It may lead him to consider new and better alternatives. It may sharpen the decision-maker's intuition and will certainly broaden his basis for judgment, thus helping him make a better decision. But value judgments, imprecise knowledge, intuitive estimates, and uncertainties about nature and the actions of others mean that a study can do little more than assess some of the implications of choosing one alternative over another. In practically no case, therefore, should the decision-maker expect the analysis to demonstrate that, beyond all reasonable doubt, a particular course of action is best.

THE LIMITATIONS

Every systems analysis has defects. Some of these are limitations inherent in all analysis of choice. Others are a consequence of the difficulties and complexities of the question. Still others are blunders or errors in thinking, which hopefully will disappear as we learn to do better and more complete analyses.

The alternatives to analysis also have their defects. One alternative is pure intuition. This is in no sense analytic, since no effort is made to structure the problem or to establish cause-and-effect relationships and operate on them to arrive at a solution. The intuitive process is to learn everything possible about the problem, to "live with it," and to let the subconscious provide the solution.

Between pure intuition, on one hand, and systems analysis, on the other, other sources of advice can, in a sense, be considered to employ analysis, although ordinarily of a less systematic, explicit, and quantitative kind. One can turn to an expert. His opinion may, in fact, be very helpful if it results from a reasonable and impartial examination of the facts, with due allowance for uncertainty, and if his assumptions and chain of logic are made *explicit*. Only then can others use his information to form their own considered opinions. But an expert, particualarly an unbiased expert, may be hard to find.

Another way to handle a problem is to turn it over to a committee. Committees, however, are much less likely than experts to make their reasoning explicit, since their findings are usually obtained by bargaining. This is not to imply that a look by a "blue ribbon" committee into such problems as poverty or the allocation of funds for foreign aid might not be useful, but a committee's greatest usefulness is likely to be in the critique of analysis done by others.

However, no matter whether the advice is supplied by an expert, a committee, or a formal study group, the analysis of a problem of choice involves the same five elements and basic structure we discussed earlier.

It is important to remember that all policy analysis falls short of being scientific research. No matter how we strive to maintain standards of scientific inquiry or how closely we attempt to follow scientific methods, we cannot turn systems analysis into science. Such analysis is designed primarily to recommend—or at least to suggest—a course of action, rather than merely to understand and predict. Like engineering, the aim is to use the results of science to do things well and cheaply. Yet, when applied to national problems, the difference from ordinary engineering is apparent in the enormous responsibility involved in the unusual difficulty of appraising—or even discovering—a value system applicable to the problems, and in the absence of ways to test the validity of the analysis.

Except for this inability to verify, systems analysis may still look like a purely rational approach to decision-making, a coldly objective, scientific method free from preconceived ideas, partisan bias, judgment and intuition.

It really is not. Judgment and intuition are used in designing the models; in deciding what alternatives to consider what factors are relevant, what the interrelations between these factors are, and what criteria to choose; and in interpreting the results of the analysis. This fact—that judgment and intuition permeate all analysis—should be remembered when we examine the apparently precise results that seem to come with such high-precision analysis.

Many flaws are the results of pitfalls faced by the analyst. It is all too easy for him to begin to believe his own assumptions and to attach undue significance to his calculations, especially if they involve bitter arguments and extended computations. The most dangerous pitfall or source of defects is an unconscious adherence to a "party line." This is frequently caused by a cherished belief or an *attention bias.* All organizations foster one to some extent; Rand, the military services, and the civilian agencies of the government are no exception. The party line is "the most important single reason for the tremendous miscalculations that are made in foreseeing and preparing for technical advances or changes in the strategic situation."[9] Examples are plentiful: the political adviser whose aim is so fixed on maintaining peace that he completely disregards what might happen should deterrence fail; the weaponeer who is so fascinated by the startling new weapons that he has invented that he assumes the politician will allow them to be used; the union leader whose attention is so fixed on current employment that he rejects an automatic device that can spread his craft into scores of new areas. In fact, this failure to realize the vital interdependence of political purpose, diplomacy, military posture, economics, and technical feasibility is the typical flaw in most practitioners' approach to national security analysis.

There are also pitfalls for the bureaucrat who commissions a study or gives inputs to it. For instance, he may specify assumptions and limit the problem arbitrarily. When a problem is first observed in one part of an organization, there is a tendency to seek a solution completely contained in that part. An administrator is thus likely to pose his problems in such a way as to bar from consideration alternatives or criteria that do not fit into his idea of the way things should be done; for example, he may not think of using ships for some tasks now being done by aircraft. Also, to act wisely on the basis of someone else's analysis one should, at the very least, understand the important and fundamental principles involved. One danger associated with analysis is that it may be employed by an administrator who is unaware of or unwilling to accept its limitations.

Pitfalls are one thing, but the inherent limitations of analysis itself are another. These limitations confine analysis to an advisory role. Three are commented on here: analysis is necessarily incomplete; measures of effectiveness are inevitably approximate; and ways to predict the future are lacking.

ANALYSIS IS NECESSARILY INCOMPLETE

Time and money costs obviously place sharp limits on how far any inquiry can be carried. The very fact that time moves on means that a correct choice at a given time may soon be outdated by events and that goals set down at the start may not be final. The need for reporting almost always forces a cutoff. Time considerations are particularly important in military analysis, for the decision-maker can wait only so long for an answer. Other costs are important here, too. For instance, we would like to find out what the Chinese Communists would do if we put an end to all military aid of Southeast Asia. One way to get this information would be to stop such aid. But while this would clearly be cheap in immediate dollar costs, the likelihood of other later costs precludes this type of investigation.

Still more important, however, is the general fact that, even with no limitations of time and money, analysis can never treat all the considerations that may be relevant. Some are too intangible—for example, how some unilateral United States action will affect NATO solidarity, or whether Congress will accept economies that disrupt cherished institutions such as the National Guard or radically change the pattern of domestic military spending. Considerations of this type should play as important a role in the recommendation of alternative policies as any idealized cost-effectiveness calculations. But ways to measure these considerations even approximately do not exist today, and they must be handled intuitively. Other immeasurable considerations involve moral judgments—for example, whether national security is better served by an increase in the budget for defense or for welfare, or under what circumstances the preservation of an immediate advantage is worth the compromise of fundamental principles. The analyst can apply his and others' judgment and intuition to these considerations, thus making them part of the study; but *bringing them to the attention of the decision-maker,* the man with the responsibility, is extremely important.

MEASURES OF EFFECTIVENESS ARE APPROXIMATE

In military comparisons, measures of effectiveness are at best reasonably satisfactory approximations for indicating the attainment of such vaguely defined objectives as deterrence or victory. Sometimes the best that can be done is to find measures that point in the right direction. Consider deterrence, for instance. It exists only in the mind—and in the enemy's mind at that. We cannot, therefore, measure the effectiveness of alternatives we hope will lead to deterrence by some scale of deterrence, but must use instead such approximations as to the potential mortalities that we might inflict or the roof cover we might destroy. Consequently, even if a comparison of two systems indicated that one could inflict 50 percent more casualities on the enemy than the other, we could not conclude that this means the system supplies 50 percent more deterrence. In fact, since in some circumstances it may be important *not* to look too dangerous, we encounter arguments that the system threatening the greatest number of casualities may provide the *least* deterrence!

Similarly, consider the objective of United States government expenditures for health. A usual measure of effectiveness is the dollar value of increased labor force participation. But, this is clearly inadequate; medical services are more often in demand because of a desire to reduce the everyday aches and pains of life. Moreover, we cannot be very confident about the accuracy of our estimates. For example, one recent and authoritative source estimates the yearly cost of cancer to the United States at $11 billion, while another equally authoritative source estimates $2.6 billion. [10]

NO SATISFACTORY WAY TO PREDICT THE FUTURE EXISTS

While it is possible to forecast events in the sense of mapping out possible futures, there is no satisfactory way to predict a single future for which we can work out the best system or determine an optimum policy. Consequently, we must consider a range of possible futures or contingencies. In any one of these we may be able to designate a preferred course of action, but we have no way to determine such action for the entire range of possibilities. We can design a force structure for a particular war in a particular place, but we have no way to work out a structure that is good for the entire spectrum of future wars in all the places they may occur.

Consequently, defense planning is rich in the kind of analysis that tells what damage could be done to the United States given a particular enemy force structure; but it is poor in the kinds of analyses that evaluate how we will actually stand in relation to the Soviets in years to come.

In spite of these limitations, it is not sensible to formulate policy or action without careful consideration of whatever relevant numbers can be discovered. In current Department of Defense practice, quantitative estimates of various kinds are used extensively. Many people, however, are vaguely uneasy about the particular way these estimates are made and their increasingly important role not only in military planning but elsewhere throughout the government.

Some skepticism may be justified, for the analytical work may not always be done competently or used with its limitations in mind. There may indeed be some dangers in relying on systems analysis, or on any similar approach to broad decisions. For one thing, since many factors fundamental to problems of federal policy are not readily amenable to quantitative treatment, they may possibly be neglected, or deliberately set aside for later consideration and then forgotten, or improperly weighed in the analysis itself, or in the decision based on such analysis. For another, a study may, on the surface, appear so scientific and quantitative that it may be assigned a validity not justified by the many subjective judgments involved. In other words, we may be so mesmerized by the beauty and precision of the numbers that we overlook the simplifications made to achieve this precision, neglect analysis of the qualitative factors, and overemphasize the importance of idealized calculations in the decision process. But without analysis we face even greater dangers in neglect of considerations and in the assignment of improper weights!

The Future

And finally, what of the future? Resistance by the military to the use of systems analysis in broad problems of strategy has gradually broken down. Both government and military planning and strategy have always involved more art than science; what is happening is that the art form is changing from an ad hoc, seat-of-the-pants approach based on intuition to one based on analysis *supported by* intuition and experience. This change may come more slowly in the nonmilitary aspects of government. For one thing, the civilian employees of the government are not so closely controlled "from the top" as those in the military; also the goals in these areas are just as vague and even more likely to be conflicting.[11] The requirements of the integrated Planning—Programming—Budgeting System will do much to speed the acceptance of analysis for other tasks, however.

With the acceptance of analysis, the computer is becoming increasingly significant—as an automaton, a process-controller, an information processor, and a decision aid. Its usefulness in serving these ends can be expected to grow. But at the same time, it is important to note that even the best computer is no more than a tool to expedite analysis. Even in the narrowest decisions, considerations not subject to any sort of quantitative analysis can always be present. Big decisions, therefore, cannot be the *automatic* consequence of a computer program or of any application of mathematical models.

For broad studies, intuitive, subjective, even *ad hoc* study schemes must continue to be used—but supplemented to an increasing extent by systems analysis. The ingredients of this analysis must include not only an increasing use of computer-based models for those problems where they are appropriate, but for treatment of the non-quantifiable aspects, a greater use of techniques for better employment of judgment, intuition, and experience. These techniques—operational gaming, "scenario" writing, and the systematic interrogation of experts—are on the way to becoming an integral part of systems analysis.

Concluding Remarks

And now to review. A systems analysis is an analytic study designed to help a decision-maker identify a preferred choice among possible alternatives. It is characterized by a systematic and rational approach, with assumptions made explicit, objectives and criteria clearly defined, and alternative courses of action compared in the light of their possible consequences. An effort is made to use quantitative methods, but computers are not essential. What is essential is a model that enables expert intuition and judgment to be applied efficiently. The method provides its answer by processes that are accessible to critical examination, capable of duplication by others, and, more or less, readily modified as new information becomes available. And, in contrast to other aids to decision-making, which share the same limitations, it extracts everything possible from scientific methods, and therefore its virtues are the virtues of those methods. At its narrowest, systems analysis has offered a way to choose the numerical quantities related to a weapon system so that they are logically consistent with each other, with an assumed objective, and with the calculator's expectation of the future. At its broadest, through providing the analytic backup for the plans, programs, and budgets of the various executive departments and establishments of the federal government, it can help guide national policy. But, even within the Department of Defense, its capabilities have yet to be fully exploited.

Notes

[1] Helmer, O., *Social Technology*, The Rand Corporation, P-3063, February 1965; presented at the Futuribles Conference in Paris, April 1965.

[2] For a further discussion of this distinction, see J. R. Schlesinger, "Quantitative Analysis and National Security," *World Politics*, 15, no. 2 (January 1963), 295–315.

[3] Or, alternatively, cost-utility and cost-benefit analysis.

[4] C. J. Hitch in E. S. Quade, ed., *Analysis for Military Decisions* (Chicago: Rand McNally, 1964), p. 23, states: "Systems analyses should be looked upon not as the antithesis of judgment but as a framework which permits the judgment of experts in numerous subfields to be utilized—to yield results which transcend any individual judgment. This is its aim and opportunity."

[5] Olaf Helmer, *op. cit.*, p. 7, puts it this way: "The advantage of employing a model lies in forcing the analyst to make explicit what elements of a situation he is taking into consideration and in imposing upon him the discipline of clarifying the concepts he is using. The model thus serves the important purpose of establishing unambiguous intersubjective communication about the subject matter at hand. Whatever intrinsic uncertainties may becloud the area of investigation, they are thus less likely to be further compounded by uncertainties due to disparate subjective interpretations."

[6] See, for example, Donald M. Fort, *Systems Analysis as an Aid in Air Transportation Planning*, P-3293, (Santa Monica, Calif.: The Rand Corporation, January 1966), pp. 12–14.

[7] O. Helmer and E. S. Quade, "An Approach to the Study of a Developing Economy by Operational Gaming," in *Recherche Operationnelle et Problemes du Tiers-Monde*, Colloquium organized by the French Society of Operational Research, with the participation of the Institute of Management Sciences, Operations Research Society of America (Paris: Dunod, 1964), pp. 43–54.

[8] O. Helmer and Norman C. Dalkey, "An Experimental Application of the Delphi Method to the Use of Experts," *Management Sciences*, 9, No. 3 (April 1963), 458–467; and O. Helmer and Nicholas Rescher, "On the Epistemology of the Inexact Sciences," *Management Sciences*, 6, No. 1 (October 1959), 25–52.

[9] *Ibid.*

[10] Kahn, H., and I. Mann, *Ten Common Pitfalls*, RM-1937 (Santa Monica, Calif.: The Rand Corporation, July 17, 1957).

[11] James R. Schlesinger, *op. cit.*, has a slightly different view: "Thus the mere uncovering of ways to increase efficiency is not sufficient. Even where a decision

is clear to the disinterested observer, it is difficult to persuade committed men that their programs or activities should be reduced or abandoned. The price of enthusiasm is that those who have a commitment will be "sold" on their specialty and are incapable of viewing it in cold analytic terms. This may be especially true of the military establishment, where the concepts of duty, honor, and country *when particularized* lead to a certain inflexibility in adjusting to technological change and the new claims of efficiency. But it is also true in the civilian world: for conservationists, foresters, water resource specialists, businessmen, union leaders, or agrarians, some aspects of their value-systems run directly counter to the claims of efficiency. The economic view strikes them all as immoral as well as misleading. (After all, is it not a value judgment on the part of economists that efficiency calculations are important?)

"Even in the case of fairly low-level decisions, if they are political, systematic quantitative analysis does not necessarily solve problems. It will not convince ardent supporters that their program is submarginal. Nevertheless, quantitative analysis remains most useful. For certain operational decisions, it either provides the decision-maker with the justification he may desire for cutting off a project or forces him to come up with a nonnumerical rationalization. It eliminates the purely subjective approach on the part of devotees of a program and forces them to change their lines of argument. They must talk about reality rather than morality. Operational research creates a bridge to budgetary problems over which planners, who previously could assume resources were free, are forced, willingly or unwillingly, to walk."

References

Marshall, A. W., *Cost/Benefit Analysis in Health*, P-3274 (Santa Monica, Calif.: The Rand Corporation, December 1965).

McKean, R. N., *Efficiency in Government Through Systems Analysis* (New York: Wiley, 1958).

Hitch, C. J., and R. N. McKean, *The Economics of Defense in the Nuclear Age* (Cambridge, Mass.: Harvard University Press, 1960).

Peck, M. J., and F. M. Scherer, *The Weapons Acquisition Process: An Economic Analysis* (Cambridge, Mass.: Harvard University Press, 1962).

Ellis, J. W., Jr., and T. E. Greene, "The Contextual Study: A Structured Approach to the Study of Limited War," *Operations Research*, 8, No. 5 (September–October 1960), 639–651.

Novick, D., ed., *Program Budgeting: Program Analysis and the Federal Budget* (Washington, D.C.: Government Printing Office, 1965; Cambridge, Mass.: Harvard University Press, 1965).

Mood, Alex M., "Diversification of Operations Research," *Operations Research*, 13, No. 2 (March–April 1965), 169–178.

Dorfman, Robert, ed.,*Measuring Benefits of Government Investments* (Washington, D.C.: The Brookings Institution, 1965).

Fisher, G. H., *The World of Program Budgeting* P-3361 (Santa Monica, Calif.: The Rand Corporation, May 1966).

13

The Role of Cost-Utility Analysis
in Program Budgeting

GENE H. FISHER

It may be inferred that program budgeting involves several essential considerations. The primary ones may be summarized under three main headings: structural (or format) aspects, analytical process considerations, and data or information system considerations to support the first two items.

The *structural* aspects of program budgeting are concerned with establishing a set of categories oriented primarily toward "end product" or "end objective" activities that are meaningful from a long-range-planning point of view.[1] In such a context emphasis is placed on provision for an extended time horizon—some five, even ten or more, years into the future. These characteristics are in marked contrast to conventional governmental budgeting, which stresses functional and/or object class categories and a very short time horizon.

Analytical process considerations pertain to various study activities conducted as an integral part of the program-budgeting process. The

Reprinted from David Novick (ed.), *Program Budgeting: Program Analysis and the Federal Government* (Cambridge, Mass.: Harvard University Press, Copyright by The Rand Corporation, 1965), pp. 61–78, by permission of the author and publishers.

primary objective of this type of analytical effort is to systematically examine alternative courses of action in terms of utility and cost, with a view to clarifying the relevant choices (and their implications) open to the decision-makers in a certain problem area.

Information system considerations are aimed at support of the first two items. There are several senses in which this is important, the primary ones being (1) progress reporting and control and (2) providing data and information to serve as a basis for the analytical process—especially to facilitate the development of estimating relationships that will permit making estimates of benefits and costs of alternative future courses of action.

The present chapter is concerned primarily with the second of the items listed above: analytical process considerations. That an analytical effort is an important part of program budgeting (at least as practiced in the Department of Defense) is made clear in a recent statement by Secretary of Defense McNamara:

> As I have pointed out in previous appearances before this committee, in adding to a defense program as large as the one we now have, we soon encounter the law of diminishing returns, where each additional increment of resources used produces a proportionately smaller increment of overall defense capability. While the benefits to be gained from each additional increment cannot be measured with precision, careful cost/effectiveness analyses can greatly assist in eliminating those program proposals which clearly contribute little to our military strength in terms of the costs involved.
>
> This principle is just as applicable to qualitative improvements in weapons systems as it is to quantitative increases in our forces. The relevant question is not only, "Do we want the very best for our military force?" but also, "Is the additional capability truly required and, if so, is this the least costly way of attaining it?"
>
> Let me give you one hypothetical example to illustrate the point. Suppose we have two tactical fighter aircraft which are identical in every important measure of performance, except one—Aircraft A can fly ten miles per hour faster than Aircraft B. However, Aircraft A costs $10,000 more per unit than Aircraft B. Thus, if we need about 1,000 aircraft, the total additional cost would be $10 million.
>
> If we approach this problem from the viewpoint of a given amount of resources, the additional combat effectiveness represented by the greater speed of Aircraft A would have to be weighed against the additional combat effectiveness which the same $10 million could produce if applied to other defense purposes—more Aircraft B, more or better aircraft munitions, or more ships, or even more military family housing. And if we approach the problem from the point of view of a given amount of combat capability, we would have to determine whether that given amount could be achieved at

less cost by buying, for example, more of Aircraft B or more aircraft munitions or better munitions, or perhaps surface-to-surface missiles. Thus, the fact that Aircraft A flies ten miles per hour faster than Aircraft B is not conclusive. We still have to determine whether the greater speed is worth the greater cost. *This kind of determination is the heart of the planning-programming-budgeting or resources allocation problem within the Defense Department.*[2]

Numerous analytical approaches may be used to support the total program-budgeting process. Here we shall focus on one of them: cost-utility analysis. Before turning to this subject, however, a few of the other types of analysis should be noted briefly.

In terms of the types of problems encountered in the total program budgeting process, perhaps one might think of a wide spectrum going all the way from the most major allocative decisions on the one hand to progress reporting and control on the other. Major allocative decisions involve such questions as: Should more resources be employed in national security in the future, or in national health programs, or in preservation and development of natural resources, etc.?[3] Ideally, the decision-makers would like to plan to allocate resources in the future so that for a given budget, for example, the estimated marginal return (or utility) in each major area of application would be equal. But this is more easily said than done; and at the current state of analytical art, no one really knows with any precision how the "grand optimum" might be attained. In the main, the analytical tools now available—particularly the quantitative ones—are just not very helpful in dealing directly with such problems. Intuition and judgment are paramount.

At the other end of the spectrum—progress reporting and control—the main problem is to keep track of programs where the major decisions have *already been made,* to try to detect impending difficulties as programs are being implemented, and to initiate remedial actions through a feedback mechanism when programs are deemed likely to get out of control in the future. Numerous techniques are available for dealing with these types of program-management problems. Examples are the following: financial and management accounting techniques;[4] network-type systems for planning, scheduling, progress reporting, and control;[5] critical path methods (within the framework of a network-type system);[6] Gantt chart techniques for program planning and control;[7] and various program-management reporting and control schemes developed in recent years in the Department of Defense to help program managers in the management of complex weapon system development and production programs.[8]

The area between the ends of the spectrum is a broad and varied one, offering the opportunity for applying a variety of analytical techniques. These techniques are focused primarily on problem areas short of dealing with determination of the "grand optimum," although they can be of real assistance in sharpening the intuition and judgment of decision-makers in grappling with the very broad allocative questions. Technically, this is called "suboptimization," and it is here that the analytical efforts are likely to have the highest payoff.[9]

In cases where a wide range of alternative future courses of action needs to be examined in a broad suboptimization context, the main subject of this chapter, cost-utility analysis,[10] may well be the most useful analytical tool. However, in other cases where the suboptimization context is much narrower and a wide range of alternatives is not available, the problem may be one of examining relatively minor variations *within* an essentially prescribed future course of action. The suboptimization context may be relatively narrow for numerous reasons—severe political constraints, lack of new technology to provide the basis for a wide range of alternatives, etc. Here, something akin to capital budgeting[11] techniques may be most appropriate.

In many instances, the above-mentioned techniques may have to be supplemented by other methods. For example, in numerous major decision problems it is not sufficient to deal only with the *direct* economic consequences of proposed alternative future courses of action, ignoring their possible indirect or spillover effects. In such instances, it may well be vitally important to consider indirect economic effects either on the economy as a whole or on specified regions or sectors of the total economic system. Certain transportation problems involve considerations of this type.[12] Also, in the case of certain national security and space decisions, especially in the higher echelons of the decision hierarchy, it is often necessary to consider possible regional or industry sector economic impacts associated with alternative weapon system development and procurement choices.[13] One way to deal with such problems is through the use of macroeconomic models that attempt to take into account key interactions among important components of the economic system: for example, interindustry (input-output) models for the economy as a whole,[14] and various types of regional models dealing with parts of the total national economy.[15]

Thus it is clear that numerous analytical methods and techniques exist that may be used to support various facets of the total program-budgeting process. We have dealt with this point at some length to emphasize that the subject of this chapter, cost-utility analysis, is not the only analytical tool that might be used in program budgeting. Let us now turn to our central theme.

What Is Cost-Utility Analysis?

Attempting to define cost-utility analysis poses somewhat of a semantics problem. Numerous terms in current use convey the same general meaning but have important different meanings to different people: "cost-benefit analysis," "cost-effectiveness analysis," "systems analysis," "operations research," "operations analysis," etc. Because of such terminological confusion, in this chapter all of these terms are rejected and "cost-utility analysis" is employed instead.

Cost-utility analysis, as envisioned here, may be distinguished by the following major characteristics:

1. A most fundamental characteristic is the systematic examination and comparison of alternative courses of action that might be taken to achieve specified objectives for some future time period. Not only is it important to systematically examine all of the relevant alternatives that can be identified initially, but also to *design additional ones* if those examined are found wanting.[16] Finally, the analysis, particularly if thoroughly and imaginatively done, may at times result in modifications of the initially specified objectives.

2. Critical examination of alternatives typically involves numerous considerations; but the two main ones are assessment of the cost (in the sense of economic resource cost) and the utility (the benefits or gains) pertaining to each of the alternatives being compared to attain the stipulated objectives.

3. The time context is the future (often the distant future—five, ten, or more years).

4. Because of the extended time horizon, the environment is one of uncertainty (very often great uncertainty). Since uncertainty is an important facet of the problem, it should be faced up to and treated explicitly in the analysis. This means, among other things, that wherever possible the analyst should avoid the use of simple expected value models.

5. Usually the context in which the analysis takes place is broad (often very broad) and the environment very complex, with numerous interactions among the key variables in the problem. This means that simple, straightforward solutions are the exception rather than the rule.

6. While quantitative methods of analysis should be used as much as possible, because of items 4 and 5 above,[17] purely quantitative work must often be heavily supplemented by qualitative analysis. In fact, we stress the importance of *good* qualitative work and of using an appropriate combination of quantitative and qualitative methods.

7. Usually the focus is on research and development and/or investment-type decision problems, although operational decisions are sometimes encountered. This does not mean, of course, that operational considerations are ignored in dealing with R & D and investment-type problems.

8. Timeliness is important. A careful, thorough analysis that comes six months after the critical time of decision may be worth essentially zero, while a less thorough—but thoughtfully done—analysis completed on time may be worth a great deal.

The Primary Purpose of Cost-Utility Analysis

In the context being considered in this chapter, let us be very clear about what the main purpose of analysis in general, and cost-utility analysis in particular, really is. Contrary to what some of the more enthusiastic advocates of quantitative analysis may think, we visualize cost-utility analysis as playing a somewhat modest, though very significant, role in the overall decision-making process. In reality, most major long-range-planning decision problems must ultimately be resolved primarily on the basis of intuition and judgment. We suggest that the main role of analysis should be to try to *sharpen* this intuition and judgment. In practically no case should it be assumed that the results of the analysis will *make* the decision. The really interesting problems are just too difficult, and there are too many intangible (e.g., political, psychological, and sociological) considerations that cannot be taken into account in the analytical process, especially in a quantitative sense. In sum, the analytical process should be directed toward assisting the decision-maker in such a way that (hopefully!) his intuition and judgment are better than it would be without the results of the analysis.[18]

Viewing the objective of cost-utility analysis in this way is likely to put the analyst in a frame of mind that will permit him to be much more useful to the decision-maker than if he takes a more hard-core view. These are two extremes here. On the one hand, it might be argued that the types of long-range-planning decision problems considered in this chapter are just too complex for the current state of analytical art to handle. Therefore, decisions must be made purely on the basis of intuition, judgment, and experience—i.e., the zero-analysis position. At the other extreme are those who (naively) think that all problems should be tackled in a purely quantitative fashion, with a view essentially to making the decision. Such a view implies explicit (usually meaning quantitative) calculations of cost and utility for all the alternatives under consideration.

This may be possible, at times, for very narrowly defined, low-level suboptimization problems; but even this is questionable.

More generally, in dealing with major decision problems of choice, if the analyst approaches his task in an inflexible hard-core frame of mind, he is likely to be in for trouble. For example, he may soon give up in complete frustration; or he may wind up with such a simplified model that the resulting calculations are essentially meaningless; or his conclusions may not be ready for presentation until two years after the critical decision time and would therefore be useless to the decision-maker.

The viewpoint taken here is that in most cases the relevant range is between the extremes mentioned above, and that in such a context there is a wide scope of analytical effort that can be useful. Furthermore, even when only a relatively incomplete set of quantitative calculations of cost and utility can be made (probably the general situation), much can be done to assist the decision-maker in the sense that the term "assistance" is used in this chapter. To repeat: The objective is to *sharpen* intuition and judgment. It is conceivable that even a small amount of sharpening may on occasion have a high payoff.

One other point seems relevant. In that rare circumstance when a fairly complete set of calculations of cost and utility is possible and a resulting conclusion about a preferred alternative is reached, it may well be that the conclusion itself is not the most useful thing to the decision-maker. For one thing, as pointed out earlier, the analysis usually cannot take everything into account—particularly some of the nebulous non-quantitative considerations. The decision-maker has to allow for these himself. But more important, most high-level decision-makers are very busy men who do not have time to structure a particular problem, think up the relevant alternatives (especially the *subtle* ones), trace out the key interactions among variables in the problem, etc. This the analyst, if he is competent, can do, and should do. And it is precisely this sort of contribution that may be most useful to the decision-maker. The fact that the analysis reaches a firm conclusion about a preferred alternative may in many instances be of secondary importance.

Some of the Major Considerations
Involved in Doing Cost-Utility Analysis

At this point, one might logically expect the title to be "How to Do Cost-Utility Analysis"—a cookbook, so to speak. We avoid this for two main reasons: (1) If such a treatise were attempted it would take an entire book; but, more important, (2) it is doubtful that even a book on the subject is possible. At the current stage of development of analytical methods, cost-utility analysis is an art rather than a science. The really significant problems to be tackled are each in a sense unique, with the result that it is not possible to give a definitive set of rules on how to do an appropriate analysis. All that can be done is to give some guidelines, principles, and illustrative examples. But books, or major parts of books, have been written on this subject.[19] Here the treatment must of necessity be more limited.

Some important guidelines to be followed in carrying out a cost-utility analysis (not necessarily in order of relative importance) are discussed in the following paragraphs.[20]

PROPER STRUCTURING OF THE PROBLEM AND DESIGN OF THE ANALYSIS

This is by far the most important of the guidelines. Given an incredibly complex environment, that which is relevant to the problem at hand must be included, and that which is irrelevant excluded. There are no formal rules to guide us. The experience, skill, imagination, and intuition of the analyst are paramount. It is at this point—the *design* of the analysis—that most cost-utility studies either flounder hopelessly or move ahead toward success. In sum, if we can structure the problem so that the *right questions* are being asked, we shall be well on the way toward a good analysis. This sounds trite, but it really is not. The author has seen all too many instances of large amounts of effort being expended on an analytical exercise addressed to the wrong questions.[21]

Another point is that typically the problem and the design of the analysis may well have to be *re*structured several times. Considerations that were initially thought to be important may, after some preliminary work, turn out to be relatively unimportant, and vice versa. Finally, in the process of doing some of the analytical work new questions and new alternatives may come to mind.

THE CONCEPTUAL FRAMEWORK

In general there are two principal conceptual approaches:[22]

1. *Fixed utility approach.* For a specified level of utility to be attained in the accomplishment of some given objective, the analysis attempts to determine that alternative (or feasible combination of alternatives) likely to achieve the specified level of utility at the lowest economic cost.

2. *Fixed budget approach.* For a specified budget level to be used in

the attainment of some given objective, the analysis attempts to determine that alternative (or feasible combination of alternatives) likely to produce the highest utility for the given budget level.

Either (or both) of these approaches may be used, depending on the context of the problem at hand. In any event, the objective is to permit *comparisons* to be made among alternatives, and for this purpose something has to be made fixed.

At this point a comment on the use of ratios (e.g., utility-to-cost ratios) seems in order. Very often such ratios are used to evaluate alternatives. The use of ratios usually poses no problem as long as the analysis is conducted in the framework outlined above (i.e., with the level of either utility or cost fixed). However, the author has on occasion seen studies where this was not done, with the result that the comparisons were essentially meaningless. For example, consider the following hypothetical illustration:

	Utility (U)	Cost (C)	U/C
Alternative A	20	10	2
Alternative B	200	100	2

If the analyst is preoccupied with ratios, the implication of the above example is a state of indifference regarding the choice between A and B. But *should* the analyst be indifferent? Most probably not, because of the wide difference in scale between A and B. In fact, with such a great difference in scale, the analyst might not even be comparing relevant alternatives at all.[23]

BUILDING THE MODEL

Here the term "model" is used in a broad sense. Depending on the nature of the problem at hand, the model used in the analysis may be formal or informal, very mathematical or not so mathematical, heavily computerized or only moderately so, etc. However, the main point is that the model need not be highly formal and mathematical to be useful. In any event, the following are some important points to keep in mind:

1. Model building is an art, not a science. It is often an experimental process.

2. The main thing is to try to include and highlight those factors that are relevant to the problem at hand, and to suppress (judiciously!) those

that are relatively unimportant. Unless the latter is done, the model is likely to be unmanageable.

3. The main purpose in designing the model is to develop a meaningful *set of relationships* among objectives, the relevant alternatives available for attaining the objectives, the estimated cost of the alternatives, and the estimated utility for each of the alternatives.

4. Provision must be made for explicit treatment of uncertainty. (There will be more on this later.)

5. Since by definition a model is an abstraction from reality, the model must be built on a set of assumptions. These assumptions must be made *explicit*. If they are not, this is to be regarded as a defect of the model design.

TREATMENT OF UNCERTAINTY

Since most really interesting and important decision problems involve major elements of uncertainty, a cost-utility analysis of such problems must provide for explicit treatment of uncertainty. This may be done in numerous ways.

For purposes of discussion, two main types of uncertainty may be distinguished:

1. Uncertainty about the state of the world in the future. In a national security context, major factors are technological uncertainty, strategic uncertainty,[24] and uncertainty about the enemy and his reactions.

2. Statistical uncertainty. This type of uncertainty stems from chance elements in the real world. It would exist even if uncertainties of the first type were zero.

Type 2 uncertainties are usually the least troublesome to handle in cost-utility studies. When necessary, Monte Carlo[25] and/or other techniques may be used to deal with statistical fluctuations; but these perturbations are usually swamped by Type 1 uncertainties, which are dominant in most long-range planning problems. The use of elaborate techniques to treat statistical uncertainties in such problems is likely to be expensive window dressing.[26]

Type 1 uncertainties are typically present in most long-range decision problems, and they are most difficult to take into account in a cost-utility analysis. Techniques that are often used are sensitivity analysis, contingency analysis, and a fortiori analysis.[27]

Sensitivity Analysis. Suppose in a given analysis there are a few key parameters about which the analyst is very uncertain. Instead of using "expected values" for these parameters, the analyst may use several values (say, high, medium, and low) in an attempt to see how sensitive the results (the ranking of the alternatives being considered) are to variations in the uncertain parameters.[28]

Contingency Analysis. This type of analysis investigates how the ranking of the alternatives under consideration holds up when a relevant change in criteria for evaluating the alternatives is postulated, or a major change in the general environment is assumed. (For example, in a military context, the enemy is assumed to be countries A and B. We might then want to investigate what would happen if C joins the A and B coalition.)

A Fortiori Analysis. Suppose that in a particular planning-decision problem the generally accepted intuitive judgment strongly favors alternative X. However, the analyst feels that X might be a poor choice and that alternative Y might be preferred. In performing an analysis of X versus Y, the analyst may choose deliberately to resolve the major uncertainties in favor of X and see how Y compares under these adverse conditions. If Y still looks good, the analyst has a very strong case in favor of Y.

Creation of a New Alternative. Although the three techniques listed above may be useful in a direct analytical sense, they may also contribute indirectly. For example, through sensitivity and contingency analyses the analyst may gain a good understanding of the really critical uncertainties in a given problem area. On the basis of this knowledge he might then be able to come up with a newly designed alternative that will provide a reasonably good hedge against a *range* of the more significant uncertainties. This is often difficult to do; but when it can be accomplished, it may offer one of the best ways to compensate for uncertainty.

TREATMENT OF PROBLEMS ASSOCIATED WITH TIME

More likely than not, the particular problem at hand will be posed in a dynamic context; or at least the problem will have some dynamic aspects to it. While a "static" type analysis can go a long way toward providing the decision-maker with useful information, very often this has to be supplemented by analytical work that takes time into account explicitly.

A case in point is with respect to the treatment of the estimated *costs* of the alternatives for a fixed level of utility.[29] The nature of the problem may be such that the costs have to be time-phased, resulting in cost streams through time for each of the alternatives. The question then arises whether the decision-maker is or is not indifferent to the time impact of the costs. If he is not indifferent about time preference, then the cost streams have to be "discounted" through time, using an appropriate rate of discount.[30] Determining specifically what rate to use can be a problem; but it is usually manageable.[31] If it is not, an upper bound rate and a lower bound rate may be used to see whether it really makes any difference in the final conclusions of the problem.

It should be pointed out that the analyst pays a price for introducing time explicitly into an analysis:[32]

1. It complicates the analysis by increasing the number of variables and hence the number of calculations. If we put time in, we may have to take something else out.

2. As implied above, it complicates the selection of a criterion for evaluating alternatives: solution X may be better for 1966 and worse for 1970; solution Y may be just the reverse.

VALIDITY CHECKING

In the preceeding paragraphs we have discussed building the analytical model, "exercising" the model (sensitivity and contingency analysis), etc. Another important consideration—often relatively neglected—is checking the validity of the model. Since the model is only a *representation* of reality, it is desirable to do some sort of checking to see if the analytical procedure used is a reasonably good representation, within the context of the problem at hand. This is difficult to do, especially in dealing with problems having a time horizon five, ten, or more years into the future.

In general, we cannot test models of this type by methods of "controlled experiment." However, the analyst might try to answer the following questions:[33]

1. Can the model describe known facts and situations reasonably well?

2. When the principal parameters involved are varied, do the results remain consistent and plausible?

3. Can it handle special cases where we already have some indication as to what the outcome should be?

4. Can it assign causes to known effects?

QUALITATIVE SUPPLEMENTATION

We have already stressed the importance of qualitative considerations in cost-utility analysis—particularly qualitative *supplementation* of the quantitative work. Introduction of qualitative considerations may take several forms:

1. Qualitative analysis per se, as an integral part of the total analytical effort.

2. Interpretation of the quantitative work.

3. Discussion of relevant nonquantitative considerations that could not be taken into account in the "formal" analysis.

The latter item can be particularly important in presenting the results of a study to the decision-maker. The idea is to present the results of the formal quantitative work, interpret these results, and then say that this is as far as the formal quantitative analysis per se will permit us to go. However, there are important *qualitative* considerations that you (the decision-maker) should try to take into account; and here they are (list them). Finally, relevant questions about each of the qualitative items can be raised and important interrelations among them discussed.

Summary Comments

We stress again that the discussion above pertains to a long-range planning context, with emphasis on specifying, clarifying, and comparing the relevant alternatives. Since comparative analysis is the prime focus, it is vitally important to continually emphasize *consistency* in the analytical concepts, methods, and techniques used. That is, instead of trying for a high degree of accuracy in an *absolute* sense (which is usually unattainable anyway), the analyst should stress development and use of procedures that will treat the alternatives being considered in an unbiased, consistent manner.

The main points presented in this chapter may be summarized as follows:

1. An analytical activity is an important part of the total program-budgeting process.

2. Cost-utility analysis pertains to the systematic examination and comparison of alternative courses of action that might be taken to achieve specified objectives for some future time period. Not only is it important to examine all relevant alternatives that can be identified initially but it is also important to design additional ones if those examined are found wanting.

3. The primary purpose of cost-utility analysis is usually not to *make* the decision, but rather to *sharpen* the intuition and judgment of the decision-makers. Identification of the relevant alternatives and clarification of their respective implications are of prime importance.

4. In a long-range planning context, the following are some of the major considerations involved in a cost-utility analysis:

(a) Proper structuring of the problem is all-important. The analysis must be addressed to the right questions.

(b) In making comparisons, an appropriate analytical framework must be used. For example, for a specified level of utility to be attained in the accomplishment of some given objective, the alternatives may be compared on the basis of their estimated economic resource impact; or (vice versa), for a given budget level, the alternatives may be compared on the basis of their estimated utility.

(c) It is usually necessary to construct a model (either formal or informal) to be used in the analytical process. Here the main purpose is to develop a set of relationships among objectives, the relevant alternatives available for attaining the objectives, the estimated cost of the alternatives, and the estimated utility for each of the alternatives.

(d) Uncertainty must be faced explicitly in the analysis. Sensitivity analysis, contingency analysis, and a fortiori analysis are three possible techniques that may be used in dealing with the problem of uncertainty.

(e) Although it complicates the analysis because of an increase in the number of variables, very often *time-phasing* of the impacts of the various alternatives is a requirement. If the decision-makers are not indifferent to time preference, the estimates of time-phased impacts must be "equalized" over time through the use of a "discounting" procedure.

(f) Since the model is only a representation of reality, it is desirable to do some validity checking of the analytical procedure; e.g., can the model describe known facts and situations reasonably well?

(g) Although cost-utility analysis stresses the use of quantitative methods, the analyst should not hesitate to supplement his quantitative work with appropriate *qualitative* analyses.

Notes

[1] In many instances, end products may in fact be *intermediate* products, especially from the point of view of the next higher level in the decision hierarchy.

[2] From the introduction of the Statement of Secretary of Defense Robert S. McNamara before the Committee on Armed Services on the Fiscal Year 1965–1969 Defense Program and 1965 Defense Budget, January 27, 1964, *Hearings on Military Posture* and H.R. 9637, House of Representatives, 88th Cong., 2d sess. (Washington, D.C.: U.S. Government Printing Office, 1964).

[3] For example, see Arthur Smithies, *Government Decision-Making and the Theory of Choice*, P-2960 (Santa Monica, Calif.: The Rand Corporation, October 1964).

[4] See Robert N. Anthony, *Management Accounting* (Homewood, Ill.: Irwin, 1960), chaps. 13–15.

[5] One example is the so-called PERT system. For a description, see *USAF PERT, Volume I, PERT Time System Description Manual,* September 1963 and *USAF PERT, Volume III, PERT Cost System Description Manual,* December 1963 (Washington, D.C.: Headquarters, Air Force Systems Command, Andrews Air Force Base, 1963).

[6] See James E. Kelly and Morgan R. Walker, "Critical-Path Planning and Scheduling," *Proceedings of the Eastern Joint Computer Conference* (Ft. Washington, Pa.: Manchly Associates, Inc., 1959), pp. 160–173; and F. K. Levy, G. L. Thompson, and J. D. Wiest, *Mathematical Basis of the Critical Path Method,* Office of Naval Research, Research Memorandum No. 86 (Pittsburgh, Pa.: Carnegie Institute of Technology, May 30, 1962).

[7] L. P. Alford and John R. Bangs, *Production Handbook* (New York: Ronald Press, 1947), pp. 216–229.

[8] For a good example, see *Systems Data Presentation and Reporting Procedures* (Rainbow Report), November 1, 1961 (with revisions as of March 9, 1962), Program Management Instruction 1–5 (Washington, D.C.: Headquarters, Air Force Systems Command, Andrews Air Force Base 1962).

[9] For a discussion of suboptimization, see Charles Hitch, "Suboptimization in Operations Problems," *Journal of the Operations Research Society of America,* 1, No. 3, May 1953, 87–99; and Charles J. Hitch and Roland N. McKean, *The Economics of Defense in the Nuclear Age* (Cambridge, Mass.: Harvard University Press, 1960), pp. 396–402.

[10] Sometimes called "systems analysis"; e.g., see Roland N. McKean, *Efficiency in Government Through Systems Analysis* (New York: Wiley, 1958).

[11] For example, see Joel Dean, *Capital Budgeting* (New York: Columbia University Press, 1951); Harold Bierman, Jr., and Seymour Smidt, *The Capital Budgeting Decision* (New York: Macmillan, 1960); and Elwood S. Buffa, *Models for Production and Operations Management* (New York: Wiley, 1963), chaps. 13 and 14.

[12] For example, see Brian V. Martin and Charles B. Warden, "Transportation Planning in Developing Countries," *Traffic Quarterly,* January 1965, pp. 59–75.

[13] See *Convertibility of Space and Defense Resources to Civilian Needs: A Search for New Employment Potentials,* compiled for the Subcommittee on Employment and Manpower of the Committee on Labor and Public Welfare, Senate, 88th Cong., 2d sess. (Washington, D.C.: U.S. Government Printing Office, 1964). Note especially Part III, "National Adjustments to Shifts in Defense Planning," and Part IV, "Studies in Regional Adjustment to Shifts in Defense Spending."

[14] W. W. Leontief et al., *Studies in the Structure of the American Economy* (New York: Oxford University Press, 1953).

[15] For example, see Walter Isard et al., *Methods of Regional Analysis: An Introduction to Regional Science* (Boston and New York: Technology Press of Massachusetts Institute of Technology and Wiley, 1960).

[16] E. S. Quade, *Military Systems Analysis* (Santa Monica, Calif.: The Rand Corporation, RM-3452-PR, January 1963), p. 1.

[17] And also because of inadequate data and information sources.

[18] Apparently this view is held by Alain C. Enthoven, Deputy Assistant Secretary for Systems Analysis, Department of Defense. He writes:

Where does this leave us? What is operations research or systems analysis at the Defense policy level all about? I think that it can best be described as a continuing dialogue between the policy-maker and the systems analyst, in which the policy-maker asks for alternative solutions to his problems, makes decisions to exlude some, and makes value judgments and policy decisions, while the analyst attempts to clarify the conceptual framework in which decisions must be made, to define alternative possible objectives and criteria, and to explore in as clear terms as possible (and quantitatively) the cost and effectiveness of alternative courses of action.

The analyst at this level is not computing optimum solutions or making decisions. In fact, computation is not his most important contribution. And he is helping someone else to make decisions. His job is to ask and find answers to the questions: "What are we trying to do?" "What are the alternative ways of achieving it?" "What would they cost, and how effective would they be?" "What does the decision-maker need to know in order to make a choice?" And to collect and organize this information for those who are responsible for deciding what the Defense program ought to be.

(Alain C. Enthoven, "Decision Theory and Systems Analysis," *The Armed Forces Comptroller,* IX, No. 1, [March 1964], 39.)

[19] For example, see Hitch and McKean, *op. cit.,* especially Part II; and McKean, *op. cit.*

[20] Observance of these guidelines will not in itself produce a good analysis, but it will most surely help. Many of the points listed here are based on Quade, *Military Systems Analysis,* pp. 8–24.

[21] Incredible as it may seem, there have been studies that started out by asking questions about which alternative would maximize gain and at the same time minimize cost—clearly an impossible situation.

[22] The fixed level of utility or budget is usually specified by someone "outside the analysis"; i.e., it is usually a datum given to the analyst. Very often the analyst will use several levels (e.g., high, medium, and low) to investigate the sensitivity of the ranking of the alternatives to the utility or budget level.

[23] For a further discussion of the possible pitfalls of using ratios, see McKean, *op. cit.,* pp. 34–37, 107–113.

[24] For example: Will there be a war in the future? If so, when? General or local? With what political constraints? Who will be our enemies? Our allies? See C. J. Hitch, *An Appreciation of Systems Analysis,* P-699 (Santa Monica, Calif.: The Rand Corporation, August 18, 1955), p. 6.

[25] For a discussion of Monte Carlo techniques, see Herman Kahn and Irwin Mann, *Monte Carlo,* P-1165 (Santa Monica, Calif.: The Rand Corporation, July 30, 1957); and E. S. Quade, *Analysis for Military Decisions,* R-387-PR (Santa Monica, Calif.: The Rand Corporation, November, 1964), pp. 407–414.

[26] Hitch, *Appreciation of Systems Analysis,* p. 7.

[27] Quade, *Military Systems Analysis,* pp. 23–24.

[28] Enthoven, *op. cit.,* pp. 16–17, talks about sensitivity analysis in the following way:

If it is a question of uncertainties about quantitative matters such as operational factors, it is generally useful to examine the available evidences and determine the bounds of the uncertainty. In many of our analyses for the Secretary of Defense, we carry three estimates through the calculations: an "optimistic," a "pessimistic," and a "best" or single most likely estimate. Although it is usually sensible to design the defense posture primarily on the basis of the best estimates, the prudent decision-maker will keep asking himself, "Would the outcome be acceptable if the worst possible happened, i.e., if all the pessimistic estimates were borne out?" Carrying three numbers through all of the calculations can increase the work load greatly. For this reason, a certain amount of judgment has to be used as to when the best guesses are satisfactory and when the full range of uncertainty needs to be explored. If there are uncertainties about context, at least one can run the calculations on the basis of several alternative assumptions so that the decision-maker can see how the outcome varies with the assumptions.

[29] Maintaining a fixed level of utility *through time* is often a tricky problem in itself. We cannot go into this matter in the present limited discussion.

[30] One may raise the question regarding under what conditions the decision-maker *would* be indifferent. Economic theorists might argue that there probably should not be any such condition. However, in practice, decision-makers often find themselves in an institutional setting (such as the Department of Defense, for example) where it is customary to be indifferent regarding time preference; hence discounting of cost streams through time is not done. This is not to say that the decision-makers are correct in principle.

It should be emphasized that the type of discounting under discussion here is purely to equalize cost streams through time with respect to time preference—not to compensate for risk.

[31] For example, see E. B. Berman, *The Normative Interest Rate,* P-1796 (Santa Monica, Calif.: The Rand Corporation, September 15, 1959).

[32] Hitch, *Appreciation of Systems Analysis,* pp. 11–12.

[33] Quade, *Military Systems Analysis,* p. 20.

VI

RELATING GOALS
TO SYSTEMS

14

Goal-Model and System-Model Criteria of Effectiveness

PERRY LEVINSON

The national investment in social welfare programs continues to expand, yet the consequences of these programs have only been partially evaluated. Without careful assessment, the relative merits of any given project will be lost while errors are repeated—or even compounded—if it serves as a prototype. The responsibility of social scientists to respond to this need for applied research has never been greater.

If asked to evaluate a social welfare program, most social scientists would make their assessment against the explicitly stated goals of the organization. The question typically posed by troubled administrators is: how close does the program come to achieving its publicized goals? Does, for example, a boy's club reduce the amount of delinquency in the neighborhood? Does a consumer education program increase buying skills? Success is thus defined as a complete, or at least a substantial, realization of a program's goals. Amitai Etzioni refers to this widely held method of evaluating organizations as the *goal-model* approach.[1]

Reprinted from *Welfare in Review*, 4, No. 10 (December 1966): 5–12, where it appeared under the title "Evaluation of Social Welfare Programs: Two Research Models," by permission of the author.

The Goal-Model Approach

One of the most sophisticated procedures designed to measure the extent to which the goals of a program have, in fact, been realized is found in the works of Clarence C. Sherwood.[2] In order to determine program success, Sherwood has suggested the study of three kinds of variables: program variables, intermediate variables, and dependent variables. Figure 1 illustrates the sequential flow of these variables and includes a fourth set of variables, population variables, to complete the outline. For the further convenience of the reader these variables have been labeled twice, once using operations research terminology (income, outcome, input, output) and once using Sherwood's terminology.

FIGURE 1
Goal-Model Approach

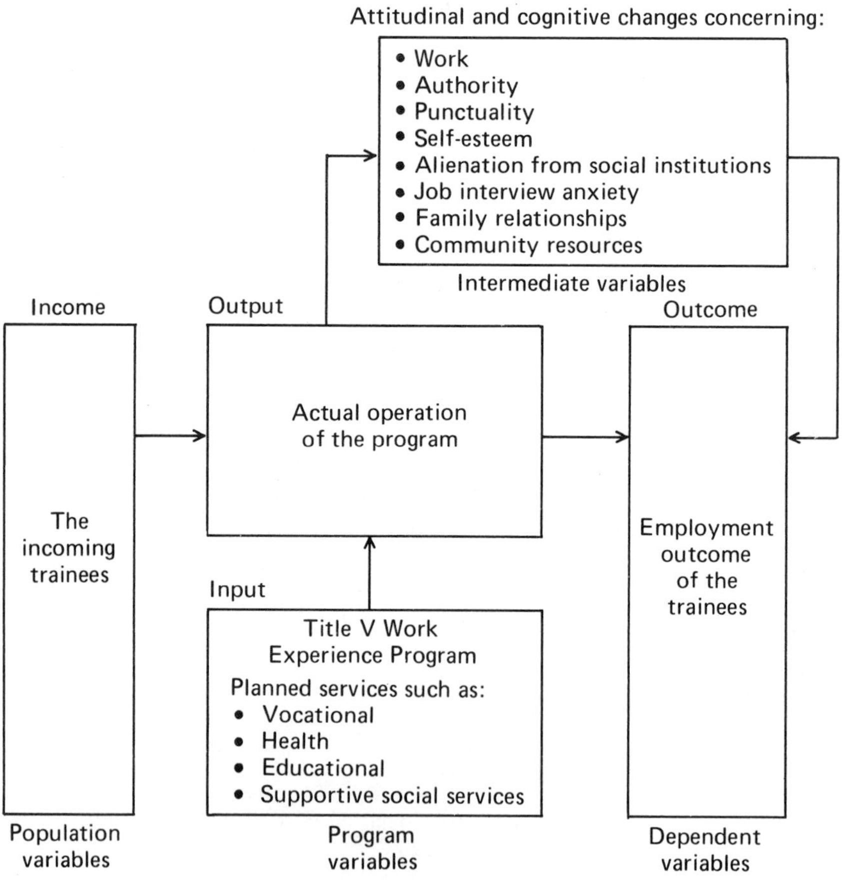

Attitudinal and cognitive changes concerning:

• Work
• Authority
• Punctuality
• Self-esteem
• Alienation from social institutions
• Job interview anxiety
• Family relationships
• Community resources

Intermediate variables

Income

Output

Outcome

Actual operation
of the program

The
incoming
trainees

Input

Employment
outcome
of the
trainees

Title V Work
Experience Program

Planned services such as:
• Vocational
• Health
• Educational
• Supportive social services

Population
variables

Program
variables

Dependent
variables

The basic flow through the *goal-model* begins with (1) an incoming group (called simply Income) possessing certain population characteristics to whom (2) something is done (the program input-output components) which in turn produces (3) a desired change (outcome), assuming that (4) certain attitudinal and cognitive changes have previously occurred (the intermediate variables). To keep a stable frame of reference throughout this paper, the *goal-model* approach has been applied to the Work Experience Program under Title V of the Economic Opportunity Act of 1964. The model can just as readily be applied to other intervention programs, such as planned parenthood, juvenile delinquency prevention, and alcoholic rehabilitation.

THE INCOMING GROUP

Obviously, the program evaluator must be familiar with the characteristics of program participants. His problem is to decide which of an infinite number of characteristics are relevant to the implementation of the program or are likely to affect chances of program success or even program participation. These relevant characteristics can be as gross as the age, sex, or occupational history of the participants or as subtle as the extent of depressed aspiration levels, anxiety, or alienation of the participants. Characteristics that are particularly important to measure at the time the group first comes into the program are those that the program assumes must be changed (the intermediate variables) before a successful outcome can occur (the dependent variable). Some of these relevant intermediate change variables will be discussed later.

THE PROGRAM VARIABLES

Sherwood has described program variables as constituting that "complex set of organized stimuli" which, if any scientific prediction is to be made concerning their effect, must be so accurately described and thoroughly understood that they can be reconstructed at another time, in another place, by other professionals. If the program works, then that which constitutes the program must be sufficiently understood so that the program can be repeated in other projects with other directors. Conversely, if the program fails, then that which constitutes the program must be sufficiently understood so that the program is *not* repeated, is *not* reorganized bearing only a new name or a new director.

However, the problem of accurately describing and thoroughly understanding program components has not been adequately solved. One possible strategy would be for program evaluators to divide the program into input and output segments. This contributes to a more accurate description of the program in that these segments coincide with the formal and informal aspects of bureaucratic structures. Just how the program was formally planned (input) should then be contrasted with just how the program actually operates in day to day practice (output). For example, if the training program is formally designated to operate over a three-month period (input), the actual attendance record of the participants (output) must be compared with the specified number of training sessions in that period. Or, for example, if project administrators express the belief that the program is to operate under the guidance of sensitive instructors who inspire confidence (input), their stated belief must be constrasted with the actual method of supervision, which may be harsh, impatient, and/or authoritarian (output). The measurement of *input* calls for a careful reading of program proposals and organizational charts; the measurement of *output* calls for the careful observation (even as a disguised participant-observer) of the work and training sessions, including the interaction between trainee and case worker, trainee and vocational educational teacher, and trainee and colleagues.

Measurement of input/output has its drawbacks, however, and must be supplemented by a second strategy. A complete description of input and output could conceivably take all of the researcher's time. Or it could be so unwieldly, bound by rigid, overspecified procedures, that it would be self-defeating: any attempt to replicate the program would never get off the ground.

The second strategy for describing program variables is to work out, with the assistance of program administrators, an *impact model.* Such a model has been described by Sherwood as "a set of theoretical concepts or ideas which trace the dynamics of how it is expected that the program will have the desired effects; a theory which logically interrelates a set of principles and procedures . . . [that] logically imply that certain decisions rather than others be made with respect to such [crucial] . . . day-to-day program situations."[3] According to this description, what must be identified are those crucial program situations which describe a standardized decision based on an explicitly stated theory of human behavior. For example, the trainees must be assigned to different job training categories. Should they choose the jobs they will train for? Should they choose their beginning level of training? How are the program answers to these questions related to a theory of interpersonal competence or for that matter to any other theory of positive mental health?

One of the latent benefits derived from program evaluation is the clarification of program goals and procedures. Other latent benefits are to:

(a) enhance the probability that such programs may have an impact; (b) provide a basis for training program personnel that does not require that a program procedure be specified for every conceivable situation; (c) provide a basis for outside monitoring of a program; (d) provide a rational basis for modifying the program design should it appear that it does not have the desired effects, and (e) provide the basis for a repeatable program which goes well beyond the mere rote repetition of isolated procedures.[4]

Developing a rigorous *impact model* is a difficult and tiresome task for program administrators and therefore a source of much of their resistance to meaningful program evaluation. Moreover, the effort required to devise an *impact model* is bound to raise the awkward question: is this particular program worth all of the trouble of evaluating it? Programs that have just begun, are in a state of transition, have no theoretical underpinnings, or are experiencing extensive personnel turnover—all may be so unstable as to defy any attempt to describe them accurately in terms of an *impact model.* This is not to infer that programs which cannot be fully evaluated should not be implemented since a trial and error period is to be expected of all new or evolving programs. But it is to suggest that programs which are well designed, have theoretical roots, and/or are likely to be emulated should be evaluated.

THE INTERMEDIATE VARIABLES AND THE DEPENDENT VARIABLE(S)

These sets of variables have been deliberately combined since there is no a priori distinction between them. This issue has been recently explored by Leonard S. Kogan and Ann W. Shyne in an incisive article in *Welfare in Review.*[5] These authors suggest that if any distinction can in fact be maintained it is largely a result of the work styles or personalities of the researchers. The dependent variable(s) has been associated with "tough-minded" evaluators; the intermediate variables with "tender-minded" evaluators.

The "tough-minded" evaluators tend to have the full support of corporation trustees, legislative committee members, fiscal officers, and other financially responsible (and oriented) administrators. They are likely to ask questions of this sort: has the school dropout rate decreased? Are program participants involved in fewer crimes? Have more alcoholics given up drinking completely? All of these questions assume relatively simple, direct, factual, and accessible criteria to depict each program's success.

The "tender-minded" evaluators tend to have the full support of the professional staff. Caseworkers are much more concerned with the intrapsychic emotions, feelings, attitudes, and interactional adjustments of their clients—whether or not they stop drinking, start working, or return to school. Kogan and Shyne explain that "at the present stage of instrument development the methods necessary to get even reasonably adequate measures of such [intermediate] variables would include the utilization of clinical judgments, often considered the ultimate of tender-mindedness on the part of evaluators."[6]

The dichotomy of "tough" and "tender-minded" approaches would seem to encourage the program evaluator to choose the kind of evaluation most compatible with his personality or ideological predispositions. Possibly the more interesting issue is to encourage the program evaluator to find not a comfortable work style but the relationship between tough-and tender-minded criteria.

Since we live in a fiscally accountable world, "tough-minded" evaluations will always be demanded of social welfare programs. As citizens we may deplore an overemphasis on hard, cold, and restrictively narrow criteria of success; as scientists we are presented with a challenging opportunity to investigate the theoretically suggested causal nexus between the intermediate ("tender-minded") variables and the dependent ("tough-minded") variable(s).

To continue with our example, the Title V Work Experience Program, let us assume that the "tough-minded" evaluators have chosen the dependent criterion of permanent employment as the basis for judging successful participation in a Work Experience Program. The number of individuals who are no longer receiving public assistance is an equally adequate "tough-minded" criterion, although it has somewhat different implications for program analysis than employment. As an example, a program geared to reuniting AFDC (Aid to Families with Dependent Children) mothers with their estranged spouses may reduce public assistance caseloads but have no effect on the unemployment rate.

But if employment is our criterion, we would hypothesize that (1) at Time $_1$, prior to participation in the training program, feelings of disengagement and alienation from the customary values placed on work and employment in our society would be of sufficiently high intensity to seriously incapacitate the trainee's ability to seek or hold a permanent job; (2) at Time $_2$, after participation in the program, the intensity of these feelings of alienation would be significantly reduced; and (3) those registering the greatest score change (in the appropriate direction) would be most likely to become permanently employed or be sufficiently motivated to look for a job even before completion of their training.[7] Thus we are testing a scientific hypothesis which presupposes a causal relationship between alienation (an intermediate variable) and employment (the dependent variable) as well as assuming a separate but significant relationship between a state of alienation in the incoming population and a change in that state as a result of the program variables. Other pertinent intermediate variables would be the trainee's level of occupational or income aspirations and his perceptions of our society's opportunity structure. We would hypothesize that, as the programs raise aspiration levels and change perceptions of the opportunity structure at $Time_2$ (compared to $Time_1$), those showing the greatest positive change would be most likely to seek and hold steady jobs.

Our interest in the intermediate variables is based not only on an assumed causal relationship between these intervening variables and the dependent variable but in the common-sense notion that an acceptable "level of employability" (personal grooming habits, minimum literacy, sufficient respect for authority and property, punctuality, and the like) is a necessary prerequisite for employment. But whether the program evaluator is looking for "deeper" psychological and sociological causal relationships or merely assuming that the trainee can be taught to look and act like an acceptable employee during an interview, he must be prepared, in either case, to measure these intermediate variables before and after the program input-output. Then he must ascertain the relationship between the extent of these before and after changes and the occurrence of the dependent variable (employment).

Before proceeding to a discussion of the *system-model* approach, a cautionary note is necessary. We have assumed a sequential flow of time-related events such that at $Time_1$ a population participating in a program during $Time_2$ undergoes certain cognitive and normative changes at $Time_3$ which result in employment at $Time_4$. We can just as easily assume that a reverse order of events can occur. For example, only after employment will some of the trainees really "understand" (register a passing score on a vocational skill test) the job skills they were trying to learn during program participation. And sometime later, after working in a semiskilled job, will they change their normative and cognitive ideas about themselves and the social institutions around them. Thus, only after achieving the dependent variable (employment) will they show changes in the intermediate and program variables.

This same idea was expressed by Herbert Krugman, who suggested that the goal of an advertising campaign should be to persuade the consumer to buy the product first in order to change his attitudes about it.[8] An extreme exemplification of this is the free distribution of product samples.

The Massimo and Shore evaluation of a delinquency treatment

program also follows this same sequential rationale.[9] Instead of a long period devoted to prevocational education and counseling services, their delinquency program was designed to help the boys obtain a manageable job as quickly as possible. That accomplished, the next goal was to provide psychotherapeutic counseling related to actual work problems and job performance. The resulting sequence (job followed by therapy, followed by changes in perception of self, authority, and use of aggression, and finally the cessation of criminal activity) reverses the original but tentative directionality of program elements that would seem to be suggested by the *goal-model* approach. Thus, the sequence of program elements not only can be empirically determined, but can be consciously manipulated.

The System-Model Approach

Although most evaluators use some variation of the *goal-model*, the research-evaluation model organizational theorists consider to be more comprehensive is referred to as the system-model.[10] However, the *goal-model* approach cannot be discounted since as later shown it forms an integral part of the *system-model.*

The *system-model* approach to the evaluation of organizational effectiveness constitutes a series of statements about relationships among the various components of an organization as it implements that single program the researcher wishes to evaluate. Typically, organizations carry out several major programs at one time (and therefore have multiple goals, including the goals of organizational preservation and continuity). Each program competes for scarce and valuable organizational resources. Ironically, a successful program could seriously drain organizational resources or be so disruptive that it would eventually have to be abandoned.

In order to draw a sharp contrast between the *goal-model* and the *system-model* approach, let us construct a hypothetical situation in which a Work Experience Program was judged to be a disappointing failure according to a well planned and executed *goal-model* evaluation. We will assume the evaluation revealed that one month after graduation from the course only 18 percent of the program trainees were employed; that few significant changes in key intermediate variables occurred among most of the trainees (although we will assume that those few trainees showing positive changes had the highest rates of employment); and that most of the trainees, the program director, the professional staff, and the mayor's committee on tax reduction were all displeased and disappointed by the results.

In spite of the results described above, a hypothetical *system-model* evaluation of the same program could not only vindicate the program, but adjudge it a resounding success. Before continuing with our example, a review of Figure 2 will help illustrate some relevant system components which are essential to an understanding of how the two models could reach such diverse conclusions.

Figure 2 depicts the division of the *system-model* approach into two major components—intraorganizational components and extraorganizational components. Within the large rectangle we have diagrammed three social service programs (P_3, P_2, and P_1) each having its own professional staff (S_3, S_2, and S_1) as well as its own incoming clients and results (outcome). The incoming clients have been designated I_3, I_2, and I_1 and

FIGURE 2
System-Model Approach
Public Assistance Agency

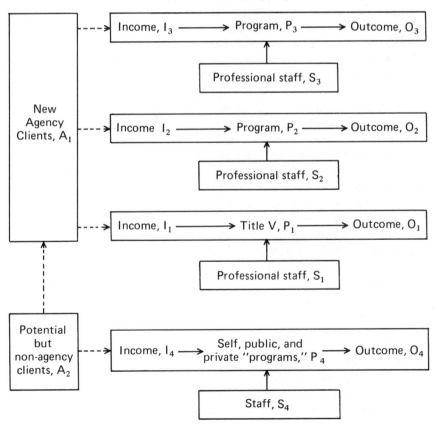

the program outcomes O_3, O_2, and O_1. All new agency clients (A_1) are potential clients for any of the three service programs.

The extraorganizational components are (1) high-risk, poverty-stricken individuals (A_2) facing similar crises that have already led others into the public assistance agency; (2) the "programs" (P_4) that individuals use to solve their problems (these would include correspondence schools, self-employment, private vocational schools, family counseling, obtaining work which offers on-the-job training, waiting-for-something-to-develop, enrolling in a program under the Manpower Development and Training Act [MDTA] or other more or less constructive "programmatic" solutions); (3) a "staff" (S_4) for each of these "programs"; and (4) a specific outcome (O_4) for each "program."

Some of the beneficial effects of a Title V program, effects which do not involve the trainees and their instructors, are to be seen within a public assistance agency:

(1) One of the most important concerns possible changes in attitudes among those professional staff members (S_3, S_2) not directly involved in the Title V program. If an agency is faced with heavily increasing caseloads and professional staff have begun seriously to doubt their ability to raise the level of client functioning significantly, a Title V Work Experience Program could change this pessimistic outlook and low morale. In spite of the Title V program's disappointing results, as disclosed by the hypothetical *goal-model* evaluation, the agency's staff may feel that a significant beginning has been made in creating a new and constructive "career" line for people trapped in economically and culturally depriving conditions. The staff's morale could also be strengthened by the support received from the community, especially from influential business executives who, along with industrial and union leaders, helped plan and organize the Work Experience Program from its inception. We have assumed that without advice and commitment from this leadership, the Title V programs have less chance of success.

(2) New clients entering the agency, or those in other types of service programs, could also favorably respond to the revitalized morale of the agency and to the possibilities that a work experience and training program opens to them. Encouraged by the success of some Title V trainees, clients who are *not* enrolled in the Title V program might be motivated to look for jobs or begin night classes. The program could have more of a beneficial impact on the self-image of the nonparticipants than on the trainees!

(3) Finally, an important feature of the *system-model* approach to program evaluation is its implied demand for comparative statistics. The rate of successful outcome in the other AFDC service programs (P_3, P_2),

as well as the rate of successful outcome of each of the "programmatic" solutions (P_4) as measured by a *goal-model* evaluation, must be used as benchmarks against which the rate of success of the Title V program can be assessed. A successful employment outcome rate of 18 percent may exceed the rates of all other official and self-help "programs" devised for or initiated by a clientele with similar characteristics. However, programs often attract clients with differing characteristics, ranging from the highly motivated to the chronically apathetic, a success rate of 18 percent may be a truly exceptional accomplishment.

Implications

Major emphasis in the above discussion is on the difference between the *goal-model* and the *system-model* approach. Yet it is evident that any evaluation which uses the *system-model* must also include several *goal-model* assessments. It is then possible to compare the relative effectiveness of any given project. Effectiveness can be defined not only in terms of the number of trainees employed, but also in terms of the number of scientifically proved hypotheses. These would include hypotheses relating changes in attitude with changes in employment status and hypotheses relating program content with changes in attitude. Each program has a differential rate of successful outcome and a differential basis of scientific validity.

Finally, we would like to suggest that differential evaluation of intervention programs should also include monetary costs, thereby providing essential information for a cost-benefit analysis.[11] Costs of intervention projects are usually assigned on a per capita basis. For example, if $100,000 is spent to train 1000 persons, the total cost per person is $100. However, a cost-benefit analysis requires the computation of effectiveness costs. If only 100 of these trainees become employed, the "benefit" per capita cost jumps to $1000. This allows a uniform assessment of cost per successful outcome.

Cost-benefit per unit of attitudinal change can also be calculated. We are suggesting that there *is* a way of assessing, in dollar terms, the statement: "Now that I've finished my Title V training, I'm more optimistic." If we find a direct relationship between feelings of appropriate optimism (for example, a high but realistic score on a level of aspiration index) and employability, we can then determine how much staff time and effort was expended (cost) in helping to achieve that high degree of optimism (benefit). A cost-benefit estimate can then be computed for the statement, "I'm more optimistic," assuming that less staff effort would produce lower optimism while more effort would produce higher optimism and also assuming that higher optimism leads to higher employment rates. Optimism (or whatever the attitudinal change found to be directly related to employment) can be achieved through the use of any one of several program elements. Since each element has its own cost factors, it would be possible to choose the least expensive. Also, two or more attitudinal or cognitive changes may lead to employment (for example, changes in job-finding skills or attitudes about punctuality).

Since only one attitudinal change may be sufficient to bring about the desired outcome, the program administrator can decide to upgrade one, eliminate the other. Provided with such cost and effectiveness factors, program specialists are better able to make difficult decisions.

Although evaluation models for social welfare programs are in the embryonic stage of development, their importance is increasingly recognized. It is hoped that this discussion has further emphasized the value of combining theoretically oriented social science research with evaluation studies as well as combining evaluation studies with cost-benefit analysis.

Notes

[1] Amitai Etzioni, *Modern Organization* (New Jersey: Prentice-Hall, 1964), ch. 2.

[2] See, Clarence C. Sherwood, "Methodological, Measurement, and Social Action Considerations Related to the Assessment of Large-Scale Demonstration Programs," paper presented at the 124th Annual Meeting of the American Statistical Association, Chicago, December, 1964; and Clarence C. Sherwood, and Howard E. Freeman, "Research in Large-Scale Intervention Programs," *Journal of Social Issues,* 21, No. 1 (January 1965), 11–27.

[3] Sherwood, "Methodological, Measurement . . .", p. 12.

[4] *Ibid.,* p. 12–13.

[5] Leonard S. Kogan, and Ann W. Shyne, "Tender-Minded and Tough-Minded Approaches in Evaluative Research," *Welfare in Review* (February 1966), pp. 12–16.

[6] *Ibid.,* p. 15.

[7] For a discussion of alienation and public assistance agencies, see Perry Levinson, "Chronic Dependency: A Conceptual Analysis," *Social Service Review,* 38 (December 1964) 371–81.

[8] Herbert E. Krugman, "The Impact of Television Advertising: Learning Without Involvement," *Public Opinion Quarterly,* 29, No. 3 (Fall 1965), 349–356.

[9] Joseph L. Massimo, and Milton F. Shore, "The Effectiveness of a Comprehensive, Vocationally Oriented Psychotherapeutic Program for Adolescent Delinquent Boys," in *Mental Health of the Poor,* Frank Riessman, Jerome Cohen, and Arthur Pearl (eds.) (New York: Free Press, 1964), pp. 540–49.

[10] Etzioni, *op. cit.*

[11] Abraham S. Levine, "Cost-Benefit Analysis and Social Welfare," *Welfare in Review,* 4, No. 1(February 1966), 1–11.

15

PPB: How Can It Be Implemented?

C. WEST CHURCHMAN
A. H. SCHAINBLATT

A recent government memorandum[1] concludes with the statement that if "PPB develops into a contest between experts and politicians, it will not be hard to pick the winners. They will be the politicians in the Congress and the White House." It is our contention in this paper that neither existing technology nor management know-how based on "experience and judgment" is capable of producing sound policies and plans with small risk of error. *All* the decisions that are being made today to implement various programs may be seriously wrong, no matter who makes them or what claims are made of expertise. Consequently, if a "contest" between PPB experts and politicians does develop, there may be no winners.

It is true that the politician manager and systems analyst have qualitatively different approaches for solving problems. These differences in style and point of view, nevertheless, need not imply a contest in which one is the winner, the other the loser. Rather, our purpose here is to indicate how an environment of debate can be created in which both are winners. To this end, we begin with a brief description of the systems approach. With this as background we will use a specific illustration of

Reprinted from the *Public Administration Review*, 29, No. 2 (March/April 1969): 178–89, by permission of the author and publisher.

PPB to show how various kinds of issues arise which can permit the most fruitful kinds of debate between manager and systems analyst, but which also may lead to a complete and disastrous breakdown of the PPB process. We shall argue that it is the debate between the two that can be the most constructive part of the entire process.

The Systems Approach

Consider how the systems analyst tries to look at organizations. The thing that strikes him most emphatically is that the different parts of an organization are not separable—the way in which one unit operates has a great deal to do with the success or failure of another unit. He also realizes that no one manager in a large organization can be aware of all that is going on or of how each effort is interrelated with other efforts. The analyst tries, therefore, to find a way of understanding this problem of organizations.

He finds, for example, that the old-fashioned manager often phrased his problem in such terms as "It is my job to do X as efficiently and cheaply as possible." What he finds the newer managers are saying is "I must look at the way X helps accomplish Y's mission." In other words, perhaps what the newer managers are saying is that one should ask how production helps marketing, or the Department of Motor Vehicles helps the Health Department, or the Air Force helps the Army. The systems analyst goes on to suggest an even more fundamental type of question: "In what way is Department X a *part* of some other department?" In other words, how is production a marketing activity, or motor vehicles a public health activity, or even how is the Air Force a part of the Army? The analyst asks these kinds of questions because of his basic need to understand the organization in terms of the central unifying concepts: its objectives and the ways in which the components of the organization assist in obtaining the objectives.

Thus, the systems analyst is perfectly willing to take a fresh look at the departmental structure of organizations. For example, suppose he looks at public health activities in a state. The manager of the Public Health Department tells him that the department's mission is to improve the health of the state's residents by introducing standards and creating clinics and hospitals to take care of emergencies, epidemics, and the normal course of disease. This mission seems quite clear-cut and easy to identify, but the analyst may begin to question how other agencies of the government also function as health agencies. What he wants here is a quantification of the Health Department's mission and then an explicit formulation of how the various other existing activities of the state contribute to it. For example, one of the Department of Motor Vehicles' missions is to preserve safety on the highways, and this entails spotting dangerous drivers either at the time they apply for licenses or later on the highways. In the performance of this mission, the Department of Motor Vehicles is the one department in the entire state that checks the "health" of the eyesight of the vast majority of the citizens. Thus, in this regard the Department of Motor Vehicles could be considered as a "part" of the Health Department, not in the old-fashioned organizational sense, but in the sense of being a component of the health system.

The aim of the systems analyst is to relate, hopefully in quantitative terms, all relevant activities of an organization to a single, unifying objective. The manager wants above all to be practical and see things in a concrete way and wants to know what to do tomorrow as well as in the long-range future. As the analyst begins to ask difficult questions about how one department's activities can be regarded as supporting what another department does, the manager may begin to lose interest because he does not see any way in which the questions can be sensibly tackled, or how the answers can benefit him. And yet there is one rather obvious link between the manager's and the analyst's approaches to the organization: they both think in terms of the allocation of resources for the sake of attaining objectives. Our position is that the current surge of PPB activity should be viewed as an expression of optimism concerning the possibility of manager-analyst collaboration on resource allocation problems. That is, those who feel confident about designing a PPB system should also feel confident that they can design an environment for productive manager-analyst interaction. The problems are one and the same. For if we examine the realities of resource allocation, we find that neither the manager nor the systems analyst can expect success without the help of the other. To illustrate this point we turn to a specific attempt to apply the PPB approach.

PPB Illustration

The specific system of our illustration is concerned with the management of a statewide alcohol-related mission. In quite general terms this mission is to lessen the extent and gravity of alcoholism and the misuse of alcoholic beverages throughout the state. The analyst will try to develop, with the manager, a more detailed and explicit formulation of the objectives and subobjectives of the alcoholism mission.

The results of such an effort might be structured in a way similar to that displayed in Table 1.[2] The six major programs of this table show one way of breaking down the broad statewide mission into more specific objectives. In order to come even closer to the operational level, these are further broken down into subprograms which are either alternative or complementary means of achieving the program objectives.

TABLE 1
**Program Structure for Management
of Statewide Alcohol-Related Mission**

I Prevention of Alcoholism
  A. Education
  B. Law and economics
  C. Research and development
II Restoration of Early-Stage Alcoholics
  A. Detection
  B. Diagnosis, evaluation, and referral
  C. Treatment, medical
  D. Rehabilitation
  E. Research and development
III Care of Chronic Alcoholics
  A. Detection
  B. Diagnosis, evaluation, and referral
  C. Treatment, medical
  D. Rehabilitation
  E. Domiciliary care
  F. Research and development
IV Control of Other Alcohol Problems
  A. Dependent families
  B. Employment-related
  C. Drinking and driving
  D. Public intoxication
  E. Felonies associated with drinking
  F. Underage drinking
  G. Personal injuries
V General Research*
  A. Medical research
  B. Behaviorial science research
  C. Operational research
VI General Support*
  A. Surveillance and measurement of
    alcohol problems
  B. Planning and evaluation at state
    level
  C. Planning and evaluation at
    community level
  D. Other

*Considered to be unallocable to
Programs I through IV.

The subprograms themselves may be broken down in order to display the different ways in which they can be carried out. For example, the subprogram II-C, medical treatment of early-stage alcoholics, may be accomplished either in specialized emergency-care centers or in general hospitals.

Such a structure is usually intended to provide the context for what we may consider to be the pivotal aspect of a PPB system—the analytical effort of the analyst. But from our point of view, the process of designing the structure itself is critical, for it marks the beginning of the dialogue between manager and analyst. If the dialogue is successful, the assumptions and implications of the objectives listed in Table 1 will be made explicit and subjected to critical examination. For example, out of the dialogue may come the following list of assumptions that are basic to Table 1:

1. Alcoholism is a disease.

2. Alcoholism can be defined in such a way that any given individual can be classified as either diseased or not diseased.

3. It is possible to prevent nonalcoholics from becoming alcoholics.

4. Alcoholism is a progressive disease and individuals who have the disease in its early stages can be detected and restored to health.

5. Alcoholism can be arrested in individuals who have the disease in its later stages.

6. There are nonmedical means which should be used to mitigate some of the undesirable consequences associated with alcoholism.

7. Resources should be allocated to eradicate alcoholism.

From the point of view of the analyst, assumption two is of critical importance. In his dialogue with the manager, he will question how alcoholism should be defined, not in some dictionary or medical-textbook fashion, but in such a way that he can begin to discover a unifying measure of merit for the alcohol-related mission. From his point of view, the *definition* of alcoholism turns out to be the formulation of the problem of alcoholism. That is, he cannot adequately decide what the problem is unless he knows how the term is to be defined; the definition of the term is also a definition of the true nature of the problem. The manager may point out that many of the common definitions of alcoholism are compatible with the spirit of E. M. Jellinek's idea: alcoholism is "any use of alcoholic beverages that causes any damage to the individual or society or both."[3] Thus, whether alcoholism is defined physiologically, psychologically, sociologically, or in terms of some combination of these, it connotes something undesirable, and this is why it is generally accepted that resources should be allocated to eradicate the problem.

But the analyst will claim that this definition is not sufficient to determine *how much* of the available resources should be so allocated. To answer this question, the analyst will apply the lost-oportunity concept: the state should stop allocating resources to alcoholism if it could eradicate more damage to the individual or society by allocating them to some other mission. In other words, the parts of a complex system like a state government are not separable, and the analyst will want the definition to reflect this point. For example, he may modify Jellinek's definition to read, "any use of alcohol beverages that causes *more* damage to the individual or society or both *than would be caused by the absence of such use.*"

The analyst would now hope to be able to translate this definition of alcoholism into a single, unifying measure of merit. Thus, for example, as a start he might define "social damage" in terms of days lost in gainful employment; hence the measure of merit could be taken to be the net increase in number of days of gainful employment (or the dollar benefits created by these days) that the alcoholism mission makes possible.

The manager and analyst would then want to reexamine Table 1. Their specific question now is of the following type: Does the breakdown of the program make sense in terms of the measure of merit? Consider Programs II and III, for example. Is it essential to distinguish between the two? Program II is concerned with the restoration of early-stage alcoholics, and Program III with the care of chronic alcoholics. The answer at this point might be that the breakdown is meaningful because these programs relate to the measure of merit in different ways and utilize different combinations of resources. On the other hand, the precise manner in which each program contributes to the measure of merit may not be clearly understood. Thus, because of resource limitations, it may be judged desirable to emphasize, say, Program III at some sacrifice to Program II. For example, there may not be sufficient funds to attempt to prevent the occasional weekend drinking binge, if indeed the absence of such drinking would represent a net improvement to the individual or society. We note that it is this kind of trade-off judgment which "cost-benefit" analyses are often expected to support.

In any event it becomes apparent that the programs listed in Table 1 are hardly separable. One must consider the manner in which the effort in one program means a sacrifice or support of effort in the other programs. In other words, in order to be able to plan for the alcoholism mission, one must not only know what has happened, and what is happening, but also what might happen if plans were to be changed. The planners must have a model of the system which shows how the different programs and subprograms are interrelated.

As a start in formulating the various interrelationships, the manager-analyst team must ask which agencies function in their day-to-day activities as a part of the alcohol-related mission. In asking this question, they are asking how the various components of the total state system contribute to the programs and subprograms of Table 1. One way of displaying this is shown in Table 2. This table is designed to show that portion of each system component's budget which is allocated, either explicitly or implicitly, to alcoholism objectives as represented by the program structure. The total of each row in Table 2 would suggest the extent to which a particular component of the total system is itself a part of the alcoholism component; the column totals would indicate the emphasis placed by the state system as a whole on the various objectives.

If the analyst could collect the data required for Table 2, he would begin to understand how the existing state system is designed to function as an alcohol management system. He might feel this would be a basis upon which to judge whether the present program activities are suitable or whether they should be modified. In other words, he assumes that an information display influences decisions and that certain types of displays produce better decisions than others.

However, because information does influence decisions—specifically, decisions concerning the size of future budgets—the managers of the various agencies may be quite cautious about supplying the figures needed in Table 2. They may disagree among themselves over rationale for choosing the data. Consider, for example, the basis for deciding how much of the Department of Corrections' budget to include in Table 2. A manager who is directly involved in the alcoholism program might welcome a large figure from the Department of Corrections, because this would give a clear indication to state legislators of the seriousness of the problem. But the managers in the Department of Corrections might feel that if a very large portion of their budget appears in Table 2, it could be misinterpreted to mean that a large amount of money is being spent by the Department of Corrections for a mission that is not directly related to its legally assigned responsibility.

Further, each side could present a "rational" argument supporting its point of view. The Department of corrections could argue that one should include in Table 2 only that portion of its budget which would have been available for other uses (either by the Department of Corrections itself or by some other department in the state) if none of the inmates had been alcoholics. A counterproposal would argue that one should include that portion of the budget which is expended on those inmates who, if they were released, would resume drinking habits that would produce more damage to themselves or society than is produced when they are in

TABLE 2
Expenditures in California on Alcohol-related Problems, FY 1964–65
($ thousands)

Source of Expenditure / Program Structure	I. Prevention of Alcoholism	A. Education	B. Law and economics	C. Research and development	II. Restoration (Early Stage)	A. Detection	B. Diagnosis, evaluation, and referral	C. Treatment	D. Rehabilitation	E. Research and development	III. Care (Chronic Alcoholics)	A. Detection	B. Diagnosis, evaluation, and referral	C. Treatment	D. Rehabilitation	E. Domiciliary care	F. Research and development	IV. Control of Other Problems	A. Dependent families	B. Employment	C. Drinking and driving	D. Public intoxication	E. Felonies	F. Underage drinking	G. Personal injuries	V. General Research	A. Medical	B. Behavioral science	C. Operations research	VI. General Support	A. Surveillance and measurement	B. State level	C. Community level	D. Other	Total
State Expenditures																																			
Governor's Office																																			
Dept. of Justice																																			
Board of Equalization																																			
Dept. of Education																																			
Dept. of Alcoholic Beverage Control																																			
Dept. of Employment																																			
Health and Welfare Agency																																			
Dept. of Mental Hygiene																																			
Dept. of Public Health																																			
Division of Alcoholism																																			
TB Sanitoria Subvention																																			
Dept. of Rehabilitation																																			
Dept. of Social Welfare																																			
Dept. of Finance																																			
Dept. of Cal. Highway Patrol																																			
Dept of Motor Vehicles																																			
Youth and Adult Correction Agency																																			
Dept. of Corrections																																			
Dept. of Youth Authority																																			
Legislative Branch																																			
Judicial Branch																																			
Total State																																			
Non-State Expenditures																																			
Federal																																			
County																																			
Municipal																																			
Private																																			
Industry																																			
Alcoholics Anonymous																																			
National Council on Alc.																																			
Salvation Army																																			
Grand Total																																			

prison. This in effect would mean including that portion of the Department of Corrections' budget that represents the imprisonment costs of people identified as alcoholics in the modified sense discussed above. The Department of Corrections could pursue its claim for a low figure by arguing that most inmates of state prisons would be in prison whether they drank or not. Managers in an alcoholism agency could counter that regardless of why an inmate were imprisoned, if he would create more social damage were he released, then the Department of Corrections was contributing to the alcoholism mission by keeping him in prison.

The systems analyst would like to believe that data collection is a nonpolitical activity. He may feel there is a "correct" set of data that should be entered in Table 2 which cannot be debated: the opportunity cost. It is not the opportunity cost associated with the *existing* organization, however, but rather those opportunities which are foregone when the system is *optimally* organized. That is, his point may be that one should first decide the optimal way of carrying out the mission of the Department of Corrections. Once this has been decided, then one might be in a position to determine which aspects of the optimal plan of this department should be considered as contributions to the alcohol-related mission. If the analyst did think this way, he would soon find himself trying to determine the optimal design of every state agency and of the whole state government, and would find himself embroiled in the problems of redesigning the entire system. Consequently, the analyst is in an odd position: he thinks that there must be a correct and objective set of entries for Table 2, but he sees that in order to find these he must go through an impossible series of steps.

The analyst would find it equally difficult to collect data on the demand for alcoholism services. For example, he may construct Table 3 to display a classification of the demand and how it relates to the program structure in terms of magnitude and cost. But the rationale behind the Department of Corrections' entries for Target Groups 13 and 15, for example, should be consistent with that portion of their budget included in Table 2. The analyst thus faces a similar dilemma here, for the "true" demand is that demand that would exist if the rest of the system were designed optimally.

It is not surprising, therefore, that managers who identify only with their part of the total organization may consider most of the information requirements imposed by PPB a burden and see no potential compensation for their efforts. The cost of data collection is apparent to them (i.e., additional data to be collected, more people required, new deadlines to meet), but the benefits are obscure since they are realized, if at all, only within the context of the larger system.

TABLE 3
Program Distribution by Target Group, FY 1966–67
($ and Target Groups in Thousands)

Total State or Community

Program Structure column headers (all data cells blank):

I. Prevention of Alcoholism — A. Education; B. Law and economics; C. Research and development

II. Restoration (Early Stage) — A. Detection; B. Diagnosis, evaluation, and referral; C. Treatment; D. Rehabilitation; E. Research and development

III. Care (Chronic Alcoholics) — A. Detection; B. Diagnosis, evaluation, and referral; C. Treatment; D. Rehabilitation; E. Domiciliary care; F. Research and development

IV. Control of Other Problems — A. Dependent families; B. Employment; C. Drinking and driving; D. Public intoxication; E. Felonies; F. Underage drinking; G. Personal injury

V. General Research — A. Medical; B. Behavioral science; C. Operations research

VI. General Support — A. Surveillance and measurement; B. State level; C. Community level; D. Other

Total

Target Group and Size	(blank data cells across all Program Structure columns)
Nonalcoholics Under 21	
1. Nondrinkers { (a) #	
{ $	
2. Drinkers { #	
{ $	
Nonalcoholics Over 21	
3. Nondrinkers { #	
{ $	
4. Drinkers { #	
{ $	
Alcoholics in Trouble	
With Employer Only (Over 21)	
5. State employees { #	
{ $	
6. Local gov't. employees { #	
{ $	
7. Poverty group empl. { #	
{ $	
8. Other alcoholics in trouble with employers { #	
{ $	
Unemployed Alcoholics only (Over 21)	
9. Skid row { #	
{ $	
10. Other unemp. alcoholics { #	
{ $	
Alcoholics in Trouble	
With Family Only (Over 21)	
11. 'Hidden housewife' (not seeking employment) { #	
{ $	
12. Other alcoholics in trouble with family { #	
{ $	
Alcoholics in Trouble	
With Law Only (Over 21)	
13. Institutionalized { #	
{ $	
14. Noninstitutionalized { #	
{ $	
Alcoholics Not Included Above	
15. All other alcoholics { #	
{ $	

The analyst is attempting to relate the various programs and sub-programs to one central measure of benefit. The manager, on the other hand, may be reluctant to come up with one specific figure. He may feel much happier when he can talk about various aspects of the mission without trying to force all the pieces together into one figure. For example, the manager might feel quite content to talk about the number of patients who have been treated in detoxification centers and in hospitals, or he may want to count the laws passed that are relevant to the alcoholism mission.

But the analyst argues that while the activity rates cited by the manager are related to the objectives of the alcohol mission, they do not, in and of themselves, provide a basis for detecting improvements in the system. In order to measure improvements, the amount of activity must be transformed into some benefit to the whole system. Thus he might try to use his idea of lost productivity or other "costs" that would be averted if the various alcohol-related programs were successful. Yet here, too, the analyst faces an impossible task. He would like to use his improvement criteria to determine how the alcoholism system should change over time. He may use a display such as that of Table 4 to depict this change in terms of costs and benefits. But the alcohol-related costs and benefits that should be entered in Table 4 are those that apply when the rest of the system is working optimally, not those under existing policies. For example, an improved design of the state highway system, at of course an additional cost, might greatly reduce the number of accidents caused by alcoholism and thereby contribute to the analyst's measure of performance.

The point of our illustration is that neither the manager nor the systems analyst alone can "get on top of" the system which they are studying. They each have something indispensable to contribute, and their contributions cannot be made in isolation from each other. For example, a manager may feel that he can ask an analyst to come up with whatever measure of performance he thinks is most suitable, present his results, and then the manager will attempt to resolve the unanswered questions. This often seems to be the attitude that writers have toward the function of cost-benefit analyses. The notion is that the analyst should generate some figures and recommendations based on his analytical techniques, but that when the manager receives these figures he should apply his own background and judgment in deciding how to use them. Yet it is at this very point that the manager and analyst should strongly interact. If the analyst does not understand why the manager modified the results of his analysis, then the analyst has learned nothing from the encounter; nor has the manager learned why the analyst performs as he

TABLE 4
Multi-year Program and Financial Plan*

Program	Subprogram	Program Element			Program Structure	FY 1964-65 Actual	FY 1965-66 Current Estimate	FY 1966-67 Budget Estimate	FY 1967-68 Program Estimate	FY 1968-69 Program Estimate	FY 1969-70 Program Estimate	FY 1970-71 Program Estimate	Total Years	Total Costs
I					Prevention of Alcoholism									
	A				Education									
	B				Law and economics									
	C				Research and development									
II					Restoration of Early-Stage Alcoholics									
	A				Detection									
	B				Diagnosis, evaluation, and referral									
	C				Treatment, medical									
		1			Emergency care centers									
		2			General hospitals									
	D				Rehabilitation									
	E				Research and development									
III					Care of Chronic Alcoholics									
	A				Detection									
	B				Diagnosis, evaluation, and referral									
	C				Treatment									
	D				Rehabilitation									
	E				Domicilary care									
	F				Research and development									
IV					Control of Other Alcohol Problems									
	A				Dependent families									
	B				Employment-related									
	C				Drinking and driving									
	D				Public intoxication									
	E				Felonies associated with drinking									
	F				Underage drinking									
	G				Personal injuries									
V					General Research									
	A				Medical research									
	B				Behavioral science research									
	C				Operations research									
VI					General Support									
	A				Surveillance and measurement of alcohol problems									
	B				Planning and evaluation at state level									
	C				Planning and evaluation at community level									
	D				Other									

*This format to be used for both costs and benefits.

does. At the very point where they could be educating each other, they fail to do so. In fact, when such a separation of the management-analyst team occurs, the chances of a successful implementation of a PPB system becomes seriously lessened.

Consequently, let us examine the ways in which the manager and analyst can interact in order to create an environment for successful implementation of good plans. We have seen that there is no sure road to exact data or correct models. The road is a rough one and the roughness of it consists of a continuing debate between the parties involved. Neither party in this debate has a superior viewpoint, but the debate itself is very important. For example, teams representing management and research, when working by themselves, inevitably engage in debate. Why, then, when they come together, should they try to remove what has been the essence of the work that has occurred before—namely, the disagreements between ideas? Obsession with obtaining a common agreement may negate the enormous benefits that can result from constructive disagreement.

The nature of this debate and the resolution of issues arising from it lead us, then, to consider the design of an environment for constructive dialogue between manager and analyst, which we believe is an essential part of the PPB process.

Formalized Debate

First we shall try to make clear the basic idea underlying our approach to a satisfactory manager-analyst interaction, and then we shall illustrate how this idea could be implemented by means of the interesting technique of formalized debate.[4]

Enough has been said in this paper to make it clear that the notion of separate functions does not work in organizations, and hence that the task of the analyst and the task of the manager are in some sense inseparable. We do not believe that the manager can make his problem clear to the analyst who then goes off and solves it, and finally presents the complete solution to the manager who implements it. Even a partial separation of functions, such as assigning data collection and analysis to the analyst, is probably a serious organizational error. As we have seen, at no stage in the development of a PPB system can either manager or analyst claim to have sufficient knowledge.

Therefore, why not give up the separation of functions idea completely? We have suggested that an excellent way to look at a department of an organization is to see in what way it is a "part" of another department in the system-analysis sense of "part." As a corollary, why not look at management and see in what way it is a "part" of the research function of the organization? In what way is management contributing to knowledge about the organization? Similarly, in what way is research contributing to management? It seems to us that these questions are among the most important that can be asked about organizations today.

Research on organizations can be regarded as a way of managing organizations, but its managerial contribution becomes weak if its function is kept separate. And perhaps even more fascinating is the way in which managing can create fundamental knowledge about organizations, since every important managerial decision can be regarded as an "experiment." It loses its experimental power, however, if its experimental nature is not evaluated. Thus the "interacting" analyst can contribute by looking at management decisions in an experimental framework. And conversely, every application of an analytical method can be regarded as a mangerial decision if there is an "interacting" manager who views the research in terms of decision making.

No doubt these remarks have an aura of impractical goodwill about them. But we believe that the idea behind them can be implemented. The first step is humility, a grace that comes hard for both manager and analyst. Each must recognize that he does not have solid answers to the questions, or even solid ways of getting the answers. After this frank admission, the two can get to work. Their work, we believe, should be in the context of debate. This means that every serious proposal at each stage in the PPB process should be confronted by a serious counter-proposal. Specifically, the grounds for accepting a proposal should be confronted by the grounds for accepting the counter-proposal. The two arguments, furthermore, must be based on exactly the same "data," where the data are given a different interpretation. By revealing the underlying interpretations, both manager and analyst can learn the hidden assumptions that each is using.

For example, consider the program called "prevention" in the alcohol-related mission. One basic issue is to decide the amount of funds to allocate to prevention versus the other programs. Consider the proposal that the majority of funds should be allocated to prevention. This, on the face of it, is an attractive proposal, because if we can prevent alcoholism from occurring, then all the resulting tragedy and social damage will be averted. The serious counter-proposal is that current prevention measures are largely a waste of time; heredity and environment invariably produce a certain amount of alcoholism no matter what we do.

Imagine now that the manager and analyst begin to develop the strongest possible arguments for each proposal using the same medical and social data. This will require imagination and ingenuity. For example, the argument for prevention may introduce the idea of inventing new drugs or using old ones that permit euphoric "escape" with less danger to health or society. Those who oppose funding prevention will view the social world in terms of the inevitable, and will convert the "data" to support their proposal. Note that the analyst characterized in the first part of this paper may feel uneasy about this assignment. He may feel that there are "facts" to prove the case for one proposal or the other. But our illustration shows that the "facts" are themselves decisions based on a way of viewing reality, i.e., the larger system. Hence each side in the debate takes the "data" and converts it in terms of its world view into a defense of its position.

Granted that this confrontation of proposals and counterproposals can occur, what then? Which one is "right"? The answer, of course, is that no one can tell for sure, but the debate will have clarified the underlying issues and enabled personal judgment to act in as unhampered a way as possible. The process of reaching a decision, therefore, is afforded the greatest opportunity of becoming a clear-cut experiment, because we can observe what happens to the underlying assumptions of each side. The managerial decision becomes a way of conducting research. But the research itself, i.e., the development of the debate, has become a way of managing.

Many people will feel a real uneasiness about the technique we have just described for implementing PPB simply because it does not generate answers to problems but only a response which clarifies the underlying issues. They may feel that science above all should give them solutions. But if they do feel this way, they have failed to understand science itself, which thrives on uncertainty, responds to hypothesis by experiment, and never answers any question in a final form.

Undoubtedly there are many other fruitful techniques of interaction between manager and systems analyst that are being or can be designed. We believe that PPB can provide an excellent proving ground for such techniques, and that the real value of PPB lies in the opportunity it offers to permit various kinds of interaction.

A Note of Caution

We end with one final word of caution: the manager-analyst interaction we have advocated does contain an inherent element of danger. The manager and the systems analyst are only a part of humanity; they are that part which concerns itself with decision and control, hypothesis and test, planning and implementation—in short, with observation, intuition, and thought. Neither manager nor analyst can make any strong claim to understanding human feelings, i.e., good versus evil, morality versus immorality, beauty versus ugliness. Indeed, both shy away from issues of ultimate value because, being deficient in the function of valuing, they regard the problem as esoteric, elusive, not their business, or meaningless. Of course we ourselves are being impressionistic in an unfeeling way at this point because we are lumping together whole classes of people and giving them labels. Our point, however, is important: if manager and analyst do begin to interact in the strong manner we have suggested, they may reinforce themselves, i.e., reinforce their own biased view of reality. But this need not happen if the opportunity is always kept open for introducing differing points of view. Even our own proposal must face, in specific instances, its strong counterproposal.

Notes

[1] *Planning-Programming-Budgeting, Initial Memorandum,* prepared by the Subcommittee on National Security and International Operations, U.S. Senate, 1967.

[2] Tables 1 through 4 resulted from a collaborative effort between TEMPO and the Division of Alcoholism, California State Department of Public Health, to explore the feasibility of applying PPB to the alcoholism mission. However, the views expressed in this paper are those of the authors and should not be interpreted as reflecting views of the Division of Alcoholism.

[3] E. M. Jellinek, *The Disease Concept of Alcoholism* (Highland Park, N.J.: Hillhouse Press, 1960), p. 35. It should be noted that Jellinek did not consider "alcoholism," as he defined the term a disease. Rather, he felt that only species of alcoholism, i.e., only certain kinds of alcohol usage, qualified as a disease.

[4] For a more detailed discussion of the technique to be described in this section, see C. W. Churchman, "Hegelian Inquiring System," Internal Working Paper No. 49, University of California, Berkeley, September 1966, and R. O. Mason, "Dialectics in Decision-Making: A Study in the Use of Counterplanning and Structural Debate in Management Information Systems," University of California, Berkeley, June 1968.

VII

IMPLEMENTING PPB

16

PPB in HEW:
Some Management Issues

DAVID R. SEIDMAN

A major value of planning, programming, and budgeting (PPB) is the power it gives a high government administrator to influence more effectively and directly the myriad decisions made by his organization. He may see more clearly what actions his organization is taking and what results it is achieving and may therefore take more informed steps to influence the orgnization's efforts toward his own priorities. Such a centralizing tendency will naturally be resisted by lower levels of officials within his own organization and by competing powers, such as legislators and lobbyists. This article assumes that the centralizing tendency of PPB is a desirable end, in terms of governmental effectiveness, though this assumption can obviously be debated.

In order to illustrate the effects of PPB on governmental programs and on the exercise of decision-making power within a public agency, the

Reprinted from the *Journal of the Institute of American Planners*, 36, No. 3 (May 1970): 168–78, by permission of the author and publisher.

The views expressed here are the author's own and do not represent official policy of either the Department of Health, Education and Welfare or the U.S. Conference of Mayors.

intricate usages of PPB in the Department of Health, Education and Welfare will be explored in some detail. First, the three formal elements required of all federal agencies by the Bureau of the Budget will be outlined: (1) Program Memoranda; (2) Program and Financial Plans; and (3) Special Analytic Studies. Then these elements will be discussed within the context of HEW, with particular emphasis on issues, such as, (1) use of the Program Memorandum as a document for issue-oriented decision-making, as opposed to an explanation of departmental plans for each program: (2) difficulties involved in merging the new program structure with the old appropriations structure, and in dealing with multiple objectives under the program structure; (3) problems in forging the necessary linkages between an effective PPB process and the budgetary and legislative processes; (4) weaknesses in current program analysis in the PPB system; and (5) complexities inherent in measures of effectiveness for program and project evaluation.

BOB's Requirements for PPB

Before going into the operation of PPB in HEW, it will be helpful, for those who have not been involved in the federal PPB effort, to briefly describe components of the annual planning cycle formally required by the Bureau of the Budget.[1] There are three basic elements of the PPB System:

1. A *Program Memorandum* (PM) presents a statement of the significant issues concerning agency programs, a comparison of the cost and effectiveness of alternative means of resolving these issues in relation to the objectives of the programs, the agency heads' decisions, and the rationale for the decisions made. These significant issues are formally referred to as Major Program Issues and are defined as questions requiring decisions in the current budget cycle and having major implications on present or future costs as well as on the direction of a program or policy choice. Since they are a highly selected set of issues, the PMs generally do not cover an agency's entire program.

2. The *Program and Financial Plan* (PFP) is a comprehensive multiyear quantitative summary of agency programs, in terms of their outputs, costs, and financing needs, over a planning period covering the budget year and four subsequent years—or longer if appropriate. (In the romantic lexicon of PPB the planning years after the budget year are called "out-years.") While PMs deal with highly selective program issues, PFPs provide a continuing year-to-year record for *all* agency programs. The PFP is organized into a hierarchy of objectives and subobjectives known as the Program Structure.

3. *Special Analytic Studies* (SAS) provide the analytic groundwork for the decisions reflected in the PMs. They are more commonly known to practitioners as program analyses. Some SASs are perfromed to resolve an issue in the current budget year; other longer range studies can continue over several years. The structure of the SASs is very flexible.

The Purpose of the Program Memorandum

The current view of the Program Memorandum as the decision document which addresses a highly *selective* list of issues and discusses nothing beyond those issues is a relatively recent development. Until 1968, the PMs were regarded as more comprehensive documents requiring some discussion of every program. During 1968, conflicting directives came from the Bureau of the Budget concerning the Program Memorandum— the PPB staff requested selectivity and the budgeting examining staff requested comprehensiveness.[2] These conflicting requests have not as yet been resolved. The fact that the presumably analytically oriented BOB should come so late to what is known in business as the "management-by-exception" principle in its prime planning document suggests the difficulty in instilling such a notion at the lower levels of the bureaucracy. At these levels the budget document was and still is a comprehensive, laudatory description that primarily attempts to justify the continuing expansion of programs. This is the form in which bureaus and agencies within HEW generally still couch the Program Memoranda they submit to the Secretary's office. For this and other reasons, the Secretary's office has had to replace or extensively revise these documents before submitting them to the Bureau of the Budget.

Even within the Office of Assistant Secretary for Planning and Evaluation (OASPE), more traditionally oriented analysts have in the past tended toward a more comprehensive, less issue-oriented document. Partly this is because the Program Memorandum has been conceived as having two conflicting roles. The first role is that of a "decision document" to be used by BOB, the Secretary, and other high department and agency officials, to make the major planning and budgeting decisions. The second role is that of an explanatory document of the department's plans—for wider dissemination, perhaps to Congress and the public—in which the department explains the reasons for its program plans.

The explanatory document might prove useful if the manpower could be found to produce it. Interest in the PPB process is rising in Congress, and there presently exists no comprehensive discussion of long-range departmental plans. However, a decision to generate a widely disseminated long-range planning document should be made with considerable caution. As many political scientists have noted, compromises are not made on the basis of accepting one another's long-term goals, but accepting one another's short-term actions.[3]

The Program Structure

The Program Structure is used to organize the financial and output data of the Program and Financial Plan. It is viewed as one of the principal differences between PPB and traditional budgeting, for it attempts to group expenditures according to their objectives or outputs rather than according to their organizational or appropriation structure. For example, the Medicaid program and the Comprehensive Health Service project grant program are both contained under the program category, "Provision of Health Services," even though the first program is under the Social and Rehabilitation Service and is authorized under Title XIX of the Social Security Act, and the second is under the Health Services and Mental Health Administration and is authorized under Section 314 of the Public Health Service Act. Thus, it is possible to determine the total amount of money being allocated toward given objectives regardless of where the money is coming from or what unit administers its expenditure. Table 1 shows the health portion of the present HEW program structure.

TABLE 1
Health Program Structure

Health
Development of health resources
Increasing knowledge
Providing facilities and equipment
Increasing and improving the health manpower pool
Improving the organization and delivery of
health services
Prevention and control of health problems
Disease prevention and control
Physical environment control
Consumer protection
Social factors affecting health
Provision of health services
Health services for the aged
Health services for the poor
Health services for indians
Health services for children and mothers
Other health services
General support
Scientific and health information
Program direction and management

When the program structure was developed in the Department of Defense, there were two reasons that it was regarded—and rightly so—as a significant advance. First, expenditures had previously been grouped by types of activities or inputs, such as motor pool, quartermaster, equipment repair, and the like. It was impossible to relate these activities to any specific objectives, and it was equally impossible to relate costs to outputs since they were not defined. Therefore, grouping costs by missions was a major advance in understanding the cost of achieving specific objectives. Second, these individually defined missions were then placed in a "hierarchy of objectives" with the highest levels having the most generalized goals. This was the first time that high-level DOD officials could see what proportions of their expenditures were being allocated to various broad goals.

The program structure for HEW achieves the second advantage. In fact, in 1968 ex-Budget Director Charles Schultze told the OASPE staff that the HEW program structure enabled him for the first time to understand what HEW was trying to do.

It is, however, interesting to note that the HEW program structure does not have the first-mentioned advantage over previous categorizations. This is because HEW has so many appropriations that budgeting by appropriation already provides a fairly meaningful allocation of funds by individual missions; it was the grouping of missions into broader goals that was missing. As Schultze points out: "The language for the Department of Defense's procurement and R&D programs—amounting to $20 billion in fiscal 1968—is contained on one page. . . . There are 50 different appropriations covering the $77 billion expenditures in the military functions of the Department of Defense. [On the other hand, for] the $14.5 billion spent by HEW [outside of the trust funds] there are 94 different appropriations—less than one-fifth the funds but twice the number of appropriations."[4] Furthermore, the overwhelming proportion of HEW non-trust (non-Social Security) funds are expended in the form of grants to provide specific services to the public, paying for nearly every expense incurred in the provision of such services. Therefore, line items for motor pools and the like were never a part of HEW budgeting procedures.

HEW appropriations provide a set of categories that come much closer to a set of defined objectives and subobjectives than do the line items of DOD. Their main problem is that they are not ordered into a hierarchy of objectives, but into a hierarchy of organizational units and legislative sections. Therefore, it makes sense to incorporate the HEW appropriation subsections into a program structure of objectives. The funds expended under a given subsection of an act—for example, 314 (e) of the Public Health Service Act—almost invariably fall under only one

HEW program category and subcategory. Thus the program structure in HEW tends to be a set of appropriation categories with a superstructure and substructure added to them. Instead of the appropriation categories being grouped by organizational unit or by legislative unit, they are instead grouped by objectives. Nevertheless, the individual subsections are generally intact.

The provision of financial data in terms of program structure via the Program and Financial Plan has been of the greatest use to high-level administrators—the Secretary, assistant secretaries, and agency administrators. However, with some important exceptions, the program structure has generally proven much less useful to bureau heads and program analysts, who find that the most meaningful detail is given by the appropriation structure.

One reason why the program structure has not proven to be as powerful a device as its original proponents speculated is that, especially in the social program area, most programs have multiple objectives and outputs which any structure has difficulty taking into account. An excellent example of this is the family planning program. Two of its most significant outputs are a reduction in poverty and a reduction in infant mortality. Family planning reduces poverty by decreasing family size, thus decreasing the amount of income required to maintain a family at some specified minimum level of well-being. It reduces infant mortality by decreasing the number of children born to older women or to women with a large number of children. (The infant mortality rate for both these classes of women is several times higher than average.) Given these two outputs—and they are both substantial—one would have to ask where to put the family planning program if the program objectives were specified purely in terms of these ultimate outputs of reducing infant mortality and reducing poverty. The problem is solved in the present structure by placing it in Health Services for Woman and Children, which is an intermediate output rather than an ultimate output. After all, health services are not an ultimate objective, but only a means to achieve the ultimate objective of physical and social well-being.

Because of the multiple outputs of many HEW programs, the current program structure is necessarily an extremely crude categorization. There is no doubt an evolutionary process at work that will gradually generate more meaningful program structures; perhaps certain programs will be noted as contributing to several objectives, and their budgets will be allocated to these objectives in proportion to their relative contributions to each. However, such a process appears quite complex and will require much time for development.

The program structure has been used with good effect to specify and demonstrate departmental priorities in the Program and Financial Plan. For example, for fiscal years 1970 through 1974, the priority items in the health category were: increasing knowledge; increasing and improving the health manpower pool, improving the organization and delivery of health services; and reducing air pollution. The Program and Financial Plan can show how much money is allocated to each of these priority categories in each planning year, what the rate of increase in these categories is, and how this compares with previous rates of increase. In this way it can be determined if the stated priorities are reflected in the financial aspects of the plan. It is, after all, not easy for a high administrator to determine if his priorities are being adhered to by lower officials. The PFP supplies the administrator with one mechanism for seeing if his organization is actually doing what he told it to and what he thinks it is doing. Care has to be taken, however, to ensure that the bureaus do not provide paper increases in the priority items by recategorizing some of their programs under these priority caregories. This can be prevented, since the Secretary's office has final control of the program structure.

The Budget and Legislative Processes

Before discussing PPB and the budget and legislative processes, it would be well to review briefly the preparation of the annual budget, which provides the Secretary's office with one of its most effective tools for implementing HEW policy and programs. Budgets are initially prepared by lower echelons and filter upward to the Secretary's office, which has very broad authority to modify these budgets. The agencies and bureaus can appeal these modifications to the Secretary, but the final decision rests with him. The budget is then reviewed and modified by the Bureau of the Budget before it is submitted to Congress. Decisions of the Bureau can be similarly appealed to the President by department and independent agency heads.

In the case of legislation, the Secretary's office also has broad review authority theoretically equivalent to its power over the budget. Proposed new legislation or amendments are submitted to the office for review and revision. The departmental "legislative package" is then sent to the Bureau of the Budget and the White House for review, modification, and submission to Congress as part of the administration's legislation proposals.

The effective difference between the budget and legislative processes is that bureaus thwarted in their legislative goals by the Secretary can nearly always find a sympathetic Congressman to submit their proposal for them, whereas the budget can be submitted only by the administration. Therefore, the bureaus tend to go around departmental and BOB decisions more frequently on legislative than budgetary matters.

The name "Planning-Programming-Budgeting Systems" indicates the intention to closely link the planning and budgeting processes. Theoretically, the first year of the planning cycle provides the administration's budget for the next fiscal year and is identical to it. In practice, there has been a marked difference between them, partly because the past few years have witnessed extraordinary and unanticipated budget cutting, and partly because it is difficult to discuss overall HEW strategy without assuming some additional funds to provide flexibility in budget allocation—unless you are willing to brave the political storms that occur when several programs are cut below their past allocations. The discrepancies between the budget and the PFP for the first year do not by any means signify that the PFP has had little impact; the budget has generally reflected the directions in which the PFP was moving, but at lower levels of increase.

The linkage between the PFP and the budget has also been weakened since some budget decisions, at least in the health area, had to be made before the Program Memorandum was completed. In the past, this was caused by bureau and agency delays in developing PFPs and Program Memoranda. The bureaus have not felt the same pressure to produce their PFPs on time as they have to produce their budgets on time; if they do not produce their budgets on time, they may not get the increases they request. The budget cycle is inexorable, ending in the appropriation of their funds; their organizational life depends on it. This has not been true with the PFP; it has not had the legal sanction of the budget. This problem might be solved by establishing a departmental requirement that agencies provide PFPs before their budgets are reviewed.

There is, however, a far more profound change now underway in the HEW planning process that, as a by-product, can solve the timing problem. In the present planning cycle for fiscal 1971, the Program and Financial Plan is being jointly developed by the Secretary's office and the agencies and bureaus rather than by the bureaus for circulation up to the agencies and then to the department. The process involves the agency and bureau staffs in a series of task forces. This single innovation may prove to be as much of a breakthrough in providing the Secretary with greater influence over the department than any other single action of the PPB process. It also carries some risks, since the Secretary's office staff can be, and in part has been overwhelmed by lower bureaucratic levels because it is too thinly spread.

Although the linkage between planning and budgeting is now fairly well understood, the linkage between planning and legislation is generally much less appreciated. Again, this is partly because PPB originated in the Defense Department, where legislation plays much less of a role in the decision-making and managerial processes than it does in HEW. Almost without exception, new program directions in HEW require new legislation. To the extent that the PPB process does not influence legislation, it is essentailly reduced to choosing an optimum allocation among existing alternatives, rather than developing new alternatives. The significance of this limitation can perhaps be best understood from a remark once made by David Hertz, a noted operations research analyst. He said that experiments he had conducted strongly indicated that *there was generally a much higher payoff in expending resources to develop innovative and imaginative alternatives than in expending resources to assure that the optimum selection is made from a set of alternatives developed in a more routine manner.* Therefore, tying the PPB process to the legislative cycle is crucial to innovation in departmental programs.

Despite the importance of this linkage, there are some difficulties in achieving it. The timing of the legislative cycle has been almost completely out of phase with the timing of the budget cycle. The budget cycle generally runs from February through September; the legislative cycle has run in the past from August through January. Hopefully, this problem will be solved by requiring agencies and bureaus to develop their legislative proposals as part of the work of the planning task forces during the budget cycle—two or three months before they would normally do so.

Another significant difficulty for the Secretary and his staff is that legislation, even more so than planning and budgeting, has generally been initiated by the bureaus. These are the organizations who are closest to the operating difficulties of the program and who are generally in the best position to determine necessary revisions for effective operation of programs. Overall allocation strategies, so meaningful for the budget, have less significance here. Furthermore, there are a relatively small number of strategies associated with allocation of funds within a given bureau, while the number of possible legislative modifications is vast. Therefore, the Secretary's office can never hope to administer the development of legislative changes with the comprehensive attention to detail it gives to the budget. It must depend on much initiative from the bureaus. To add to the difficulties, in the past few years major legislative revisions have often been proposed by the White House after the budget has been submitted and just before Congress convenes, as well as at various other times.

A PPB staff can recommend a relatively small number of significant new pieces of legislation. For example, one legislative initiative of OASPE was the development of early case-finding and treatment projects under the Crippled Children's Program. This resulted from a program analysis in child health care which indicated there was a potential high payoff in the early diagnosis and treatment of potentially crippling conditions in young children. [5]

An often overlooked extention of the legislative cycle is the writing of program guidelines and regulations after the statute has been enacted. These guidelines provide a potentially high payoff to the PPB staff. Very often the enabling legislation for a specific program consists of a page, whereas the guidelines run to a small book. Often the real structure of a program—determination of what it is going to do and how it is going to operate—is determined by administrative guidelines and regulations, not by legislation. There is the additional advantage that these guidelines are much more under the control of the department, within the constraints of legislative intent. For these reasons, it makes sense for the PPB staff to review guidelines proposed by the bureaus. This review need not be comprehensive in nature, but it should concentrate on a few major points in each guideline that the PPB staff believes can significantly influence the priority and effectiveness of the program, particularly if these are backed up by an analytic study. For example, the guidelines for the Children's Bureau's new family planning program were reviewed from the vantage point of a recently completed program analysis on family planning. As a result, several modifications were made to the guidelines.

During the course of the discussion on these family planning guidelines, an interesting question arose concerning the proper role of OASPE. The guidelines, after all, are the sacred teachings of the bureau, and interference from outside is generally regarded as heresy. Such interference in the details of the bureau's operations is fought off in part by pointing out that the Secretary's office in general, and OASPE in particular, has been given no specific authority for such review and, therefore, it can provide policy guidance only. It is true that the present delegation of authority to OASPE is only in terms of developing the PM and PFP, developing long-range objectives, conducting economic analyses, and overseeing program evaluation. It has no legally specified role in developing or reviewing proposals for legislation, regulations, or, for that matter, the budget.

Clearly, in order to have an impact on the on-going programs of the department, OASPE needs more specific authority that will accord it a formal role in the processes that generate current departmental policy. Without such authority, the office is in jeopardy of being frozen out by other administrators who want no intrusions on their areas of authority.

By its very nature PPB must intrude into the detailed operations of a program; thus, it also needs some rather general authority to make detailed recommendations on program operations on the basis of its analyses and evaluations.

The reader will have noted here the emphasis on the use of PPB in effecting decisions concerning the next one or two fiscal years. Not only is this a shorter range than the five-year planning period required by BOB, but it is also far shorter than the twenty-five-year periods many city and regional planners are accustomed to. This is partly because of the very long lags between plans and implementation in the construction programs considered by planners.

Much of the difference, however, stems from the context in which OASPE operates. It is crucial to the continued success of PPB that it maintain the support of the high administrators of the governmental unit in which it lies. Therefore, OASPE concentrated particularly heavily on the next budget year in order to prove to key department decision-makers that the PPB process can be useful to them in the decisions they *must* make. Since these decision-makers are not used to making decisions over the long-range and have not felt the legal force of such decisions as they do the budget decisions, the OASPE staff elected to supply information that would prove most useful and meaningful to these administrators in the decisions they considered of utmost importance. Over the longer run—once PPB has been accepted by these officials as an important tool to be employed by them in their decisions, then more emphasis can be placed on planning over longer periods of time. Such a beginning strategy is probably necessary for survival in nearly all initiations of the PPB system.

The city planner will also be frustrated by the lack of discussion here on the relation between PPB and urban, regional, and state planning. While the federal experience is not directly relevant, Mushkin et al. have provided an excellent discussion of PPB and planning agencies at subnational levels.[6]

The Role of Program Analysis

Program analyses, or Special Analytic Studies as they are officially known by the Bureau of the Budget, define some objectives to be reached and specify a set of alternative means for reaching each objective. Each alternative is then analyzed to determine its relative economic effectiveness in reaching the objective. These analyses are usually called cost-effectiveness studies or cost-benefit studies.

Sometimes a problem is broken up into several parts with several alternatives for each part. For example, in the family planning study mentioned earlier, the family planning program was split into methods of attracting patients to the clinic; methods of following up patients who failed to keep appointments; geographic and institutional types of locations for clinics; types of contraceptive and other services offered in the clinic; and the like. For each of these components several alternatives were analyzed and relative cost and effectiveness assessed for each.

These analytic studies must be considered the backbone of the PPB operation. Without program analyses, the OASPE staff could provide the form but not the substance of the PPB process. It would then become merely another advocate in a mob of advocates inside and outside the government unit, with nothing to substantiate its position. The potential of its specialized skills would be lost, and the advantage of a disinterested analytic approach would be unrealized. To quote Mushkin et al., "The formal [PPB] system without analyses is a paper-shuffling exercise."[7]

Unfortunately, it is all too easy to let the analytic studies drift into the background. Very often the PPB staff is severely undermanned, and there are many operations that are rigid requirements, such as developing the PFPs and writing Program Memoranda. The PPB office is also often required to respond to urgent issues arising in the Secretary's office, and it is difficult and usually unwise to refrain from becoming involved. Because of all these pressures, it can be very difficult to develop the program analyses that are known to be needed. The implications of this fact are that, when a PPB operation is established, the administration of an agency must be willing to commit itself to providing sufficient numbers of persons to carry out all functions of the PPB process, including the critically needed program analyses.

An enormous impetus to the PPB process including program analysis will occur in HEW when 1 percent or .5 percent of funds for each program (less for Medicaid and Medicare) are earmarked for program evaluation. This earmarking is insignificant in terms of the total program cost, but can have enormous payoffs in determining means for improving program effectiveness. A small proportion of this money could be used to augment inhouse PPB staffs.

Since program analyses are time-consuming, the question arises: how can we be sure they are used effectively? To answer this, we must consider another question concerning the role of PPB in the Secretary's office. Staffs in Secretarys' offices have generally regarded themselves as assistants to the Secretary in his decision-making processes. This may be an excessively narrow interpretation of the PPB role at this level, especially when strong PPB staffs do not exist at lower echelons.

Perhaps the PPB operation should be seen as having as its objective improving the decision-making processes in the entire system of—in our case—health, education, and welfare. If the health system, for example, can be improved most significantly by improving the decision-making power at the local level, then perhaps the OASPE staff should concentrate its efforts on improving the decision-making process here.

Certainly one way in which federal PPB staffs could improve decision-making at subnational levels is by making the program analyses they execute for federal decisions more useful to others: these analyses have the potential of being a major resource to administrators and PPB analysts in state and local governments and in individual projects. The information on methodology, data sources, and bibliographic references can be extremely helpful to someone trying to develop a similar analysis. Yet in HEW, and presumably elsewhere, such information is usually left out of the finished documents. It would be very profitable if significant analyses done at any level of government, in a university, or a consulting firm provided a technical supplement that allowed other analysts to use the recommendations, methodology, data sources, or references. Federal agencies should consider this as part of their responsibility to their counterparts at other governmental levels. In short, program analysts everywhere should take a more scholarly approach to their finished products.

Beyond making analyses for federal decisions more useful to nonfederal officials, HEW and other departments should consider supporting analyses dealing specifically with decisions at state and local levels, starting with the decisions of directors of federally sponsored projects. Beginning state and local PPB efforts have found it difficult to support the development of full-scale program analyses. In this situation, Mushkin et al. argue for the use of issue papers as a partial substitute. The issue paper examines thoroughly the first stage of a program analysis—that of problem definition. It raises alternative methods for solving the defined problem but does not analyze the costs and effectiveness of each. This placing of governmental problems in improved perspective can be of significant assistance to decision-makers. However, unless outside analyses can be brought to bear on the issue, the weighing of alternatives in the issue paper remains a primarily judgmental process based on inadequate information. For this reason, subnational governmental units may always have to depend heavily on centrally executed or funded program analyses.

Some of these analyses could be merely extensions of federal program analyses; other would be completely separate analyses supported by federal grants to consultants, federal project grantees, or subnational governments. Because of widely varied local conditions, such analyses will not, of course, be able to provide uniformly valid conclusions. Rather the analyses could provide the framework into which parameters representing local conditions could be inserted; the significant factors to consider should not vary from place to place.

An often overlooked output from program analysis is identification of essential additional research and data collection. OASPE experience suggests that program analysts in the social policy field generally find out more about what they do not know than what they do know, what information is most needed, and where the required knowledge fits into the overall scheme. Thus, a standard part of program analysis should be specific recommendations for further research. They should state precisely what relationships need to be better defined and what type of research should be undertaken toward that end. They should identify what new data are required, in what form they are to be collected, and what methods of collection might be utilized. These gaps in knowledge uncovered by program analyses should also generate experiments, including demonstration projects specifically tailored to fill in these gaps and provide the required missing parameters in the analytic process.

Program Evaluation

Program evaluation has several features in common with program analysis, but there is one major difference. Program evaluation is performed to assess impact and effectiveness of an *existing* program in meeting its objectives. Program analysis, on the other hand, may be used to define a problem—whether or not any program exists—for example, identifying health needs of the poor and barriers to health service delivery, and then considering alternative means of solving this newly specified problem. Program analysis can compare several existing programs and design alternative programs that do not presently exist. Thus, program analysis is concerned with problems or suspected problems: needs that are not currently being attacked by existing programs; programs that are not effective in attacking the needs to which they are addressed because of misdirection, poor structuring, under-funding, and the like. It is addressed to subject areas in which some major change may need to take place: a new program; a restructured program; a greatly augmented program. For this reason, program analysis tends to have a one-shot nature. Once the analysis is completed, the analysts go on to another program and do not return to the first program unless another major restructuring is being considered.

Program evaluation, on the other hand, is expected to be an ongoing, repetitive operation, a continual monitoring process done on programs year after year. The emphasis in program evaluation is not necessarily on possible *major* changes in programs, but can be instead on improvement of the program through more gradual modifications. Certainly, decisions to make fundamental changes might result from a program evaluation, but it is unlikely they would be made purely on the basis of the evaluation, since evaluation does not necessarily consider markedly different ways of working toward the same objectives. Program evaluation is thus more of an incremental process in which a presumably optimum program is approached through a series of corrective steps.

Because of its continuing nature, program evaluation places a much greater emphasis on collection of basic data concerning program impact and cost. Program analysis, because of its generally short-run nature, does not usually have time to develop a collection system to supply data ideally suited for its needs; it must instead seek existing data most relevant to its purposes. Program evaluation, however, can develop a data collection system over several years, and this data collection activity is a major and necessary part of the program evaluation process.[8] Again, because of its emphasis on existing programs, program evaluation can investigate the managerial questions of how well a program is organized and administered.

More than any other part of the PPB system, program evaluation can be viewed as the function that closes the feedback loop in the program development process of discerning and articulating a need, developing a program to alleviate that need, and implementing the program. Program evaluation measures how well the program has satisfied the need to which it was addressed.

MEASURES OF EFFECTIVENESS

One of the crucial tasks in PPB is development of measures of effectiveness needed for program evaluation. Such measures can be set in a hierarchical order, with the low end containing concrete measures of administrative effectiveness of specific projects and programs, primarily of use for short-term administrative control. Examples of these are the number of clients enrolled or the proportion of a target group reached by a program. At the high end, on the other hand, are measures of the actual benefits of the program, generally in terms of changes in the overall status of a community or a nation with respect to certain important attributes. Such measures have a high level of "intrinsic significance." Examples of these are decreases in the infant mortality rate and in the crime rate.

A desirable characteristic of each of the highest level measures is that it have *normative* value; that is, if the particular measure changes in the "right" direction while other things remain equal, then we can agree that the condition of our society has improved. Thus, figures on mortality rates or crime rates qualify, but statistics on numbers of doctors and policemen do not. The reason for this relates to the important distinction between input and output. Doctors and policemen must be considered as inputs into a process intended to improve the outputs of health status and crime prevention. They have significance only as they affect these and other outputs or objectives.

All programs may not be able to satisfy this criterion. For example, the ultimate output of a professional manpower training program is a person adequately discharging the duties of the job for which he was trained. The value of this job can be assessed in given settings, but the variety of possible settings makes difficult assessment of the overall value of a profession. Therefore, evaluation measures for professional manpower training will probably stop short of having normative value.

To illustrate these hierarchical concepts, we can consider a specific set of evaluation measures that relate to family planning programs. For this program, four levels of intrinsic significance can be defined:

Level 1—Project administration measures. These are to be measured on individual family planning projects and aggregated to national totals. They include such factors as total number of women and of new women seen per year; percent of unwed and high risk mothers enrolled; cost per patient year; and the like.

Level 2—Sampling survey questions. These are asked of persons in the target area of a family planning project or in a more general area such as a city or metropolitan region. They are intended to determine what impact a family planning project is having in a community in terms of knowledge, attitudes, and practice. The surveys seek changes in the percentage knowing of family planning and of the specific family planning project, approving the concept of family planning, practicing family planning, and similar questions.

Level 3—Basic output measures. It is assumed here that the desired basic objective of a family planning program is prevention of unwanted and untimely births.[9] Therefore, basic output measures include total number of births averted;[10] changes in fertility rates; cost per birth averted; and the like. Some of these measures, such as fertility rates, can be obtained directly and routinely; others may have to be partially inferred—such as births averted.

Level 4—Measure of benefits. This is the highest level of significance and corresponds to the level of social indicators. Measures of benefit could include such things as changes in infant mortality rates, selected infant morbidity rates, abortion rates or deaths attributed to abortions, illegitimacy rates, number of families avoiding poverty (because of smaller family size), increased family income due to ability of the mother to work, and the like.

As mentioned earlier, ascribing these measures of benefits to a family planning program is a difficult inference to make. This is one reason that the lower level, more clearly causally related measures are used to assist in evaluating specific programs. Furthermore, these lower level measures can often be used as a step in the estimation of benefits. For example, expected decreases in poverty because of smaller family size can be inferred by using OEO's estimate of $500 additional income needed per child to stay out of poverty and multiplying this by the estimated decreases in family size.

An example of a more complex inferential chain is the use of statistical analysis to determine the extent to which each of several independent variables affect a selected benefit measure. Then, estimates of program impacts on the independent variables can be used to estimate program impact on the benefit measure. Here is where the development of mathematical models is sorely needed in so many program areas. For example, a multiple regression analysis of infant mortality, done on individual maternity records, could indicate the extent to which age, number of children, and pregnancy interval relate to infant mortality rates. From our knowledge of changes caused in these independent variables by family planning, we could then estimate the effect of a specific family planning program on infant mortality.

Besides using this sequential chain of inferences, we can sometimes attempt to measure the impact of a program on certain social indicators more directly by a properly designed statistical experiment. For example, we might attempt to develop experimental and control areas of comparable initial conditions, and develop a family planning program in one area and not in the other. Then, differences in the trends of these indicators could be ascribed to the family planning program.

A hierarchy of measures similar to that described before should be capable of development for every program. There will not always be the same types or numbers of levels; in some cases there may only be administrative measures and benefit measures. Nevertheless, such a hierarchy should always prove useful, by providing a range of measures for evaluating different aspects of a program's operation. Several analysts have referred to this hierarchy, sometimes calling the lower level measures impact measures or public good measures and the higher level benefits measures or effectiveness measures.[11]

Project Evaluation

In addition to the overall evaluation of a program, there is need for the evaluation of individual projects. In the federal context a project can be defined as the recipient of a project grant. Many of the programs funded by HEW and other federal agencies consist of projects directed toward the same general objectives. For example, most of the health service and manpower training programs fall in this category. Yet, many federal program managers can cite cases to show that individual projects vary in effectiveness by several orders of magnitude.

For programs consisting of projects with similar objectives, evaluation measures for the program can also be used to evaluate the effectiveness of individual projects. For example, the evaluation measures for family planning can be and should be used on the project level. Their use will be helpful in several ways: (1) it will help individual project directors compare themselves with other projects and analyze where their strengths and weaknesses lie; (2) it will assist federal and state program managers to determine where significant difficulties exist in projects; (3) it will help program managers to determine what techniques are and are not effective and to demonstrate and promote proven effective methods among other project directors; and (4) it will provide much more concrete evidence to program managers in reaching and justifying decisions that certain project grants should be suspended or terminated.[12]

NEED FOR OUTPUT MEASURES

With the development of program evaluation, it is possible to supply the output measures required in the PFP. Although the Bureau of the Budget requires output measures in the PFP, this was not mentioned in the discussion of the PPB process in HEW. The output measures developed so far have been virtually useless, primarily due to the great difficulty in generating them and the short time that has been available to develop the basic data required for them. Occasionally, the measures submitted by the agencies have been ridiculous. For example, output measures were requested for the various medical services provided by the Medicaid program, such as physician services, hospital services, and the like. The measure submitted initially was "the number of potential recipients" and was the same number for each service category. Upon inquiry, this proved to be simply the total number of persons enrolled in the Medicaid program. Not only had the effort sunk so low as to count *bodies,* but *potential bodies* at that.

There are three ways in which HEW, and presumably other agencies, can improve this situation. The first is through central program evaluation. The second, closely related, is through the central reports clearance function. This clearance function is a result of the Federal Reports Act of 1942, which requires that all questionnaires used for the collection of information on identical items from ten or more persons be submitted to the Bureau of the Budget for approval and, generally, reapproval every three years. Before this is done, they are first approved by the department and agency staffs, giving the central PPB staff the opportunity to include certain questions deemed important, particularly of an output nature.

The third way of assuring better output measures is by insisting that they be provided once the basic data required for them have been developed. Given the proper format and the proper incentives for accurate reporting, this could be an almost automatic activity. However, during the interim a number of basic issues must be confronted and much hard work must be done.

Notes

[1] Most of the discussion on federal PPB requirements is taken from Bulletin 68–9, April 12, 1968, of the Bureau of the Budget.

[2] See, BOB Bulletin 68–9, April 12, 1968; and BOB Circular A-11, Section 24.3, June 23, 1969.

[3] See, Aaron Wildavsky, *Politics of the Budgetary Process* (New York: Little, Brown, 1964); and Edward C. Banfield, *Political Influence* (New York: Free Press, Macmillan, 1961).

[4] Charles Schultze, "The Rowan Gaither Lectures," Lecture 1, April 8, 1968 (unpublished draft).

[5] Program Analysis: Maternal and Child Health Care Programs, P.A. 1966-6, HEW.

[6] Selma Mushkin et al., *Implementing PPB in State, City, and County* (Washington, D.C.: State-Local Finances Project, George Washington University, June 1969).

[7] *Ibid.*, p. 71.

[8] The author is indebted to Wayne Kimmel for his thoughts on the differentiation between program evaluation and program analysis.

[9] Not a trivial assumption; many physicians believe the primary purpose of a family planning program is to reduce the infant mortality rate.

[10] It has been assumed here that a birth averted is not a benefit in itself, but a means of obtaining certain benefits, such as decreased poverty. Others may disagree and wish to merge Levels 3 and 4. Since decreasing the birth rate of the poor will have little effect on the national birth rate, that benefit has not been considered sufficiently significant to warrant placing births averted under Level 4.

[11] Jack W. Carlson, Speech presented to the Washington Chapter, American Society of Public Administration, April 17, 1969.

[12] For an example, see, Worth Bateman, "Assessing Program Effectiveness—A Rating System for Identifying Relative Project Success," *Welfare in Review* (January-February 1968), 1–10.

17

Program and Responsibility Cost Accounting

FRANCIS E. McGILVERY

The advent of planning, programming, and budgeting (PPB)[1] has some-times served to distract attention from a prior requirement for extensive improvements in financial management in the Executive Branch of the federal government. Since 1950 and even before, the combined weight of the Congress as expressed in legislation[2] and of the Comptroller General of the United States,[3] has been focused on causing the achievements of certain specified improvements in budgeting, accounting, and other financial management processes. These improvements, if they had been achieved, would have immensely benefited PPB from its start. In their absence, appropriate financial management data for the purposes of PPB are often not available and in some cases new financial data systems have been conceived and initiated under the PPB heading. One of the effects of this is a tendency to depart from long-standing principles and objectives, particularly with regard to "cost" data.

It should be noted that in PPB documentation cost is defined as New Obligation Authority (NOA) and Total Obligation Authority (TOA). This

Reprinted from the *Public Administration Review*, 28, No. 2 (March/April 1968): 148–54, by permission of the publisher.

would be considered an expediency, directly transferred from the Department of Defense. The expediency is chosen in both cases simply because cost data, in the conventional sense of goods and services used, are not available. However, in the long run and in depth, PPB analysis and evaluation of alternatives in terms of output and cost relationships must utilize conventional costs in order to arrive at conclusions useful to management. The term "cost" as used herein is described by the Comptroller General in this way:

> Any qualified representation as to cost implies that all significant elements of cost, in terms of financial, property, and personnel *resources consumed* in carrying out a given purpose, are included in the amount reported as total cost. Such factors as (a) differences in methods of financing the resources used, (b) prescribed requirements for obtaining reimbursement or setting prices for sales of goods or services, and (c) administrative policies relating to budgeting, accounting, and financial reporting do not constitute valid basis for excluding items of cost that are otherwise applicable. [Italics supplied.][4]

PPB Data Problems

PPB, which derives from systems analysis concepts and practices at the Secretary's level in the Department of Defense, employs a new form for appraising the relative effectiveness of governmental programs. Quantification of program output is a necessity, and quantified program output is related to program cost. In this way, alternatives are posed and analyzed in terms of relative output and relative cost.

PPB is employed at the highest levels of government organization— the Bureau of the Budget and the secretary or equivalent levels of departments and agencies. Consequently the massive and diverse programs of government must be simplified, distilled, summarized, and compacted. This leads to a great number of problems, some procedural and some judgmental. Aside from problems of judgment, procedural problems divide into:

(a) How to quantify and how to secure output quantities to reflect program end services rendered (and in how much detail)

(b) What is cost and how to secure cost data.

To most departments and agencies both of these problems are immensely complex, and large sums of money are being spent trying to solve them. This article is concerned with the second procedural problem:

what is cost and how to gather and bring cost data up from the operating levels to serve purposes of highest-level PPB analysis and decision making.

Why Is This a Problem?

It has been observed in two major departments that efforts are being made to gather costs at operating levels directly against elements of the high-level PPB structure. These elements are functional and broad enough to cut across major organizational components. Except in rare instances, they do not coincide with organizational arrangements for accomplishing work and incurring cost. In traditional management accounting concepts, operating cost account structures are designed to reflect responsibilities of key individuals for portions of the work program, and, therefore, the responsibilities of key individuals for accomplishing work and incurring costs. These responsibility cost centers also become points of responsibility for planning, programming, and budgeting for output and cost at the operating or working levels.

Thus, a simply stated problem of designing a cost account structure is posed:

(a) Should the structure be a direct extension of a PPB structure down to the lowest levels of operation, or

(b) Should the conventional concepts of responsibility accounting dictate the structure design?

If the former is chosen, the practical advantages of responsibility accounting and budgeting are lost. In its place data for use at higher levels, but of only limited value at operating levels, is accumulated. If the latter course is chosen, nothing is lost to PPB, yet the operating level will gain the advantages of traditional cost planning, budgeting, and control. Nothing is lost to PPB because conventional accounting procedures provide means for reexpressing cost data in a variety of forms for analytic purposes which readily serve purposes of PPB.

If a department or agency builds its management cost accounting system around the PPB element structure, several consequences can be predicted:

1. The operating levels of management will not have an effective management control system.

2. The accounting system will not produce cost reports which are useful to operating management.

3. Cost accounting systems which already exist will continue to exist, resulting in duplication.

4. If element costing proves not to be viable (and there is little evidence to suggest that it will) it will be abandoned or overhauled at great expense.

5. It is probable that element cost structures will be found not to satisfy the Principles and Standards of the Comptroller General and the statutory requirements from which they are derived.

The Case for Responsibility Accounting

It is not unusual in our society to find that long-established rules and principles occasionally need to be restated. In recent years the Supreme Court has handed down notable decisions which apply, in today's context, certain rules and principles long ago stated in our Constitution. So, perhaps it would be useful to cite authoritative sources which define, recommend, explain, and require responsibility accounting as a basis for planning, budgeting, and management control.

DEFINITION

Let us begin by calling upon a most modern source for current insight into the long-standing concept of responsibility accounting.

> *A responsibility center* is simply an organization unit headed by a responsible person. The center is responsible for performing some function, which is its *output,* and for using resources, or *inputs,* as efficiently as possible in performing this function.
>
> Cost centers are often production departments, and these departments are also responsibility centers since the department foreman is a responsible supervisor. When individual machines or other segments of a department are used as cost centers, costs for the responsibility center can be obtained simply by adding up the relevant costs of these separate cost centers. At the other extreme, if the whole factory is a single cost center (as is the case when a plant-wide overhead rate is used), separate accounts are set up to collect the controllable costs for the individual responsibility centers in the plant. Likewise, if cost centers are departments and responsibility centers are individual work shifts or other departmental subdivisions, separate accounts for these subdivisions are required. In short, costs are collected for the cost center or the responsibility center, whichever is the smaller unit, and costs for the other are obtained by addition. Thus the fact that a cost center is not necessarily the same as a responsibility center raises no particular problem of cost collection.

Service centers headed by responsible supervisors, such as the maintenance department, the personnel department, the accounting department, and so on, are also responsibility centers. Service centers that are mere aggregates of cost without reference to personal responsibility are not. An example of the latter is the occupancy service center which is not in itself a responsibility center, although its costs are part of the responsibility center of the plant manager.[5]

RECOMMENDATION

The most comprehensive and knowledgeable examination of federal financial management practices was made by the Second Hoover Commission in 1955. In its Task Force report it stated, among other things:

The operating budgets should coincide with the organizational pattern by which responsibility has been established within an agency. Operating budgets should disclose the projected programs and workloads, be based on reliable cost information, and indicate the funds required to finance operation.[6]

EXPLANATION

An early and most lucid explanation of the technical application of responsibility accounting in a federal department or agency was developed by E. Reece Harrill in the early 1950s. The doctrine he developed and published was based on his actual experience in systems design and installation of such improvements in federal agencies. Relevant quotations from his *Responsibility and Activity Accounting in the Federal Government* follow:

Responsibility and activity accounting is the classification and accumulation of transactions by organizational units, further segregated according to the various lines of work carried on by an organizational unit.

If accounts are properly selected, the basic data accumulated will reflect the various activities of each center and this information can be reshuffled, summarized, or analyzed to provide answers to any reasonable inquiries raised by management.

The activity accounts for current expenses which are subsidiaries to the current expenses control account should be established according to "responsibility centers" and thereunder according to functions being performed by each center.

The activity accounts should correspond to the organizational units according to assignment of responsibility. In some agencies the organizational structure parallels the activities, without any one organization performing more than one activity. In other agencies, the activities are diverse and the organization is more complex.

Responsibility and activity accounts can and must be used to develop ways and means of gathering, evaluating and compiling the necessary control data at a minimum of cost and effort.[7]

STATUTORY REQUIREMENTS

Public Law 863, 84th Congress, which amended the Budget and Accounting Act of 1921 and the Budget and Accounting Procedures Act of 1950, had among its notable provisions:

Amendments to the Budget and Accounting Act, 1921
The requests of the department and establishments for appropriations shall, in such manner and at such times as may be determined by the President, be developed from cost-based budgets.

For purposes of administration and operation, such cost-based budgets shall be used by all departments and establishments and their subordinate units. Administrative subdivisions of appropriations or funds shall be made on the basis of such cost-based budgets.

Amendments to the Budget and Accounting Procedures Act, 1950
The head of each executive agency shall, in consultation with the Director of the Bureau of the Budget, take whatever action may be necessary to achieve, insofar as is possible, (1) consistency in accounting and budget classifications, (2) synchronization between accounting and budget classifications and organizational structure, and (3) support of the budget justifications by information on performance and program costs by organizational units.[8]

The foregoing citations make the point that the concept of responsibility accounting has the endorsement of one of the accounting profession's foremost scholars; that is recommended for use by a most competent study of federal financial management; that it has long ago been applied and its practical application explained by a man who is a national and international authority; and that it is required by law.

Costs for Varied Purposes

Basic data at responsibility levels can be arranged and rearranged to serve a variety of purposes through cost analysis. The relevant purposes in this discussion are:

1. Cost-based appropriations presentations in the President's budget.

2. Internal management control through operating cost budgets, which are related to the appropriations.

3. PPB element and output unit costing.

If costs are first gathered against responsibility cost centers, the problem of ultimately reaching an element cost per unit of output is not unlike the commercial problem of arriving at a unit of production cost for product pricing purposes. It is a problem of gathering direct costs and assigning an appropriate share of distributive costs. A very recent publication of the American Institute of Certified Public Accountants examines this problem in a variety of forms and clearly explains the relatively simple and wholly conventional procedures and principles involved in its solution.[9] The only other problem in serving the three purposes cited above through one system is to identify the contribution of responsibility cost centers in terms of the functional or program activities (budget activities) in the appropriations' structures.

Table 1 illustrates, in sequence, how each of these three purposes is served.

TABLE 1
Cost Analysis Sequence

	Appropriation			
Organization	*BA*	*BA*	*BA*	*BA*
DIVISION A				
Branch A$_1$				
Branch A$_2$	Cost center			
Branch A$_3$				
DIVISION B			Cost center	
Branch B$_1$				
Branch B$_2$				
Section X				
Section Y		Cost center		
Section Z				
Total Cost	XXXX			

BA = Budget activity

Each intersection of BA and organization unit is a cost center. Any cost center can be further subdivided into any number of subsidiary cost centers as necessary to have un-mixed identification of functional (BA) occurence within an organization, and to measure the organization's contribution to that function.

PPB Elements

	E I	E II	E III	E IV
Cost center A				
Sub-cost ctr. A_1	100	20		75
Sub-cost ctr. A_2		50	75	
Sub-cost ctr. A_3	25			100
Total cost	125	70	75	175

Costs are distributed to PPB Elements on the basis of man-hour reports, end product counts, or other ratios to show the organization's contribution to each element.

PPB Element IV End Product (EP)
Unit Costs
(When an element has more than one output)

	EP_1	EP_2	EP_3	EP_4
Sub-cost ctr. A_1 (75)				
Sub-cost ctr. A_3 (100)				
Total cost				

Unit cost = Total cost # units
Again, costs are distributed to end products on the basis of man-hour or other ratios as appropriate.

The following analysis is really a restatement, and extension to PPB unit costs, of concepts in the 1953 article by Harrill. [10] The relationship of program budget activities to organizations through the responsibility cost center concept is also explained and diagrammed by Kohler and Wright in *Accounting in the Federal Government.* [11] The additional point illustrated by the following diagrams is the extension of their basic methodology to the problem of costing PPB elements and outputs.

Probably the most highly developed and generally comparable solution to the need to move from costs accumulated by responsibility centers to an end product unit cost is found in hospital accounting. Hospitals uniformly deal in the ultimate cost of hospital care for "inpatients" and "outpatients." These are a hospital's primary outputs: i.e., the number and unit costs of patients treated, divided between inpatient and outpatient status, because the costs vary markedly between the two types of care. The method for determining unit costs of handling patients through the whole complex of hospital activity is called cost finding. It is a method through which costs gathered in responsibility cost centers are distributed first from common service or other distributive responsibility cost centers. These total costs are then distributed or allocated to the across-the-board functions of inpatient and outpatient care. The unit cost per patient is thereafter a simple matter of long division. This method is explained and illustrated in the American Hospital Association's publication *Cost Finding in Hospitals.*[12]

Thus the unit costs of program and functional outputs for PPB or any other purpose can be determined through a variety of cost analysis techniques if the concept of responsibility cost accounting is used as the basis for collecting costs at operating levels.

Key Features of the Problem

The introduction of a major system concept like PPB by the President and the Bureau of the Budget generates a tremendous response effort by the departments and agencies. It might be characterized as a vast effort to accumulate, process, and present huge quantities of data about the work of the departments and agencies. In terms of cost data, we begin with the fact that present systems accumulate very little cost data and often none at all. It is easy to understand that the forces involved in implementing PPB would go directly to gathering costs against the PPB structure. They would say: "If new cost accounting systems have to be installed, why not start at the very bottom with costing the elements of the PPB structure— then there is a simple and direct flow of data in the form required for ultimate use." As far as "responsibility accounting" is concerned, merely make individuals up and down the line responsible for elements and subelements and then it can be said that accounting is in terms of responsibilities of operating managers.

Herein lies one of the major points of the problem. The foregoing is not logic, it is sophistry. The assignment of responsibility to an operating manager for an element or subelement is an *additional* responsibility assignment—on top of his responsibility for managing an organization or operation. The former (PPB element or subelement responsibility) is new, ill-defined, and perhaps transitory. Responsibility accounting has deep-rooted meaning, importance, and permanence. It cannot be arbitrarily defined to mean something else.

This particular aspect of the problem results from the fact that the PPB structures of programs or categories, elements, and subelements do not, and should not, coincide with organization structure. Therefore, to PPBers the PPB structure is preferable to the organization structure. But organization structure is the formal expression of the way in which management responsibilities are assigned and is the appropriate framework for responsibility accounting.

A second major point is the matter of properly charging or allocating costs to end purposes. This is a basic consideration of all cost accounting, whether costing for purposes of pricing products for sale, or costing the work of organizations for budget control purposes, or costing functional program or category elements for PPB purposes. Within this the allocation of overhead, support, and common service costs is of particular concern.

Allocation of overhead and support costs is an analytical function in which the appropriate assessments are based on ratios and percentages approximating usage or benefit. The analytical process can vary depending on the purpose for which it is being performed. It occurs whether responsibility accounting is followed or not because there are always multipurpose organizations whose primary functions receive common service and support. It is sounder to accomplish distribution at operating levels where cost is incurred and understood and where it is useful to operating management. It is sounder also to allocate the costs to primary responsibility cost centers because the participation of responsibility and knowledgeable people is brought into necessary judgments as to fairness and accuracy of the distributions. If higher authority would prescribe reports of data in the form it wants, and perhaps criteria for allocation for its purposes, then the purposes of PPB can be served without distorting the traditional principles for gathering and using costs at operating levels.

The basic principles of integrated programming, budgeting, and accounting which have been evolving in the Executive Branch since the early 1950s are the indispensable basis for both achieving the data requirements of PPB and complying with requirements of the Budget and Accounting Procedures Act of 1950 as amended and the Principles and Standards of the Comptroller General of the United States.

Those principles are reflected in the authoritative sources previously cited, including the statutes. They hold, in essence, that operating budgets should be based on work programs planned in advance; that they should reflect the costs of goods and services to be consumed; that accounting data should reflect actual costs and work output in relation to programs and budgets, and that all of the foregoing should be based on a common classification of accounts (responsibility centers).

None of the requirements of the Budget and Accounting Procedures Act of 1950 are amended or changed because of the advent of PPB. Its provisions are still the ground rules for budgeting and accounting in federal departments and agencies. It must be assumed that if an agency meets requirements of the statutes, it can reasonably provide cost data for PPB. If this cannot be assumed, then agencies have two huge, overlapping systems requirements placed on them—one by law and one by Bureau of the Budget directive.

Compliance with applicable statutes is the foremost task facing federal departments and agencies. Systems designed to meet those criteria can be tailored to provide PPB cost data. The key is responsibility accounting from lowest levels upward and uniform cost finding techniques to organize data for reporting to highest levels for PPB purposes.

Notes

[1] Bureau of the Budget Bulletin No. 66-3, Subject: "Planning-Programming -Budgeting," October 12, 1965.

[2] The Budget and Accounting Procedures Act, 64 Stat. 834, 31 USC 665, approved September 12, 1950.

[3] *General Accounting Office Policy and Procedures Manual for Guidance of Federal Agencies*, Title 2, The Comptroller General of the United States, June 30, 1965.

[4] *Ibid.*, pp. 2–51.

[5] Robert N. Anthony, *Management Accounting: Text and Cases* (Homewood, Ill.: Irwin, 1965), pp. 367, 440.

[6] Task Force on Budget and Accounting, *Report on Budget and Accounting in the United States Government*, June 1955, p. 47.

[7] E. Reece Harrill, "Responsibility and Activity Accounting in the Federal Government," *The Federal Accountant*, 3, No. 2 (Washington, D.C.: The Federal Government Accountants Association, 1953). See also Eric L. Kohler and Howard W. Wright, *Accounting in the Federal Government* (Englewood Cliffs, N.J.: Prentice-Hall, 1956), pp. 1–12.

[8] Public Law 84-863, approved August 1, 1956, pp. 83–86.

[9] *Cost Analysis for Product Line Decisions*, Management Service Technical Study No. 1 (New York: The American Institute of Certified Public Accountants, 1965).

[10] Harrill, *op. cit.*

[11] Kohler and Wright, *op. cit.*, p. 188.

[12] *Cost Finding in Hospitals* (Chicago: American Hospital Association, 1957), p. 188.

18

PPBS in Fairfax County:
A Practical Experience

ROBERT A. LUTHER

The budget system of Fairfax County, prior to the attempt to develop
PPB, was traditional line item-object budgeting with an increasing emphasis on the use of management studies and systems analyses. These
two, though an important factor in PPB, were still on a line-object
orientation rather than program orientation. Since 1950, however, radical
changes have occurred in the county that have required considerable
attention to the development of improved systems rather than a modification of the old concept.

Fairfax County has experienced a population growth of over 300
percent in the span of less than twenty years, going from a population of
98,000 in 1950 to over 400,000 in 1968. In addition, the character of the
community, itself, has taken a radical change. Twenty years ago, the
county was a rural, even somewhat agrarian, area disassociated from the
developing metropolitan Washington area. It is now an almost self-
contained sector of this same urban complex which it once skirted. As a
necessary result, both the nature of the community and the types of

Reprinted from *Municipal Finance* (August 1968): 34–42, by permission of
the author and publisher.

services demanded changed drastically from those of a rural community to those of an urban area. Faced with this, the county organization and collection of services to meet these demands grew vastly.

In order to cope with the problems of multiplicity of programs, frequently duplicated, and the struggle for departmental autonomy, a continuous and effective program of management analysis was adopted. Again, the county was faced with the problem of having to treat the symptoms of the disease, and at the same time, trying to cure the disease itself. These studies, performed by the budget and research division, a staff arm of the office of the county executive, became and continue to be in-depth analyses of organization-wide problems and, in essence, have become a more systems-oriented approach to the old expenditure control techniques used in the traditional line item-object budgeting process. A good example of this was a problem of printing and printing facilities maintained by county departments. Each department controlled and maintained its own facility for all printing which was a massive duplication of effort—inefficient and uneconomical. Through a detailed analysis of the procedures, needs of individual departments, and demands on the total county organization, a central self-supporting county agency for printing was created.

If the transitions were as simple and as smooth as this, one would say that management studies, in the final analysis, are the answer to the overall budget-management-systems syndrome that faces all local governments in the same situation. Two problems, however, can be pointed out that restrict their effectiveness. First, the semiautonomous departments were, and are, reluctant to accept the solution. Department heads are reluctant to give up complete control. Consequently, there is a continuous effort on their part to return to the old system. Second, the management study was, in fact, a stopgap measure to correct an existing situation and not an attempt to return to the original need, i.e., develop a new system for the total organization and proceed accordingly. Management studies, therefore, as used in the context of a total system or, eventually in a PPB approach, have been but successful attempts to alleviate an immediate problem which was brought on by this onrush of growth and "changing community character."

Further illustration of this problem was brought out in a recent report prepared for the county government:

> Not all problems can be studied by a staff unless that staff is of considerable size ... Staff recommendations no matter how good do not carry the necessary weight to gain implementation of the recommendations, i.e., there is a tendency for difficult recommendations to be ignored ... there are also recommendations difficult for staff people to make since the recommendations necessarily imply

criticism of present, and past practices, and objectivity is lost in some cases because of the internal relationship with the organization being studied.

Closely related to management analysis, and possibly more closely associated with PPB as an organization moves toward that end, is a program of systems analysis. In Fairfax County, however, systems analysis is specifically "machine problem" oriented. That is, individual departments are confronted with specific tasks which can be either improved or made more efficient through the use of data processing type equipment. The data processing division systems analyst develops a computer "system" to perform a specific task required by the department. There is, and will continue to be, an effort to develop an overall management information system. Again, however, as with management studies, in many cases the practical problem of finding successful remedies for immediate problems and demands is foremost. There is, presently, a continually increasing need to develop comprehensive systems utilizing data-processing equipment to cope with basically clerical type workloads. Machine-oriented systems developed to date include accounting and clerical processes for tax billing, payrolls, welfare payrolls, voter registration and budget preparation. A significant step toward any systems approach to budgeting requires improvement and purification of computer procedures for these clerical tasks before total organization programs and systems may be developed.

Performance Budgeting

An attempt was made several years ago to adopt some of the facets of performance budgeting. It was felt that the traditional budgeting process, because of its orientation to individual items, did not permit an adequate analysis and review of the effectiveness of services provided to county citizens. Work program forms were included with annual budget request forms requiring each agency to quantify, itemize, and estimate cost of work units related to each of the services performed. The ultimate goal was to be a county-wide costing of services that cover more than one department. This budget technique was used for several cycles but was eventually abandoned for several reasons.

First, there was considerable difficulty on the part of participating departments and agencies to quantify, or even categorize within their department, units of work. The problem was, indeed, legitimate for the difference between a process and a work unit is difficult to make. For example, does the buildings and grounds division quantify custodial supplies or custodial services; or, does the library administration quantify all procedures associated with the receipt and issue of a book or record or lump all procedures into one work unit? In the former case, the division chief simply did nothing: in the latter, the chief lumped all procedures into one. Neither is acceptable.

Second, with only a few exceptions, the collection of these work units became nothing more than another budget procedure begun, collected, completed and submitted in the span of one month's time. Consequently, all data given was an estimate and not a particularly accurate one. Only those departments that used this type of data in their day-to-day operation, e.g., police department, presented accurate current data. Third, and probably most important in the long-run approach to PPB, the entire concept of this data collection and the need for it was questioned by department heads. Consequently, each work unit activity and service was viewed as an acceptable, unquestionable program with views only toward expansion rather than possible alteration of the activity or service. Without this vitally needed departmental cooperation, the program was destined to be only a budget exercise.

Program Budget

The use of the work program technique was replaced in 1967 with a program budget consisting of all known or determinable activities. Each was determined and identified without regard to conventional organizational or fiscal breakdown: this technique permitted closer scrutiny of services or programs with the aim of determining county performance and reasons for this performance of any particular function. Following the general concept used by the federal government each program included a general description of goals, possible quantitative measures and known trends.

Initial identification of programs was provided by the individual departments during the submission of budget requests. Staff instructions to the department heads asked them to: list programs to be performed: give particular consideration to all departmental operations: and define and state the purpose and goal of each defined program.

As was the case previously with the work unit approach, the resulting information was inadequate and, in some cases, not even germane to the request. One department, for example, provided as its program information a detailed justification of personnel requests for the fiscal year and a detailed breakdown of a proposed reorganization in the department. This information was relatively useless in program analysis. Another department submitted detailed statistical data which would have been much more appropriate in the preceding year's work unit requests. The result was a somewhat one-sided determination by the staff of program definition, deliniation, and objective. From this, one hundred and four separate programs were defined with a cost estimate attached to each.

This program grouping and analysis which was included with the formal budget document was well received in the community for several reasons. It provided a summary of the budget *in toto* in an easily understood format. Additionally, it served somewhat of a public relations function, for many interested citizens had seen and read about the PPB system in operation in the federal government. Criticism too, was to be expected. For example, 104 programs were far too many. This early acceptance and interest in the program budget led to the formulation of a plan of action to develop a PPB system in Fairfax County.

Many reasons have been given for this development: two, however, as stated below present all quite succinctly:

(1) It has become increasingly difficult to evaluate and make decisions about requests for funds among competing programs within agencies—it has been especially difficult to determine longer range implications of budget decisions made on an annual basis.

(2) As demonstrated by the approval of the 1967 program budget, the community needs and demands more each year a more understandable and sensible budget process. The various departments and accounting alignments have complicated the substantive program aspects of the budget to a point where it has made citizen participation in the budget and planning process difficult.

A major problem with which the county was confronted, however, was the general confusion and conflicting statements about what PPB was. Also, a total absence of a complete system in any local government put the county in a pioneering position.

The county's approach to PPB recognized four central characteristics of PPB which, together, make up a single cohesive system.

(1) Identification of the fundamental objectives or goals of the government, and a determination of how government programs relate to the achievement of these objectives.

(2) Projection of programs into the future on a planned and controlled basis, so that budgeting is a continuing process.

(3) Consideration of all pertinent costs of programs including capital outlays.

(4) Analysis of costs and effectiveness of alternative ways of reaching objectives.

Plans to develop and implement the system were in several phases:

The *first phase* was to involve identification of existing programs to determine what government objectives apparently were. Although some work had been done along these lines in the 1967 program budget, it was felt that more work should be done in close collaboration with department and agency heads to be accurate and to encompass capital improvement, debt service and trust funds. Specifically, forms would be designed to be used by department heads to determine in what meaningful programs their agency was participating. Emphasis was to be on discussions with department heads by staff people in order to provide an understanding of the concepts involved in PPB. Budget instructions would include the 1967 program summary to be used as a guide in identifying new programs or modifying those listed. It was to be pointed out that programs identified were to portray the direct service to the public or the support of a direct service provided by another agency or group of agencies. Dollar requirements were also to be determined.

The information obtained from the agencies would be used in describing objectives and grouping programs as they related to the achievement of objectives. It was to be implied in instructions that there should be a definite reason for a program to exist and that grouping of reasons into general objectives should give a framework for analysis. Work in this phase would be included in the 1968 budget document.

Phase two would involve projecting into the future all interrelated programs over a five-year period—and that it would be desirable to formalize the work into a carefully defined system capable of using data processing equipment. This would eliminate much detail work in the annual updating of the plan and should also make it possible to test alternative program emphasis. It was planned that forms for this phase also be designed and distributed to all department heads and that the budget staff personally contact them and work with them on the development of their program requests for the future five years. This phase was to also encourage agency heads to consider what mix of programs would be most effective in achieving desired goals over the time period.

Phase three would involve a compiling of agency projections into a summarized form showing programs grouped under related objectives and projected over the future five years. Results of the findings were to be discussed with the County Planning Commission staff and Board of Supervisors prior to proceeding to the next phase.

Phases four through seven were to involve testing the feasibility of projections by drawing schedules showing the projected revenues over the time period including bond sales and federal and state aid; conversion of completed work to data processing; preparation of a procedural manual; and preparation of a survey report on progress achieved and further work required.

The following questions were asked in order to obtain necessary information for the planned PPB program: Does each program correspond to any listed in the 1967 program summary, or is it a modification of one listed or is it a new program? What are the goals and purposes of the program? What are your agency's contribution to this program? Who is the coordinator of the various programs? What other agencies participate in the program and what are their contributions as you see them? What, if any, statistical data is available relative to performance? Other comments?

Realizing the problems that had occurred in the past with particular reference to cooperation of the individual department heads, the staff worked closely with each department. Each budget analyst normally in charge of the preparation and review of the agency's budget entered into discussion involving agency participation in specific programs and methods of assigning costs. Probably most important was the attempt over several months to orient department personnel to the concept of many departments contributing to the achievement of one program.

Though the results were not as successful as earlier anticipated, major improvement was made in: (1) refinement of the elements within the individual programs; (2) a better understanding of what the budget staff was attempting to do. Again, as before, several of the department heads were still unable to comprehend the concept of an interdepartmental program. Consequently, considerable information provided was but an explanation of the activities submitted in previous years under the work program concept.

Much of the information was presented in the form of "canned" answers which were indicative of either failure to understand the questions asked or, hopefully, inability to grapple with the needed information. The latter case demonstrated, at least, an effort to cooperate. In summary, department heads, though not so much as in previous attempts, demonstrated a general apathy or possible fear of the approaching system. Conversely, some department heads cooperated fully but were faced with legitimate problems of the elements constituting the program. A common error was the inclusion of "administration" as an agency program, which was obviously a task or function not a program. Owing to the ingrained conventional system, there was a basic resistance to any change, justified or not. One further observation need be made with respect to the entire process: on returning to speak with department heads after the submission of the initial data, the staff attempted to clarify and logically extend some of the data. In some cases these department heads were reluctant to offer any additional assistance and, in others, they became almost vehement in their denunciation of the program, for the essence of the clarifications was the question of justification of departmental existence. This could be taken initially as a rejection of the entire concept; however, it would seem more logical that this attitude reflected an awareness rather of the eventual worth of the system and its possible ramifications in changing either the department thoroughly or, at least, seriously revamping existing programs and procedures.

In order to complete a significant portion of Phase I, programs were costed and grouped based on both the data provided from the submitted forms and from the various discussions with department heads. Because of a time lapse, it was impossible to include portions of this in the formal 1968 budget presentation; however, after completion of staff preparation, a status report on Phase I became available during the fiscal year. The purpose here was to stimulate interest among the department heads with particular regard again to education in the concept of PPB.

The process of preparation of the program listing and costs allocated to them created, if nothing more, considerable introspective thought on the budget process itself. It refined the staff's awareness of the problems facing the county and, possibly more important, it made the staff more sympathetic toward the problems facing the individual department heads.

The major program definition was, by and large, a four stage process. It was necessary, initially, to prepare a list of all funds and agencies within those funds, including additionally the more difficult capital outlay, debt service and trust funds in order to determine departmental participation in the total program picture. The second list included all programs and functions as submitted by the individual departments. Function was included here because departments were, in many cases, unable to differentiate between a "function" and a "program." A third list was prepared in which the staff refined actual programs, excluding what were believed to be functions. Each program in this listing was, then, assigned to each individual performing department. Necessarily, in many cases there was multi-participation by several departments in one program. The fourth listing was a further refinement of the program definitions wherein the actual number of programs was reduced by collecting what was initially determined to be small programs in individual agencies into broader programs encompassing several agencies. Actually, it could be considered an extension and refinement of the third listing rather than a totally new listing. The complexities of these refinements of and limitations to the programs were formidable.

The tracing of the cost requirements was also complex, for in some funds which act as collecting accounts for miscellaneous expenditures the specific assignment to one program was either difficult to determine or, once determined, difficult to compute. "Unclassified Administrative Costs Account," for example, was of this type. Included are such items as county contribution to insurance programs, social security, et cetera. In that each determined program used personnel in some form or another, costing of that program would require, certainly, partial assignment of these unclassified personnel costs. The control of minutia that this entails is readily apparent. It was evident that the most practical approach to this was an additional governmental objective to be named "Supportive Services" with the stated objective of providing administrative support to enable the effective and efficient accomplishment of the other major objectives of the government. This definition had an uncomfortable similarity to many agency descriptions of their program goals. Any contribution or unclassified cost that could not be specifically assigned to a specific program was placed in this category.

The same was true with respect to the "Contributions Account," in which are included all contributions to outside organizations, supplementing the services and programs of individual operating departments in the county.

Eight objectives determined into which all programs could be placed. (See Figure 1.) The relating of specific programs to the broad objectives was another complex and difficult procedure. It was difficult to determine, for example, whether welfare programs such as aid to dependent children, foster child care or old-age assistance belong under health or welfare departments, for both departments seem intrinsically involved. Contributions to various private community agencies could be grouped with individual agencies or in a collecting objective. All programs involving youth could be grouped into one objective or placed with the other adult-oriented objectives. The library system in some respects is certainly oriented to the educational objective but it, too, is an important part of the leisure time objective. The final decisions are indicated in Figure 1.

At the staff level, some attempt was also made to determine measurable criteria for the eight objectives. The major problem in this process involved quantification. The not-so-readily-quantifiably were, for example, in the objective of "Administration of Justice": length of time between filing and final disposition of cases: length of time to appellate review; the relationship between caseload and workload capacity of judges, and the number of judges and courtrooms available; the availability of court-appointed attorneys: public attitudes including creating confidence in the judicial system; and recidivism. The objective of "Control of Environment" created assignment problems with respect to such matters as making miles of sidewalk, storm sewers, and rapid transit the measurement of "improving the environment."

Some interesting observations were brought out in this process. A

FIGURE 1
Fairfax County Program Structure

I—Protection of persons and property
Goal: To minimize injury to persons and loss of property from unexpected events or violent acts.
Police protection
Fire suppression
Fire prevention
Rescue and first aid
School safety program
Control of dogs and other animals
Inspection of building construction
Inspection of electrical installations
Street lighting
Civil defense
Contribution to Fairfax County Safety Council

II—Administration of justice
Goal: To settle disputes between individuals in the community and between the government and individuals and to assess and provide penalties or rehabilitative service to those found guilty of criminal acts.
Courts
Sheriff (including service of process and court bailiffs)
Prosecution of criminal and traffic offenders
Prisoner confinement
Law library
Contribution to regional detention home
Contribution to district probation and parole office
Contribution to legal aid association

III—Protection of health and welfare
Goal: To protect people in general from sickness and disease, both physical and mental; and specifically to provide for those who are unable to help themselves.
Hospital and health center commission
Construction of hospital facilities
Construction of health centers
Home nursing services
School health nurse program
Control of environmental health
General health clinics
Mentally retarded centers
Institutional and other care
Housing advisor
Fairfax House
Juvenile and domestic relations counseling
Public assistance to adults
Aid to dependent children
Foster care of children
Child protective services
Construction of sanitary sewers
Inspection of plumbing and sewer systems
Collection and treatment of sanitary sewage
Contribution to Cerebral Palsy Development Center
Contribution to Mental Health Center
Contribution to Alexandria Community Health Center
Contribution to District Home
Contribution to District Nursing Home
Contribution to Higher Horizons Day Care Center
Contribution to Coop. School for Handicapped

IV—Education
Goal: To give all people the opportunity to develop their intellectual resources to the maximum
Construction of school facilities
Operation and maintenance of schools
Support of higher education
Construction of library facilities
Operation of library system

V—Control of environment

Goal: To provide for pleasant, orderly and effective environment in the County by regulating and controlling its physical aspects.

Planning commission
Comprehensive planning
Rezoning processing
Land use control
Zoning administration
Sidewalk construction
Other public works construction
Public works engineering
Control of streets and subdivision design
Drainage and storm sewer maintenance
Soil analysis and conservation
Contribution to Northern Virginia Regional Planning Commission
Contribution to Historical Landmark Commission
Contribution to Northern Virginia Transportation Commission
Contribution to Washington Metropolitan Transportation Authority

VI—Leisure time opportunities

Goal: To provide opportunities and facilities for constructive and healthful use of recreational and leisure time.

Acquisition and development of park and playground areas
Operation and maintenance of parks
Community playgrounds and recreation
Organization of sports
Recreation activity classes
Support of 4-H Clubs
Farm and garden advisory
Homemaking demonstration services
Contribution to youth council
Contribution to teen centers
Contribution to Fairfax County Cultural Association

VII—Community services

Goal: To accomplish those objectives desired by the citizens of the County which can best be accomplished by group action of the government as contrasted to individual action.

Collection of refuse from homes
Roadside refuse service
Operation of sanitary landfill
Promotion of industrial development
Recording of deeds and other legal documents
Condemnation of Alexandria water company
Public Utilities Commission

VIII—Supportive services

Goal: To provide administrative support to enable the effective and efficient accomplishment of the other major objectives of the government.

Legislative services (board of supervisors)
County Executive
County Attorney
Fiscal and management analysis
Central data processing service
Personnel administration
Purchasing and warehousing
Real property assessment
Personal property assessment
Business tax assessment
State Income Tax Administration
Accounting and treasury management
Employee benefits
Office facilities
Miscellaneous administrative support
Voter registration
Elections

common assumption concerning health and welfare programs is that the poor segment of the community benefits from governmental activities. In fiscal 1968, eighty percent of the Health and Welfare Objective would finance programs not benefiting just the poor, but all citizens regardless of level of income. Operations of the sanitary sewer system and construction of hospitals were two of the more obvious benefiting all citizens. In the "Administration of Justice" objective, over eighty percent of costs of achieving the goal was in the area of prosecution, court administration and prisoner confinement. Only twenty percent was rehabilitative costs. Also to be noted was that dollar amounts indicated in this PPB category did not include federal or state assistance.

Five-Year Projection

With the completion of the Phase I status report, portions of Phase II were attempted, including the determination of program requirements over a five-year period. Forms again were designed and submitted to agencies and contained objectives and related programs peculiar to each agency. Additionally, private organizations supported in part by the county government were requested to estimate program requirements for the approaching five-year period. Each agency was instructed to review in detail programs with which it was concerned and determine financial requirements for both capital and operating for the future five-year period. To assist in this determination, the staff suggested that projections be based on historical growth, inflationary trends, and anticipated demands. In order to provide the broad picture of development, the staff, itself, prepared all estimates of debt service and supportative programs.

As a whole, information received was somewhat better than that obtained in past inquiries; however, most projections were estimated on a purely mathematical historical basis. Again, as an observation, this was due largely to lack of knowledge or training on the part of county agencies, and, with regard to the outside private agencies, lack of ability or staff to provide such data. A partial reason for this, too, was the lack of major policy decisions which determine the general direction toward which long-run planning must direct itself.

Those projections which the staff determined as valid were included in the "Plan for Orderly Growth," an annual capital improvement plan compiled by the staff each year. Alternatives were not determined by the individual departments, which limited in many respects the accuracy of the report. However, the most recent 1969 edition pointed out that the purpose was to provide a basis for considering the achievement of county goals within resource limitations over the next five years.

Criticism of this plan indicated some of the broad problems involved in developing an effective PPB system. Though certainly some of the criticisms were unwarranted, some, indeed, showed merit and demonstrated an understanding of the problems facing the staff as it proceeds toward a more effective system. There was and continues to be a lack of broad political policy-making decisions which seriously affects any attempt at an effective PPB system. This was particularly noted with respect to overall total county land use planning. As stated, a statement of alternatives was not proposed. This is, of course, the core of the system, and closely associated with this, alternatives should be viewed in the light of cost-benefit analyses, minimizing cost and maximizing service performance to the citizens of the county.

Conclusions

The development of the PPB system in Fairfax County has been an evolutionary one; possibly this is the one "universally applicable" observation that may be made. It was a process of trial and error in which the input from departments caused the staff to reevaluate the techniques of the system and return again to the operating agencies. In this sense the county has moved forward from the original work unit technique first envisioned.

It has been demonstrated that a necessary reciprocal cooperation is imperative between the implementing staff and the line departments. Without this cooperation, the system will be destined for failure. In many cases there was frustration on the part of the budget staff as it tried to build up interest for the system in department heads. However, this forced the staff to refine and clarify its techniques which, in the end, was a step forward.

Difficulty in communication of the worth of the system itself and the specific techniques were created by a lack of technical knowledge on the part of both staff and department heads. Consequently, an essential factor in the development of PPB is a trained technical staff to deal with the problems of establishing accurate criteria and quantification of inputs and the actual use of this data once collected.

Another very important result of the process was the effect on the budgeting system as a whole. It forced the staff to be more rigorous in its analysis of the entire budgeting process; and, possibly more important, it forced the department heads, some for the first time, to take an objective, critical view of their own operations and goals, with particular emphasis not on expansion alone but on study of their programs as they relate to benefits to be derived by citizens of the county.

19

The Use of PPBS
in a Public System
of Higher Education:
Is It Cost-Effective?

JAMES S. DYER

Introduction

Systematic approaches to decision-making and resource allocation seem to be least developed in such areas as public higher education, in which potential returns from such techniques may be the greatest. Although such a situation may seem paradoxical, this results in part from the desire of individuals to select problems for study of such a nature that tractable models and elegant mathematical techniques can be applied to achieve uncontestable results. Unfortunately, most public systems are classified by systems analysts as "ill-structured," and they do not possess the clear input-output relationships required for complete mathematical modeling. However, some significant steps are being taken toward increasing the adequacy of the analytic study of complex, large-scale systems.

For example, the conventional myopic techniques of planning and budgeting in higher education are being augmented by the new theories of

Reprinted from the *Academy of Management Journal,* 13, No. 3 (September 1970): 285–99,, by permission of the author and publisher. Footnotes have been renumbered.

the Planning-Programming-Budgeting System (PPBS), which will be used to denote the combined activities of structuring a program budget, generating alternative systems designs, evaluating alternative systems, and allocating scarce resources. For an introductory discussion of PPBS, see the work by D. Novick.[1]

Several public institutions of higher education, including the University of California, the Ohio State University, and the University of Pittsburgh, have adopted PPBS (or at least the program budgeting feature of the total, systematic approach to planning) as the conceptual framework for the analysis of their activities. Several researchers have also contributed to this area.[2] Unfortunately, the experience of these institutions and researchers is not yet sufficient for a complete evaluation of the system; therefore, the following question is still one of legitimate concern: Is the use of PPBS within a public system of higher education a fad, or does it provide enough additional, relevant information to justify the alteration of an existing budgeting system? In the language of PPBS, is its use in higher education "cost effective?"

One of the first things that an analyst learns to appreciate is that *all* questions cannot be answered quantitatively on a cost-effectiveness basis. The question pertaining to the value of PPBS is of this nature. The answer will depend on such factors as the status of the individual system, particularly with regard to its size and complexity; the availability of resources; the availability of trained personnel; the attitude of the administrators and faculty; and the degree to which the existing planning and budgeting system is considered inadequate.

Costs associated with the use of PPBS will include the costs of hiring or training analysts, of acquiring and synthesizing new data, and, most importantly, the monetary and nonmonetary costs associated with altering the roles and functions of an existing organizational structure and decision-making process. These costs, it should be noted, may be substantial.

The remainder of this paper will consist of a qualitative discussion of the potential benefits to be derived from the use of PPBS in public higher education. The discussion is divided into three primary sections. The first section will briefly describe the existing classical techniques of planning and budgeting for public systems of higher education; the limitations inherent in these approaches will be considered. The second section will present suggestions for the application of PPBS to a public higher education system. The problems of identifying the objectives of higher education, of developing satisfactory measures of effectiveness for evaluating the attainment of these objectives, and of structuring a program budgeting format that will assist decision-making with regard to resource allocation will be described. The third section will be concerned with the effect of PPBS on the relationships between the organizational units of the system, with particular emphasis being placed on questions of authority and power redistribution.

Existing Budgeting Techniques—A Critical Appraisal

The primary considerations in the classical planning and budgeting techniques of public systems of higher education are the following: (1) efficiency, (2) reaction to environmental demands, and (3) comparison with peers. This section will examine the implications of this situation.

EFFICIENCY

By emphasizing efficiency, the planner in higher education concentrates on analysis of such ratios as cost per full-time equivalent student (FTE), student-faculty ratio, cost per student credit hour (SCH), and percent of usage of classroom space. Certainly, this discussion does not mean to imply that "inefficient" operation in terms of these statistics is desirable. On the contrary, the efficient pursuit of proper objectives is to be expected; however, the "efficient" operation of a system which is not properly designed to achieve its primary objectives can hardly be considered "efficient" in a global sense. The reliance on these statistics for planning and operating decisions can screen or cloud the perception of the purpose and responsibilities of a system of higher education.

An emphasis on efficiency instead of on the objectives of an organization may be the result of an attempt to circumvent the problems inherent in the identification of the goals of higher education and their related measures of effectiveness. An extension of this approach has been used in a previous application of PPBS to higher education. The basic philosophy implied by a logical adherence to the criteria of efficiency is that the "ends" of an organization are really the last "means" and that there can be no separation of goals and objectives from the approaches and operations used to reach them. Thus, the question of differentiation between outputs and objectives becomes purely academic and requires no answer.[3] This philosophy may have considerable merit for planning over a short time period; however, in the dynamic environment of higher education, the use of this approach in planning over a time horizon of several years could lead to a tragically myopic result. To note an obvious parallel from private industry, even the most efficient producers of such items as buggy whips and trolley cars were doomed to a slow demise.

Although these industries were stifled by technological changes, who is to say that the social and cultural changes of the 1960s may not have even greater ramifications in institutions of higher education?

REACTION TO ENVIRONMENTAL DEMANDS

A second technique of planning and budgeting in public systems of higher education is based on projections of enrollment. One of two methods of enrollment projection is generally used. In the first, the historical enrollment data are used as the basis for "fitting" a trend line that is projected into the future. In the second, estimates are made of the number of high school graduates in an area in future years, and a ratio, based on historical data, is applied to these figures to develop enrollment estimates. The same "ratio" technique may be used to obtain estimates for each institution, and, within each institution, for each grade level and program. A desired student-teacher ratio is then assumed, and a complete budget including estimated faculty needs and costs is produced as a result.

Reliance on such techniques implies that institutions of higher education are passive in nature and only *react* to the demands of potential students. In actuality, this conclusion is not valid. Research has shown that policy questions, especially those having economic implications for potential students, may significantly affect enrollments.[4] Obviously, raising or lowering admission policy standards can alter enrollment. Less obviously, changes in the quality of education or in the programs and courses offered by an institution can have a similar effect. While enrollment projections *do* provide useful information, the really important questions require decisions which may destroy their validity. A more complete understanding of these relationships is required.

COMPARISON WITH PEERS

The use of such statistics as the student-teacher ratio was discussed previously with respect to both evaluating system efficiency and determining future budgets as a consequence of their application to enrollment projections. The method for selecting the "proper" or "desirable" ratio will now be considered.

The most commonly used technique for ratio selection is a comparison with the operation of "peers." Institutions of "similar" size in states with "similar" socioeconomic conditions are chosen for a comparative analysis. In most cases, several such institutions are selected and such ratios as the student-teacher ratio are computed for each. Ignoring the problems of determining the criteria sufficient for the proper identification of a "similar" institution, we will only consider the use of the results.

Those who espouse the provisions of "adequate" education by the state may consider the mean, or perhaps the median or mode, of these ratios to be a desirable figure. Unfortunately, those concerned with efficiency may feel that the highest student-teacher ratio in the group should be selected as a standard, while those concerned with educational quality may prefer the lowest. Thus, the problem is not actually resolved.

Further consideration makes the use of this technique appear even more suspect. What if each of these other institutions also determines their "key ratios" by comparison with "similar" institutions? Although this situation may seem ludicrous, there can be little doubt that it does exist, at least to a limited extent. Surely, this must qualify as a classic example of "the blind leading the blind."

The following section will be concerned with the development of a more logical, objective-oriented system for planning in higher education.

PPBS

The essential activities involved in the application of PPBS are the following: (1) identification of objectives, (2) organization of activities into programs designed to achieve these objectives, and (3) analysis of alternative systems designs to develop the final resource allocation.

The following discussion will consider the potential contribution of each of these activities in a public system of higher education.

OBJECTIVES AND MEASURES OF EFFECTIVENESS

One of the most important steps in the use of PPBS involves the proper identification of system objectives. The significance of this activity is magnified by the fact that alternative system configurations and resource allocations will be evaluated according to their contributions to objective attainment. Unfortunately, the objectives of higher education are complex and are not clearly defined.

For example, the higher education system may be identified as part of a larger system involved in the production and distribution of knowledge, a function which may be considered to be a valid goal, and to be independent from its importance as a means to the attainment of other objectives. Higher education is also involved in the creation of human capital. In this respect, higher education may be viewed as an investment whose purpose is the development of a skilled labor force that will provide additional personal income to the participants while contributing to economic growth, prosperity, technological advances, and the national security. Education has also become a source of social mobility, which is generally considered to have great social value and to be a legitimate objective of a government. In addition, education provides students with the joys and satisfaction of learning; in this latter respect, expenditures on education must be regarded as consumption. Other functions, such as preserving the culture of a society, may also be considered as objectives of education.

In order to provide a basis for discussion, an objective-oriented framework for public higher education will now be proposed based on a normative concept of the role of higher education within a state. These comments are not definitive and are only offered as an example of the *approach* that should be taken, not as the final result.

The goals of a public system of higher education may be conveniently divided into two distinct types. The first, which we will designate as the set of *primary objectives,* denotes the results which are expected to be achieved by the educational system. These primary objectives could include the following:

I. Student development
   A. Developing political maturity
   B. Developing social maturity
     1. Basic intellectual skills
     2. Individual development
   C. Developing the capacity for economic achievement
     1. Educators
     2. Industrial
     3. Public service
     4. Arts
     5. Other professional programs
II. Expansion of knowledge
   A. Applied research
   B. Theoretical research
III. Public service

The second type of system goal, which we will define as a *constraining consideration,* relates to policy matters which are not actual functions of the educational system and which can seldom be analyzed objectively in terms of their value. Although not exhaustive, a list of these constraining considerations might include the following:

1. The system should not discriminate on the basis of race, sex, religion, social status, or wealth;

2. The system should avoid dehumanization;

3. The percentage of out-of-state-students should remain above 20 percent but below 35 percent; and

4. The system should maintain a "high" quality of education.

For illustrative purposes, we shall assume that the above lists of primary objectives and constraining considerations are valid for the higher education system of a particular state; they should now be associated with quantifiable measures of effectiveness. Unfortunately, because of the nature of the educational process, the degree of quantification of results will differ among the categories. For example, economic contributions can be estimated more easily than political and social returns.

The first primary objective is that of assisting the political, economic, and social development of the students. The results of political and social development defy complete quantification. Of course, one may be able to infer some relevant information with regard to political development from a study of the voting rates among college graduates versus noncollege graduates, and from a study of political activism as measured by participation in campaigns and political parties. Also, the degree to which college-educated persons seem to be better informed on national and local political issues may be considered significant. In addition, standardized tests could be administered to determine whether certain basic facts and concepts have been conveyed to the students. Such tests would also represent a source of valuable data for a cost-effectiveness evaluation of teaching methods. Finally, the actual percentage of college work which the "average" graduate takes in areas relating to political development, such as history, government, and political science, may be a helpful, although not ideal, measure. This latter measurement is actually an "input" from the system to the student; ideally, we wish to measure the *effects* of these inputs. However, when the assessment of *effects* is difficult, information on inputs may serve as a less desirable aid to decision-making.

Similar problems arise in estimating the results and value of attempts at social development. Research related to this problem might involve efforts to determine the degree of job satisfaction, the self-image, the self-perception, etc., of college-educated persons versus noncollege educated persons. Other indications, such as comparative crime rates, may also be relevant. Research into questions concerning the effect of higher education on a person's appreciation of the arts, as revealed through his reading and leisure habits, may also produce significant results. Unfortunately, such suggestions as the latter are loaded with value judgments and imply, perhaps, that it is "better" for an individual to spend a Sunday afternoon at the symphony than at a professional football game. Extreme care must be taken in the interpretation of such results.

Economic contributions, although presenting difficulties, are much more amenable to measurement. Data are available from the census and from other research which relate average income figures to educational achievement. Such data for college graduates and for high school graduates not attending institutions of higher education are of particular importance. Similar data related to a particular institution or educational system could be obtained from questionnaires. These figures, when adjusted for individual ability and socioeconomic factors, may be used as the basis for the computation of expected discounted economic returns to individuals and to the state which result directly from public higher education.[5] Although the data are cross-sectional, a discount rate (such as 10 percent) minimizes the effect of errors produced by their use in projections of future incomes.

The second primary objective, expanding knowledge, includes a suggested categorization into "applied" and "theoretical" research. Applied research may be directed toward solving problems of immediate concern, such as pollution, transportation, national security, and defense, etc. Theoretical research may be considered to include efforts to expand man's knowledge without regard to immediate returns. Much of the research in the humanities may fall into this category. Although the relationships are admittedly weak, some evaluation of the success of these efforts may be derived from the resulting patents and publications.

Public service activities include consulting on immediate problems, the provision of continuing education for the professions, and the provision of a center for art and cultural activities on campus. Although difficulties would be involved, measures of effectiveness similar to those previously suggested could be developed.

The set of constraining considerations also requires the development of some measures of effectiveness to insure that the proposed system alternatives do not infringe on policies. For example, a breakdown of enrollment by socioeconomic backgrounds could produce valuable information related to policy questions. In particular, any modifications or policy changes involving economic considerations either directly, as via tuition rates, or indirectly, as through the location of additional institutions, could be evaluated in terms of their effects on enrollment. Of particular importance should be an estimate of the proportion of the population that is effectively "priced out" of the system. For example, research has shown that approximately 20 percent of the eligible college-age population of Texas cannot be expected to attend an institution of higher education unless they can *commute* to a *public* facility.[6]

This section would not be complete without a final caveat. While the use of PPBS increases the availability of relevant, quantified data to the decision-maker, the measures are still incomplete and imperfect. For example, the informal effects of peer and faculty interactions in institutions of higher education are not considered in the above discussion. Such experiences may contribute significantly to the "political and social development" of the student. Unfortunately, their omission from the program budget may result in their omission from consideration, even in decisions related to dormitory construction and policies. Sole reliance on the information obtained from PPBS should be avoided.

A restatement of the primary objectives appears in Table 1, along with some suggested measures of effectiveness. The following section will discuss the implications of these objectives on the development of a program budgeting structure.

FORMAT OF PROGRAM BUDGET

The format of a program budget should be flexible enough to provide assistance in the analysis of questions relating to different problem areas. In particular, the format should allow determination of *what* is done, *when* it is done, and to *whom*. The *effects* of these actions are evaluated in the creation of the budget.

With respect to the first consideration, the budget should be classified by programs. These programs will be the same as those objectives shown in Table 1; each program will consist of a set of *program elements* whose combined activities promote the accomplishments of one of the objectives. One additional program, Support Activities, will be required to include those activities not directly related to the accomplishment of any of these objectives; therefore, these activities are also not amenable to logical allocation among them. This inability to allocate "indirect costs" should not be considered to pose a problem, as only *incremental* costs resulting from system modification are of primary importance. However, changes within the primary objective-oriented programs may effect these support costs. These incremental cost differences should be estimated for the purpose of system comparison.

If possible, the "program elements" should consist of the existing and proposed departments and colleges of the institutions. Of course, the process of programming may emphasize the need to combine some existing departments, separate others into new departments, and increase or decrease the size of others. Unfortunately, some of the "program elements" may require the artificial division of departments. Such a case could occur when lower level course offerings in an area are designed for

TABLE 1
Objectives and Measures of Effectiveness

Objectives	Measures of effectiveness
Student development	e_1 = instruction
Political	e_{11} = political effectiveness
	e_{111} = voting rate
	e_{112} = participation
	e_{113} = informed on issues
	e_{114} = standardized test scores
	e_{115} = percent of courses
Social	e_{12} = social effectiveness
	e_{121} = job satisfaction
	e_{122} = self-image
	e_{123} = crime rates
	e_{124} = participation in cultural activities
Economic	e_{13} = economic effectiveness
	e_{131} = economic returns to individuals
	e_{132} = economic returns to the state
	e_{1321} = economic returns to the state economy
	e_{1322} = economic returns from increased tax revenue
Expanding knowledge	e_2 = research
Applied research	e_{21} = answers to questions
	e_{211} = patents
	e_{212} = contracts
	e_{213} = publications
Theoretical research	e_{22} = general investigation
Public service	e_3 = service
	e_{31} = consulting
	e_{32} = workshops
	e_{33} = public cultural activities

the social or political development of students, but higher level courses in the same area are intended for the development of professional competence.

Emphasizing planning rather than mere budgeting, the use of PPBS requires estimates of *when* changes are to be made in a system. Once a goal or desired system configuration has been determined, the steps required to attain the necessary modifications in the existing system can be time-phased in the budgeting plans of the future so that a logical, stepwise progression toward the goal is accomplished. The speed with which the existing system is transformed should be a function of available resources and the degree to which the existing system is deemed inadequate.

The question of to *whom* the advantages of higher education are made available can be considered from two aspects. The first logical categorization is by level. The number of students at the freshman-sophomore levels, junior-senior levels, and graduate levels can have a significant impact on resource requirements.

The second important categorization relating to the students is by socioeconomic characteristics. These figures are required for evaluating the effects of proposed system alterations on those "constraining considerations" relating to policies against discrimination, de jure or de facto.

Not all of these suggested categories will be important in every use of the program budget. However, the budgeting format should be made so flexible that any of the breakdowns may be used in any order. Such a requirement would necessitate the use of the computer. However, the activities of planning and budgeting will make other demands requiring computerization of data, so these additional programming requirements should not be considered excessive.

The effects of the proposed multiclassification scheme are shown graphically in Figure 1. An abbreviated budget format is shown in Table 2.

FIGURE 1
A Multidimensioned Budgeting Format

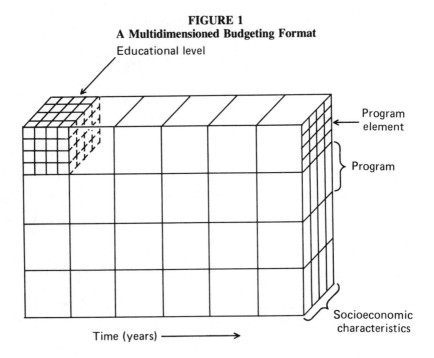

TABLE 2
An Abbreviated Budgeting Format

I. Student development
  A. Political maturity
    1. Freshman-sophomore
      a. Department of Government
      b. Department of History
      c. Department of Political Science
    2. Junior-senior
      a. Department of Government
      b. Department of History
        ·
        ·
        ·
        ·
    3. Graduate
      a. Department of Government
        ·
        ·
        ·
        ·
  B. Social maturity
    1. Freshman-sophomore
      a. College of Fine Arts
      b. Department of Sociology
      c. Department of Psychology
        ·
        ·
        ·
        ·
    2. Junior-senior
        ·
        ·
        ·
        ·
  C. Economic development
    1. Freshman-sophomore
      a. College of Business Administration
      b. College of Engineering
        ·
        ·
        ·
II. Expansion of knowledge
        ·
        ·
        ·
        ·

This table uses programs as a primary category, educational level as the secondary category, and program elements as the third. Other permutations of the suggested classification are also possible.

The simple categorization of resource allocations in higher education according to objectives produces a significant aid to planning. For the first time, an administrator is able to see clearly how trade-offs among departments have effects relating to the attainment of total system objectives. For example, increasing the budget of the Department of Fine Arts at the freshman-sophomore level at the expense of the Department of Business Administration can now be perceived as an alteration in emphasis from activities designed to enhance the economic development of students to those activities which increase their social maturity. While such relationships may have been understood intuitively in the past, the use of a program budgeting format makes the implications of these actions explicit.

Unfortunately, it seems doubtful that the tools of analysis associated with PPBS can be of much assistance in determining the proper allocation of resources among the programs designed to achieve the primary objectives of higher education. These programs are addressed to different objectives, and the problem of quantitatively determining the *optimal* levels of an individual's political, social, and economic development, of the efforts expended in the expansion of knowledge and in public service, is so involved with value judgments that a simple answer should not be expected.

However, *within* each of these categories, such techniques as cost-effectiveness analysis may be of value in attempts to determine "better" approaches to objective attainment. In addition, if the results indicate that even small improvements in the functioning of one of the programs is comparatively expensive, indicating high marginal costs, some consideration should be given to shifting resources to other programs where the response to increased resources is greater.

The Effect of PPBS on Organizational Relationships

This section will be concerned with the impact of PPBS on the relationships among the organizational units of a system of public higher education. The organizational structures of different systems vary greatly, so that certain assumptions and definitions are required as an aid to the discussion. Each *campus* of a public higher education system will be considered to be composed of *departments;* the central figure of authority on each campus will be referred to as the *chancellor,* while the total system of public higher education will be assumed to be the responsibility of the *president.* Finally, a committee serving as an interface between the state's government and the operating system will be assumed to exist, and will be designated as the *coordinating board.* The use of PPBS should have profound effects on the relationships among all of these centers of authority and responsibility.

Some authors have suggested that the use of PPBS centralizes authority within an organization. In actuality, while the result of its use may be an increase in the centralization of authority with respect to the *previously* existing arrangement, PPBS tends to *restore* the authority for decision-making to the originally intended units within the organizational structure by reducing the uncertainty inherent in decisions. For example, most budgeting systems for a campus are based on the requests for resources from the various department heads. Classical budgeting techniques make no attempt to assess the contribution of each department toward organizational goals. Thus, the chancellor of a campus has no rational basis on which to evaluate the requests from the departments. Such a situation generally results in a *forced* delegation of the chancellor's authority with regard to resource allocations to each department. Therefore, each department tends to develop autonomously with respect to the other departments and to the goals of the individual campuses. The power and the prestige of the department heads become the dominating factors in the competition for scarce resources.

The use of PPBS would require that requests for budgets be *justified* in terms of expected results. Even more important, the adoption of PPBS would require that the activities and contribution of all departments be evaluated as objectively as possible in terms of their contribution to the attainment of the goals of the campus. Such activity could result in significant changes in emphasis within each campus. In particular, the chancellor would be provided with information that would increase the rationality of his decisions regarding the allocation of scarce resources.

Similar remarks are valid with respect to all of the administrative relationships. Authority is restored to the originally intended organizational levels through the reduction of uncertainty in the decisions. For example, PPBS should better equip the president to make logical allocation decisions among the different campuses. Such questions as the following can be subjected to analysis: Should high quality upper-level and graudate courses in all areas be offered at all campuses, or should some campuses emphasize programs in the liberal arts while the others specialize in science and engineering?

The requirements of program justification do not imply that existing programs or future budget requests will be reduced. In fact, the opposite effect may result. For example, the dialogue between the coordinating board and the higher education system of a state should be enhanced by concrete proposals and estimates of their effects and their returns to the state. Certainly, the coordinating board would be willing to recommend the expansion of existing facilities or the construction of new campuses and institutions to a state legislature if such proposals were accompanied by competent studies revealing significant positive contributions to the state and her citizens.

Once again, the positions of both the coordinating board and the higher education system with respect to a state's government should be strengthened by PPBS. In times of rising taxes, legislatures are understandably hesitant to continue voting for increased spending in higher education without some idea of the benefits expected from such investments. However, budget requests accompanied by figures estimating the results of proposed programs in terms of increased voting rates, expected increases in individual incomes, expected increases in state tax revenues (which help offset a proportion of the costs), expected contribution to the trained manpower pool, etc., should receive much more favorable consideration.

Thus, the use of PPBS centralizes authority only to the extent that it helps return it to the originally intended level of the orgnization. In addition, the results of analysis should be a definite aid in justifying requests for resource allocations for worthy programs.

Conclusions

An attempt has been made to identify and analyze qualitatively the "costs" and "benefits" associated with the use of PPBS as an aid to planning and budgeting in a public system of higher education. While the costs were recognized as significant, the potential benefits also appear to be great.

The existing techniques of long-range planning currently in use in most public systems of higher education are of negligible value for evaluating alternative programs, and do not even question the suitablility of the existing system. Therefore, another approach to planning seems desirable.

Although presenting no panacea, PPBS does offer a logical, objective-oriented approach to planning. Potentially, PPBS would allow administrators to evaluate the anticipated results of proposed programs and system alternations, and to compare results from different proposals in search of a "best," or "satisficing," alternative. In addition, this form of analysis would allow requests for resources to be justified in terms of expected returns, as opposed to being ambiguously requested on the basis of 10 percent more than last year's budget. Thus, the relationships among the managerial units involved in a public system of higher education should be strengthened.

Although PPBS offers no escape from a reliance on managerial judgments, the more relevant information generated by its associated activities should improve both the perception and understanding of an exceedingly complex system. If so, the potential gains from the increased "effectiveness" of the decision-making should far outweigh the associated costs.

Notes

[1] David Novick (ed.), *Program Budgeting: Program Analysis and the Federal Budget* (Cambridge, Mass: Harvard University Press, 1965).

[2] S. A. Haggart et al., *Program Budgeting for School District Planning: Concepts and Application*, RM-6116-RC (The Rand Corporation, November 1969), Paul H. Hamelman, "Academic Planning with Program Budgeting," presented at the Thirty-second National Meeting of the Operations Research Society of America, and Harry J. Hartley, *Educational Planning-Programming-Budgeting: A Systems Approach* (Englewood Cliffs, N.J.: Prentice-Hall, 1968).

[3] See Albert Shapero, "A Planning, Programming and Budgeting (PPBS) Approach to the University of Texas System" (internal report at the University of Texas at Austin, October 24, 1967), p. 4.

[4] James S. Dyer, *Cost-Effectiveness Analysis for Higher Education*, (PhD dissertation, The University of Texas at Austin, 1969).

[5] James S. Dyer, *Measure of Effectiveness in Higher Education: Interactions and Implications*, Working Paper 69-47 (The University of Texas at Austin: Graduate School of Business, March 1969).

[6] Dyer, *Cost-Effectiveness . . .* , *op. cit.*

20

The Politics of Evaluation:
The Case of Head Start

WALTER WILLIAMS
JOHN W. EVANS

A far-reaching controversy has flared over a recent Westinghouse Learning Corporation—Ohio University evaluation study showing that Head Start children now in the first, second, and third grades differed little, on a series of academic achievement and attitudinal measures, from comparable children who did not attend Head Start.

In the heat of the public controversy, there have been some old-fashioned political innuendos based on vile motives, but, in the main, the principal weapons in the battle have been the esoteric paraphernalia of modern statistical analysis. This is appropriate; the methodoligical validity of the Head Start study is a critical part of the debate. However,

Reprinted from the *Annals of the American Journal of Political and Sacial Science*, 385 (September 1969): 118–32, by permission of the authors and publisher.

Robert A. Levine, The Urban Institute, and Tom Glennan, The Rand Corporation, have provided helpful comments on earlier drafts of this paper.

The views expressed are those of the authors, and not necessarily those of the organizations with which they are affiliated.

the *real battle is not over the methodological purity of this particular study, but, rather, involves fundamental issues of how the federal government will develop large-scale programs and evaluate their results.*

At this deeper level of the debate, what we are seeing is a head-on collision between two sets of ideas developed in the mid-1960s. On the one hand, there was the implicit premise of the early years of the war on poverty that effective programs could be launched *full-scale,* and could yield significant improvements in the lives of the poor. Head Start was the archetype of this hope. Born in late 1964, the program was serving over a half-million children by the end of the following summer. On the other hand, the federal government, during roughly the same period, implemented the Planning-Programming-Budgeting System (PPBS), founded on the premise that rigorous analysis could produce a flow of information that would greatly improve the basis for decision-making. And the notion of evaluating both ongoing programs and new program ideas was fundamental to this type of thinking.

To see the dimensions and ramifications of this clash, it is necessary to return to those halycon days in which the basic ideas of the war on poverty and PPBS were formulated. Only then can we explore the present Head Start controversy to see what we may learn from it for the future.

The Early Days of the War on Poverty

On June 4, 1965, President Johnson said in his Howard University Address, entitled, "To Fulfill These Rights":

> To move beyond opportunity to achievement . . . I pledge you tonight this will be a chief goal of my administration, and of my program next year, and in years to come. And I hope, and I pray, and I believe, it will be a part of the program of all America. . . . It is the glorious opportunity of this generation to end the one huge wrong of the American Nation and, in so doing, to find America for ourselves, with the same immense thrill of discovery which gripped those who first began to realize that here, at last, was a home for freedom.

The speech rang with hope—a call for basic changes that seemed well within our grasp. Viewed from the present, the address marked a distinct watershed. It was the crest of our domestic tranquility, based on the strong belief that black and white could work together in harmony as a nation. The speech also marked the high point of our faith in our ability to bring about significant change. Despite some of the rhetoric of the time to the effect that change would not be easy, it is fair to say that the faith was there that giant steps could be taken quickly. On that June day, there was the strong belief that the concentrated effort of the war on poverty, launched less than a year before, could bind the nation together.

This faith had two dimensions—first, that there could be a redistribution of funds and power toward the disadvantaged and, second, that, with such a redistribution, new programs could bring substantial improvement in the lot of the disadvantaged. The first was both more clearly perceived and more glamorous. To wrest power and money from the entrenched forces was heady stuff. Less clearly perceived was that redistribution was a necessary, but not a sufficient, condition of progress. New programs had to be devised, not just in broad brush strokes, but in the nitty-gritty detail of techniques and organization. Taking young black men from the ghettos to the wilderness of an isolated Job Corp Center was not a solution in itself. One had to worry about such mundane things as curriculum and the morale of these young men in a Spartan, female-absent environment. This atmosphere of confidence and enthusiasm led us to push aside the fact that *we had neither the benefit of experience in such programs nor much realization of the difficulties involved in developing effective techniques.*

Standing in 1969 on the battle-scarred ground of the war on poverty, it is easy to see the naiveté and innocence of that time—scarcely half a decade ago. Events were to crash upon us quickly. Vietnam was to end any hope for large funds. Riots, militancy, and the rise of separatism made the earlier ideas of harmony seem quaint. Those with established power did not yield easily either to moral suasion or to more forceful means. Real power is still a well-guarded commodity.

Most important for this discussion, we have found, over a wide range of social action programs, both how unyielding the causes of poverty are and how little we really know about workable techniques for helping the disadvantaged. The point is not that we are unable to derive "reasonable" programs from bits and pieces of information and hard thinking. We *can,* we *have.* But our experience seems to point up, over and over again, the almost insurmountable difficulty of bridging the gap between brilliantly conceived programs and those which work in the field. Great pressures exist for new "solutions" to social problems to be rushed into national implementation as soon as they are conceived. But the attempts to go directly from sound ideas to full-scale programs seem so often to end in frustration and disappointment.

The Origins of Analysis Within the Government

In the early 1960s, Secretary Robert McNamara relied on a conceptual framework, formulated at The Rand Corporation, to make analysis a critical factor in the decision-making process of the Department of Defense. In October 1965, drawing on this experience, the Bureau of the Budget issued Bulletin No. 66–3, establishing the Planning-Programming-Budgeting System within all federal departments and agencies. The departments and agencies were instructed to "establish an adequate central staff or staffs for analysis, planning, and programming [with] . . . the head of the central analytical staff . . . directly responsible to the head of the agency or his deputy." These central offices were to be interposed between the head of the agency and the operating programs and were charged with undertaking analysis that would provide a hard quantitative basis on which to make decisions. For social action agencies, this was a radical change in the way of doing business.

Before PPBS, not much progress had been made in analyzing social action programs. Although the broad approach developed at the Department of Defense might be used in such analyses, the relevance of particular methodological tools was less clear. For example, there was little actual experience with the kinds of evaluations which seek to measure the effects of a social action program on its participants or the external world. And a host of formidable problems existed, such as the lack of good operational definitions for key variables, the shortage of adequate test instruments, and the difficulties of developing valid control groups. Thus, the usefulness of evaluative analysis for social action programs would have to be proved in particular situations.

Beyond this was the political question of bringing analysis into the agency's policy-making process. As analytical studies were quite new to social action programs, their results—especially those measuring the effectiveness of ongoing programs—were seen as a threat by those with established decision-making positions. Unfavorable evaluation results have a potential either to restrict a program's funds or to force major changes in the direction of the program. One can hardly assume passive acceptance of such an outcome by the managers and operators of programs.

Thus, one can see how the tiny dark cloud of the Head Start controversy formed at this early date. The push toward new operating programs and the emerging PPBS brought about a role conflict between those who ran programs (and believed in them) and those who analyzed these programs (and whose job it was to be skeptical of them). As former Director of the Bureau of the Budget Charles L. Schultze has observed:

> [In the] relationship between the political process and the decision-making process as envisaged by PPB . . . I do not believe that there is an irreconcilable conflict. . . . But they are different kinds of systems representing different ways of arriving at decisions. The two systems are so closely interrelated that PPB and its associated

analytic method can be an effective tool for aiding decisions only when its relationships with the political process have been carefully articulated and the appropriate roles of each defined. . . . It may, indeed, be necessary to guard against the naiveté of the systems analyst who ignores *political* constraints and believes that efficiency alone produces virtue. But it is equally necessary to guard against the naiveté of the decision maker who ignores *resource* constraints and believes that virtue alone produces efficiency.[1]

Looking in retrospect, at the early PPBS vis-à-vis social action programs, it may be said that: (1) the absolute power of analysis was oversold and (2) the conflicts in the system between the analytical staff and the operators of the programs was underestimated. Hence, the politics of evaluation—in essence, the clash between methodology, political forces, and bureaucracy—looms much larger than was imagined in those early days. At the same time, knowing more today about how difficult it is to develop and operate effective programs, the need for analysis—the need to assess both our current operations and our new ideas—seems even more pressing than in the less troubled days of 1965.[2]

Background of the Head Start Study

With these general considerations as background, we now need to look briefly at the key elements within OEO: the Head Start program; OEO's analytical office, the Office of Research, Plans, Programs, and Evaluation (RPP&E); and the general state of evaluation of the antipoverty programs prior to the Westinghouse study.

HEAD START

The concepts underlying Head Start were based on the thinking of some of the best people in the child development area and on a variety of research findings (probably relatively rich compared to most other new programs) suggesting a real potential for early childhood training, *but offering few and often conflicting guidelines as to the detailed types of programs to be developed.* In fact, the original concept of Head Start was that it was to be an explicitly experimental program reaching a limited number of children. The idea, however, was too good. It was an ideal symbol for the new war on poverty. It generated immediate national support and produced few political opponents. In this atmosphere, one decision led easily to another, and Head Start was quickly expanded to a

$100 million national program serving a half-million children. In the beginning, Head Start consisted mainly of six-to-eight-week summer projects under a variety of sponsors (school systems, churches, and community action agencies, for example) with a high degree of local autonomy concerning how the project was to be carried out. Later, Head Start funded a significant number of full-year projects with a similar policy of flexibility and local autonomy.

The immense popularity of the early days carried over. Head Start remained OEO's showcase program, supported strongly by the Congress, communities, poor mothers, and a deeply committed band of educators (many with a significant personal involvement in the program).

RPP&E

Analysis came early to OEO because its Office of Research, Plans, Programs, and Evaluation was one of the original independent staff offices reporting directly to the head of the agency. RPP&E predated the *PPBS Bulletin,* but was, in many ways, the epitome of the PPBS analytical staff, in that it was headed by Rand alumni who stressed the power of analysis. RPP&E was both a major developer of analytical data and a key factor in the agency's decision-making process. As one might expect, in this role it had more than once clashed with program-operators.

EVALUATION AT OEO

Critical to our discussion is the fact that RPP&E did not establish a separate Evaluation Division until the autumn of 1967. Prior to that time, most of the responsibility for evaluation rested with the programs, but RPP&E had had some involvement, particularly in trying to use data developed by the programs to make over-all program assessments.

In the case of Head Start, the program itself had initiated a large number of *individual* project-evaluations, mainly of the summer program. Across a wide range of these projects it was found that, in general, participants who had been given various cognitive and affective tests at the beginning of the Head Start program showed gains when tested again at the end of the program. However, virtually all the follow-up studies found that any differences which had been observed between the Head Start and control groups immediately after the end of Head Start were largely gone by the end of the first year of school. The meaning of this "catch up" by the control group has been and still is subject to considerable debate, ranging from doubts that the immediate post-program gains were anything more than test-retest artifacts, to assertions that the superior Head Start children raise the performance levels of their non-Head Start classmates.

RPP&E had tried fairly early to develop its own national assessments of Head Start, but found little support for such undertakings within the program. Two such studies were developed, but the results were marred by technical and analytical problems. At the time of the establishment of the Evaluation Division, therefore, no good evidence existed as to overall Head Start effectiveness—a fact that was beginning to concern the agency, the Bureau of the Budget, and some members of Congress.[3]

As one might guess, the program offices hardly greeted the newly created Evaluation Division with enthusiasm—no one was happy with a staff office looking over its shoulder. In a formal division of labor, three types of evaluation were recognized. RPP&E was given primary responsibility for evaluation of the overall effectiveness of all OEO programs (Type I). The programs retained primary responsibility for both the evaluation of the relative effectiveness of different program strategies and techniques, for example, different curricula in Head Start (Type II) and the on-site monitoring of individual projects (Type III). The basic logic of this division of labor was to ensure that Type I overall evaluations would be carried out, to locate the responsibility for these evaluations at a staff-office level removed from the programs, and, at the same time, to place the Type II and Type III evaluation-responsibilities at the program level because of the greater need for detailed program-knowledge that these kinds of evaluation require.

This division of labor also matches the type of evaluation with the types of decisions for which different levels within the organization have primary responsibility—the overall mixture of programs and resource-allocation at the top (Type I), and program design (Type II) and management (Type III) at the program level.

The Westinghouse Study

Thus, it was out of this total complex of conditions that the Westinghouse evaluation of Head Start originated:

1. The explosive expansion of Head Start from what was originally conceived as a limited experimental program to a large national program almost overnight.

2. A developing commitment throughout the government to increasing analysis and assessment of all government programs.

3. The national popularity of the Head Start program and the widespread equation of this popularity with effectiveness.

4. Previous evaluations of Head Start that did not provide adequate information on the program's overall impact.

5. The development of a new staff-level evaluation function at OEO charged with producing timely and policy-relevant evaluations of the overall impact of all OEO programs.

As one in a series of national evaluations of the major OEO programs, the new RPP&E Evaluation Division proposed for the Head Start program an ex post facto study design in which former Head Start children, now in the first, second, and third grades of school, were to be tested on a series of cognitive and affective measures, and their scores compared with those of a control group. Because the program was in its third year and there was, as yet, no useful assessment of its overall effects, time was an important consideration in deciding on an ex post facto design. Such a design would produce results relatively soon (less than a year), as compared with a methodologically more desirable longitudinal study which would take considerably longer.

Within the agency, Head Start administrators opposed the study on a number of grounds, including the inadequacy of the ex post facto design, the weakness of available test instruments, and the failure to include other Head Start goals such as health, nutrition, and community involvement. In sum, Head Start contended that this limited study might yield misleading negative results which could shake the morale of those associated with Head Start and bring unwarranted cutbacks in the program. RPP&E evaluators did not deny the multiplicity of goals, but maintained that cognitive improvement was a primary goal of Head Start and, moreover, was an outcome which reflected, indirectly, the success of certain other activities (for example, better health should facilitate better school performance). Further, the study's proponents in RPP&E recognized the risks outlined by Head Start officials, but argued that the need for evaluative evidence in order to improve the decision-making process makes it necessary to run these risks. After much internal debate, the Director of OEO ordered that the study should be done, and a contract was made in June 1968 with the Westinghouse Learning Corporation and Ohio University.

The study proceeded in relative quiet, but as it neared completion, hints came out of its negative findings. Because President Nixon was preparing to make a major address on the poverty program, including a discussion of Head Start, the White House inquired about the study and was alerted to the preliminary negative results. In his Economic Opportunity Message to the Congress on February 19, 1969, President Nixon alluded to the study and noted that "the long-term effect of Head Start appears to be extremely weak."

This teaser caused a flood of requests for a full disclosure of the study's findings. In the Congress, where hearings were being held on OEO legislation, strong claims were made that OEO was holding back the results to protect Head Start. This was not the case, but the demands did present a real dilemma for the agency—particularly RPP&E. For the results at that time were quite preliminary, and Westinghouse was in the process of performing further analysis and verification of the data. Hence, RPP&E, which, in general, was anxious for evaluative analysis to have an impact at the highest levels of government, did not want to suffer the embarrassment of a national debate over tentative results that might change materially in the later analysis. However, after much pressure, an early, incomplete version of the study was released. In June, the final report was published, and it confirmed the preliminary findings.

These background facts are important in order to understand why the controversy rose to such a crescendo, as it ranged over the executive branch and the Congress, with wide coverage in the press. The Westinghouse study is, perhaps unfortunately, an instructive example of public reaction to evaluations of social action programs. As we turn now to a brief description of the study, its findings, and a discussion of its methodological and conceptual base, this milieu must be kept in mind.

The study and its major conclusions are summarized succinctly in the following statement by the contractor:

> The basic question posed by the study was:
> *To what extent are the children now in the first, second, and third grades who attended Head Start programs different in their intellectual and social-personal development from comparable children who did not attend?*

To answer this question, a sample of one hundred and four Head Start centers across the country was chosen. A sample of children from these centers who had gone on to the first, second, and third grades in local area schools and a matched sample of control children from the same grades and schools who had not attended Head Start were administered a series of tests covering various aspects of cognitive and affective development [The Metropolitan Readiness Test, the Illinois Test of Psycholinguistic Abilities, the Stanford Achievement Test, the Children's Self-Concept Index, and the like]. The parents of both the former Head Start enrollees and the control children were interviewed and a broad range of attitudinal, social, and economic data was collected. Directors or other officials of all the centers were interviewed and information was collected on various characteristics of the current local Head Start programs. The primary grade teachers rated both groups of children on achievement motivation and supplied a description of the intellectual and emotional environment of their elementary schools.

Viewed in broad perspective, the major conclusions of the study are:

1. Summer programs appear to be ineffective in producing any gains in cognitive and affective development that persist into the early elementary grades.

2. Full-year programs appear to be ineffective as measured by the tests of affective development used in the study, but are marginally effective in producing gains in cognitive development that could be detected in grades one, two, and three. Programs appeared to be of greater effectiveness for certain subgroups of centers, notably in mainly Negro centers, in scattered programs in the central cities, and in Southeastern centers.

3. Head Start children, whether from summer or from full-year programs, still appear to be considerably below national norms for the standardized tests of language development and scholastic achievement, while performance on school readiness at grade one approaches the national norm.

4. Parents of Head Start enrollees voiced strong approval of the program and its influence on their children. They reported substantial participation in the activities of the centers. In sum, the Head Start children cannot be said to be *appreciably* different from their peers in the elementary grades who did not attend Head Start in most aspects of cognitive and affective development measured in this study, with the exception of the slight, but nonetheless significant, superiority of full-year Head Start children on certain measures of cognitive development.[4]

Methodological Issues

We now turn to the methodological and conceptual validity of the study—the *explicit* focal point of the controversy—and this presents difficult problems of exposition. First, both of us are protagonists on one side of the controversy, with Evans being one of the major participants in the debate. Second, a presentation of the methodological questions in sufficient detail to allow the reader to form his own opinions would require an extensive discussion. The final Westinghouse report comprises several hundred pages, with a significant portion of it directed specifically to methodological issues. Under these circumstances, we will summarize the major criticisms that have been made of the study and comment on them briefly in this section. Then, in the next major section, we will set out *our* judgment as to the overall technical adequacy of the report and its usefulness for decision-making.

CRITICISMS OF THE STUDY

1. The study is too narrow. It focuses only on cognitive and affective outcomes. Head Start is a much broader program which includes health, nutrition, and community objectives, and any proper evaluation must evaluate it on all these objectives.

Our experience has been that one of the reasons for the failure of so many evaluations is that they have aspired to do too much. We did not think that it was possible to cover all of the Head Start objectives in the same study; therefore, we purposely limited the study's focus to those which we considered most important. Despite its many other objectives, in the final analysis Head Start should be evaluated mainly on the basis of the extent to which it has affected the life-chances of the children involved. In order to achieve such effects, cognitive and motivational changes seem essential.

2. The study fails to give adequate attention to variations among the Head Start programs. It lumps the programs together into an overall average and does not explore what variation there may be in effectiveness as a function of differing program styles and characteristics. The study, therefore, fails to give any guidance concerning what detailed changes (for example, types of curricula) should be made in the program.

This is essentially correct. As discussed earlier, the purpose of the evaluation was to measure the overall effect of the Head Start program in a reasonably short period of time. This in no way denies the need for a study to get at the question of variation among the programs. The fact is that both overall and detailed information are frequently needed, but the latter generally takes much longer to develop.

3. The sample of full-year centers in the study is too small to provide confidence in the study's findings. Because of such a small sample, the lack of statistically significant differences between the Head Start and control groups is to be expected, and gives a misleading indication that the

programs had no effect. With such a small sample, it would take quite large differences to reach a satisfactory level of statistical significance.

The 104 Head Start centers, selected at random, were chosen in order to provide an adequate *total* sample. This was then broken down into an approximate 70–30 division in order to approximate the actual distribution of summer and full-year programs. If we were doing the study over, we would select a larger number of full-year centers. The main advantage, however, would be to allow more analysis of subgroups within the full-year sample. It is very unlikely that the study's principal conclusions about the overall effectiveness of the program would be altered by a larger sample. A detailed "power of the test" analysis showed that with the present sample size and variance, the statistical tests are capable of detecting differences between the experimental and control groups below the level of what would be practically meaningful. Forgetting the statistical complexities for a minute, the simple fact is that the differences between the Head Start and control group scores were quite small. Even in the cases in which differences were statistically significant, they were so small as to have little practical importance.

4. The sample is not representative. Many of the original randomly chosen centers had to be eliminated.

The study suffered a loss of some of the centers specified in the original sample because (1) some small rural areas had all their eligible children in the Head Start program (and hence no controls could be found) and (2) some communities prohibited the testing of children in the school system. Centers were substituted randomly, and a comparison of the final chosen sample with the total universe of Head Start centers showed the two to be very similar on a large number of factors (for example, rural-urban location, racial composition, and the like).

5. The test instruments used in this study, and indeed all existing instruments for measuring cognitive and affective states in children, are primitive. They were not developed for disadvantaged populations, and they are probably so gross and insensitive that they are unable to pick up many of the real and important changes that Head Start has produced in children.

It is entirely possible that this is true. However, most of the cognitive measures are the same ones being used by other child-development and Head Start researchers doing work on disadvantaged children. In those cases (relatively few) where previous studies have shown positive changes on these very same measures, they have seldom been questioned or disregarded because of the inadequacy of the instruments. In the affective area, Westinghouse found no appropriate test instruments and had to devise its own. Hence, the results should be viewed as suggestive, but no more. The Westinghouse study used the best instruments available, and with these instruments, few appreciable differences are found between children who had been part of a Head Start program and those who had not.

6. The study is based on an ex post facto design which is inherently faulty because it attempts to generate a control group by matching former Head Start children with other non-Head Start children. A vast number of factors, either alone or acting together, could produce a superior non-Head Start group which would obscure the effect of the program.

It is always possible in any ex post facto study that failure to achieve adequate matching on all relevant variables (particularly self-selectivity factors) can occur. Ex post facto studies, however, are a respected and widely used scientific procedure, although one which does not provide the greater certainty which results from the classic before-after experimental design carried out in controlled laboratory conditions.

In the Westinghouse study, the two groups were matched on age, sex, race, and kindergarten attendance. Any residual differences in socioeconomic status were equated by two different statistical procedures: a random-replication-covariance analysis and a nonparametric matching procedure. Both statistical techniques, which equated the two groups on parent's occupation, education, and per capita income, yielded the same basic results on the cognitive and affective comparisons between Head Start and control-group children.

7. The study tested the children in the first, second, and third grades of elementary school—after they had left Head Start. Its findings merely demonstrate that Head Start achievements do not persist after the children return to poverty homes and ghetto schools. Rather than demonstrating that Head Start does not have appreciable effects, the study merely shows that these effects tend to fade out when the Head Start children return to a poverty environment.

It is possible that poor teachers, impoverished environment, and other similar factors, eliminated a significant cognitive advantage gained by Head Start children during the Head Start period. But even if this is true, we must have real doubts about the current course of the program. Unless Head Start *alone* can be improved so as to have positive effects which do not disappear, or unless Follow Through or some other program can be developed to provide subsequent reinforcement that solidifies the gains of Head Start children, the *present* worth of the gains seems negligible. Whatever the cause, the fact that the learning gains are transitory is a most compelling fact for determining future policy.

8. The study's comparison of Head Start with non-Head Start children in the same classrooms fails to take into account secondary or spillover effects from the Head Start children. The children who have had Head Start are likely to infect their non-Head Start peers with their own greater motivation and interest in learning. Their presence in the class-room is also likely to cause the elementary school teacher to upgrade her entire level of teaching or to give more attention to, and therefore produce greater gains in, the less advanced non-Head Start group. Thus, the study minimizes Head Start's effect by comparing the Head Start children with another group of children which has been indirectly improved by the Head Start children themselves.

This is certainly a possibility. However, most of the previous before-after studies of Head Start's cognitive effects have shown, at most, small gains—so small that it is hard to imagine their having such major secondary effect on teachers and peers. Moreover, the first-grade children in the Westinghouse study were tested during the early part of their first-grade year—prior to the time when such secondary influence on teachers or peer children would have had a chance to occur. In results of direct measurements of the children (Metropolitan Readiness Test, Illinois Test of Psycholinguistic Abilities, and the like), there were only marginal differences between the Head Start and control-group children at that time. Also, on the Children's Behavior Inventory, an instrument which obtained teachers' ratings of the children, there were few significant differences between the two groups, indicating that the teachers were not able to perceive any differences between the motivation of the Head Start and non-Head Start children. In the light of these findings, it is hard to see how spillover or secondary effects could have occurred to an extent which contaminated the control group.

An Assessment

Our overall assessment of the study is as follows:

(1) In terms of its methodological and conceptual base, the study is a *relatively* good one. This in no way denies that many of the criticisms made of the study are valid. However, for the most part, they are the kind

of criticisms that can be made of most pieces of social science research conducted outside the laboratory, in a real-world setting, with all of the logistical and measurement problems that such studies entail. And these methodological flaws open the door to the more political issues. Thus, one needs not only to examine the methodological substance of the criticisms which have been made of the study, but also to understand the social concern which lies behind them as well. Head Start has elicited national sympathy and has had the support and involvement of the educational profession. It is understandable that so many should rush to the defense of such a popular and humane program. But how many of the concerns over the size of the sample, control-group equivalency, and the appropriateness of covariance analysis, for example, would have been registered if the study had found positive differences in favor of Head Start?

(2) The scope of the study was *limited,* and it therefore failed to provide the answers to many questions which would have been useful in determining what specific changes should be made in the programs.

(3) Longitudinal studies, based on larger samples and covering a broader range of objectives, would be better, and should be undertaken. But until they are instituted, this study provides a useful piece of information that we can fit into a pattern of other reasonable evidence to improve our basis for decision-making. Thus, the Westinghouse study extends our knowledge, but does not fly in the face of past evidence. For the summer program, the study of a national sample shows what smaller studies have indicated—no lasting gain for the Head Start children relative to their peers. This may deflate some myths, but does not affect any hard facts. For the full-year program, the evidence of some limited effect is about as favorable as any we have found to date.

We imagine that this type of positive, but qualified assessment will fit any *relatively* good evaluation for some time to come. For we have never seen a field evaluation of a social action program that could not be faulted legitimately by good methodologists, and we may never see one. But, if we are willing to accept real-world imperfections, and to use evaluative analysis with prudence, then such analysis can provide a far better basis for decision-making than we have had in the past.

What, then, does the Westinghouse study provide that will help in making decisions? First, the negative findings indicate that the program is failing, on the average, to produce discernible school success for its participants. Put more bluntly, the study shows that along the key cognitive and affective dimension, the program is not working at all well. And from this, one can infer, directly, that we should search hard for, and test, new techniques to make learning gains in the Head Start classroom more permanent and, indirectly, that the years before and after Head Start should also be looked at carefully. Second, the evidence suggests the superiority of the full-year over the summer programs. Most of all, we believe that the value of the study consists in the *credible, validating* evidence which it provides, that the honeymoon of the last few years really ought to be over, and that the hard work of finding effective techniques should start in earnest.

Thus, the study pushes policy-makers toward certain decisions, particularly those involving within-program tradeoffs—more experimentation and more full-year projects in place of summer projects. Yet, and this would be true no matter how good the study was, the evidence is not a sufficient condition for major program-decisions. The last statement holds even for the within-program choices (tradeoffs, but not overall cutbacks) and takes on greater cogency when one seeks implications for decisions concerning the need for more, or fewer, resources. The evaluative evidence must be considered in the light of other pieces of information and various highly important political judgments. For example: How deleterious would a program cutback be for program morale, or for our commitment to increase the outlays going to the disadvantaged for education? Surely, no reasonable person would claim that evaluative evidence alone is sufficient. Rather, such choices ought to be political, in the broad sense of that term, with credible evaluative data—a commodity heretofore in short supply—being considered as one of the inputs in the choice process.[5]

Conclusions

In this section, we shall first present a number of inferences which, in our opinion, can be drawn concerning the larger issues of this controversy and then touch on the unknowns that still plague us. The former fall into two categories—program operations and evaluation.

OPERATIONS

(1) *We should be far more skeptical than in the past of our technical capability to mount effective large-scale programs, particularly in those areas in which the main program goal is to provide a material, positive change in an individual's capacity to earn or to learn.* We should distinguish clearly between such "opportunity" programs and maintenance programs in which the primary goal is to deliver a service that is itself a highly valued commodity, for example, money and food. The

technical problems of the latter are relatively simple compared to those of programs which attempt to offer earning or educational opportunities. For example, politics aside, it would not be difficult, *technically*, to mount a large-scale food-or income-maintenance program far superior to the ones we have presently. But in programs which specialize in opportunity, we often simply do not *know* what to do technically in order to reach our goals.

(2) *For opportunity programs, we need to start, as a highest-priority activity, a systematic, concerted effort to develop new ideas for restructuring on-going programs or creating new ones, and to test the merits of these ideas, on a small scale, before mounting large-scale national programs.* Clearly, political concerns will often override this dictum of testing on a small scale. A government program cannot be managed by the procedures which are effective in a research laboratory. Large-scale programs will often start without a prior tested model. But, at the margin, an effort to test may both produce useful tested models and make us think harder about starting large-scale programs without such testing. It is our belief that a commitment by the government to the systematic search for new ideas is a key point which has great potential for improving opportunity programs. Analysis cannot (and should not) replace politics, but it can, over time, facilitate better political decisions.

EVALUATION

(1) We urgently need to evaluate the effectiveness of present programs.

(2) In many areas, we now have methodological tools that will allow us to do evaluations much superior to those done in the past.

(3) These evaluations will have limitations, both in terms of scope and in terms of techniques. However, if used in conjunction with other reasonable evidence, such studies can materially improve our base of decision-making information.

(4) The milieu for meaningful program evaluation involves an interaction of methodology, bureaucracy, and politics; it will therefore often be the case that attacks which are methodological in form but ideological in concern will be made against evaluations.

(5) Major evaluations of programs should be performed by an office and staff removed from the operating program. Self-evaluation is an almost impossible task for a manager who has strong convictions about the value of his program. A separate office can at least *institutionalize* a relative degree of objectivity, in that it can be charged specifically, within the agency, with the task of program-measurement, not program-defense.

Some people, however, feel that even this may be illusory inasmuch as the staff office will be serving the agency head, who, after all, is the program's *chief manager*. One cannot escape the fact that evaluation, with its potential for indicating that a program is not working, is a weapon of the arsenal of analysis which is difficult to handle.

(6) Finally, for those of us who urge more evaluation, it is well to remember that evaluation is only one of many inputs—political, bureaucratic, and the like—in the decision-making process, and does not serve as a substitute for good judgment.

THE REMAINING UNKNOWNS

We have come down strongly on the side of analysis—measuring ongoing programs and testing new ones. At the same time, we have recognized the technical limitations of evaluation and have warned that they must be used with prudence in the light of these limitations. But is this not a politically naive warning, and hence really a below-the-belt punch to the argument for expanding social programs? As *The New York Times* reported on April 18, 1969: "A number of social scientists . . . have expressed fears that Congress or the Administration will seize upon the [Westinghouse] report's generally negative conclusions as an excuse to downgrade or discard the Head Start Program." Even when administrators and legislators are pure of heart (but relatively ignorant of the limitations of analytical techniques), will they not overvalue, and hence overreact to, quantitative evaluations because of their aura of scientific accuracy? Will the guideline "test and prove before operating on a large scale" become a facade for disparaging all new ideas and retrenching our commitment to the disadvantaged?

These are profound and difficult problems for which there are no simple solutions. For example, a legitimate question to ask us, on the basis of our stated convictions, is whether we would have opted for a large-scale Head Start program at its inception. Even given today's knowledge, we might have done so, because the *redistributive* kinds of changes, which we discussed earlier, are a critical need. At the same time, we would not today urge either an increase in the program, as now constituted, or new starts on a large scale in the educational area, without prior testing.

We recognize the danger that the results of evaluation and systematic testing can be ill-used. But what course of action is not dangerous? What "good" approach cannot be turned to evil? Is it not even more hazardous to proceed boldly—as if we know, when we do not? Does it seem wise to launch new large-cale *opportunity* programs—amid verbal paeans, but with no solid evidence of success—and to continue to believe our earlier words without a thought of investigating the outcome?

As we pose these questions, we trail off into gray areas of nagging doubts, without a burst of penetrating truth. This seems fitting—for to stand unsurely in a morass of conflicting issues simply mirrors the larger reality of today. The confidence of 1965 is literally light years behind us.

Notes

[1] Charles L. Schultze, *The Politics and Economics of Public Spending* (Washington, D.C.: Brookings Institution, 1968), pp. 16–17, 76.

[2] PPBS has recently been subjected to a searching appraisal by a number of scholars (including several major practitioners) in the Joint Economic Committee's three-volume study, *The Analysis and Evaluation of Public Expenditures: The PPBS System* (Washington, D.C.: Government Printing Office, 1969). The weight of opinion is that PPBS—the *formal system* in which analysis is carried out—is having its problems and may well be in political trouble. At the same time, there is general agreement concerning the urgent need for sound analysis. What is at issue, then, is the format for analysis. For example: Should analysis such as that of PPBS be tied to the budget process? But this issue need not be addressed here, for the main concern of the paper is analysis, and not necessarily its particular formal wrapping. Of course, whatever the formal structure, analysis will still have to confront politics and bureaucracy.

[3] Later, Head Start made its own attempt at national evaluation through its network of university-based evaluation and research centers. But failure to create control groups and comparable procedures made the results unsatisfactory, and the evaluation component of these centers was discontinued in 1969.

[4] *The Impact of Head Start: An Evaluation of the Effects of Head Start on Children's Cognitive and Affective Development,* Westinghouse Learning Corporation-Ohio University, July 12, 1969, pp. 2, 7–8.

[5] It is important to note that Mr. Nixon's speech which first suggested the negative results called, not for a cutback in Head Start, but for continuing commitment to early childhood programs and an extensive effort to find new ways to meet the educational needs of the disadvantaged. For what it is worth, this is also the authors' view.

VIII

PPB: CRITIQUES AND PROSPECTS

21

The Impact of Management Science on Political Decision Making

MICHAEL J. WHITE

In the past 75 years in the United States and other industrialized countries a large number of managerial and scientific technologies have penetrated organizations, public and private, and been integrated into the routine fabric of institutional activities. McKean's list includes scientific management, financial analysis, consumer research, market research, operations research, and systems analysis.[1] To these we could add long-range planning, research and development, industrial engineering, PPBS, and futuristics. Currently into the American federal government, and into many state and local governments, several of these technologies are being

Revised version of a paper delivered at the 66th Annual Convention of the American Political Science Association, Los Angeles, September 8–12, 1970. Reprinted by permission of the author and the Association.

The research upon which this paper is based has been supported by NASA Grant NGL 14–007–058 and a grant from the Booz-Allen-Hamilton Foundation to the Cooperative International Program of Studies of Operations Research and the Management Sciences, Graduate School of Management, Northwestern University. Among the many people who have helped me, I am particularly indebted to Michael Radnor and Fred Vetter.

integrated: operations research, systems analysis, and PPBS. For the purposes of this paper, no particular distinction will be drawn between these three, and all will be considered OR/MS (for operations research—management science). In common with other managerial technologies, OR/MS has the following attributes: it is rationalistic in that it assumes that explicit human intelligence can lead to improvement; it is research oriented; it involves esoteric techniques and uncommon cognitive perspectives; it is oriented toward increasing the viability and effectiveness of complex organizations in increasingly complex environments; and, it leads to the routine production of new ideas. Further, OR/MS shares with other managerial technologies two organizational attributes: it is usually organized into specialized organizational units and has been accompanied by a parallel process of institutionalization in the academic world.[2]

Whether known as PPBS, systems analysis, or operations research (each claims the others as either offsprings or siblings), the application of these and related technologies has caused much controversy in federal civilian agencies, just as it has in defense and industrial settings. Among others, the professional practitioners of OR/MS engage in vigorous and spirited debate about their performance as a profession. Their writings often contain the most broad, perceptive, and constructive of all criticisms of OR/MS. However as James Schlesinger writes:

> Analysts themselves may be self-doubting, bemused by uncertainties, frighteningly candid, but different tactics have been required of the missionaries who have proselytized in behalf of analysis.[3]

Consequently, Mosher and others find OR/MS oversold[4], and there is a general reaction against their hyperbolic claims. These practitioners, or *analysts,* are often equally vigorous in their criticisms of the institutions that employ them and the people and policies they find there. This is, of course, as it should be: for analysts are change-agents and their job is constructive criticism. They are more than ordinary change agents also. They are, in the phrase of Michael Radnor, "change-squared" agents. The consequence of their activity is not only discrete changes but also change in the way change itself occurs in institutional settings. OR/MS analysts and OR/MS are thus doubly threatening. It should be no surprise that the reaction to them is sharp and sometimes confused.

Criticisms of OR/MS can be divided into those that are *optimistic* and those that are *pessimistic* in the following sense. Some criticisms seem to have as their underlying assumption that OR/MS will have a significant impact on public policy and organizational decision making. OR/MS recommendations will be implemented and OR/MS analysts will achieve a position of power and influence in important matters of state. Criticisms making or implying this assumption shall be called *optimistic*. On the other hand, many criticisms seem to assume that OR/MS will have little or no impact. OR/MS recommendations will not be implemented and OR/MS analysts will not achieve positions of power and influence. Criticisms making or implying this assumption will be called *pessimistic*. At times, I shall restate criticisms of OR/MS. In doing so, there is some danger that criticisms will be taken beyond the original intent of the authors. The distortion is moderated, in my view, by the common organizational consequences of the component OR/MS technologies. We shall treat the controversy in the setting of federal civilian agencies and shall proceed with comments on specific criticisms of OR/MS.

The Pessimistic Critique, Part I: It Can't Be Done

When most forthright, the pessimistic critique says that OR/MS is simply impossible. Victor Thompson writes: [5]

> I must be blunt: science cannot solve social problems. Suppose, for example, that we ask medicine to solve the problem of race prejudice. As a medical problem the "solution" might turn out to be some drug. However, the social problem would still remain.

The same holds true for the solutions of management scientists, the "econologists" who have seized the opportunity for power presented by PPBS. Thompson continues:

> the solution of a social problem is properly described with such words as "compromise," "consensus," "majority," "negotiation," "bargaining," "coercion," etc. If the "solution" cannot be described in such terms, then it is not the solution of a social problem.

Wildavsky reacts to PPBS in an equally abrupt manner: PPBS cannot be done because no one knows how to do it. [6]

These are strong statements. It is obvious that recommendations must be implemented before they become "solutions." Or is it? A recommendation can be implemented and still not be a solution. We have many cases of that. And a recommendation need not be described in Thompson's vocabulary to be a solution. Recently, there has been much writing on "incentives." [7] Too many of these incentives are within the discretion of administration for Thompson's vocabulary to be given unqualified allegiance. But perhaps this is quibbling with words. Thompson's criticism is less inaccurate than it is trivial. [8] The statement that no one knows how to do PPBS is both inaccurate and trivial. PPBS was being done prior to 1965 in the Defense Department and in several large corporations and, in a prototype form, in several federal civilian agencies as well. Whether the PPBS that was, or is, practiced happens to meet some set of explicit personal criteria is another matter, but Wildavsky does not offer such criteria.

If PPBS or some other form of OR/MS can be done, it can be misdone as well. Wildavsky suggests that benefit-cost analyses can be "fudged" by adding in benefits such as "recreation" or through the manipulation of the discount rate or through opportunistic aggregation.[9] In a later paper he castigates economists for adding in aesthetic factors in order to make their analyses come out "right."[10] James Schlesinger notes the criticisms of OR/MS in the Defense Department based on military fiascos such as the TFX or the Vietnam (or is it "SEA") War, although he acquits OR/MS of the charges.[11] I once forced this criticism upon a group of civilian agency analysts and their response is appropriate here. They argued that when and if this happened other analysts would step in and let it be known. Professional criticism would in most cases be sufficient control. Professional criticism is also the channel through which Wildavsky was able to learn about the methodological peculiarities that he notes.

OR/MS CRITICIZED FOR LACK OF POLITICAL AND SOCIAL REALISM

It is easiest to list some specifics and then list comments. (a) Thompson feels that econologicians "vastly underestimate the complexity of the units with which they deal."[12] (b) He also feels that they do not consider adequately how people will react to the systems they design.[13] (c) Mosher feels that PPBS involves an oversimplified view of the world, one that is too market-oriented.[14] (d) Wildavsky feels that "economic rationality, however laudable in its own sphere, ought not to swallow up political rationality—but will do so if political rationality continues to lack trained and adept defenders."[15] (e) Fenno notes that many budget reform proposals—more coordination, more integration, more comprehensive consideration—are rejected by congressmen not because congressmen are less intelligent or less concerned with the public interest than anyone else, but because they do not feel these reforms "are likely to help them perform their function any better."[16] (f) Wildavsky sees program budgeting as tying the President's hands to five-year expenditure commitments while Presidents like to maintain their freedom.[17]

The environment of federal civilian programs is both complex and reactive. It is reactive both in the market sense and in the game-theory sense. Thompson's criticisms—(a) and (b)—represent serious obstacles to OR/MS in any institution. They can be and are being overcome through the accumulation of experience and through the inclusion of a mix of professional skills in analytical units. Yet the units with which politicians or sociologists deal are also more complex than they realize; if they were not, either our policies would be better or sociologists would be kings.

OR/MS may be econological rather than sociological, but the model of economic man has proven itself to give, at least in this culture, more consistently reliable predictions than any other has.[18] Political sensitivity is important, but attempts to breathe some useful life into this concept have involved its explication in terms which OR/MS analysts find congenial: political resources, exchange costs, and opportunity costs.[19] Wildavsky's interpretation of five-year expenditure projections as a politically unrealistic attempt to tie the President's hands is unsupported by either practice or theory; proof of political insensitivity need rest on more than that misrepresentation. These allegations discriminate neither among tactics appropriate for diverse political arenas (Congress, bureaucracy, or community, for example), nor between what Wildavsky distinguishes as "systems" and "policy" politics.[20] Fenno's comment (e) introduces the factor of purpose. His notion is stated elegantly by two prominent management scientists in an essay, the reception and wide circulation of which is evidence that the analytical community has not neglected Fenno's point.[21]

Even if OR/MS analysts are politically insensitive, they operate in a bureaucratic environment conducive to learning that skill. They are, generally by choice, "on tap and not on top."[22] This criticism is generally appropriate but hardly profound; in general it applies as well to any human activity transcending epistemological and political fatalism.

CRITICAL VARIABLES ARE NOT MEASURABLE

This is a related criticism and has, as a corollary, the claim that consequently the analysts will solve the problem that remains after these critical variables have been ignored. Thompson writes:

> The neo-Taylorites set up self-serving rules that assure their being able to reach determinate solutions. That is, they solve what problems they can, not the problems that most need to be solved.[23]

Both parts of this charge are too familiar to require further documentation. Implicit in such a charge are the assumptions that all problems that OR/MS analysts face are, in fact, unamenable to quantification of the most salient variables and that analysts are unimaginative in their efforts at quantification. Neither of these assumptions is particularly true. Many problems in the areas such as housing, transportation, banking, and agriculture involve the expression of public preferences through market mechanisms. In reading critiques of this type, one might assume that the government is involved only in mental health, education, and efforts to increase human feelings of self-worth and that many analysts are skillful users of behavioral measures.

In "soft" policy areas, primary goals may be measurable and the "unmeasurable" goals only secondary at best. An illustrative *cause celebre* is the Westinghouse Learning Corporation's study of Head Start. Reflecting on that controversy, Williams and Evans state that it is necessary to limit the scope of analytical studies:

> Despite its many other objectives, in the final analysis Head Start should be evaluated mainly on the extent to which it has affected the life chances of the children.[24]

The key indicators of this were measures of enduring cognitive and motivational change. When enduring changes were found in a small fraction of the previous studies that used these same measures, the critics of the Westinghouse study remained quiet. Williams and Evans conclude:

> The milieu for meaningful program evaluation involves an interaction of methodology, bureaucracy, and politics; it will therefore often be the case that attacks against evaluations will be made which are methodological in form but ideological in concern.[25]

There is evident a great amount of progress in the social sciences in the measurement of variables long felt to be immeasurable. The problem is rarely that variables cannot be quantified nor even that analysts will not try when they can be; sometimes rather it is that politicians will not allow the use of behavioral science measuring instruments that are available.[26]

Wildavsky has commented on the problem of making interpersonal comparisons of utility. He notes that "public works projects have a multitude of objectives and consequences," that "no single welfare function can encompass these diverse objectives,"[27] and that "No one knows how to deal with interpersonal comparisons of utility."[28] Further, he observes that "The process we have developed for dealing with interpersonal comparisons in government is not economic but political."[29]

Anti-pluralists like McConnell and Wolff show that in American politics explicit interpersonal comparisons of utility are avoided through a variety of institutional and ideological mechanisms.[30] Yet giving the marginal dollar to the SST rather than to OEO makes the comparison anyway, in effect. Perhaps the critics fear making comparisons explicit. If so, they ought to reject all valid knowledge from policy making. OR/MS can contribute usefully to an understanding of means-ends relations and of relations among ends. It cannot provide algorithmic solutions to complex value choices: although it changes the argument, it does not replace politics. For the latter, OR/MS should not be faulted.

COSTS OF CALCULATION

Bertram Gross, among others, has alerted us to the danger of "paralysis by analysis."[31] Wildavsky has argued that "policy analysis is expensive in terms of time, talent, and money,"[32] and he criticizes the "paper-pushing" aspects of PPBS—program structures, PMs and PFPs. He writes approvingly in his study of zero-base budgeting of such calculation aids as "what Congress would approve, what the statutes required, what could be done with available resources."[33] In *The Politics of the Budgetary Process* he even offers the example of the voter's use of party preference as the type of calculation short-cut to be admired.[34] Yet problems can be over-studied, and politicians have developed devices for intentional paralysis.[35] Wildavsky's criticisms of "paper-pushing" were anticipated by Budget Bureau action.[36] The simplicity of calculation in present policy making and budgeting procedures may be overrated. Clearly there is a lot of calculation going on, as one year's collection of budget hearings, Congressional Records, and agency studies would testify. One must assume that congressmen and agency officials actively seek information and might well like better information than they have. Through screening and filtering processes, these officials might well find a way to drop the least valuable item of information from their attention list and replace it with something better. At the same time, some of the calculation aids listed by Wildavsky become less useful upon inspection. Statutes are often not very clear and judges spend years determining what the law is.[37] What can be done with available personnel and resources is also not so easy to discover, and this is one reason why operations researchers command GS–14 and –15 slots in Washington. Whether OR/MS in any of its forms adds an unbearable burden of calculation is contingent upon whether it replaces or supplements other calculations. It may be that it at first supplements and then replaces other calculations. Redundance would seem an advisable interim tactic and the general criticism is probably a function of the temporary novelty of new ways of making decisions rather than a permanent fixture.

Each of the preceding criticisms suggests that OR/MS in civilian government is either impossible or not worth the effort. Some of them are trivial and undeserving of sustained discussion as posed. Other arguments are dependent for their relevance on the fast-disappearing novelty of OR/MS or upon an inadequate appreciation of OR/MS in a social context. Some of the criticisms are fast losing their relevance because of the actions taken by analysts before the criticisms became widespread outside of professional analytical circles. But each deserves consideration for its social function. Even those who argue that OR/MS is impossible may, as they provide needed elaboration of their critiques, stimulate better performance on the part of analysts and more realistic expectations about OR/MS on the part of political decision makers.

The Pessimistic Critique, Part II: No Improvement

It is not enough to say that OR/MS is difficult or impossible. Were we not accustomed to it, the way that decisions are currently made might also seem impossible. The second half of the pessimistic critique states that, even though OR/MS is possible, it will not be an improvement upon present methods. Present methods for making decisions are far more rational than they appear, the argument continues. Whereas Wildavsky is the best known proponent of the first part of the pessimistic critique, Charles E. Lindblom is identified intimately with the second. His writings have opened new areas of inquiry in more than one discipline[38] and have won deserved acclaim. Five themes run through his work from his early articles to the present, and for the sake of brevity most references will be to well-known and widely circulated articles.

FAILURE OF COMPREHENSIVENESS

The first theme is the inadequacy of central coordination and comprehensive inquiry. Each concept, according to Lindblom, suffers from a failure to account for man's limited capacities for calculation and information processing and from the frequent impossibility of casting a problem into a means-ends framework.[39] Lindblom offers a caricature of synoptic rationality that approximates the recommendations offered by some budgetary reformers and writers of textbooks in administrative practice.[40] The outlines are familiar. He ascribes it to OR/MS advocates and thus it becomes of interest here. In making this ascription Lindblom has, I feel, made a fundamental error. To see why, it is necessary to distinguish three uses of the comprehensive model: (1) as an ideal for the sociopolitical solution of problems; (2) as an ideal in individual inquiry; and (3) as a model for reconstructed logic. Used as either (1) or (2), the model may be impossible. But that does not mean it is worthless. Rather, the comprehensive model is best seen as a checklist: the analyst evaluates his own work or social and political decision processes to see if they can be reconstructed in the comprehensive model. Making the reconstruction is a way of checking to see what has been left out and therefore the reconstruction provides a basis for an *incremental* process of planning and inquiry. In other words, the comprehensive model is a discipline, as is suggested by Roger Jones in his comments on Lindblom and by the research project histories collected by Hammond.[41] The failure to see the comprehensive model as the discipline of reconstructed logic can lead one to view OR/MS as inferior, particularly for large-scale problems.[42]

SUPERIORITY OF INCREMENTALISM

Incrementalism refers both to a strategy for policy development and to a strategy for social change. Lindblom writes:

> The incremental method is characterized by its practitioner's preoccupation with: (1) only that limited set of policy alternatives that are politically relevant, these typically being policies only incrementally different from existing policies: (2) analysis of only those aspects of policies with respect to which the alternatives differ; (3) a view of the policy choice as one in a succession of choices; (4) the *marginal* values of various social objectives and constraints; (5) an intermixture of evaluation and empirical analysis of the consequences of policies for objectives independently determined; and (6) only a small number out of all the important relevant values.[43]

Supposedly, policy making proceeding in this fashion will be more rational than that which emerges from a more comprehensive analysis. The incremental model has been applied most frequently to budgeting.[44] Yet congressional budgeting can be modeled adequately by a few linear equations, a fact that led Otto Davis to testify that

> one can abolish the appropriations committees. They are not needed because their behavior is even more predictable than the executive branch's behavior.[45]

Such a predictable system may not be all bad; its rationality is somewhat elusive, however.

Justifications of the superiority of either incremental or "comprehensive" processes usually have the same defect: they ignore output and concentrate on secondary criteria.[46] No process can justify the egregious policies that have happened to us incrementally, such as our farm programs, urban renewal, and the "Vietnam" war. Incrementalism seems particularly inappropriate in situations where some objectives are far more important than others; for over time, other, less relevant objectives may become equally well served. Subsidy programs also can be distorted more easily and less noticeably through incremental rather than through "comprehensive" processes. Lastly, in incremental processes, undesirable side effects may become institutionalized. The value of the comprehensive approach as reconstructed logic can be seen here. It builds in an evaluation of consequences of both kinds: are we reaching our goals, and are we having unintended consequences?

At its best, incrementalism is more than a strategy for policy making that ignores consequences and outputs. It can also be an experimental epistemology in the sense discussed by Karl Popper in his interesting essay, "On the Sources of Knowledge and of Ignorance."[47] Well-known management scientists interpret OR/MS in much the same way.[48] We approximate knowledge through continual "conjectures and refutations." We continually examine purposes and proposals logically and empirically because we are faced with multiple goals and changing environments for all our interesting problems. If *incrementalism at its best* is superior to OR/MS, it is because its involvement of a wider number of actors in the conjecture and refutation process leads to better output.

INCREMENTALISM AND PARTICIPATION

If we must evaluate policy on the basis of output we can still look at participation under the hypothesis that scope of participation is positively related to quality of output. Pluralist doctrine assures us that all relevant interests will be represented. Wildavsky discusses how altruistic citizens, entrepreneurial politicans, and imperialistic bureaucrats will make sure of that.[49] Yet we know that there are strictly technical barriers to interest mobilization and organization, and I hope that we know that politicians and bureaucrats have effective ways of suppressing or ignoring some interests.[50] Some political arenas are effectively closed to large segments of the public; for example, most of administrative law. Analysis is one method that can be used to include in the policy-making process interests and potential or real consequences that would otherwise be neglected. In this way, analysis may be superior to incrementalism even when incrementalism is working at its best. The analyst is not only a "partisan efficiency advocate,"[51] but may also be an advocate of otherwise unrepresented interests.

GOALS, MEANS, AND AGREEMENT

Yes, the devotee of Lindblom's writings will answer, but what about the problem of getting agreement? There is, supposedly, some value in not making one's goals explicit in the political process: unstated values and ideologies do not prevent agreement on marginal values or on means: considered in actual choice situations alternatives may weigh in differently than they do in the abstract.[52] As an ethical statement, it is far more appropriate to the marketing of vegetables than it is for the expenditure of tax money.

At the same time analysis, while requiring explicit statements of goals, does not compel their appearance on the front page of the *Washington Post*. They need not be known beyond the agency. The goals of the analyst can be and often are tactically concealed.

Goals often change through the consideration of means. This is true in OR/MS and in incrementalism.[53] This in itself is not an argument for keeping goals hidden from the outset. It may be the reverse: the conjecture and refutation process may be facilitated if goals are stated. One large class of decisions where this may be true are those over which interaction can be described as "analytical" rather than "bargaining."[54] Even if this is not the situation, we are still not in a position to assert the superiority of incrementalism. Both game theory and classical economics gain validity as more people know about them.[55]

The argument that goals should not be made explicit has another aspect. Lowi has argued that part of the current national malaise results from the government's failure to state and pursue explicit goals. Contemporary laws are written as broad and rather empty statements of good intentions and the government itself becomes only one of many interests contesting to determine what the specific goals will be.[56] (This fact implies, of course, that it is easier to get agreement on ends than on means!) It is clear that the incrementalist position on stating goals is more than a methodological recommendation or even a neutral political recommendation. Rather, it is part and parcel of the dominant American "public philosophy" of "interest-group liberalism." The OR/MS position on stating goals is at this time still an exclusively methodological one; it has not been linked to an articulated political philosophy.[57] It has political implications however, and therefore the relative superiority of either incremental or OR/MS approaches to political decision making can be resolved on only partially technical grounds.

COERCION AND INCENTIVES

We cannot dismiss the notion of conflict yet however. Elsewhere, Lowi has noted the paradox that in recent years, political scientists writing about policy making have ignored coercion while many economists writing about the same topic find coercion important.[58] Lindblom is concerned with removing coercion more conventionally because of its inefficiency. He argues for the manipulation of a price system rather than the use of production quotas or priority rationing as means of achieving national economic goals. If price systems are recognized as separate from free markets they will be seen as important aids to rational administration.[59] In an earlier book he and Dahl wrote that a price system involves "spontaneous field control," which is, paradoxically, "both tyrannical and free."[60] For the decade of the 1970s the term is, rather, "incentives." Incentives are superior to central administration because they are cheaper and easier to operate, and probably more effective.[61] Former Budget Director Charles L. Schultze finds that the manipulation of incentives is essential for the implementation of policies involving dispersed and delegated power and program operation. Yet the incentives are difficult to design and demand a careful attention to goals.[62] Former OEO planner Robert Levine concludes that a cost of using incentives systems arises from their potential for individual abuse. While net losses may be small, they still must be controlled. Yet it is OR/MS that offers the models and techniques suitable for this task.[63] If a price or incentives system (an idea that derives from the incrementalist argument) is superior to an administered system (an idea more commonly associated with planners and OR/MS analysts), the former cannot be effective without large inputs from the management sciences both in design and operation.

Several more brief comments about Lindblom's ideas and their relation to OR/MS are necessary before this section can be summarized. (1) the incrementalist approach is under attack from "anti-pluralists" as leading to unjust policy outcomes.[64] That systemic morality results from the morality of the subsystems seems a fundamental assumption of contemporary pluralist thought. This has been challenged outside of the partisan confines of the pluralist–anti-pluralist debate by the philosopher and management scientist C. West Churchman[65] and deserves greater attention than it has received from "incrementalists." (2) Central coordination is a concept that needs rethinking. The design and implementation of incentives systems assumes a greater degree of centralization than is normally considered desirable in incrementalist arguments. Dahl and Lindblom's early comments on the tyranny of "spontaneous field control" should be revived. (3) There have been important improvements in the methodology of systems design. Lindblom's writings have certainly been seminal. Simon's discussion of "nearly decomposable systems" implies the possibility of significant simplification in social design.[66] Finally, Forrester argues that too often we mistake coincident symptoms for cause and that incremental adjustment is based on the logic of first-order negative-feedback systems. But all social systems are "high-order, multiple-loop, nonlinear feedback structures" that require for their management the discovery of completely nonobvious relationships. Failure to appreciate this may lead designers (including politicians) to make heavy-handed and countereffective interventions when minor but nonobvious adjustments would be effective.[67] The strategy of incremental policy change may simply be intellectually inadequate unless supplemented by prior, more comprehensive analysis.

The case for incrementalism rests upon a failure to distinguish reconstructed logic from a design algorithm, and upon a dogmatic moral perspective. When both incrementalism and OR/MS are properly conceived, the two are often complementary and sometimes identical in part. Where they differ, the superiority of incrementalism even on the criteria chosen by its advocates is in every case questionable. Incrementalism as a strategy of policy change, rather than as a method of inquiry and debate, may depend on significant OR/MS inputs. Finally, recent developments in the methodology of systems design make possible more comprehensive analysis and coordination. These developments include the significant and articulate contributions of Lindblom and other incrementalists.

The Optimistic Critique

The major component of the optimistic critique is the perceived effect of OR/MS on governmental institutions and, specifically, the effects of PPBS and analysis on budgetary politics. Wildavsky makes the strongest statements on this topic in his belated discovery that PPBS affects policy by affecting the way decisions are made ("system politics").

> My contention is that the thrust of program budgeting makes it an integral part of system politics.[68]

Having discovered this fact, Wildavsky appears convinced of the impending disaster. Yet "system politics" have been effectively practiced by commercial interests. Walton Hamilton, in arguing that industry has been the major source of twentieth-century constitutional innovations in America, makes it clear that he is writing about "system politics."[69]

Congressional committees even play system politics with PPBS by withholding funds and positions for department-level PPBS staffs,[70] a practice consistent with "the traditional unwillingness to allow the Office of the Secretary to be properly staffed."[71]

Perhaps the fear is not so much of "system politics" as it is of program budgeting itself. Budgeting involves questions of who shall prevail regarding what is in the budget:

> If we substitute the words "what the government ought to do" for the words "ought to be in the budget" it becomes clear that a normative theory of budgeting would be a comprehensive and specific political theory detailing what the government's activities ought to be at a particular time.[72]

Normative budget theories are "totalitarian" in Wildavsky's view. His conclusion demands from such theories a degree of precise elaboration that neither exists nor is forthcoming and again there seems some overreaction. All normative budget theories, including Wildavsky's own defense of the budget practice that currently obtains, have the consequence of indulging some and depriving others in fairly regular patterns. One is left with the suspicion that Wildavsky's fears rest on unstated, undefended policy and constitutional preferences.

Fenno also argues that "no budgetary reform is neutral." He feels that the appropriations process is the key source of the House's power and that its members realize that budget reforms begun in the executive branch are threatening to them. Consequently, congressmen will, and those sympathetic to them should, scrutinize PPBS for its effects on the power of the purse.[73] Otto Davis, however, finds that Congress follows executive budget proposals so closely that:

> If one is worried about the implication of PPB for Congressional control, and if one thinks that the additional complexities in the budgetary process caused by PPB analysis might in some way cause Congress to lose control of the budgetary process, then one is really worrying about a fictitious issue.[74]

OR/MS, if used by congressmen, might have an effect opposite to what Wildavsky and Fenno anticipate: It might strengthen congressional control by directing it to important policy issues.

Several other fears are included in the optimistic critique. One is that OR/MS will lead to a major increase in political conflict. This is a reasonable deduction from some of Dahl's work[75] and has been discussed under the second part of the pessimistic critique. The counterarguments would be essentially similar. Another is more apocalyptic. Bertram Gross counters the suggestion that the PPB methods will lead to "professional-ization, large-scale institutionalization, and 'depolitization' of politics through monopoly by technocratic politics of what Wildavsky calls 'total efficiency' rationality." He suggests that in the context of the development of "post-industrial service societies," present-day systems analysis may be seen as one of the technological factors that tend to promote disorder and discontinuity rather than social systematization.[76] He continues:

> The diffusion of systems analysis of the more narrow variety could provoke continued enlargement of anti-institutional politics—particularly if systems analysis is used by political leaders as window dressing for a "welfare-warfare State."[77]

Such hyperbolic language is hard to take seriously. It sounds like a stump speech in the vagueness of its rhetoric. At the same time, the claims offered on behalf of systems analysis are so extensive as to be, I hope, ridiculous on even casual inspection. Is systems analysis really necessary for a "welfare-warfare State?" I think not.

In general, preoccupation of both critics and advocates of OR/MS with the budget process has been misplaced. First, much of the government's activity is funded through: (a) trust funds; (b) permanent and indefinite appropriations (interest on national debt); (c) fixed charges (expenditures determined by eligibility requirements and/or statutory formulae like veteran's benefits); and (d) ongoing projects (what does the government do with half a bridge?).[78] Fenno notes (e) public debt transactions as another way of circumventing the budget process.[79] Combined, these alternatives include about half of the annual federal expenditures. But this half is amenable to analysis even if it is not effectively in the budget.

Secondly, budgeting is more complex as well as less relevant for the use of OR/MS than it first appears. Schick ascribes three functions to budgets—planning, management, and control—and contends that:

> Multipurpose budget systems are a vital part of the future of budgeting. Although many of the problems have not been solved or even recognized, budgeting in the future will not be able to neglect its planning role or abandon its investment in control and management.[80]

The use of the budget as an instrument of rational policy choice is in practice reconciled to these other functions.

Of course, the amount of money appropriated does have an impact on what the consequences of a program will be. Particularly with a new program, the budget process is often critical. In general, Fenno observes, "the separation between appropriations and legislation is difficult to maintain."[81] Yet maintained to a large degree it is, according to his mammoth study of the appropriations process.[82] There are institutional norms and enforceable expectations concerning policy making by the appropriations committees. Critical decisions are made in authorization committees that jealously guard their policy-making prerogatives. Further, much critical policy has a high degree of independence from appropriations (for example, rules governing the sale of securities or rules for tax accounting). In discussing the impact of possibility of OR/MS the fixation upon the budget process is misplaced.

New Directions in the Analysis of Analysis

OR/MS must be seen as a complex phenomenon. It penetrates throughout the federal establishment and no single defect will significantly retard its diffusion. Because it is complex, its effects on the government and society cannot be captured in felicitous phrases or catchwords. We come to Charles Schultze's more realistic question of how OR/MS can fit into the political decision process.[83]

Schultze offers some hypotheses about which kinds of programs will be, politically, the most feasible to analyze. He concludes that

> analysis can operate with fewer constraints and can profit from consideration of a wider range of alternatives in programs that produce a pure public good and do not directly affect the structure of institutional and political power than in programs that produce a quasi-public good, fundamentally affect income distribution, or impinge on the power structure.[84]

He notes, a bit forlornly, that the programs for which there is the greatest relevance of market criteria as well as the best data and prior theoretical and empirical work are just those programs that involve income subsidies to powerful groups.[85] A corollary is that analysis will be more feasible for new and rapidly expanding programs than it will be for these subsidy programs.[86]

Wildavsky suggests:

> Policy analysis is facilitated when: (a) goals are easily specified, (b) a large margin of error is allowable, (c) the cost of the contemplated policy makes large expenditures on analysis worthwhile.[87]

Some exceptions may be taken; regarding costs, for example, OR/MS has been applied to such minor government activities as the helium program at the direction of the Budget Bureau.[88] But these propositions represent a first step toward an empirical evaluation of the potential for analyzing government programs systematically.

A second new direction involves the listing of preconditions for the success of an OR/MS staff in an organization. Mosher and Harr find that the following conditions facilitated the use of PPBS in the Department of Defense: (a) the many prior years of analytical work and the many available and experienced defense analysts; (b) clarity of the DOD mission, (c) the strength, abilities, and sympathies of the Secretary; (d) a relatively simple appropriations structure; and (e) a bias toward the procurement of hardware. In the civilian agencies, in contrast, all these conditions are reversed. Furthermore, (a) mission boundaries differ from organization ones; (b) measures of objectives are hard to obtain; (c) programs often involve grants or loans to spenders outside the immediate control of the agency; and (d) political feedback is immediate and ubiquitous.[89] Reflecting this excellent list against the conclusions from their study of programming systems in the State Department, one finds almost complete descrepancy. Aside from legal and personal leadership weaknesses, Mosher and Harr find that intraorganizational, intergroup, and interpersonal factors are responsible for the failure of the programming innovations they studied. Chance, expressed in external events and in the location of key personalities, was also a factor.[90] In other words, they find that the real barriers to OR/MS are the same ones common to all attempted organizational change. The conclusion I draw from this is that most discussions of why the civilian agencies cannot do PPBS (Schultze's comments above are an exception) are either lists of temporary obstacles or, worse, simply irrelevant. In the former category fit most discussions of technical obstacles and in the latter fit most discussions derived from pluralist dogma.

We can begin to see the importance of organizational factors even more surely when the recommendations for improving OR/MS in civilian government are revealed. Take, for example, some of the recommendations of Aaron Wildavsky. He advocates "policy analysis" or management science supplemented with behavioral sciences.[91] For his policy analysis units, Wildavsky recommends spending only half of their time on short range projects with the other half reserved for long-range analyses. He is sensitive to the tension between organizational demands for immediate results and the mission of long-range analysis. He recommends that the policy analysis unit report "directly to the Secretary or the agency head" to show that it "is meant to be taken seriously." Policy analysis must have the support of agency top management, and policy analysis should be "geared to the direct requirements of top management."[92] Each of these recommendations shares a common attribute: they could be found in just about any of hundreds of articles on how to start an operations research group which appeared in trade, engineering, and management journals around the world during the past twenty-five years.[93] This is like saying, however, that the recommendations are truisms with all the wisdom—but also the validity—that truisms offer. Each of these recommendations can be evaluated against the insights derived from several years of studying OR/MS staffs.[94] An example of such an evaluation follows:

It is rare that an OR/MS staff has complete control over the fraction of its time that it allocates to long-range studies. The priority problems of management, the legitimacy accorded to the research mission by managers, the technical skills of the analysts, their familiarity with organizational problems and procedures, and the extent to which they have developed stable relations of understanding and confidence with top and operating management all affect the way they allocate their time. The impact of each of these factors varies with the location of the staff in what is actually a lengthy (as much as ten years) process of becoming integrated into the organization. Only the best OR/MS staffs, then, are able to control their own time; "best" refers to technical skills, a record of proven results, and adroit staff leadership. Even such a staff is likely to devote a significant part of its time to matters that cannot even be considered short-term projects. There will be a continuing need to service requests for advice with a turnaround time of 48 hours or less. By doing so the staff builds and maintains the confidence that managers have in it. Long-term projects tend to be allowed under either of two circumstances: the managers do not understand what the staff should be doing, or the staff has reached an advanced stage of development. The latter, as has been implied, requires a careful cultivation of relationships with operating managers unless the staff works only for top management. But that option is possible only if the staff needs little or no cooperation from operating managers in the collection of data or the implementation of recommendations. The fraction of time devoted to long-range analysis projects also depends on the way in which the staff has developed. An OR/MS staff may attempt to compel radical changes in organizational goals or procedures; alternatively, it may accept the rates of change imposed upon it by the managers in the organization. Sometimes it will be forced to choose the latter option because its presence will not be tolerated otherwise. The whole question of how time will be allocated among projects with different time frames is about as important as any question one could ask about an OR/MS staff. It cannot be decided by *fiat*, especially from outside the organization, and the specific figure of 50 percent long-term and 50 percent short-term even if taken as an approximation is unlikely to result from anything but chance.

In other words, policy analysis brings us back to where we began. A new managerial technology is emerging. It is really new only in its organizational setting, and not all that new there either. Policy analysis is management science for the civilian government, and its emergence in the academic cloisters of political science is evidence that management science—or policy analysis if you wish—is now having that parallel institutionalization in the relevant academic areas that has been characteristic of all managerial technologies. At the same time, "policy analysis" is evidence that the future of analysis in civilian government is assured and that organization theorists and other students of public organizations can move from the ideological debate over whether OR/MS can work to the scientific study of how OR/MS analysts behave in organizations and how organizations react to their presence.

New Ways of Thinking About Policy Making

Our understanding of the role of analysis in political decision making will be improved if policy-making systems are appreciated in ways different from those current in political science today.

1. The dominant frame of appreciation is one derived from pluralist theory and incremental models of decision processes. Like "Professor Easton's Political Science,"[95] the pluralist-incremental frame of appreciation is devoid of either social or ethical content.[96] OR/MS advocates, however adequately, have shown themselves to be concerned with the ethics of policy substance[97] although they have been less sensitive to the social dimensions of policy implementation.[98] Lowi has pioneered in the use of policy attributes as independent variables in the study of policy making processes.[99] We need to expand upon his categories and begin to look at more specific attributes of policy, such as specificity of means, amount of delegation, complexity, and specificity of goals for their behavioral implications. The analysis of the social and ethical consequences of law seems considerably more vital both within and outside of the discipline. That the substance of policy itself has behavioral implications is the first thing that should be added to our frame of appreciation.

2. We must therefore change our image of policy-making processes in another way. Unlike most organization theorists,[100] political scientists have long perceived that decision making is a process of developing a coalition large enough to enforce its will upon those who, for whatever reason, disagree with it. The coalition agrees on a commitment to take

specific actions in the future, possibly only under certain contingencies. Decisions and policies have futures! After the decision has been made there is a process of maintaining and revising the commitment. First, there is the dimension of to *what* individual and institutional actors are committed. Pluralist-incremental models suggest that members of the coalition will have different conceptions of the commitment and that these conceptions will change as their knowledge of its implications increases, changes occur in the environment, and their social roles impinge upon coalition members. Second, there is the dimension of the composition of the coalition. In implementing the commitment, some members will drop out, but other must be added. For example, one of the problematical features of many recent laws is that for their successful implementation, the coalition must be expanded to include multitudinous state and local officials. This expansion of the coalition is difficult to execute and occasions much of the current discussion of "incentive systems," as has been noted.[101] Attention to the half of policy making that occurs after the coalition has reached agreement is a necessary addition to the frame of appreciation of both pluralist-incremental theorists and to OR/MS analysts.

3. Policy-making processes are not just divided into pre- and post-decision phases. There are a series of decisions in a policy-making process and most decisions are neglected in favor of the study of the major policy-making process. This is not a plea for the use of a decision-making paradigm such as that suggested by Polsby:[102] initiation, incubation, formulation, etc. Rather, the stimulus here is the work of Bachrach and Baratz. We should begin looking at policy making with the question of initiation, but the next step is not incubation. It is a decision to make any decision at all. The next step, once a decision to decide has been made, is a decision on whether or not to proceed to a resolution of the issue. Most issues that are raised are probably not resolved in a way at all favorable to the initiators. The response may be, instead, repression, a court fight, a circulation of the issue to someone else, a request for further study, a barrage of propaganda and symbolic reassurance, etc. This part of the policy-making process has been studied most carefully by those scholars concerned with the poor and other politically powerless.[103] But it is equally relevant for the study of OR/MS analysts in government. They, too, can be given a "runaround," or be given symbolic reassurances. Their work can be ignored if there is a decision made that no decision will be made on their proposal. Vincent Davis's[104] study of innovations in the Navy is a pioneer attempt to analyze the multiphase decision process that envelops innovative proposals in organizations, and further work should be done on this important aspect of public administration.

4. It is easy to assume, on the basis of pluralist-incrementalist literature, that bargaining is the essence of policy making and that knowledge and the quest for knowledge plays little if any part in it. Even Lindblom, who acknowledges the importance of knowledge in policy making, quietly makes bargaining and coalition the central focus of his descriptive essay on policy making.[105] Policy making is, however, a search for some form of truth as well as a search for some agreement among partisan and self-interested actors.[106] Pluralist-incremental models sell politicians short. Through the adversary process, in their own way, they search for knowledge about the social system, about human behavior, about economic laws, about the relation of science to society, and other matters. If, in Rivers and Harbors, analysis is used to make incremental adjustments on political bargains perhaps in other areas of policy—welfare, some aspects of transportation, housing, education, and macroeconomics are possibilities—bargaining is used to make incremental adjustments on analytical recommendations. The salience of knowledge in different policy areas is a new topic for research and the conception of policy-making processes as searches for knowledge is the fourth needed addition to our appreciation of these processes.

Implications of a Rosy Future

If none of the arguments against OR/MS in civilian politics are particularly valid, and the key factors determining its success are intraorganizational ones, what does this tell us about American society and its policy-making processes? First, it suggests that most of us, particularly those who are not part of the emerging student "counter-culture," accept the economic model of man that underlies OR/MS. The suggestion has two parts. One is that we tend to be predominantly responsive to reinforcement schedules based on economic incentives and expect others to be likewise. The other part is that in the design of policy we tend to think exclusively in terms of economic means. The pluralist-political philosophy has largely eliminated from the active consideration of policy makers and most other Americans the alternative of coercion.[107] Deeply rooted democratic values make us resistant to the use of propaganda and psychological manipulation as overt policy instruments except in those policy areas where our national phobia regarding Communism is operative. That, of course, is no small exception. A third alternative, policy means based on humane social and interpersonal incentives is currently not realistically available. While politicians have long manipulated these kinds of factors in pernicious ways—such as racism—a social science adequate for use in the design of policy means has been developing only since the 1930s.[108] (Economic science has a head start of over 150 years if it is dated from Adam Smith.) This alternative is developing in feasibility quite rapidly. Applications of social science in business organizations are becoming more common daily.

This leads to the second implication of the apparently bright future for OR/MS, one that can be raised but not answered. If OR/MS is having an impact on public policy decisions and will have a greater impact in the future, one can ask why? Wildavsky is certainly right when he argues that budget reforms are not neutral. To shed some light on this question, let me propose two variables. Each is admittedly empirically problematic: 1. The effect of OR/MS on the distribution of political power; and 2. The effect of governmental decisions on society. For the purposes here they can each be dichotomized to yield the following table.

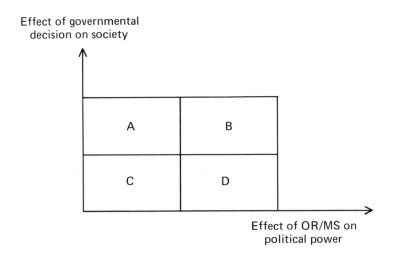

A society can be changed significantly and its power structure remain largely the same. If OR/MS fits the situation described by Box A, that means that OR/MS reinforces an existing structure of power even if it leads to other important changes. For example, OR/MS might contribute to the design of construction techniques and incentives for homebuilding that would revolutionize American residence standards. These same designs could lead to concentration of the presently fragmented homebuilding industry into large economic units controlled by the same numerically large but relatively small financial and managerial elite that controls most other large economic enterprises. These organizations could be just as powerful politically as the present homebuilding industry.

To the extent that the existing distribution of power is based upon the continued salience of a value structure based on economic incentives, Box A is a real possibility! OR/MS might succeed because it augments an existing distribution of power.

As we are considering the use of OR/MS in federal civilian government, Box D is irrelevant. Lowi's analysis of the American political system as one in which the government is just one of many interest groups (and often not the most powerful one) [109] implies that Box C describes the situation. Government decisions have little effect on the distribution of power. OR/MS may succeed because it is irrelevant to political power.

OR/MS could fit Box B; the counterarguments to the optimistic critique of OR/MS suggest this as the least probable of the alternatives. Analysis of the half of policy making that occurs after the coalition has reached agreement should also suggest that this is a low probability alternative. [110] The optimistic critique can be inadequate and still not exhaust the issue it raises, however. In the immediate future, the impact of OR/MS on society through its role in governmental decision making will likely be slight. The question remains unanswered in the longer run even if certain alternatives can be eliminated.

Conclusion

It is conceivable that the consequences of many laws are not the ones intended by the legislators who passed them. There is no a priori reason to assume that the majority of Congress intended farm programs to have the redistributional effects they have clearly had, for example. [111] It is possible that if policy makers had different kinds of knowledge readily available that policies themselves would be different. We have at this time no adequate understanding of the impact of knowledge on policy. In fact, we know very little about the relations between attributes of the policy making process and their consequences, in terms of either policies on paper or policies in action. *Until we know something about these relationships, we will know very little about American politics.* Pluralist-incremental doctrine, because it directs us away from questions of substance, suppresses this whole line of inquiry. Incremental models of policy making taken instead as description facilitate this line of inquiry by delineating attributes of policy making processes. The study of the impact of OR/MS on political decision making, properly conceived and executed, is as likely a place as any to start the study of the impact of knowledge on policy and, through this, of the relation between process and substance in American politics.

Notes

[1] Roland N. McKean, *Efficiency in Government Through Systems Analysis, with Emphasis on Water Resources Development*, ORSA Publications in Operations Research No. 3 (New York: Wiley, 1958), pp. 6–7.

[2] See the suggestive paper by Terry Clark, "Institutionalization of Innovations in Higher Education: Four Models," *Administrative Science Quarterly* 13:1 (June 1968) 1–25.

[3] James R. Schlesinger, *Uses and Abuses of Analysis* (Washington, D.C.: U.S. Government Printing Office, 1968), p. 5, memorandum prepared at the request of the Subcommittee on National Security and International Operations, Committee on Government Operations, U.S. Senate.

[4] Frederick C. Mosher, "Limitations and Problems of PPBS in the States," *Public Administration Review* 29:2 (March 1969), 160.

[5] Victor Thompson, *Bureaucracy and Innovation* (University, Ala.: University of Alabama Press, 1969), p. 57.

[6] Aaron Wildavsky, "Rescuing Policy Analysis from PPBS," *Public Administration Review* 29:2 (March 1969) 193–194.

[7] This will be discussed *infra* with appropriate citations.

[8] In the sense that zero is a *trivial* solution for the equation, $X^3 - 4X = O$.

[9] Aaron Wildavsky, "The Political Economy of Efficiency," *Public Administration Review* 26:4 (December 1966) 292–310, reprinted in James W. Davis, ed., *Politics, Programs, and Budgets* (Englewood Cliffs, N.J.: Prentice Hall, 1969) p. 235.

[10] Aaron Wildavsky, "Aesthetic Power or the Triumph of the Sensitive Minority over the Vulgar Mass: A Political Analysis of the New Economics," *Daedalus* 96:4 (Fall 1967), 1118.

[11] Schlesinger, *Uses and Abuses of Analysis*, p. 3.

[12] Thompson, *Bureaucracy and Innovation*, p. 54.

[13] *Ibid.*, pp. 53*ff.*

[14] Mosher, *Limitations and Problems*, pp. 161–162.

[15] Wildavsky, "The Political Economy of Efficiency," p. 252.

[16] Richard Fenno, "Comment," in Robert L. Chartrand et al., eds., *Information Support, Program Budgeting, and the Congress* (New York: Spartan Books, 1968), p. 214.

[17] Wildavsky, "The Political Economy of Efficiency," p. 247.

[18] I shall not elaborate now on the social and political implications of that statement here except to note that there are societies where the statement would have far less validity. This tells us something about the possible effectiveness of OR/MS solutions as well as something about American culture.

[19] Specifically, Wildavsky, "The Political Economy of Efficiency"; Robert A. Dahl, *Who Governs?* (New Haven, Conn.: Yale University Press, 1961), Books IV and V; Edward M. Epstein, *The Corporation in American Politics* (Englewood Cliffs, N.J.: Prentice-Hall, 1969).

[20] Wildavsky, "The Political Economy of Efficiency," p. 246.

[21] C. W. Churchman and A. H. Schainblatt, "The Researcher and the Manager: A Dialectic of Implementation," *Management Science* 11:4 (February 1965), B-69–B-88.

[22] In my interviews I have twice come across instances where OR/MS groups were having forced upon them what Leonard Sayles calles a "stabilization

relationship," in which the group is given the power of advance approval or disapproval of some actions in the workflow [*Managerial Behavior* (New York: McGraw-Hill, 1964), Ch. 6]. In both cases, the group viewed this as an imposition upon it, potentially damaging to both its research mission and its relations with operating management.

[23] Thompson, *Bureaucracy and Innovation,* p. 56.

[24] Walter Williams and John W. Evans, "The Politics of Evaluation: The Case of Head Start," mimeographed (July 14, 1969), p. 24. Both authors were connected with the study at OEO but they maintain that the views expressed in the paper are not necessarily official.

[25] *Ibid.,* p. 24.

[26] MacAlister Brown, "The Demise of State Department Public Opinion Polls: A Study of Legislative Oversight," *Midwest Journal of Political Science* 5:1 (March 1961), 1–17.

[27] Wildavsky, "The Political Economy of Efficiency," p. 234.

[28] *Ibid.,* p. 233.

[29] Aaron Wildavsky, *The Politics of the Budgetary Process* (Boston: Little, Brown, 1964), p. 130.

[30] Grant McConnell, *Private Power and American Democracy* (New York: Knopf, 1965); Robert Paul Wolff, "Tolerance," in *The Poverty of Liberalism* (Boston: Beacon Press, 1968).

[31] Bertram Gross, "The New Systems Budgeting," *Public Administration Review* 29:2 (March 1969), 128.

[32] Wildavsky, "Rescuing Policy Analysis," p. 191.

[33] Aaron Wildavsky and Arthur Hammann, "Comprehensive Versus Incremental Budgeting in the Department of Agriculture," *Administrative Science Quarterly* 10:3 (December 1965), 321–346, reprinted in Fremont J. Lyden and Ernest G. Miller, eds, *Planning Programming Budgeting: A Systems Approach to Management,* first edition (Chicago: Markham 1968), p. 145. This article and its conclusions should be considered in the context of the Department's thirty-year experience with program budgets and in the context of political events surrounding the Department during the period discussed. The authors consider neither, but on the former, see "Planning, Programming, and Budgeting in USDA," a paper based on a presentation by William A. Carlson during a Civil Service Commission seminar in PPB, Alexandria, Va., December 1–12, 1969.

[34] Wildavsky, *The Politics of the Budgetary Process,* p. 147.

[35] Elizabeth B. Drew, "On Giving Oneself a Hotfoot: Government by Commission," *The Atlantic* 221:5 (May 1968), 45–49.

[36] Charles L. Schultze, *The Politics and Economics of Public Spending* (Washington, D.C.: Brookings, 1968), pp. 79*ff.*

[37] Theodore Lowi, "Liberal Jurisprudence," in *The End of Liberalsim* (New York: Norton, 1969); Victor Rosenblum, *Law as a Political Instrument* (New York: Random House, 1955).

[38] Consider his *The Intelligence of Democracy* (New York: Free Press, 1965) as a theoretical essay in organization and management.

[39] Charles E. Lindblom, "Decision-Making in Taxation and Expenditures," in National Bureau of Economic Research, *Public Finances: Needs, Sources, and Utilization* (Princeton, N.J.: Princeton University Press, 1961), excerpted in Alan A. Altshuler, ed., *The Politics of the Federal Bureaucracy* (New York: Dodd-Mead, 1968), p. 170.

[40] Altshuler, ed., *The Politics of the Federal Bureaucracy,* p. 165–166;

Lindblom, "The Science of 'Muddling Through,'" *Public Administration Review* 19:2, (Spring 1959), 79–88, reprinted in Robert T. Golembiewski et al., eds., *Public Administration: Readings in Institutions, Processes, Behavior* (Chicago: Rand McNally, 1966), p. 295.

[41] Roger Jones, "The Model as Decision Maker's Dilemma," *Public Administration Review* 24:3 (Sept. 1964), 158–160; Philip E. Hammond, ed., *Sociologists at Work* (Garden City, N.Y.: Doubleday-Anchor, 1967).

[42] Note Lindblom's approving use of the quotation from Hitch in "The Science of 'Muddling Through,'" p. 80.

[43] Lindblom, "Decision-Making in Taxation and Expenditures," p. 172.

[44] This literature is ably reviewed by David Caputo in "Normative and Empirical Implications of Budgetary Processes," paper presented at the 1970 annual meeting of the American Political Science Association, Los Angeles, September, 1970.

[45] U.S. Congress, Subcommittee on Economy in Government of the Joint Economic Committee, *The Planning-Programming-Budgeting System: Progress and Potentials,* 90th Cong. 1st sess. (Washington, D.C.: U.S. Government Printing Office, 1967), hereafter cited as *Progress and Potentials.*

[46] See Yehezkel Dror, *Public Policymaking Reexamined* (San Francisco: Chandler, 1968), Chs. 1–6.

[47] In Karl Popper, *Conjectures and Refutations: The Growth of Scientific Knowledge* (New York: Harper Torchbooks, 1963), pp. 3–30.

[48] Stafford Beer, "The Aborting Corporate Plan: A Cybernetic Account of the Interface Between Planning and Action," in Erich Jantsch, ed., *Perspectives of Planning* (Paris: OECD, 1969), pp. 397–422; C. West Churchman, "Setting the Objectives of Organizations," Internal working paper no. 110, 12 pp., and "Suggestive, Predictive, Decisive, and Systemic Measurement," Internal working paper no. 95, 12 pp. (Space Sciences laboratory, Social Sciences Project, University of California, Berkeley).

[49] Wildavsky, *The Politics of the Budgetary Process,* pp. 156–160; Lindblom is less dogmatic on this point, "The Science of 'Muddling Through,'" p. 300.

[50] Mancur Olson, Jr., *The Logic of Collective Action* (New York: Schocken Books, 1968); Michael Parenti, "Power and Pluralism: A View from the Bottom," *Journal of Politics* 32:3 (August 1970), 501–530.

[51] Charles L. Schultze, *The Politics and Economics of Public Spending,* p. 96.

[52] Lindblom, "Decision-Making in Taxation and Expenditures," p. 174.

[53] E. S. Quade, in E. S. Quade and W. I. Boucher, eds., *Systems Analysis and Policy Planning: Applications in Defense* (New York: American Elsevier, 1968) pp. 13, 36, and 423; and Quade, "The Selection and Use of Strategic Air Bases: A Case History," in E. S. Quade, ed., *Analysis for Military Decisions* (Chicago : Rand McNally, 1966), pp. 24–63.

[54] Using the terms as in James G. March and Herbert A. Simon, with the collaboration of Harold Guetzkow, *Organizations* (New York: Wiley, 1958), p. 130.

[55] Ithiel de Sola Pool, "Political Information Systems," in Jantsch, ed., *Perspectives of Planning,* pp. 307–325.

[56] Lowi, *The End of Liberalism, passim.*

[57] In spite of Robert Boguslaw, *The New Utopians* (Englewood Cliffs, N.J.: Prentice-Hall, 1965).

[58] Theodore Lowi, "Decision Making vs. Policy Making: Toward an Antidote for Technocracy," *Public Administration Review* 30:3 (May 1970), 315.

[59] Charles E. Lindblom, "Economics and the Administration of National Planning," *Public Administration Review* 25:4 (Dec. 1965), 274–283.

[60] Robert A. Dahl and Charles E. Lindblom, *Politics, Economics, and Welfare* (New York: Harper Torchbooks, 1963, first edition, 1953), p. 100.

[61] Lindblom, "Economics and the Administration of National Planning"; also, Lindblom, *The Intelligence of Democracy.*

[62] Schultze, *The Politics and Economics of Public Spending,* Ch. 6.

[63] Robert A. Levine, "Redesigning Social Systems—A Note on Bureaucracy, Creative Federalism, Business, and the War on Poverty in the United States," in Jantsch, ed., *Perspectives of Planning,* pp. 449–467. See also Charles L. Schultze, "The Role of Incentives, Penalties, and Rewards in Attaining Effective Policy," in Robert Haveman, ed., *Analysis and Evaluation of Public Expenditures: The PPB System* (Washington, D.C.: U.S. Government Printing Office, 1969), Vol. I, pp. 201–25. A compendium of papers submitted to the Subcommittee on Economy in Government, Joint Economic Committee, Congress of the United States, 91st Cong., 1st Sess., hereafter cited as *Analysis and Evaluation.*

[64] Allen Schick, "Systems Politics and Systems Budgeting," *Public Administration Review* 29:2 (March 1969), 137–151; David Kettler, "The Politics of Social Change: The Relevance of Democratic Approaches," in William E. Connolly, ed., *The Bias of Pluralism* (New York: Atherton, 1969), pp. 213–249.

[65] C. West Churchman, *Challenge to Reason* (New York: McGraw-Hill, 1968).

[66] Herbert A. Simon, *The Sciences of the Artificial* (Cambridge, Mass.: MIT Press, 1969).

[67] Jay W. Forrester, "Planning Under the Dynamic Influences of Complex Social Systems," in Jantsch, ed., *Perspectives of Planning,* pp. 237–254.

[68] Wildavsky, "The Political Economy of Efficiency," p. 246.

[69] Walton Hamilton, *The Politics of Industry* (New York: Vintage Books, 1967, first edition, 1957).

[70] As was the case in the State Department, as related by F. C. Mosher and John Harr, *Program Budgeting Visits Foreign Affairs* (Syracuse, N.Y.: Inter-University Case Program, Inc., 1969), p. IV-9.

[71] William Capron, "Comment," in Chartrand, et al., eds., *Information Support, Program Budgeting, and the Congress,* p. 193.

[72] Wildavsky, *The Politics of the Budgetary Process,* p. 129.

[73] Richard Fenno, "The Impact of PPBS on the Congressional Appropriations Process," in Chartrand, et al., eds., *Information Support, Program Budgeting, and the Congress,* pp. 175–176.

[74] From testimony reported in *Progress and Potentials, op cit.,* pp. 207–208.

[75] For example, *Pluralist Democracy in the United States* (Chicago: Rand McNally, 1967).

[76] Gross, "The New Systems Budgeting," p. 127.

[77] *Ibid.,* p. 128.

[78] Murray Weidenbaum, *The Modern Public Sector* (New York: Basic Books, 1969), pp. 172–179.

[79] Richard Fenno, *The Power of the Purse* (Boston: Little, Brown, 1966), pp. 46ff.

[80] Allen Schick, *Some Problems with Multi-Purpose Budget Systems,* (Washington, D.C.: Bureau of the Budget, Program Evaluation Staff, December, 1966), p. 22.

[81] Fenno, *The Power of the Purse,* p. 22.

[82] *Ibid.*

[83] Schultze, *The Politics and Economics of Public Spending,* p. 1.

[84] *Ibid.,* pp. 85–86.

[85] *Ibid.,* pp. 88–89.

[86] *Ibid.*

[87] Wildavsky, "Rescuing Policy Analysis," p. 191.

[88] See the list given by Jack Carlson in "The Status and Next Steps for Planning, Programming, and Budgeting' in Haveman, ed., *Analysis and Evaluation,* Vol. II, p. 628, and also Attachment 12 in the same volume, pp. 763–785. A more recent list of analytical studies is submitted by Carlson in *Economic Analysis and the Efficiency of Government* (Washington, D.C.: U.S. Government Printing Office, 1969), Vol. III, pp. 695–697. Hearings before the Subcommittee on Economy in Government of the Joint Economic Committee, 91st Cong., 1st Sess.

[89] Mosher and Harr, *Program Budgeting Visits Foreign Affairs,* pp. I–10 to I–13.

[90] *Ibid.,* Chapter VII.

[91] Wildavsky, "Rescuing Policy Analysis," pp. 196–200; cf. Michael Radnor, "Management Sciences and Policy Sciences," in *Policy Sciences,* forthcoming, 1971.

[92] Wildavsky, "Rescuing Policy Analysis," p. 196.

[93] See Radnor and David Mylan, "Preliminary Annotated Bibliography on the Management of Operations Research and Management Science," Cooperative International Program on the Management of Operations Research and the Management Sciences, Northwestern University, Evanston, Illinois, 1969.

[94] Michael J. White, *Management Science in Federal Civilian Agencies,* dissertation in process, Northwestern University, Department of Political Science, 1971.

[95] The term is from Paul Kress, "Self, System, and Significance: Reflections on Professor Easton's Political Science," *Ethics* 77:1 (Oct. 1966), 1–13.

[96] See Schick's criticism of Wildavsky in "Systems Politics and Systems Budgeting," and Wildavsky's reply in *Public Administration Review* 30:2 (March 1970), 198–200.

[97] For Example, Paul Feldman, "Prescriptions for an Effective Government: Ethics, Politics, and PPBS," in Haveman, ed., *Analysis and Evaluation,* Vol. III, pp. 865–885.

[98] Mosher, "Limitations and Problems of PPBS in the States," pp. 163–164.

[99] Lowi, "Decision Making vs. Policy Making: Toward an Antidote for Technocracy."

[100] Richard Cyert and James G. March, *A Behavioral Theory of the Firm* (Englewood Cliffs, N.J.: Prentice-Hall, 1963) is an exception.

[101] *Supra,* fns. 62–63.

[102] Nelson Polsby, "Policy Analysis and Congress," in Haveman, ed., *Analysis and Evaluation,* Vol. III, pp. 943–952.

[103] Parenti, "Power and Pluralism," and references therein.

[104] Vincent Davis, "The Politics of Innovation: Patterns in Navy Cases," *Monograph Series in World Affairs* 4:3 (1966–1967). (Denver: The University of Denver Social Science Foundation and Graduate School of International Studies).

[105] Charles E. Lindblom, *The Policy Making Process* (Englewood Cliffs, N.J.: Prentice-Hall, 1968).

[106] This perspective is evident in James L. Sundquist, *Politics and Policy* (Washington, D.C.: Brookings, 1968).

[107] Lowi, *The End of Liberalsim*, Chs. 2–3. Note that even politically deviant students are punished by having scholarships withdrawn.

[108] See Dorwin Cartwright's introduction to Kurt Lewin, *Field Theory in Social Science* (New York: Harper, 1951).

[109] Lowi, *The End of Liberalism*.

[110] As does Grant McConnell.

[111] Analyzed in James T. Bonnen, "The Distribution of Benefits from Cotton Price Supports," in Samuel B. Chase, ed., *Problems in Public Expenditure Analysis* (Washington, D.C.: Brookings, 1968), pp. 223–254.